MW01225316

AGING

CANADIAN PERSPECTIVES

AGING

CANADIAN PERSPECTIVES

edited by
Victor W. Marshall
& Barry D. McPherson

broadview press/Journal of Canadian Studies

Canadian Cataloguing in Publication Data

Aging: Canadian perspectives
Papers originally published in a special edition of Journal of Canadian Studies.
Includes bibliographical references.
ISBN 1-55111-012-1

1. Aged — Canada. I. Marshall, Victor W.
II. McPherson, Barry D.

HQ1064.C3A45 1994   305.26'0971   C94-931404-8

©1994 broadview press Ltd./Journal of Canadian Studies

Broadview Press
Post Office Box 1243, Peterborough, Ontario, Canada, K9J 7H5

in the United States of America
3576 California Road, Orchard Park, NY 14127

in the United Kingdom
c/o Drake Marketing, Saint Fagan's Road, Fairwater, Cardiff, CF53AE

Broadview Press gratefully acknowledges the support of the Canada Council,
the Ontario Arts Council, the Ontario Publishing Centre,
and the Ministry of National Heritage.

Cover design by Don LePan

PRINTED IN CANADA
5 4 3 2   98 99

Contents

Introduction:
Aging: Canadian Perspectives

VICTOR W. MARSHALL AND BARRY D. McPHERSON

Introduction

This book is an expansion of a special issue published as Volume 28, no. 1 of *Journal of Canadian Studies*. We have added three original articles and we reprint another two, to provide greater depth and to broaden the coverage somewhat. As with the special issue, the topics and authors included in this book have been selected with the conviction that this area of study has much to offer scholars interested in all aspects of the humanities and social sciences. Aging, after all, is one way to consider the experience of living. Moreover, the aging of individuals occurs in social, economic, political and environmental contexts that are changing as well, partly due to another form of aging, demographic or population aging. Consequently, we must study aging individuals in an aging society.

The chapters in this book focus on demographic aspects of aging and on the impact of population aging on major social institutions such as the community, work, leisure, and the family. This introduction links these structural concerns to some issues about the meaning of aging and old age for the aging individual. We begin by examining (1) demographic aspects of aging, (2) the structure of the life course, (3) socioeconomic issues, and (4) health issues. We then turn to a consideration of psychosocial concerns associated with aging: dependency and independence; family life; attitudes toward aging; and the association between aging and the anticipation of, and preparation for, death.

Demographic Aspects

Canada has an aging population. Whereas at the beginning of this century, less than 6% of the Canadian population were aged 65 and older, today almost 12% fall into that category, and this proportion will rise to almost 25% by 2031. The proportion that will be old around 2021 and 2031 is now projected to be quite a bit higher than had been projected fifteen or twenty years ago because demographers no longer anticipate large increases in fertility, and because recent decreases in later-life mortality have been significant.

Women live much longer than men. Life expectancy at birth is just 70.2 years for men but it is 77.5 years for women. These life expectancy differences persist at later ages. To illustrate, a man born in 1980-1982 has a 75% chance of living to age 65; but a woman born in that period has an 86% chance. At age 65, a man can expect to live an additional 14.6 years, whereas a woman can expect to live an additional 18.9 years. Because women are increasing their advantage in life expectancy over men, the world of the aged is becoming a world dominated by women. This has profound implications for women, who become a majority group, and for men, who become the new minority. This shift in the sex ratio also has a profound impact on younger cohorts in terms of economic support and caregiving that may be needed, and on such public policy areas as housing, transportation, community support, health promotion and institutional and health care.

Another important aspect of the age structure of the population is the changing median age. This is the age at which you would say, "half of all Canadians are younger than this age". The current median age of the Canadian population is 30. In 1971 it was just 26.2 years. By the end of this century it is projected to have risen to 37.2 years; and when all the baby boomers are old by 2031, the median age may be as high as 41.6 years. As a larger and larger proportion of our population reach age 65 and beyond, the overall composition of Canadian society will become, in a way, more "mature".

Another interesting and important trend is that, considered as a population in itself, the group over age 65 is aging. That is, growth in the very advanced ages (80+) is happening at a greater rate than among younger old people. This, however, will change after 2010, when the first of the baby boomers start to enter the 65+ category. By 2031, about one in twenty Canadians will be aged 85 or older.[1]

The Structure of the Life Course

The "structure of the life course" refers to typical patterns of the ordering and timing of major life events, such as marriage, retirement, the empty nest, and widowhood. For example, in Chapter 10, Rosenthal and Gladstone describe how the life course has changed in terms of the family.

The life course is becoming more structured over time in that there is much less variability than there once was around the average years at which these events occur. In statistical terms, the standard deviation has been reduced for the mean age of marriage, the birth of first child, the birth of last child, the last child leaving home, and widowhood.

In addition, there have been changes in the mean ages at which the events occurred. The mean age of marriage and birth of first and, especially last child has fallen; the age of entering the "empty nest" stage of family life when the children are likely to have left home has also declined. In contrast, the age of widowhood has risen, on average. These changes have led to a new stage of family life, the "empty nest" period. The average Canadian born 100 years ago did not experience an empty nest period of more than a year or two, because widowhood could come at any time and because the last child in a family did not leave home until the father or mother died. Now, the typical Canadian can expect several years in the empty nest stage. Then, typically, the male dies and the woman can expect eight or so years of widowhood.[2]

Another important life course event is retirement. The average Canadian born 100 years ago did not experience retirement as we know it today. Retirement is an invention which has become popular only in this century. Young people who entered the labour force in 1900 would not reasonably expect to retire (or be retired) at the age of 65. Most did not do so. Hence, retirement is another aspect of the structure of the life course, and it increasingly structures the later life of both men and women who have been in the paid labour force.[3]

These are structural issues, but they have social psychological impacts. The impacts of a given life-course event on an individual will vary depending on how much he or she anticipates and interprets the events, and on how typical one's particular life course is in comparison to the norm. Most people live beyond the time they expected to live. In terms of retirement, many people live their working lives without giving much thought to the fact that they can anticipate a very large number of years in retirement.

Given the changes in the structure of the family life course, which are described in Chapter 10 by Rosenthal and Gladstone, we suspect that few people, while young, have a clear anticipation of what their family structure will be like. Most of us, for example, think of older people as having children. However, about one in five persons aged 65 or older have no living child, and another one in five have only one living child. Some people never marry, some are infertile, some are voluntarily childless and some outlive their children. The result is that a significant minority of older people have few or no children as possible resources in time of need.

Socioeconomic Status

Most older people are excluded from the labour market by the social institution of retirement. In addition, for the current cohort of older women, many never have worked in the paid labour force (although they certainly worked!). Loss of the ability to work means loss of income. As a nation, we have not faced the fact that pension income, or retirement income of which pension income is but one component, is not high. Our public income security programs (e.g., OAS, GIS and CPP) replace only about 40% of pre-retirement income on the average. The private pension system is a dismal failure, with only 13% of pension income being derived from private plans (only 9% of female retirement income). This occurs because only 41.6% of men and 31.0% of women in the paid labour force are covered by such plans and because portability and vesting provisions mean that many people who contribute, and whose employers contribute, to pension plans on their behalf, never see the money.[4]

The result is poverty and near poverty for a significant minority of Canada's aged. In 1990, 35% of unattached seniors, but just 4% of elderly couples, had incomes placing them below the federal government poverty line. Unattached elderly women, however, were more likely to be poor, with 38% falling below the line compared to just 26% of unattached elderly men.[5] Fortunately, the majority of Canada's elderly (72% of families with an elderly head, and 38% of elderly unattached individuals) own their homes completely.[6] It is fair to say, however, that few of Canada's elderly are wealthy. Moreover, significant subgroups among the elderly—widows, those renting apartments and so forth— experience some degree of poverty in Canadian society.

Health

Most people retain adequate levels of health until well into the later years. Severe health problems, or cognitive and sensory declines, may lead to institutionalization, as described by Rule et al., in Chapter 5. However, as Haldemann and Wister point out in Chapter 3, only about 7% of people over age 65 are institutionalized. Even among people aged 85 and older, only 39% live in institutionalized settings. The typical older person, then, lives in a home-like setting in the community. However, over half of these community-dwelling elderly, if they are over age 65, will experience some permanent limitation of their major activities, although they may require only limited assistance.

A commonly used measure of the need for assistance is the Activities of Daily Living Inventory (ADL), which is described by Chappell in Chapter 6. Depending on the study, about 10% of respondents over age 65 might require assistance with any one item on the ADL inventory. The proportion requiring help with at least one item rises to about 30-50% among people aged 85 and older. The vast majority of older people are in fact quite independent, with only a minority being quite severely ill and limited in their independence.

Psychosocial Concerns

We have described a number of demographic and family structure phenomena which, with socioeconomic status and health conditions, determine who among the older are coping and who are at risk. Now we introduce four social psychological concerns related to aging and the aged.

Dependency and Independence

Older people generally want to be independent for as long as possible. However, women, especially women who are now old, have spent much of their lives submerging their own identities, not to mention their energies, in the care and feeding of their husbands. In later life, their responsibilities often increase, as Aronson notes in Chapter 11. The majority of men die, so to speak, in the arms of their spouse; while the majority of women are already widowed by the time they need assistance. This is one of the factors which, in addition to gendered role definitions, leads to women providing the majority of care to the elderly.

There are other implications. Living alone is in itself a new challenge for countless older people, but it is a special challenge for older women. Studies show that the aged are not more lonely than other age groups, but these studies also show that significant minorities of people of all ages are lonely. Living alone is the preferred living arrangement of the majority of older widows and widowers, who rarely wish to live with an adult child. The challenge here, as the chapters by Haldemann and Wister, Joseph and Martin Matthews, and Gee and McDaniel note, is to provide environments as well as formal and informal support systems to assist these people to maintain their independence.

Family

From a social psychological point of view, it is important to recognize how changes in one family dimension affect others. When a woman becomes a mother, her parents become grand-parents. When the oldest generation dies, the younger generations each move up a rank in seniority and in maturity and family responsibility. At the same time, increasing age may threaten the authority of the oldest generation because the adult children wish to assume greater authority in the family. We can see this in the changing location of important family events such as Christmas. There is a period when the adult children continue to return to their parental home for Christmas, Thanksgiving and other important celebrations; but there is also, almost always, a time when the oldest generation loses control over such family ritual occasions and celebrates Christmas alone or in one of their children's homes. This symbolizes the passing of authority, within families, from generation to generation and it changes, perhaps threatens, the sense of familial place of the oldest member of the family.

Rosenthal and Gladstone, in Chapter 10, provide ample evidence of the supportiveness of families toward their elders, and it is clear that, if aged parents need assistance, then children provide it—whether they feel close or affectionate towards their parents or not. The normative pressures in our society are so strongly supportive of taking care of one's parents that few would dare to go against this basic principle of "filial piety" that is shared by almost everyone in our society. While we hear of "elder abuse" these days, and surely some is present, as Rosenthal and Gladstone point out, there is no solid evidence that elder abuse is widespread or epidemic. As another aspect of intergenerational relations, in Chapter 12 Connidis shows that the elderly provide a good deal of assistance and support to younger generations.

Attitudes Toward the Aged

Ambivalent attitudes toward the aged are pervasive in our society. We have been called an ageist society, yet no societies in world history have provided a larger proportion of societal wealth to provide income security, health care and shelter for the aged. We have been called ageist, yet our political leaders, judges, and religious leaders tend to be much older than the median age of the society. We have been called ageist, yet most younger people have living parents whom they love and against whom they do not behave in a manner that can be called ageist.

There are stereotypes, mostly negative, about the aged; but Chen and Zhou's presentation in Chapter 13 shows that some stereotypes are positive. The negative stereotypes are held by the aged almost as strongly as they are held by the young—they are learned while young and this knowledge persists through the years. But most older people exempt themselves from the stereotypes. While they may see old people, in general, as rigid, slow, conservative, or stuffy, they report that they are exceptions to these generalizations. Furthermore, most older people report that they feel "young" for their age or "healthier than the average person" of their age.

One of the most damaging stereotypes about old age is the view that aging is naturally associated with illness and physical decline. This is a stereotype widely shared by young people, who greatly overestimate the proportion of older people who live in institutions; but it is also a stereotype still shared by many of the aged, who are more sedentary than they ought to be, because they think it inappropriate or dangerous to be physically active. The stereotype is also all too often reinforced by the medical and health professions. One result, as the research summarized by Ouellette in chapter 9 shows, is a high level of passive leisure activity. Fortunately, cultural expectations are changing, but there is still far more hesitation among older people than there should be about activity and independence. There is concern about whether certain activity patterns are appropriate in later life. In the family context, we see a great deal of delicate negotiation between elderly parents and their adult children, as the latter attempt to provide appropriate security and assistance to their parents without creating or reinforcing dependency. Our general ambivalence in this area is apparent in popular culture. For example, in many movies adults are portrayed as if they had lived their entire lives without parents playing any role in their lives. Similarly, if older persons are included as characters in movies, they are frequently portrayed as dependent or as interfering in the lives of their adult children.

Concerns about independence versus dependency are likely to grow in prevalence simply because of the extension of life expectancy. As death itself is postponed until later years, morbidity and functional limitations are not postponed to the same extent. For example, while deaths from cardiological causes are decreasing, we can not delay the onset of osteoporosis, vision difficulties and many other physical conditions that make the older person at least partially dependent on others.

Preparing for Death

With increasing age, people become more aware that their own time on earth is limited. Research in the area of aging and dying suggests that the vast majority of older people do come to terms with their mortality, but that these concerns do not become salient for most people until sometime in their seventies. At that time, they experience more and more of their peers dying, and they become concerned that their own dying be appropriate. Appropriateness requires that the life which death brings to a close is also appropriate. People, or at least most people, do not want to live forever. But they want to die feeling that their life has been meaningful and dignified. That is why factors such as the ability to remain independent, both physically and economically, and the ability to maintain family and affectional bonds are so critically important to the aged.

One major and typical way in which older people try to prepare for impending death is through the process of the "life review". Robert Butler has described this process as a naturally-occurring, universal process through which the aged person systematically recalls and evaluates his or her past life in order to arrive at a sense that it has been meaningful. In particular, past conflicts, and the decisions that might have been wrong or at least problematic, become the focus in a search for meaning. Because conflicts from the past are brought into consciousness, people engaged in a life review often exhibit irritability while working through these conflicts. Family members, or care-giving staff in institutional settings for the aged, tend to demean reminiscence and worry about the older person "living in the past" and incessantly repeating all those old stories. However, it is important to recognize the therapeutic effects of such reminiscence.

People will readily tell you, "I'd rather die than lose my faculties"; and this speaks to an important concern of the aged. We ought not to forget the problems of cognitive decline in later life (see Chapter 5), but we also ought to reduce unwarranted fears in this area by noting that only about 14% of any birth cohort will suffer serious cognitive decline or dementia (including Alzheimer's disease) at a clinical level, before they die. In other words, the vast majority of older people die with their faculties intact.

In this introductory section, we have described some demographic aspects of aging in Canada, raised some of the social psychological issues and concerns associated with aging, and linked these to structural and policy concerns discussed in other chapters in this book. In particular, we have suggested that many psychological concerns and anxieties that may be prevalent in later life are rooted in basic structural features such as demographic changes, the impact of such changes on family structure, and the way in which we have structured our economy. Each of these background features that has an impact on the social psychological concerns of older people should be included in the assessment of the older person, in the design of supportive and remedial environments, programs and services for the elderly, and in health promotion programs for the elderly. If Canadians are to understand the lives of our increasing numbers and proportion of older persons, it is essential to relate earlier life conditions and experiences to later life conditions.

Topical Overview

Having set the stage for an analysis of aging in Canada, this section presents a preview of the other chapters included in the book. To develop the special issue of the *Journal of Canadian Studies*, which forms the core of this book, we first sought to include contributions from as many of the most creative and prolific Canadian scholars on aging as possible. Moreover, where appropriate, we forced a marriage between two authors with similar expertise but different perspectives on the topic. In many cases, these authors had not had an opportunity to collaborate in the past. In some instances we were not successful in finding authors or in obtaining an agreement to write an overview article on a specific topic, or to review the literature in a specific discipline. We have provided a small corrective to the resultant gaps with the additional papers included in this book. Even so, the collection does not include a discussion of literature, history, politics, or multiculturalism in relation to aging. Nevertheless, we believe the contents of this book represent a reasonably complete and up-to-date inventory of current aging topics and issues facing Canadians and Canadian society.

The next four chapters review issues pertaining to the current environment and aging. In Chapter 2, Joseph and Martin Matthews indicate where Canada's old population lives, and the consequences for later life of living in a large urban place, a small urban place, or a rural area. Focusing on the older population living in rural areas or dispersed small towns with less than 5,000 population, they note that the latter are aging communities with much higher proportions of their populations being old than the proportion found in the general population. They describe a subset of rural small towns where 30% or more of the population is aged 65 or older. Size, proximity to urban areas, and migration patterns affect the nature of these communities as living environments for the elderly. For example, many smaller towns may have a nursing home but few other services to assist the elderly to remain in their own homes. The result is often premature institutionalization. While it is difficult to generalize about the wide variety of rural and small town living environments, general living conditions as indexed by factors such as age and quality of housing, and such amenities as flush toilets or hot water are poorer outside the urban environment. Another common feature is "transportation dependency" or "transportation deficits". Large proportions of seniors living in small communities report difficulties in getting around their communities, which often lack bus or taxi services. Hence, they are dependent on access to a privately-owned automobile. But many, especially older widows, may not drive at all or may no longer be able to drive themselves.

Haldemann and Wister (Chapter 3) focus on housing issues in the urban environment. Just as Joseph and Martin Matthews stress heterogeneity of living environments at the community level, Haldemann and Wister stress the presence of heterogeneity at the level of the built environment. Housing for the elderly is no longer confined to the "total institution" located on the fringes of urban places. Housing for older adults may include public and non-profit housing with varying levels of supportive services and at varying levels of affordability. Current challenges include providing housing for people with different needs, and for meeting the changing housing needs of individuals over time. With increased housing options, there will nonetheless continue to be a demand for the institutional setting, which can optimize care provision for the very frail and ill elderly.

Yet another treatment of the distribution of the older Canadian population is provided in Chapter 4 by geographers Moore and Rosenberg, who draw on several recent Canadian sources of data to examine two kinds of geographical mobility of the elderly. Residential mobility refers to changes in permanent residence within a given labour market, i.e., a short-distance move. Migration, on the other hand, refers to long-distance moves between labour markets. They examine such moves in a life course perspective, in relation to critical life events such as retirement, health changes, or widowhood. While the elderly move less often than the young, these moves are often related to major changes and call for important adjustments. In the aggregate, the patterns of such migration have important policy consequences for society.

Concluding the set of chapters on living environments, in Chapter 5, Rule, Milke and Dobbs review the evidence about older people's experience of sensory, cognitive and social deficits that affect their interaction with the environment. They distinguish between the cognitively impaired resident of an institution for the aged and the resident who is not cognitively impaired, and make specific recommendations for the design of facilities for the cognitively impaired,

Chappell's chapter on technology, which follows, also deals to some extent with living environments for the aged. She provides insights into the possibilities of supporting older people who wish to live in their own home environments. Technology can enhance safety and overcome physical limitations, and its potential to support independent living of the elderly is just beginning to be tapped. Technology can be "high-tech", such as in-home medical monitoring devices, or "low-tech", such as better-designed doors, utensils and clothing. The living environments of the elderly are likely to become more technological in the future, but this technology is generally appreciated by people of all ages — good design is good for everyone, including potential caregivers. Chappell also describes how technology for the aged is beginning to constitute an important new market for entrepreneurs.

The next three articles address the domains of work and leisure. In Chapter 7, Foot and Gibson begin by reminding us that no country has matched Canada in post-war labour force growth. This record was achieved because Canada had the largest baby boom, which entered the labour force in the 1960s and 1970s. With persistent low fertility, the entry of younger people into the labour force has declined and the labour force is aging. Current trends toward early retirement may have to be countered if we are to meet future demands for labour. In addition, educational changes will be required to create a more generalist, flexible worker who might well be expected to change career paths several times, and to adapt to new technology. The re-education and retraining of middle-aged and older workers will assume greater importance in the future.

McDonald and Chen reinforce the same theme in Chapter 8, arguing that older workers can fill the emerging labour force needs, if only they can be enticed to remain in or re-enter the labour force. The aging of the labour force is, they argue, more accurately described as a "middle-aging". Keeping such workers in the labour force will require enhanced introduction of part-time, flex-time and part-year work, job redesign and programs that allow workers to ease their transition into retirement. These changes will require innovative thinking and policies on the part of management and of labour.

In Chapter 9, Ouellette takes us into a different institutional sector, defined in one sense as "non-work" — the domain of leisure. In the context of Canadian research on aging and leisure, he reviews several studies done by himself and others in New Brunswick. Physical activity is an increasingly important leisure pursuit for the elderly, but by no means the only one. The elderly are posing new demands on the educational system and creating new organizations for recreational, tourist and sedentary leisure pursuits.

Any person's life can be quite fully described in terms of the three domains of work, leisure, and family. The next three chapters in the book deal with this third domain, the family.

The impact of population aging on family life is described by Rosenthal and Gladstone in Chapter 10. The family is neither dead nor dying, but its structure is different, with the typical family having more generations but fewer people at each generational level. People have more opportunities, over a longer period of time than in earlier historical periods, to live out family relationships with parents and grandparents, siblings and children. With the oldest generation living longer, the family is the major source of support to frail or ill elderly. Since women carry the brunt of caregiving, important dilemmas for women are posed as they try to maintain occupational careers while meeting family obligations. The authors suggest that governments can play important roles to strengthen the family's ability to fulfil its support functions.

The next chapter, by Aronson, pursues the issue of women's roles in family care provision to the elderly. She notes that it is taken for granted in our society that the family is the first resort for care provision, including care for the elderly. Public policies that increasingly emphasize community care rely on and reinforce this assumption. While the gendered nature of family care for the elderly is profoundly influenced by large-scale features of the political economy, Aronson focuses this contribution by describing the meaning of caring and felt obligations to care, for women.

In Chapter 12, Connidis makes some further observations of family life, in order to complement the earlier chapters that deal with the family. She focuses on the neglected areas of unmarried and childless elderly, and sibling relationships in later life. She also highlights some areas of aging and family that have been distorted in media or even professional accounts. Here, she looks at grandparenthood, later life marriage, and intergenerational relations. Family ties over the life course, Connidis argues, have pervasive influences on individuals.

Leaving the area of the family, the next chapter, by Chen and Zhou, indicates a growing awareness of the importance of the seniors market or "grey market". This is complementary to Chappell's argument about the growing importance of the senior as a consumer. Based on a content analysis of general-audience and specialized magazines targeted to the older population, Chen and Zhou find an increased representation of older characters in Canadian magazine advertisements, compared to an earlier study. The portrayal of the elderly is also more positive, more social and integrative, and more active than that found in many previous studies. However, the portrayal of the aged is not totally realistic. For example, older males are over-represented, while racial minorities are not well represented in this media portrait of the elderly.

The final three chapters of the book focus on the policy area. In Chapter 14, Gee and McDaniel provide a general framework for understanding policy debates in the aging area, and emphasize the importance of gender issues for social policy. Their discussion of the need for age-sensitive workplace policies resonates nicely with points raised by McDonald and Chen, and by Rosenthal and Gladstone. Gee and McDaniel argue strongly that Canadians should not adopt a crisis mentality about the impact of population aging. While the policy issues are complex, they call for careful, information-based creativity and planning, not panic. Their hope, however, is that population aging will see creative social policy and not simply more economic policies.

Marshal, in Chapter 15, outlines a desired policy process for aging and health, based on the principles of "healthy public policy". He then describes several barriers to the realization of such a policy process, including narrow foci based on demographic determinism, the reduction of social policy to economic policy (see also Chapter 14), a medicalization of health policy, and ageism. Additional structural barriers noted by Marshall include the complex array of competing or over-lapping policy structures of the provinces and the federal governments, a weak pool of policy experts, lack of basic data and the need for intersectoral coordination mechanisms.

In the final chapter, Béland and Shapiro narrow the policy focus to the area of long-term care, but broaden the scope of the analysis to examine recent long-term care reform policy documents from all Canadian provinces. They include a description of the values underlying long-term care reform in the various provinces, the organizational principles and structure of the long-term care systems, and the financial aspects of the systems. While within Canada the provincial systems may appear to be quite different from one another, when viewed in a larger, international context, the various provincial systems appear to be quite similar in values, organizational principles and financing, and to be well integrated with broader aspects of health and social policy in Canada.

Notes

1. Statistical data are found in Victor W. Marshall and Blossom T. Wigdor, "Services for the Elderly in Canada", in Jordan I. Kosberg (Ed.) (1994) *International Handbook on Services to the Elderly*. Westport, Conn.: Greenwood Publishers; and in Statistics Canada (1992), *The Nation*. Ottawa: Statistics Canada Cat. 93-310.

2. Ellen M. Gee (1987). "Historical change in the family life course of men and women" In Victor W. Marshall (Ed.), *Aging in Canada: Social Perspectives, 2nd edition*. Markham: Fitzhenry and Whiteside. It should be stressed that there is considerable variability, with not everyone encountering the life event we are discussing in the same order or sequence. However, the great majority of life courses vary little from this standard sequence.

3. Canadian research on retirement is presented in Lynn McDonald and Richard A. Wanner (1990). *Retirement in Canada*. Toronto: Butterworths.

4. Gee, Ellen M., and McDaniel, Susan A. (1991). "Pension politics and challenges: Retirement policy implications." *Canadian Public Policy 17* (4): 456-472.

5. Ng, Edward (1992). "Children and elderly people: Sharing public income resources". *Canadian Social Trends*, no. 25, 12-15.

6. National Advisory Council on Aging (1991). *The Economic Situation of Canada's Seniors. A Fact Book*. Ottawa: Ministry of Supply and Services Cat. no. H71-3/14-1991E.

7. For discussions of aging and dying issues, see Victor W. Marshall, *Last Chapters: A Sociology of Aging and Dying*. Monterey, California: Brooks/Cole (1980), and "A sociological perspective on aging and dying", In V.W. Marshall (Ed.), *Later Life: The Social Psychology of Aging*. Beverly Hills, California: Sage (1986), pp. 125-146.

AUTHORS' NOTE

Work on this paper (and on this book) was supported in part by CARNET: The Canadian Aging Research Network, funded by the federal Networks of Centres of Excellence Program.

Growing Old in Aging Communities

ALUN E. JOSEPH AND ANNE MARTIN MATTHEWS

About one in every three elderly Canadians resides in communities well outside the typical cityscape. In 1981, 21.9 percent of Canadians aged 65 or older lived in rural areas.[1] A further 8.1 percent of Canada's elderly population lived in small urban places of 1,000-4,999 people.[2] Given the considerable degree of cohesiveness that exists between (dispersed) rural and small-town Canada, we believe that there are very good grounds for considering many of these communities of 1,000-4,999 inhabitants as integral elements of the *rural* settlement system, even though strictly speaking they are defined as urban in census terms.[3] Indeed, it is these rural small towns which most characterize the phenomenon of "growing old in aging communities."

The overall objective of this paper is to provide a descriptive analysis of the experience of population aging in rural small towns from the complementary perspectives of communities and their aging residents. Throughout our discussion, we attempt to examine the interrelationships between the aging individual and the local community in order to understand more fully the typical as well as the unique features of growing old in aging communities.

We begin by considering the demography of aging rural communities, but subsequently extend our discussion to embrace their broader social attributes. We then consider the socio-economic characteristics of the rural elderly and the major features of their social world. These community and individual perspectives on rural aging provide the platform for the section of the paper that deals directly with the recursive relationship between person and place, between aging individuals and their aging communities. In this pivotal part of the discussion, we focus on voluntarism as a substantive and dynamic link between individual and community.

A central theme overall is that the problems which individuals experience can be treated as "personal troubles" to be dealt with privately by those directly involved, or they can be generalized as "public issues" of concern to society as a whole.[4] While some of the problems that men and women experience as part of the aging process can appropriately be considered personal troubles, other events and conditions central to the experience of growing old in aging communities may also be defined as public issues governed by policy and legislation. For example, issues of failing health or loneliness may be considered personal troubles to be surmounted by an elderly person. However, some of the repercussions of declining independence, such as increased demands on formal helping services, may lead to concerns about the availability of appropriate service facilities or the provision of adequate transportation. Such concerns fall within the purview of public policy. Thus, this paper concludes with a consideration of several policy issues central to the individual and collective experience of growing old in aging rural communities.

The Demography of the Aging Community

Population aging is one of the unifying features of rural regions across Canada.[5] However, within most rural regions there exists a "demographic divide" between *nucleated* rural communities with generally high, or very high, proportions of elderly in their total populations and *dispersed* rural communities with substantially lower proportions of elderly. Indeed, the small towns of Canada are home to a disproportionate share of our elderly population. In 1981, settlements with 1,000-4,999 people had, in aggregate, 12.9 percent of their population aged 65 or older. This compared with 9.7 percent for the country as a whole. At the same time, these communities had, in aggregate, a high proportion of persons aged 80 and over — 2.9 percent, compared to the national figure of 1.9 percent.[6] However, these summary data conceal important variations within the rural milieu. In particular, they mask the existence of a significant subset of rural small towns with proportions of elderly population exceeding 30 percent and correspondingly high percentages of the very old.[7] It is in communities such as these that the social ramifications of population aging are most keenly felt.

In discussing the nature and implications of population aging in small towns, a distinction must be made between the "congregation" and the "relative concentration" of the elderly. Congregation considers numbers of elderly people without reference to the remainder of the population. The congregational dimension of population aging is important because it captures the notions of "target populations" and "threshold populations" for seniors' programs. In contrast, the number of elderly people as a proportion of the total population in a community is a question of relative concentration.[8] As the relative concentration of the elderly in community populations increases, a shift in the pattern of service needs may occur, such that there is an expansion of demands for special programs targeted to the elderly and a contraction of demands for services and facilities used by younger groups. It is the relative concentration of elderly people in small towns, often running at two to three times the national average, that has drawn the attention of policy-makers and analysts.

In addition to noting characteristic congregation and relative concentration levels, we need to acknowledge that the population structures of aging communities are the cumulative, often distinctive, record of past patterns of fertility, longevity and migration. Migration is usually the most important and volatile source of variation in population structures, and rural small towns may be particularly affected by *elderly* migration. By adding to the numbers of those who have lived in the same community for their whole lives, or "aged-in-place," the in-migration of older adults can lead to a greater (absolute) congregation of the elderly in a community. If the size of younger cohorts remains the same, or decreases through out-migration, an increase in relative concentration will also occur. In this way, high proportions of elderly can arise from different community demographic histories, and it is likely that these histories will create very different socio-environmental contexts for aging.[9]

What are Aging Communities Like?

We have identified the demographic parameters, notably high levels of elderly concentration overall and disproportionately high shares of the very old in particular, that distinguish many small, mostly rural, communities from the large towns and cities of Canada. Prior to considering the environmental context for aging that these communities provide, we must acknowledge once again that they are by no means homogeneous. Indeed, we argue strongly for the recognition of the heterogeneity of the environments in which rural Canadians, including rural small-town residents, find themselves growing old. Unfortunately, the richness of the rural mosaic is frequently ignored. As Raymond T. Coward notes, "In the zeal to characterize environmental similarities, the mistake of overgeneralizing the concept of rurality has too often been made, and in the process has obliterated the diversity which exists in rural environments."[10] While agreeing in principle with Coward, we maintain that at various levels of inquiry, ranging from the community itself (the "macro" level) to the immediate circumstance of the home (the "micro" level), it is possible, and indeed necessary, to generalize about the contrasting environmental contexts in which elderly persons in rural small towns find themselves. Here, we are particularly interested in the macro, community context of aging.

Three factors discriminate quite effectively amongst small towns at the macro level: population size, urban proximity, and migration experience. Various commentators have proposed population size as a primary discriminator of small-town environments. Most emphasize the service dimension, noting that service availability and choice are positively correlated with community size. Gerald Hodge and Mohammad A. Qadeer, for instance, suggest that small rural towns of 1,000-2,500 inhabitants provide significantly fewer services to their residents than do rural towns of greater size.[11] Of particular relevance to the elderly is the fact that smaller communities typically lack housing and services catering to those who require limited assistance to maintain independence.[12] Since many small towns have nursing homes (or other institutional housing forms), this lack of intermediate housing options may translate all too often into an uncomfortable choice between premature institutionalization and "struggling on" at home.

Urban proximity is also important in terms of the service and housing options available to small-town residents. For example, communities located near large urban centres provide their residents with greater potential access to specialized health care services and age-targeted housing developments than do more isolated communities. However, urban proximity may also have a pervasive effect on the overall character of communities. Most urban-proximate small towns have been heavily affected by "spillover" urban growth,[13] such that many of them have effectively lost their distinctiveness, often becoming bedroom or dormitory communities. Indeed, most of these urban-proximate small towns are, to all intents and purposes, part of urban Canada, and they have little in common with their rural counterparts. Within the large residual category of "non urban-proximate" small towns, a variety of communities represent the various faces of *rural* small-town Canada. Among these communities, an important distinction has to be made between settlements in the agricultural core regions of Canada and those in the resource hinterlands of the north and coastal regions.[14] Isolated communities in resource hinterlands consistently present more limited service profiles and more restricted catchment areas. These small towns also exhibit a greater reliance on large, often resource-based industries for job creation, which adds to their distinctive character.

In terms of migration experience, the third of our discriminating factors, communities that have aged primarily through out-migration of younger cohorts or through aging-in-place, will be very different from those that have aged primarily through in-migration of older persons. Furthermore, small towns that have attracted mostly local, generally older migrants seeking more appropriate housing or better services need to be distinguished from communities that have attracted long-distance, generally younger migrants seeking specific amenities. There is not always consensus, though, about the implications of such a differentiation for important themes like service provision. For example, some commentators contend that because long-distance in-migrants are generally married, healthier and wealthier, they are less likely to become dependent on formal health and social support services than are local in-migrants or elderly persons who have aged in place.[15] However, others argue that the lack of informal supports built up through kinship and over long years of residence may lead long-distance in-migrants to lean more heavily on formal supports.[16] As

Graham D. Rowles notes, this may be the case even for migrants who are returning to their "home" communities:

> Elderly return migrants, although they may have been born in the community, have spent most of their working lives elsewhere, often in an urban environment, before "coming home" to retire. They are less likely to be integrated into local support networks and are unable to count on the accumulated social credit and earned status in the community that provides the context for assistance available to lifelong residents.[17]

Although they are often treated individually, we believe that it is more appropriate to consider population size, urban proximity and migration experience as interdependent descriptors of communities. This is particularly true in terms of service provision. For example, on the supply side of the equation, an urban-proximate community might have fewer services, yet provide better access to city-based services, than a smaller town isolated from service-rich urban centres. On the demand side, communities similar in size and urban proximity might differ in terms of the migration-influenced age mix of elderly residents drawing on local services. The lesson is clear — it is necessary but difficult to generalize about the nature of aging communities. Similar challenges exist in pronouncing on the lives of elderly residents, and it is to the individual perspective on growing old in aging communities that we now turn.

The Characteristics of the Rural Elderly

In a recent analysis of town and village life in Canada, Gerald Hodge and Mohammed A. Qadeer comment on the salience of the concept of rurality in the lives of Canadians today. They conclude that "...while the conventional rural-urban differences have eroded, new factors have come into play which distinguish small and large communities.... Towns and villages may not be a separate universe, but they certainly are a distinct genre of the contemporary urban species."[18] Several features are known to characterize small-town and rural Canada: generally, families are larger, birth rates and out-migration are higher, labour force participation rates are lower, service sector employment is less important, educational and income levels are lower, and access to communication media is inferior.[19]

In addition, several socio-demographic characteristics distinguish the rural and urban elderly. Historically, there has been an inverse relationship between community size and the ratio of men to women in the older population.[20] In 1981, urban areas of 500,000 or more residents had only 65 men per 100 women aged 65 and over, while at the other end of the rural-urban continuum, rural dispersed communities had more men than women in their elderly population.[21] However, recent studies of rural aging have reported a dramatic fall in the sex ratio, with some commentators venturing to suggest that small towns may increasingly become centres of elderly women.[22] The rural aged are also more likely than the urban to be married.[23]

However, in the key area of economic security, there is some debate as to whether the rural aged are financially disadvantaged in comparison to their urban counterparts. A report of the National Council of Welfare indicates no substantial variation in the risk of poverty for *families* living in different-sized communities, and notes that *individuals* living in rural areas face the lowest risk of falling below the low-income line.[24] Contrary to these claims, several local and regional studies report that elderly (headed) households in rural areas have lower family incomes than do those in urban areas.[25] For instance, in Manitoba, the mean monthly incomes reported by rural elders in the early 1980s were consistently lower than those reported by their urban peers.[26] It appears, however, that these conflicting results may well be the artifact of definitional problems. In Canada, low-income cut-offs are adjusted by degree of urbanization, and are consequently higher in urban areas. Therefore, in a comparison of two financially distressed seniors, the rural small-town elder could have the lower income, but only the urban resident would be classified as "poor." It is also possible that the comparison of communities of like size across unlike regions has produced spurious results. For instance, for over 50 years per capita personal income in Ontario has been almost exactly double that in Prince Edward Island as well as Newfoundland and Labrador. Such contrasts reflect the distinctive economic bases of the regions and subregions wherein the elderly reside. They constitute an overarching, regional component of the environmental context of aging.

Regardless of the definitional and regional issues that plague national contrasts in income levels, the rural elderly repeatedly come second to their urban counterparts in terms of general living conditions. Rural households headed by the elderly are less likely to have such taken-for-granted amenities as piped hot and cold water or the convenience of freezers, dishwashers, or automobiles than are urban households.[27] The incidence of this deprivation in living conditions is likely to be greater in poorer provinces.

The Social World of the Rural Elderly

There is, of course, more to being rural, to being a resident of a small town, than these aggregate characteristics of elderly residents suggest. Data on the objective circumstances of life are obviously relevant to the discussion of growing old in aging rural communities, but they give an incomplete picture of the social world of the elderly, and generally understate the importance of "community" as the medium through which individuals collectively experience aging. The social world of the rural elderly thus requires attention.

In our discussion of the social milieu we will consider, in turn, prevalent patterns of informal social support and of access to formal support services. This focus on "support" is somewhat restrictive in the sense that it avoids discussion of the attitudes or beliefs that may underlie rural-urban contrasts in various types of behaviour. Indeed, as Norah C. Keating notes, "Rurality must not be seen as an objective circumstance outside the individual, but as an internal creation, an element of the way in which individuals organize and construe their lifeworlds."[28] Despite this caveat, we believe that a focus on support themes not only provides a window on the strengths and weaknesses, and freedoms and constraints, intrinsic to the social world of the rural elderly, but also provides an appropriate backdrop for the analysis of the aging individual in the aging community.

Comparisons of social support patterns, especially informal exchanges among families of rural versus urban elderly, are fraught with conflicting findings. The debate involves whether rural elders are more or less integrated into a supportive family network than are urban elders. Some studies report that the rural elderly are less likely than the urban elderly to rely on family members for assistance, and more likely to rely on neighbours and friends. This finding is particularly intriguing when one considers that other studies have reported that the rural elderly have significantly larger family networks than do the urban elderly, and that these networks are geographically more proximate.[29]

Overall, then, there is little evidence of significant differences in patterns of family support between the rural and urban elderly. The rural aged are no more likely than their urban peers to share a household with other family members. They are also no more likely to include different types of kin (children, nieces, cousins) in descriptions of their family networks, although they do report higher levels of contact with brothers and sisters.

Within the local environs of the rural community, neighbours provide more casual contacts for the elderly than appears to be the case in urban areas, although planned social events may primarily involve kinfolk, especially children and their families, as is the norm in urban centres. It also appears that older rural women depend primarily on their age peers for friendship, and that friendship bonds are strengthened by duration of residential stability.[30] But there are often certain dysfunctions in this non-kin component of the support system. Given the town and village clustering of the aged, there is a strong probability that their friends and neighbours are also elderly women living alone, thus limiting the amount of practical assistance to be offered by neighbours. This may help to explain why neighbours apparently contribute so little in terms of practical support to the rural elderly, even with such traditional neighbourly activities as cutting grass or shovelling driveways in winter.[31] The likelihood of having a confidante also declines with age, and with widowhood, in spite of the concentration of elderly widows in small settlements where access is not a problem and the women are known to one another. Indeed, it appears that rural elders have contact with relatively few people, considering their potential network of acquaintances.

On the basis of these varied and disparate observations, what are we able to conclude about the social world of the rural elderly? There is evidence that certain regions of the country have strong familistic orientations which guarantee high levels of support to the aged.[32] For the most part, the rural elderly are as integrated as the urban elderly into family and non-family support systems, and perhaps even more so. The reliability of these informal supports is, however, probably more precarious: children live farther away, the rural elderly receive fewer personal visits, and they have older neighbours. In other words, rural seniors may be as "vulnerable" to dependence on formal support services as their urban counterparts. But are these services as available and as accessible?

Rural Canada is generally well served in terms of institutional facilities like hospitals and nursing homes. Nova Scotia has the largest proportion (24 percent) of such facilities in rural areas, compared to a low of three percent in Manitoba. It is noteworthy, though, that all the provinces except Prince Edward Island, Ontario, and British Columbia have the largest proportion of their institutional facilities located in small towns with 1,000-4,999 residents.[33] Overall, it appears that in rural and small-town Canada, services are readily available for the elderly who are ill and in need of institutional facilities, but much less so for those whose ability to remain living in the community is dependent upon limited assistance with tasks of daily living. This is as true of special housing options (such as small congregate homes or serviced apartments) as it is of health and home support services (such as home nursing and Meals-on-Wheels). It follows that seniors in need of limited formal support may be faced by uncomfortable choices: either struggling on in inappropriate housing or accepting premature institutionalization in a local facility; or perhaps either staying on in a familiar community or moving to one that offers more appropriate housing/support. It is in these sorts of deliberations that the local (un)availability of formal support services (including housing) and the accessibility of alternatives elsewhere become central questions.

We will address general issues of local service availability and choice in the concluding section as they are very much related to policy concerns that stem from the tension between the "personal troubles" and "public issues" views of aging introduced earlier in the paper. Here, the focus is on a specific feature of the service accessibility issue — "rural transportation" — a feature that has been closely associated with the very nature of rurality.

While the lack of access to adequate transportation has consistently been identified as a major concern of rural elders, estimates of need vary considerably, both within and between provinces and according to the nature of the inquiry.[34] However, there is no doubt that, compared to their urban counterparts, rural elders have less access to transportation, as many small towns and villages do not have public transit systems and some do not have private taxis.

Overall, it is estimated that approximately 20 percent of the rural elderly have a serious transportation problem to almost all destinations. A further 20 percent have difficulty getting around in their local town at least once a week, and approximately a quarter have trouble getting to a larger centre at least once a month.[35] These individuals are often referred to as "transport dependent" in that they usually depend on others for their mobility. The likelihood of transport dependence increases with age; those with the most serious transportation problems are typically very aged, widowed women who live alone on a low income and do not own a car. Among such women, few ever were drivers, and even fewer have driven in winter. Reliant on their husbands as a primary source of transportation, their widowhood occasions a significant loss of ready access to all sorts of destinations.[36] Such a disadvantage is particularly acute in the rural context, where various degrees of transportation dependence may severely circumscribe the options of elderly residents seeking better support or more suitable housing.

The geographic dispersion of the population, of facilities and services, and the distance factor make access to adequate transportation the *sine qua non* of rural life for the elderly. It is not so much that support services are totally unavailable in rural areas, but rather that they are frequently inaccessible. A medical specialist may be available, but located in a large town 60 kilometres away. A day centre program may be in place, but distantly located and therefore difficult to reach during winter months when it is most needed. The continuing challenge of service provision to rural elders is thus the need to enhance the accessibility as well as the availability of programs.

The Individual in the Aging Community

How do rural villages and towns cope with the needs of their aging residents and how do elderly individuals get along in their aging communities? These questions lie at the core of the discussion of growing old in aging communities, but we must recognize that they are part of a more general issue, "community sustainability," that permeates all levels of the debate on rural communities and rural life.[37] The sustainability of aging rural communities depends upon the extent to which they remain "economically viable," in terms of their capacity to support growing numbers of the elderly, and "socially vital" in the face of high levels of relative concentration of the elderly.

Without denying the importance of economic viability, we believe that the social vitality of communities is of more immediate relevance to the life experience of aging rural residents. Following Ralph Matthews, we will distinguish between the formal and informal dimensions of social vitality:

The institutions and organizations which formalize on-going daily activity and which structure social life constitute the *formal level of community social vitality*. Underlying the formal institutional level there is an *informal level of community social vitality*. Here the focus is on the attitudes and values of the community members and on their *involvement and commitment* to community life ... and on the *pattern of leadership* and the *extent of community co-operation*.[38]

To date, this paper has addressed both dimensions of social vitality. In terms of the formal level of community social vitality, we have focused on the extent to which services (particularly transportation and community-based versus institutional services) are available within different kinds of rural communities. In addition, we considered the ways in which the availability and accessibility of services in communities structure the social lives of their elderly residents. Issues associated with the informal level of community social vitality have been addressed in terms of the social world of the rural elderly, especially their social support patterns and family and friendship ties.

However, in order to emphasize the dynamic interplay between the formal and informal levels of social vitality, and to assess the implications of that interplay for the lives of elderly individuals in aging communities, we turn to a consideration of "voluntarism." We believe that voluntarism lies squarely at the intersection of the formal and informal components of social vitality; voluntarism is an informal social activity that promotes the vitality of formal institutions. We would further argue that voluntarism provides a window through which the interconnection of broad community attributes (like population size and proportions of elderly) and the individual experience of aging can be glimpsed.

Voluntarism is becoming increasingly important in social-service provision as national governments devolve responsibility for particular programs to lower levels of government and/or to the voluntary and private sectors.[39] This is not new to the provision of social support for the elderly, because churches, social clubs and charitable organizations have long been active in the field. What is new, though, is the degree of pressure placed on the resources of these organizations, especially in small towns where the elderly constitute a high proportion of the total population. This is not to say that the congregation of the elderly in small towns is not a relevant consideration. Indeed, all too often, the small number of elderly persons with particular needs in small towns has translated into irregular hours of service, extended service catchment areas, or "homogenized" services. However, assuming sufficient demand for services, we believe that the high relative concentration of elderly persons in small rural towns profoundly affects the provision of volunteer-reliant services.

The role of local volunteers in raising funds and in setting up and delivering services has become extremely important in recent years, especially for services like Meals-on-Wheels and the provision of transportation.[40] But how does the proportion of elderly people in community populations affect the availability of volunteers? First, it should be acknowledged that the impact of relative concentrations of the elderly on patterns of voluntarism is intertwined with that of community size. Small communities, regardless of the exact proportions of the population that is elderly, often find it difficult to sustain necessary levels of voluntarism, either in service initiation and administration or in fundraising and service-delivery activities. For example, in order to secure a provincial government subsidy for its operations, a Meals-on-Wheels program in Ontario serving 25 elderly persons must go through the same set-up procedures as one serving 200 persons. The program must have a volunteer board (to oversee its activities), a service co-ordinator and volunteer fundraisers, as well as volunteers to prepare and deliver meals. There are clearly economies of scale in voluntarism that work against small communities, making it difficult to launch and sustain local initiatives. It is worth noting that the absence of economies of scale in voluntarism in small communities may be paralleled by the scale problems in service demand mentioned earlier. The congregation of elderly in a small community may simply be insufficient to support a particular service.

A high proportion of elderly persons exacerbates "generic" problems of mounting and sustaining local service initiatives in small communities. The relationship between the number of potential volunteers and potential clients in a community population is critical in determining the likely magnitude of impacts. This can be crudely assessed by calculating an elderly dependency ratio. As an illustration, Alun Joseph and Denise Cloutier report that, for Ontario as a whole, the ratio of population aged 20-64 to population aged 65 or over was 5.59: 1 in 1986. In contrast, for (predominantly rural) Grey County it was 3.54: 1; for towns in Grey County it was 2.88: 1; and for villages in Grey County it was 2.70: 1.[41] Taken at face value, these ratios suggest that the relative concentration of the elderly (reflected in the dependency ratio) provides an important indicator of the ability of communities to cope with the implications of population aging for voluntary service provision. The situation is, however, more complicated than this because the elderly themselves are invariably part of the volunteer pool in small towns.

There is consistent evidence for the participation of younger elderly persons in voluntary service-related activities, especially as drivers in transportation schemes. However, volunteers for physically demanding services like caregiver relief (sometimes referred to as "respite care") tend to be middle-aged women.[42] It is unlikely that the overall role of seniors as volunteers will expand greatly. Younger elderly people (usually women), otherwise potentially available to assume voluntary care-giving roles, may already be providing care to a spouse.[43] Migration, another of the rural community attributes discussed earlier, may also play a role in limiting involvement by the elderly in volunteer activities.

Several studies have reported that elderly migrants to rural small towns tend to be drawn disproportionately from higher socio-economic groups, such that "oldtimers" and "newcomers" may differ as much by class and income as they do by length of residence. This may inhibit the participation of in-migrants as volunteers in service provision when client groups are dominated by persons who have aged-in-place and who have different class affiliations, perhaps compounding the social polarization between those who need help and those who are in a position to give it.[44]

A second, and possibly more important, impact of migration on voluntarism stems from the high incidence of seasonal migration among elderly Canadians, a factor often referred to as the "snowbird" phenomenon. Snowbirds tend to have the same profile (relatively young, healthy and affluent) as elderly volunteers, so that seasonal migration of the elderly to warmer climes undoubtedly removes people from the volunteer pool for a part of the fall/winter season (typically three to six months), although precise numbers are not known.[45] The population of the elderly left behind will contain proportionately more older, frailer and less affluent persons. This all occurs at a time when the Canadian winter places pressure on service delivery systems in rural areas. Communities with large numbers of elderly in-migrants who fit the profile of snowbirds are particularly prone to this winter depletion of seniors from the volunteer pool, although long-term residents may also join in the seasonal exodus. The net result is that in winter the elderly populations of many rural small towns are more likely to be dominated by those in need of help, at the very time when there are comparatively few elderly volunteer providers. In addition, there is evidence that once snowbirds develop significant health problems, they cease their pattern of seasonal migration, thereby swelling the ranks of those needing assistance in winter months.[46]

Voluntarism is an excellent example of a social activity that ties the individual to the community and the community to the individual. Institutions in aging communities are strengthened by voluntarism. Aging individuals benefit generally from this expression of the social vitality of their community and may also be the recipients of services. Some elderly people will also draw satisfaction from being volunteers themselves. However, it would be unwise to be overly captivated by the dynamic relationship between individual and community that is embodied in voluntarism. We believe rather that the larger, overarching issue governing the experience of growing old in aging rural communities stems from the tension between individual responsibility and state responsibility, between personal troubles and public issues.

Personal Troubles versus Public Issues

At several points in this paper, we have noted that rural small towns are often hard pressed to cope effectively with elderly residents in need of limited assistance to maintain their independence. This lack of "intermediate" options, lying between the extremes of institutionalization and "struggling on," is particularly evident in the area of housing, where the urban elderly are consistently presented with a more extensive and varied menu of choices than are the rural elderly. It is in the context of this housing issue that it is important to explore some of the important policy questions associated with the experience of growing old in aging rural communities.

First, it is important to remember that housing is more than shelter. The home represents the point of access to the surrounding physical and social environments. It is also the locus for social exchange, for the receipt of social support, and for the consumption of services. These various attributes of the home are generally more important for the elderly than they are for younger age groups. Older people generally spend more time in the home, especially after retirement. Moreover, the aging process can produce a dissonance between the supportive characteristics of the home and the needs of the individual, or what M. Powell Lawton and others have referred to as "environmental press."[47] It is not the intention here to reiterate these theories or to catalogue supporting empirical evidence. Instead, it is sufficient to invoke this literature as context and rationale for the use of housing choice to illustrate the interconnection of personal troubles and public issues.

Housing choice is a behaviour that binds the aging individual to the community. It also spans the divide between the objective characteristics of communities and their (perceived) subjective status in the eyes of elderly residents. It is the existence of a subjective dimension in housing choice that promotes what often appear to be irrational decisions, such as staying on in the local community despite offers of more suitable accommodation elsewhere. Such determination to stay in a community is testimony to the power of place, to the importance of attachments built up over a lifetime.[48] Public policy has the tools to deal with the objective problems of housing the elderly. For example, building codes and standards can be used to promote the design of built environments that facilitate continuing independence. However, public policy does not deal at all well with subjectively based housing decisions, or with their outcomes.

It is through the outcomes of decisions to stay on that the personal troubles of the elderly become a public policy issue. To what extent should the state extend support to elderly people who choose to remain in inappropriate housing in small, difficult-to-service rural communities? Should in-home support services, for instance, be equally available, and of similar quality, in urban and rural communities? In most jurisdictions in Canada, the answer has been a qualified yes; responsible agencies have struggled to provide standard services to rural communities. Indeed, many rural small towns have flourished as the location of employment-generating social service agencies. But there is evidence that this may not continue indefinitely. Across Canada, rural post offices, long a focal point of the social life of rural communities, are being down-graded or closed. In some provinces, notably Saskatchewan, rural hospitals are under serious threat, with important ramifications for physician services. Such changes may well be a harbinger of the further decline of the objective quality-of-life in rural Canada. For a glimpse of where long-term public policy could lead, one can look to the antipodes, where New Zealand presents a stark picture of a restructured rural society in which the local post office, bank, drugstore, general practitioner and dentist have all but disappeared from towns of 1,000-2,500 people, over the space of only seven years.[49] In this way, shifts in public policy can turn responsibility for coping with the difficulties of growing old in an aging rural community back upon the individual, thereby creating the potential for more personal troubles.

In such a climate, aging rural communities in Canada will be caught between shifting public policy and the mounting personal troubles of their elderly residents in the years ahead. Rural small towns will strive to cope with the needs of an increasing congregation of elderly residents and to maintain their social vitality in the face of high relative concentrations of the aged. Their success in maintaining informal support networks, in nurturing the voluntary sector, and in retaining formal support services and institutions will shape the future experience of growing old in aging communities.

NOTES

We are grateful to Ms. Bonnie Dunnett, who ably assisted in the compilation of statistics and provided critical comments on earlier versions of the paper.

1. These data are drawn from Statistics Canada, Census of Canada, Catalogue 92-901, Table 6 (1982). Statistics Canada defines the rural population as that which remains in an area after the urban population has been defined. This means that comparison of rural counts over time are confounded by various reclassification effects. These include definitional boundary crossing in both directions at the urban threshold of 1,000 people and the physical expansion of urban boundaries. Readers are directed to A.E. Joseph, P.D. Keddie and B. Smit, "Unravelling the Population Turnaround in Rural Canada," *The Canadian Geographer* 32.1 (1988): 17-30 for a general discussion of these issues. A specific example of reclassification effects is presented by P.D. Keddie and A.E. Joseph, "Reclassification and Rural-versus-Urban Population Change: A Tale of Two Definitions," *The Canadian Geographer* 35.4 (1991): 412-20.

2. Data for 1981 are used throughout this paper. Unfortunately, in the 1986 Census small-town population counts are available only for areas outside Census Metropolitan Areas (CMAs) and Census Agglomerations (CAs). The 1991 data have not yet been published, but it is likely that they will share the above-mentioned limitation of the 1986 data. An overview of the 1981 data is presented in A. Martin-Matthews, "Aging in Rural Canada," in *North American Elders: United States and Canadian Perspectives*, E. Rathbone-McCuan and B. Havens (eds.), (New York: Greenwood Press, 1988), 143-60.

3. The case for considering small towns located in rural regions as an integral part of rural Canada is made in G. Hodge and M. Qadeer, *Towns and Villages in Canada: the Importance of Being Unimportant* (Toronto: Butterworths, 1983); A. Martin-Matthews, "Variations in the Conceptualization and Measurement of Rurality: Conflicting Findings on the Elderly Widowed," *Journal of Rural Studies* 4.2 (1988): 141-50.

4. This distinction was introduced by C. Mills, *The Sociological Imagination* (New York: Grove Press, 1959).

5. Martin-Matthews, "Aging in Rural Canada"; see also A.E. Joseph and A.M. Fuller, "Towards an Integrative Perspective on the Housing, Services and Transportation Implications of Rural Aging," *Canadian Journal on Aging* 10.2 (1991): 127-48. G. Hodge, *The Elderly in Canada's Small Towns: Recent Trends and Their Implications* (University of British Columbia: Centre for Human Settlement Occasional Paper 43, 1987) provides census data to support this point.

6. Statistics Canada.

7. This issue is raised in Ontario Advisory Council on Senior Citizens, *Toward an Understanding of the Rural Elderly* (Toronto: Queen's Printer, 1980). Specific examples of rural communities with very high proportions of elderly, again from Ontario, are considered in more detail in A.E. Joseph and D.S. Cloutier, "Elderly Migration and its Implications for Service Provision in Rural Communities: an Ontario Perspective," *Journal of Rural Studies* 7.4 (1991): 433-44. Martin Matthews, "Aging in Rural Canada," draws attention to equally high, or higher, proportions of the aged in small towns in Manitoba and Saskatchewan.

8. Joseph and Cloutier apply the concepts of "congregation" and "concentration" in their descriptive analysis of rural population aging in Grey County, Ontario.

9. See Joseph and Cloutier.

10. R.T. Coward, "Planning Community Services for the Rural Elderly: Implications from Research," *The Gerontologist* 19.3 (1979): 275-82, 277.

11. We believe that recent restructuring of rural service provision, including the closure of many small-town post offices, has "inflated" the threshold effect noted by Hodge and Qadeer, perhaps to the 5,000 population level invoked frequently in this paper.

12. The limited range of housing options in small rural towns is discussed at length in Joseph and Fuller.

13. Supporting data are provided in P.D. Keddie and A.E. Joseph, "The Turnaround of the Turnaround? Rural Population Change in Canada, 1976-1986," *The Canadian Geographer* 35.4 (1991): 367-79.

14. Joseph, Keddie and Smit provide population growth data in support of the distinction between rural communities in agricultural core regions and those in resource hinterlands.

15. H.C. Northcott, *Changing Residence: The Geographic Mobility of Elderly Canadians* (Toronto: Butterworths, 1988) provides an extensive review of research on elderly migration in Canada.

16. Joseph and Cloutier provide data that offer qualified support for this position.

17. G.D. Rowles, "What's Rural about Rural Aging? An Appalachian Perspective," *Journal of Rural Studies* 4.2 (1988): 115-24, 17.

18. Hodge and Qadeer, 84.

19. See R. Thompson, *Persistence and Change: The Social and Economic Development of Rural Newfoundland and Labrador, 1971 to 1981* (Government of Newfoundland and Labrador, Department of Rural, Agricultural and Northern Development, 1983).

20. This is supported by data for a sub-region in Quebec reported in R. Santerre, "Masculinité et Vieillissement dans la Bas-Saint-Laurent: Notes de Recherche," *Anthropologie et Sociétés* 6.3 (1982): 115-28, as well as by evidence presented in Saskatchewan Senior Citizens' Provincial Council, *Profile '83: The Senior Populations in Saskatchewan I: Demographics* (Regina: The Council, 1983).

21. Government of Canada, *Canadian Government Report on Aging* (Ottawa: Ministry of Supply and Services, 1982).

22. For example, see Hodge.

23. A comprehensive overview of these contrasts is presented in United Senior Citizens of Ontario, *Elderly Residents in Ontario: Rural-urban Differences* (Toronto: Ministry of Community and Social Services, 1985).

24. National Council of Welfare, *Poverty Profile* (Ottawa: Ministry of Supply and Services, 1985).

25. For example, see Ontario Advisory Council on Senior Citizens.

26. E. Shapiro and L.L. Roos, "Using Health Care: Rural/Urban Differences among the Manitoba Elderly," *The Gerontologist* 24.3 (1984): 270-74.

27. This point was made strongly in Ontario Advisory Council on Senior Citizens.

28. N.C. Keating, *Aging in Rural Canada* (Toronto: Butterworths, 1991), 105.

29. For example, see P.R. Grant and B. Rice, "Transportation Problems of the Rural Elderly," *Canadian Journal on Aging* 2 (March, 1983): 30-35. Evidence of geographic proximity is provided in two Quebec studies: E. Corin, "Manières de Vivre, Manières de Dire: Reseau Social et Socialité Quotidienne des Personnes Agées au Québec," *La Culture et L'age. Questions de Culture* 6.1 (1984): 157-86; E. Corin, J. Tremblay, T. Sherif and L. Bergeron, "Strategies et Tactiques: Les Modalités d'affrontement des Problèmes Chez des Personnes Agées de Milieu Urbain et Rural," *Sociologie et Sociétés* (Numéro Spécial sur le Vieillissement) 16.2 (1984): 89-104.

30. E. Cape, "Aging Women in Rural Settings," in *Aging in Canada: Social Perspectives* (2nd edition), V.M. Marshall (ed.) (Toronto: Fitzhenry and Whiteside, 1987), 84-99, discusses various features of the social world of rural elderly women.

31. Reported by Cape.

32. A. Martin, *Up-Along: Newfoundland Families in Hamilton* (Hamilton: McMaster University M.A. Thesis, 1974) shows that these familistic orientations are strong enough to withstand the impacts of migration.

33. Conference Planning Committee, 4th Manitoba Conference on Aging, *The Provincial Fact Book on Aging — Manitoba* (Winnipeg: Manitoba Council on Aging, 1985).

34. See for instance, Grant and Rice; G. Hodge and L. McKay, *Small Town Seniors and Their Freedom to Move: Improving Transportation for Seniors in British Columbia's Small Towns* (Vancouver: Final Report on Seniors' Independence Project, Health and Welfare Canada, 1992).

35. Grant and Rice.

36. Cape.

37. The concept of "community sustainability" is discussed in A.M. Fuller, P. Ehrenshaft and M. Gertler, "Sustaining Rural Communities in Canada: Issues and Prospects," in *Sustainable*

Rural Communities in Canada, M.E. Gertler and H.R. Baker (eds.) (Saskatoon: The Canadian Agriculture and Rural Restructuring Group, 1990), 1-41.

38. R. Matthews, *"There's No Better Place Than Here": Social Change in Three Newfoundland Communities* (Toronto: Peter Martin Associates Ltd., 1976), 49-50.

39. J.L. Brudney, "The Availability of Volunteers: Implications for Local Governments," *Administration and Society* 21.4 (1990): 413-24.

40. A. Martin-Matthews and A.E. Joseph, *The Home Support Services Review: Agency Survey and Area/District Office Survey* (Toronto: Ministry of Community and Social Services, 1990) report that home support agencies are, almost universally, sensitive to the need to attract and maintain volunteers.

41. Data presented by Joseph and Cloutier suggest that these contrasts have existed at least since the early 1970s.

42. Reported in Martin-Matthews and Joseph. The increased involvement of middle-aged women in the workforce means that the pool of volunteers for these services will become smaller. See A.E. Joseph and A. Martin Matthews, "Caring for Elderly Persons: Workforce Issues and Development Questions," in *Health and Development*, D. Phillips and Y. Verhasselt (eds.) (London: Routledge, in press).

43. The extreme case is reported in A.P. Fengler and R. Goodrich, "Wives of Elderly Disabled Men: The Hidden Patients," *The Gerontologist* 19.2 (1979): 175-83.

44. A.E. Joseph and B. Smit, "Rural Residential Development and Municipal Service Provision: a Canadian Study," *Journal of Rural Studies* 1.4 (1985): 321-57 provide data for a township in Ontario to support this contention. Class-related issues are discussed at length in H. Newby, *Green and Pleasant Land? Social Change in Rural England* (Harmondsworth: Penguin, 1980).

45. The "snowbird" phenomenon is discussed in various contributions to L.C. Mullins and R.D. Tucker (eds.), *Snowbirds in the Sunbelt: Older Canadians in Florida* (Tampa, Florida: International Exchange Center on Gerontology, University of South Florida, 1988).

46. J. Daciuk and V. Marshall, "Health Care Utilization of Canadian Snowbirds: An Example of Strategic Planning," in Mullins and Tucker, *Snowbirds in the Sunbelt*, 53-68.

47. M.P. Lawton, *Environment and Aging* (Monterey, Calif.: Brooks/Cole Publishing, 1980).

48. See, for instance, A.E. Joseph, "On the Importance of Place in Studies of Rural Aging," *Journal of Rural Studies* 8.1 (1992): 111-19.

49. This extraordinary decline in the fortunes of small rural towns in New Zealand is documented in S. Britton, R. LeHeron and E. Pawson, *Changing Places: The Geography of Restructuring in New Zealand* (Christchurch: New Zealand Geographical Society, 1992).

Alun E. Joseph is Professor and Chair of the Department of Geography and an associate member of the Gerontology Research Centre at the University of Guelph, and a member of the Canadian Aging Research Network (CARNET). Anne Martin-Matthews is a Professor in the Department of Family Studies and Director of the Gerontology Research Centre at the University of Guelph, and Director of the Work and Eldercare Research Group of CARNET.

Environment and Aging

VERENA HALDEMANN AND ANDREW WISTER

Introduction

For more than 30 years, the interface of aging and environment has been on the agenda of researchers in the field of social gerontology. The focus has primarily been on the ways that aging individuals adjust to the environment in the face of age-related change.[1] Aging as a biological, psychological, and social process is seen to influence the way in which individuals experience their environment.[2] Furthermore, the space of daily living is viewed as becoming more limited and more salient as the individual's ability to respond adaptively in the areas of functional health, social roles, and cognition deteriorates with age.[3] Invariably, a person's interaction with the environment is modified in a number of significant ways.[4] Because aging is largely defined in terms of decline, restriction and losses, the dominant hypothesis is that aging individuals and their psychological well being become more dependent on their environment than younger people.[5]

Research on this topic has been dominated by an ecological approach.[6] Conceptual frameworks have introduced *environmental docility* — the tendency for more competent individuals to withstand more demanding physical or social environmental conditions and vice-versa;[7] *person-environment congruence* — the fit between a person's functional ability and the environment;[8] the *human ecosystem* — the interrelated components of the person-environment relation, namely the individual, significant others, social neighbourhood, social structure, and physical features;[9] the *ecological actor* — environmental actions as products of an ongoing interpretive process;[10] the notion of *proactivity* — the volitional, creative contribution that the individual makes to the social structure;[11] and the *meaning of space* — the environmental experience linked to life history.[12] Within this general ecological approach, differences appear in the relative importance given to the individual's capacity as an actor or to the constraining power of the environment. Variations are also found in the weight afforded to age compared to other attributes such as gender, class, ethnicity, or spatial setting (rural-urban).

The objective of this paper is to provide an overview of primarily Canadian research on the physical environment and aging. The focus will be on the elderly living in urban settings, since they represent approximately 80 percent of all Canadians aged 65 and over, and since rural aging and migration are discussed in other papers in this issue.[13] In Canadian research, as well as in the work of other countries, environment related to population aging is mainly perceived and treated in terms of shelter, affordability, and other housing problems of the aging individual. Neighbourhood, transportation, access to services, and more general environmental issues are considered, but overall they receive less attention.

Two major features of Canadian society are important for research on environment and aging, namely the transformations in the welfare state and the physical and demographic change of cities over the last 30 years.[14] We shall present research on environment and aging in relation to the way in which the welfare state has dealt with the issue of shelter for the aged, leaving the link with restructured urban settings to be acknowledged when pertinent.

Three Perspectives on Environment and Aging

We can identify three distinct approaches to dealing with the shelter of the aged in Canada, each of which has developed in succession by building upon the foundations of preceding models but shifting the relative importance of resources attributed to each. The first mode is *institutionalization and purpose-built housing*. After the traditional asylum for the poor, the nursing home was offered by the new welfare state to the elderly as an alternative for people who could not stay at home for a wide variety of reasons (health, income, social isolation, etc.). This resulted in the relocation of significant numbers of elderly people. As a relatively new phenomenon, it gave rise to studies on life in institutions (nursing homes, hospitals), and on the advantages and disadvantages of relocation.

With the rising demand for nursing homes during the 1970s and the concomitant rise in costs, access to this kind of shelter was restricted to people with serious health problems. Elderly people with housing problems related to low income or isolation were largely overlooked. Efforts were made to construct low income housing accessible to the elderly (public housing, non-profit private housing). During this period, research concentrated on planned housing, including cost, equity, and acceptability of public programs. Location of housing within the general urban setting and in relation to service access became an important issue, as did the age segregation/integration problem.

The second approach can be termed *housing alternatives and maximization of choice*. According to this perspective, which surfaced in the late 1970s, people at different times in their life require different types of shelter. Recognizing the heterogeneity of the older population, accentuated by growing numbers of people leaving the labour force at younger ages and by the very old surviving longer, it gradually became more difficult to promote a single model of shelter as the ideal for all or for even a majority of seniors. This difficulty was magnified by specific characteristics of recent aging cohorts, particularly, the wide range in their level of education, the great number of home-owners and the access some individuals enjoyed to good private pensions. Knowledge of the heterogeneity of aging people implied the need to provide a greater variety of shelter as well as affording more flexibility in the system for achieving adequate environments. On the one hand, researchers emphasized the study of heterogeneity and its sources, concentrating on needs and on special groups. On the other hand, they investigated a wide range of housing alternatives, living arrangements, and financial supports. Moreover, they applied residential decision-making models to assemble the web of factors that determine residential choice in different life situations.

The third approach has been coined *aging in place* and gained popularity in the mid-1980s. The demand for nursing homes continued to rise in spite of public housing efforts, while the state experienced growing fiscal austerity. Aging in place appeared to be one solution to these developments. Furthermore, the demand for institutionalization was interpreted in part as the result of the absence of social support, which was viewed as a factor at least as relevant as severe health problems. Attention was given to broadening formal sources of support and strengthening informal support from family and the community in order to maintain people in their own homes for as long as possible. Research efforts were realigned to investigate social networks and support for the elderly, as well as the interface between informal support and formal services. Research also identified living arrangements and ordinary neighbourhoods as social and physical support.

More recently, additional orientations have become important in research on environments for the aged. These approaches have been driven largely by a rethinking of person-environment theory. First, there is a concern for the role that individuals play in adapting to the constraints of environment through social psychological processes (familiarity and attachment, control, cohort-related experience, and other normative and value systems). Second, there is interest in the environmental experience and the residential decisions of aging people, as well as the interplay of these with public policy. These trends will be discussed under "developing perspectives," although they are not mutually exclusive of the three principal approaches which are reviewed next.

Institutionalization and Purpose-built Housing

For many years, institutions have been the traditional shelter for needy elderly people, need referring to a variety of problems including income, social isolation, and physical and mental health. With the developing welfare state and with the growing proportion of older Canadians, institutions became an important component of "old age policies." Financial input from governments induced the growth of many types of institutional care for which elderly people became the main consumers.[15]

A wide array of institutions became available, especially during the 1970s. These ranged from residential care, providing mainly a convenient residential setting for old people, to extended and long-term care, covering more serious disabilities that require higher levels of care. For this reason, the long-term facility of today is frequently thought of as the "total institution."[16] The time has passed when entering an asylum translates into a social stigma. Today, citizens are viewed as having social rights, including the right to minimum income and shelter in old age. In other words, shelter for the aged is a public concern, analogous to old-age pensions. Therefore, governments have to know what types of shelter are needed and who among the older citizens should be given priority in accessing sheltered housing supported by public finance. Researchers are expected to assess the needs emerging from population aging and individual aging, as well as to provide tools for evaluating the performance of institutions.

One pragmatic way to assess need consists of evaluating the capacity of the individual to accomplish Activities of Daily Living (ADLs) at home. According to the functional incapacities found, the older person is relocated to another environmental setting that can compensate for his or her "losses." Leaving home and relocating to a new environment is considered to be a stressful life-event by researchers, one which requires considerable adaptation.

While adjustments to a new environment have been proven to be positive in situations of voluntary residential relocation, they are more problematic for individuals moving from their own home into institutional settings.[17] Research has shown not only high mortality rates among relocated institutional residents, but also low physical, psychological and social well being.[18] However, conceptual and methodological problems have brought these findings into question, suggesting that if relocation is stressful, it does not significantly affect mortality rates or explain problematic behaviour or low morale among institutionalized older people.[19] Indeed, by using indicators other than mortality, such as "perceived well being" or "problematic behaviour," more positive outcomes of institutionalization have been demonstrated.

The overall results of research on relocation to institutions have been ambiguous, if not contradictory.[20] They have nevertheless been used as a basis for the ongoing discussion of institutionalization. Canada's high rate of institutionalized older people, inducing a growing financial burden for the state, combined with the perception that institutions are alienating places, has fueled debate on the virtues and shortcomings of institutional versus non-institutional environments for the aged.

This debate has opposed a "bureaucratic" and a "welfare" model of institutions. The first focuses on alienation due to the loss of personal control implied by the very nature of institutional organization.[21] The second centres on rewards directed at the relief of those people who have experienced alienating situations in the general society.[22] The dominant orientation in care for older people adopted a "trend away from institutionalization," one that has been perceived by many as more related to fiscal austerity than to humanistic considerations.[23]

In an attempt to transcend this dualistic view, some researchers insist on acknowledging and stressing differentiation.[24] All institutions are not the same, and more knowledge of the organizational and environmental features of institutions has been shown to be important. Life in institutions has become a research focus for such fields as design and architecture, social work, and psychology.[25] Moreover, it has become obvious that individuals relocated to institutions have different functional incapacities deriving from variant economic, social, and personal living conditions throughout their lives. Their needs have been defined in terms of low income, physical and mental health problems, and social isolation, each of which have been viewed as influencing the demand for institutionalization. From this view, specific problems are addressed by the allocation of specific resources to specific environments. For example, low-income problems require subsidized housing and health problems necessitate sheltered housing with some level of care.

Within this perspective, the main concern has been to avoid institutionalization for people without serious health problems. The state has freed money for purpose-built housing, mainly public housing for the aged and non-profit private housing for independent or semi-dependent elderly people.[26] Work has been conducted on motives for the demand of institutionalization, on the one hand, and on the adequacy of planned environments to meet the needs of physically and cognitively impaired elderly on the other.[27] The latter include architectural features and design, location of the buildings, ethnic homogeneity or heterogeneity, and the segregation of environments with different levels of care.[28]

Housing Alternatives and Maximization of Choice

The principle of planning community-based environments that respond to specific needs has partly developed out of the high costs of institutionalization. The identification of a particular need of an individual and the matching of this need to a limited resource is viewed as cost-effective. Concurrently, breaking up the "total" institution (homes for the aged, nursing homes) into a number of specific resources has underestimated the interplay between different changes experienced by elderly people. This interplay has been dealt with by coordinating various separate resources, considered to be on a continuum ranging from financial assistance to assisted living.

It is recognized that different changes not only combine and accumulate, but that this personal "constellation" of needs changes over time. In this way, older people who enter a public housing project because of low income may experience a decline in health and, at some point in time, require special care. The question is how to respond to this issue. Is it by successive relocation of residents, which is not advisable because of relocation stress? Or is it by integrating some form of care into otherwise independent housing, which means somehow returning to quasi-institutional types of shelter? From a maximization of choice perspective, the answer to this problem has been primarily left with the individual who has to "choose" between a variety of housing alternatives offered at various costs by both the public and the private sector. Included in this choice is the decision to relocate or to alter presently occupied housing to improve its fit with evolving needs. Thus, "variety" and "flexibility" have become major requirements when planning adequate environments for older adults.[29]

An important underlying assumption of these developments is that intervention on the built environment can compensate for changes in personal competence and, thus, significantly influence the "outcome" of the behaviour and morale of aging people. This "investment in bricks" (*aide à la pierre*) presupposes access to support services; however, public home support services were poorly developed before the 1980s.

Research has begun to address the problem of relating the housing career to the continuum of care or, in other words, the need to identify housing-related needs of the elderly and their change over time.[30] Heterogeneity of income, location, living arrangements, availability of support services and care have been acknowledged;[31] as well, special groups have been identified as being particularly at risk, such as women living alone, ethnic groups and immigrants, the rural elderly, and the very old in the community.[32] Efforts continue to assess new forms of housing and living arrangements, most of them related to the intermediary stage of the housing continuum, like private sector congregate housing, granny flats, home sharing, accessory apartments, and non-profit and cooperative housing developments.[33]

It has become evident that affordability is one of the most important problems faced by the aged, notwithstanding their increased income through pensions. Indeed, one experienced researcher in the field asked if there was a housing problem or an income problem.[34] This question exemplifies the importance of the latter to the former. The "core housing needs" of elderly renters have also been recognized.[35] In this context, developing housing alternatives for supported independent living appears to be inefficient, because some of the options are unaffordable for many older people.

Affordability and adequacy of housing for the aged have been not only related to pension income, but also strongly associated with the quality of the existing housing stock and the changes occurring in inner-city areas where elderly households are concentrated.[36] Urban renewal and gentrification of downtown and surrounding areas have been shown to result in high rents and growing tax expenditures, along with rising costs for housing maintenance.[37] Neighbourhoods have been destroyed and social support networks disconnected during these transformations. These problems have not been fully acknowledged by governments who continue to limit their responsibility for housing to special-need groups. Albeit, there has been a fringe of solvent older people, mainly ex-homeowners who prefer to relocate to supported housing. The private sector has provided various types of self-contained but serviced housing at very high costs. However, this market niche appears to be saturated, leaving the less affluent elderly with their problems.

Aging in Place

By 1980, government funding had shifted from public housing for independent living to mostly private non-profit housing for supported independent living.[38] Whatever the success of these options, the demand for institutionalization has not decreased. Interestingly, research has shown that the propensity for entering an institutional setting is linked not only to disability or health problems, but also to living arrangements and social support.[39] In response to a greater valuation of privacy, independence and autonomy, as well as social norms of expected separateness, living alone has been identified as the residential option among increasing numbers of older people, especially women.[40] Concurrently, this arrangement has brought a feeling of insecurity in the face of potential emergencies of all kinds. As a result, research on various kinds of living arrangments and related support systems and their impact on the well being of elderly people has increased.

The focus of this research has been on informal social support studied in terms of family relations and social networks.[41] The functioning of the modern "modified extended family" and the restructuring of urban neighbourhoods have been shown to alter older people's networks. However, research also demonstrates that the modern family has not left older people socially abandoned, and that quantity and quality of contact should be distinguished when investigating exchanges of support.[42] It has also been established that the family and the larger informal support network provide most of the assistance necessary for older people to stay at home.[43] However, the contribution of the informal support network has been shown to be insufficient, so that complementary formal home support services were initiated by local public and private agencies. Research has therefore centred on the interface between formal and informal home support for the elderly and its variation by socio-economic and spatial milieu.[44] Generally more attention is given to urban neighbourhoods, assessing the physical and social support offered to elderly residents, as well as to the availability of transportation and access to services.[45] Other studies examine how the elderly perceive their spatial setting in terms of security and cognitive orientation.[46]

In summary, then, there has been extensive work on what may be called the social competence of the elderly, in terms of family and community resources that they can activate to deal with the environment when aging compromises their personal competence. In spite of this focus, the physical environment has remained an important concern. While funding of purpose-built housing has become scarce and while formal social support for aging in place depends on local initiatives largely supported by provincial monies, older people continue to make up a growing proportion of housing consumers. Aging in place implies adequate homes, but a significant number of older people have been unable to keep up their home, for a wide range of reasons.[47] The "staying put" philosophy, therefore, has been concerned with physical aspects of the existing housing stock, such as structural repair and rehabilitation, and the conversion of large residences into smaller units.[48] These general programs of maintaining and revitalizing the existing housing and neighbourhoods are supposed to benefit older as well as younger people.[49]

A variety of special programs have been established in this area by provincial governments.[50] However, their impact is not well known. For example, while upgrading inner-city housing seems to benefit some elderly supported by valuable assets, it may be harmful to others who cannot absorb the rising rents or maintenance costs. The economic rationale of "creating value" by rehabilitation and subdivision of housing units omits the needs of the less fortunate residents and may actually increase their "core needs," if it does not exclude them from the market.[51] Some elderly people, however, organize themselves within small, family-owned multi-story houses where they have access to low-cost self-contained dwellings.[52]

In this context, new tools for financial assistance have been developed. Rental allowances have been implemented in several provinces, despite the fact that they are sometimes perceived as a form of subsidizing private property. Various forms of tax relief and the freeing of home equity through reverse mortgages have also been encouraged. Yet, the situation of the aged within the housing market has remained difficult and government subsidies continue to favour access to home ownership for younger people.

Researchers are now more interested in the way in which older people living in the community organize themselves. Several community studies have focused on the aged and work has been undertaken on the housing conditions and the home range of older people in metropolitan areas, on local migration, on elderly people in family-owned multi-story houses, and on the situation of the elderly in the private market.[53] Another recent research interest has been the role of technology for the home environment.[54] Environmental control, barrier-free design, and reduction of home hazards have begun to receive needed attention in the literature.

Developing Perspectives

Canadian research has largely borrowed theoretical frameworks from the literature in the United States. The ecological perspective, led by the work of Powell Lawton and his associates, has been widely endorsed. Environmental behaviour and well being are understood as the result of a dynamic balance or fit between environmental press and individual competence.[55] This perspective implicitly assumes that an ideal environment can be created given any set of individual attributes; it supports the maximization of choice and aging in place perspectives, which promote the increase of available housing, living arrangements and social support options.

In response to relatively meager findings and several criticisms of the major concepts used in this research, the ecological model of aging has been revised to increase the emphasis placed on the individual side of the person-environment formula.[56] This has shifted attention from the impact of environment to the role that individuals play in the interpretation and shaping of their environment.[57]

Recent years have witnessed a growth in research on *decision-making* in the areas of relocation to more manageable residences and long-term care facilities, alterations to the design of the home, changes in living arrangements, and service utilization.[58] Consistent findings from this literature indicate that older persons articulate more positive appraisals of their residential worlds than do professionals, that they are often reluctant to make significant changes to their physical or social environment until a crisis has occurred, and that they tend to display lower utilization rates of formal ancillary health services than implied by need studies.[59] This has raised several questions about intervention strategies for supporting the frail elderly.

Studies on *living arrangement decisions* have acknowledged the pervasive influence of present and past life-style norms and beliefs on the elderly. For example, the increasing number of persons living alone has been linked to preferences for independence, privacy, and autonomy in living style, in addition to other factors (health, income, home support programs, age/sex/marital status change).[60] One prevailing issue is the effect of living arrangment changes on family relationships and support.

The *meaning of home* to the individual has received attention by researchers studying housing satisfaction and by those studying relocation.[61] Familiarity and attachment to personal objects, the home, neighbourhood and community are identified as important domains affecting housing satisfaction.[62] This work suggests that an individual's self-identity is expressed and preserved by family and personal histories, attachment to possessions, and relation to the immediate physical environment.

While studies of social psychological adaptation enhance the diversity of levels on which the person-environment transaction operates, there is also an increasing concern for *temporal issues*. Several authors use the term "environmental experience," which is to be understood as the product of on-going processes of interpretation and decison-making.[63] The present way of relating to the environment is thus linked to previous experience and to the whole life story of the individual.

These developing perspectives remain within the micro-analyses of housing for older people, merely expanding the existing dominant paradigm of environmental psychology. Other developments may also contribute to a better understanding of environment and aging, namely those adopting a *long-term perspective* and those giving more attention to the *social structural features* that shape the environmental experience of older people. For example, we should look more closely at the "housing careers" (succession of dwellings occupied over a life time) and the successive living arrangments experienced by the aged individual, as well as the way in which these have been shaped by public policies during mid-life and later life.

Conclusion

Governments and researchers have dealt with the environmental issues of aging in a way that is still best reflected by the "shelter for the aged" formula, despite the fact that everybody claims to go "beyond shelter." For quite some time, psychologists and architects have been interested in this field, while few sociologists, anthropologists, geographers and economists have appeared on the scene until recently. Indeed, the social aspects of the environmental experience of older people have thus far received less attention. Among the unanswered questions are those related to the social use of environments.

First, *meaning of space* is related to social norms and values as well as to the context of the person-environment interaction. There is research in progress that attempts to develop a better understanding of what the home means by linking it to the personal and family life history of the aging individual. However, it is also necessary to grasp the meaning of home through its links with the general bearing of property, and especially real estate property, and on the self-image and social status of the individual in Canadian society. Moreover, it is important to show the function of ownership in intergenerational relations and the transmission of cultural and economic assets.

Second, *control over space* is, without doubt, related to functional health. But control is not only the ability to know and perceive a space correctly and to move one's body through it easily. Control over space also means having something to say about how to use this space, what activities are to be held in it, how to modify it and, if necessary, to leave it and to relocate. Control also relates to tenure and to position in the housing market. These forms of control are linked to the individual's social and economic position within groups and social structures. The description of one extreme position given in the 1970s is that of the powerless inmate of a total institution whose administrators are actually the "space managers."[64]

Third, physical environments should be examined not only as barriers for declining personal competence but also as *contexts for social interaction*. While this has been acknowledged by researchers on housing for older people, there has not been a systematic program of research on the use of space by the aged outside their home. Some interesting work has been undertaken on the use of shopping malls by inner-city elderly, but we still know very little about the spatial aspects of neighbourhood relations and the use by the elderly of various public spaces in the city.[65] Other aspects of the social use of more macro spaces should be investigated, such as the life-cycle of neighbourhoods and its bearing on the aged, or the experience of winter by those living in our cities.[66]

Fourth, the direct and indirect impact of *government programs* related to the housing of the aged is not well known; moreover, the effects of such programs in relation to other public policies are even more obscure. A systematic investigation of the relative effect of housing and other policies on the aged, as well as on the interface between different policies, is long overdue. Housing policies operate at various levels and some fiscal regulations (such as tax savings and mortgage advantages) may have a greater impact on the situation of older people than direct expenditures on housing.[67] This kind of research would afford more information about inequalities, such as the increasing discrepancies noted between older owners and renters, or the reason why older women are considered to be increasingly at risk.

In summary, research on environment and aging is both precipitating and responding to governmental action and public concern. While Canadian research has provided the groundwork for better environmental planning, it is hoped that researchers will increasingly take a leading role in addressing and defining the most important questions to ask, including both socio-political and scientific domains of inquiry.

NOTES

1. M.P. Lawton, "Housing and Living Environments of Older People," in R. Binstock and E. Shanas, eds., *Handbook of Aging and the Social Sciences* (New York: Van Nostrand & Reinhold, 1985), 450-77.

2. B.D. McPherson, *Aging as a Social Process: An Introduction to Individual and Population Aging* 2nd Edition (Toronto: Butterworths, 1990).

3. M.P. Lawton and L. Nahemov, "Ecology and the Aging Process," in E. Eisdorfer and M.P. Lawton, eds., *Psychology of Adult Development and Aging* (Washington: American Psychological Association, 1973), 619-74.

4. G.D. Rowles, *Prisoners of Space? Exploring the Geographical Experience of Older People* (Boulder, Colorado: Westview Press, 1978). G.D. Rowles and R.J. Ohta, eds., *Aging and Milieu: Environmental Perspectives on Growing Old* (New York: Academic Press, 1983).

5. M.P. Lawton, "Competence, Environmental Press, and the Adaptation of Older People," in M.P. Lawton, P. Windley and T.O. Byerts, eds., *Aging and the Environment: Theoretical Approaches* (New York: Springer Publishing Company, 1982), 33-57.

6. V. Bernardin-Haldemann, "Ecology and Aging: A Critical Review," *Canadian Journal on Aging* 7, 4 (1988), 458-71.

7. Lawton, 1982.

8. E. Kahana, "A Congruence Model of Person-environment Interaction," in M.P. Lawton, P. Windley and T.O. Byerts, eds., *Aging and the Environment: Theoretical Approaches,* 97-121.

9. M.P. Lawton, "Ecology and Aging" in L.A. Pastalan and D.H. Carson, eds., *The Spatial Behaviour of Older People* (Ann Arbor: University of Michigan, Institute of Gerontology, 1970), 40-66. J.F. Gubrium, *Late Life: Communities and Environment Policy* (Springfield, Ill: Charles Thomas Publisher, 1974).

10. R.A. Ward, M. La Gory and S.R. Sherman, *The Environment for Aging. Interpersonal, Social and Spatial Contexts* (Tuscaloosa: The University of Alabama Press, 1988).

11. M.P. Lawton, *Behavior-Relevant Ecological Factors,* unpublished, 1987a.

12. S. Golant, *A Place to Grow Old: The Meaning of Environment in Old Age* (New York: Columbia University Press, 1984). G.D. Rowles, "The Grand Fiction of a Personal Odyssey," *Journal of Environmental Psychology* 7, 7 (1987), 357-65.

13. Statistics Canada, *A Portrait of Seniors in Canada* Catalogue 89-519 (Ottawa: Ministry of Supply and Services, 1990).

14. J. Myles and L. Teichroew, "The Politics of Dualism: Pension Policy in Canada," in J. Myles and J. Quadagno, eds., *States, Labour Markets, and the Future of Old-Age Policies* (Philadelphia: Temple University Press, 1991), 84-104. On demographic changes, see S.M. Golant, "The Locational-Environmental Perspective on Old-Age Segregated Residential Areas in the United States," in R.J. Johnson and D.T. Herbert, eds., *Geography and the Urban Environment* (New York: Wiley, 1980).

15. W.F. Forbes, J.A. Jackson and A.S. Kraus, *Institutionalization of the Elderly in Canada* (Toronto: Butterworths, 1987).

16. M. Penning and N. Chappell, "A Reformulation of Basic Assumptions about Institutions for the Elderly," in V.W. Marshall, ed., *Aging in Canada: Social Perspectives* (Don Mills: Fitzhenry & Whiteside, 1980), 269-80.

17. F.M. Carp, "Short-term and Long-term Prediction of Adjustment to a New Environment," *Journal of Gerontology: Social Sciences* 29, 4 (1974), 444-53. L. Bélanger and M.A. Delisle, *Les habitations à loyer modique pour personnes âgées: effets psychologiques et sociaux de l'entrée en HLM et de refus de la demande d'admission* (Québec: Université Laval, Laboratoire de gérontologie sociale, 1981). See also discussion by D.L. Rutman and J.L. Freedman, "Anticipating Relocation: Coping Strategies and the Meaning of Home for Older People," *Canadian Journal on Aging* 7, 1 (1988), 17-31.

18. For a review, see J.H. Borup, "Relocation Mortality Research: Assessment, Reply, and the Need to Refocus on the Issues," *The Gerontologist* 23, 3 (1983), 235-41.

19. For a review, see T.C. Coffman, "Relocation and Survival of Institutional Aged: A Re-examination of the Evidence," *The Gerontologist* 21 (1981), 483-500.

20. N. Chappell and M. Penning, "The Trend Away from Institutionalization," *Research on Aging* 1, 3 (1979), 361-87.

21. "The bureaucratic model, derived largely from Goffman's concept of total institutions (1961), argues that the process of bureaucratization leads to withdrawal, self-mortification, and sick-role identification.... (because of) the fact that all aspects of life are conducted in the same place under the same single authority; that all phases of the resident's daily activities are carried out in the immediate company of others, all of whom receive similar treatment; that all aspects of daily life are tightly scheduled and imposed from above through a system of explicit formal rulings and administered by a body of officials; and that the contents of such activities are regarded as rationally planned, supposedly designed to fulfill the goals of the particular institution." (Penning and Chappell, 1980, 270, citing E. Goffman, *Asylums* [Garden City, N.Y.: Doubleday, 1961], 6).

22. "Differing from the bureaucratic perspective, the social welfare model argues that the same dimension is operative for both the institutionalized and community elderly. Illness, poverty, and social isolation are considered the primary factors within either environment, but it is argued that their impact is decreased within the institutional environment designed specifically for their relief." (Penning and Chappell, 1980, 271). See especially J. Myles, "Institutionalizing the Elderly: A Critical Assesment of the Sociology of Total Institutions," in V.W. Marshall, ed., *Aging in Canada: Social Perspectives,* 257-68.

23. Penning and Chappell, 1980.

24. Chappell and Penning, 1979.

25. P. Cluff, "Design-related Issues and Solutions for Meeting the Needs of the Very Old in Institutional Settings," in G. Gutman and N. Blackie, eds., *Housing the Very Old* (Vancouver: Gerontology Research Center, 1988), 45-62. S.Brink and J.R. Champagne, *Designing Homes for the Aged,* Building Practice Note 60 (Ottawa: National Research Council of Canada, Division of Building Research, 1985). A.W. Cluff and P. Cluff, *Cost and Design of Housing for Disabled Persons: Case Studies* (Ottawa: Canada Mortgage and Housing Corporation, 1983). A. Girouard-Lefebvre, *Les comportements psycho-sociaux des personnes âgées*

hébergées, rapport analytique (Montréal: Association des centres de services sociaux du Québec, 1986). D.H. Coons, "The Therapeutic Milieu: Social Psychological Aspects of Treatment," in W. Reichel, ed. *Clinical Aspects of Aging* 2nd Edition (London: Williams and Wilkins, 1983), 137-50.

26. M.J. Audain, *Beyond Shelter: A Study of NHA Financed Housing for the Elderly* (Ottawa: Canadian Council on Social Development, 1973). S. Goldblatt, "The Federal Government's Role in Housing Elderly Canadians," in G. Gutman and N. Blackie, eds. *Aging in Place* (Vancouver: Gerontology Research Center, 1986), 99-103. J.J. Syrotuik, *Public Housing for the Low Income Elderly: Locational Aspects and Financial Considerations* (MA Thesis, University of Regina, 1987).

27. F. Béland, "Les désirs d'hébergement et les modes de cohabitation des personnes âgées," *Cahiers de l'ACFAS* 13 (Montréal, 1982), 89-100. G. Gutman, ed., *Shelter and Care of Persons with Dementia* (Vancouver: Gerontology Research Center, Simon Fraser University, 1992).

28. S. Weaverdyck and D. Coons, "Designing a Dementia Residential Care Unit: Addressing Cognitive Changes with the Wesley-Hall Model," in G. Gutman and N. Blackie, eds. *Housing the Very Old*, 63-83. G. Gutman and J. Mercer, *Residential and Life Satisfaction of the Elderly in Institutions: A Study of the Locational Suitability of Fifteen Personal and Intermediate Care Facilities in Greater Vancouver* (Ottawa: Canadian Mortgage and Housing Corporation, 1979). I. Pereira, *Homogenous Versus Heterogenous Environments for Portuguese and Italian Elderly in Toronto* (MA Thesis, University of Waterloo, 1991). G. Gutman, *Senior Citizens Housing Study* – Report No. 3: The Long Term Impact of Multi-level, Multi-service Accommodation for Seniors (Ottawa: Canadian Mortgage and Housing Corporation, 1983).

29. B. Wigdor and L. Ford, *Housing for an Aging Population: Alternatives* (Toronto: University of Toronto Press, 1981).

30. This housing continuum is divided into three stages: independent living, supported independent living, and dependent living. Housing-related needs are income, location, support services, special design and health care, whose relative importance differs at each stage of the housing continuum (Brink, 1985).

31. N. Blackie, "The Option of Staying Put," in G. Gutman and N. Blackie, eds., *Aging in Place,* 1-12.

32. S. Fletcher and L.O. Stone, *The Living Arrangements of Canada's Older Women*, Statistics Canada Catalogue 86-503 (Ottawa: Ministry of Supply and Services, 1982). A.V. Wister, "Living Arrangements and Informal Support among the Elderly," *Journal for the Elderly* 6, 1, 2 (1990), 33-43. K. Thomas and A.V. Wister, "Living Arrangements of Older Women: The Ethnic Dimension," *Journal of Marriage and the Family* 46, 2 (1984), 301-12. K.V. Ujimoto, "The Ethnic Dimension of Aging in Canada," in V.W. Marshall, ed. *Aging in Canada: Social Perspectives,* 2nd Edition, 111-37. A. Martin Matthews, "Social Support of the Rural Widowed Elderly," *Journal of Rural Health* 4, 3 (1988), 57-70. G.Gutman and N. Blackie, eds. *Housing the Very Old.*

33. G. Gutman and N. Blackie, eds. *Innovations in Housing and Living Arrangements for Seniors* (Vancouver: Gerontology Research Center, 1985). G.Gutman and N. Blackie, eds. *Aging in Place.* V. Doyle, *Congregate Housing and Care Facilities: Learning from Non-Profit and Co-operative Developments,* paper delivered at Congregate Housing and Care Facilities, Vancouver, March 1991 (Toronto: The Canadian Institute, 1991).

34. R. Leblanc, "Le problème de l'accessibilité financière au logement chez les personnes âgées," *Actualité Immobilière* 9, 4 (1986), 50-54. L.O. Stone, "Shelter Poverty and the Elderly," *Journal of Aging and Social Policy* 2, 2 (1990), 61-83. A. Rose, "Social Policy Issues for Housing an Aging Population," in B. Wigdor and L. Ford, eds., *Housing for an Aging Population: Alternatives,* 69-93.

35. Households unable to afford adequate, uncrowded housing without paying more than 30 percent of gross income. See S. Brink, "Housing Elderly People in Canada: Working towards a Continuum of Housing Choices Appropriate to their Needs," in G. Gutman and N. Blackie, eds. *Innovations in Housing and Living Arrangements for Seniors,* 1-23.

36. McPherson, 1990.

37. S.M. Golant, "Understanding the Diverse Housing Environments of the Elderly," *Environments* 18, 3 (1986), 35-51. M. Bédard, "Conséquences de la restauration domiciliaire du quartier St-Sauveur de Québec," *Service social* 33, 1 (1984), 73-85. J.R. Henig, "Gentrification and Displacement of the Elderly," *The Gerontologist* 21, 1 (1981), 67-75.

38. Goldblatt, 1986.

39. F. Béland, "The Family and Adults 65 Years of Age and Over: Co-Residency and Availability of Help," *Canadian Review of Sociology and Anthropology* 21, 3 (1984), 302-17. E. Shapiro and N.P. Roos, "Predictors, Patterns and Consequences of Nursing Home Use in One Canadian Province," in V.W. Marshall, ed., *Aging in Canada: Social Perspectives,* 2nd edition, 520-37.

40. G.E. Priest, "Living arrangements of Canada's Older Elderly Population," *Canadian Social Trends* 10 (1988), 26-30. L.O. Stone and S. Fletcher, "The Hypothesis of Age Patterns in Living Arrangement Passages," in V.W. Marshall, ed. *Aging in Canada: Social Perspectives,* 2nd edition, 288-310. A.V. Wister, "Living Arrangement Choices among the Elderly," *Canadian Journal on Aging* 4, 3 (1985), 127-44. N.J. Gnaedinger, *Elderly Widows who Live Alone in their Own Houses: Assessments of Risk* (MA Thesis, Carleton University, 1986).

41. For review, see N.L. Chappell, *Social Support and Aging* (Toronto: Butterworths, 1992) and C.J. Rosenthal, "Aging and Intergenerational Relations in Canada," in V.W. Marshall, ed., *Aging in Canada: Social Perspectives,* 2nd Edition, 311-42.

42. E.Corin, T. Sherif et L. Bergeron, *Le fonctionnement des systèmes de support naturel des personnes âgées* (Québec: Laboratoire de gérontologie sociale, Université Laval, 1983).

43. N.L. Chappell, "Informal Support Networks among the Elderly," *Research on Aging* 5, 1 (1983), 77-99.

44. Chappell, 1992. E. Corin, "The Relationship between Formal and Informal Social Support Networks in Rural and Urban Contexts," in V.W. Marshall, ed. *Aging in Canada,* 2nd edition, 367-94.

45. V. Regnier, "Neighborhoods as Service Systems," in M.P. Lawton, R. Newcomer and T. Byerts, eds. *Community Planning for an Aging Society: Designing Services and Facilities* (Stroudsburg, PA: Dowden, Hutchinson and Ross, 1976), 240-57. M. Wexler, "Vers un environnement résidentiel socialement adapté aux besoins des personnes âgées," *Actualité immobilière* 9 (1986), 44-49. Y. Bussière, "Effets du vieillissement démographique sur la demande de transport dans la région métropolitaine de Montréal, 1986-2001," *Cahiers québécois de démographie* 19 (1990), 325-50.

46. V. Regnier, "Urban Neighborhood Cognition: Relationship between Functional and Symbolic Community Environments," in G.D. Rowles and R.J. Ohta, eds. *Aging and Milieu,* 63-82.

47. Blackie, 1986.

48. R. Wheeler, "Staying Put: A New Development in Policy?" *Aging and Society* 2, 3 (1982), 299-329. Champagne, 1986. M.H. Choko, "Émergence du marché du condominium dans la restauration résidentielle à Montréal et ses conséquences," *Actualité immobilière* 9, 3 (1985), 18-26. M. Stegman, "Urban Displacement and Condominium Conversions," in M.P. Lawton and T.O. Byerts, eds. *Housing an Aging Society,* 151-60.

49. R.J. Struyk and B.J. Soldo, *Improving the Elderly's Housing: A Key to Preserving the Nation's Housing Stock and Neighborhoods* (Cambridge, MA: Ballinger Publishing Company, 1980). ·

50. Gutman and Blackie, 1986.

51. Choko, 1985. V. Bernardin-Haldemann, *Vieillir et se loger au Québec: de l'écologie aux rapports sociaux* (Thèse de doctorat, Département de sociologie, Université de Montréal, 1987).

52. M. Wexler, *Residential Adjustments of the Elderly: A Comparison of Non Mobile and Mobile Elderly in Montreal, (Québec)* (Ph.D. Dissertation, University of Pennsylvania, 1988).

53. T. Sherif, R.L. Tremblay et J. Alain, *Vivre et vieillir chez soi à St-Émile* (Québec: Centre des services sociaux de Québec, 1986); C. Laliberté, *Vieillir à Charny. Les conditions du vieillissement dans une ville de chemin de fer* (Mémoire de maîtrise, Département d'anthropologie, Université Laval, Québec, 1985). Golant, 1986. V. Bernardin-Haldemann, "L'habitat des personnes âgées à Québec," *Service social* 34, 1 (1985a), 90-106. R. Kirouac, *La mobilité résidentielle à l'âge de la retraite dans la région urbaine de Québec* (thèse de doctorat, Département de géographie, Université Laval, Québec, 1986). H.C. Northcott *Changing Residence: The Geographic Mobility of Elderly Canadians* (Toronto: Butterworths, 1988). M. Wexler and B. Mishara, "Considérations sur la mobilité et l'immobilité résidentielle des personnes âgées," *Actualité immobilière* 9, 2 (1985), 12-22. E. Berger, R. Godin and A.C. Harvey, "Older Canadians: Housing Market Characteristics and Demands," in G. Gutman and N. Blackie, eds. *Aging in Place,* 49-69.

54. For a review, see J.R. Watzke and B. Kemp, "Safety for Older Adults: The Role of Technology and the Home Environment," *Topics in Geriatric Rehabilitation* 7, 4 (1992), 9-21, and Chappell, this issue.

55. Lawton, 1982.

56. See especially Rowles and Ohta, 1983. F.M. Carp, "A Complementary/Congruence Model of Well-being or Mental Health for the Community Elderly," in I. Altman, M.P. Lawton and J. Wohlwill, eds. *Human Behavior and the Environment: The Elderly and the Physical Environment* (New York: Plenum, 1984), 279-336. Bernardin-Haldemann, 1988.

57. In recent years, Lawton has put forth the Environmental Proactivity Model. In this revised model of ecology and aging, competence is extended to include personal resources and environmental press to include environmental resources. The proactivity hypotheses states that the greater the competence of the person, the greater the number of environmental resources that may be used in the pursuit of personal needs and wishes. This model recognizes the proactive role that the individual may take in shaping their environment. See Lawton, 1987a, and M.P. Lawton, "Aging and Proactivity in the Residential Environment," paper presented at the annual meeting of the American Psychological Association, New York City, 1987b.

58. For a review, see A.V. Wister, "Privacy, Independence and Separation in Living Arrangements Selections among the Elderly: Research and Implications for Housing Policy," *Environments* 20, 2 (1989a), 26-35.

59. Golant, 1986. A.V. Wister, "Environmental Adaptation by Persons in their Later Life," *Research on Aging* 11, 3 (1989b), 267-91. T.T.H. Wan and B.G. Odell, "Factors Affecting the Use of Social and Health Services among the Elderly," *Ageing and Society* 1, 1 (1981), 95-115.

60. I. Connidis, "Living Arrangements Choices of Older Residents: Assessing Quantitative Results with Qualitative Data," *Canadian Journal of Sociology* 8, 4 (1983), 359-75. Béland, 1984. Wister, 1985.

61. R.L. Rubinstein, "The Home Environment of Older People: A Description of the Psychosocial Processes Linking Person to Place," *Journal of Gerontology: Social Sciences* 44, 2 (1989), 45-53. Rutman and Freedman, 1988.

62. R. Rubinstein, "The Significance of Personal Objects to Older People," *Journal of Aging Studies* 1, 3 (1987), 225-38.

63. Rowles, 1987.

64. R. Sommer, "Small Groups Ecology in Institutions for the Elderly," in L. Pastalan and D. Carson, eds., *Spatial Behavior of Older People*, 25-39.

65. D.F. Graham, I. Graham and M. MacLean, "Going to the Mall: A Leisure Activity of Urban Elderly People," *Canadian Journal on Aging* 10, 4 (1991), 345-58.

66. K. Fitzpatrick and J. Logan, "The Aging of the Suburbs, 1960-1980," *American Sociological Review* 50, 1 (1985), 106-17. National Advisory Council on Aging, *Seniors and Winter Living* (Ottawa: Minister of Supply and Services Canada, 1989).

67. H.L. Kendig, "Comparative perspectives on housing, aging, and social structure," in R.H. Binstock and L.K. George, eds., *Handbook of Aging and the Social Sciences* (San Diego, CA: Academic Press, 1990), 288-306. V. Bernardin-Haldemann, "Se loger au Québec: les règles du jeu," *Relations* 509 (1985b), 89-91.

Verena Haldemann is a research associate in the Sociology Department and member of the Centre for Studies of Community Based Services (Centre de recherche sur les services communautaires) at Laval University, Québec. Andrew Wister is an Assistant Professor in the Gerontology Program at Simon Fraser University.

Residential Mobility and Migration Among Canada's Elderly

ERIC G. MOORE AND MARK W. ROSENBERG

Introduction

Changing residence is a pervasive characteristic of individual and community experience in Canadian society. The average Canadian can expect to move about a dozen times during the course of a lifetime. While most of these moves are concentrated among younger members of the population, the elderly are by no means immobile and changes of residence for this group have important consequences both for themselves and for the larger society. For elderly individuals, moves contribute to the ongoing process of adjustment to changing needs and desires with respect to housing, to physical and cultural amenity and to support from family, friends and social agencies. For the larger society, the aggregate result of these moves produces a redistribution of the population both geographically and with respect to the supply of housing in private, public and institutional settings with corresponding shifts in pressures on the allocation of resources.

In this paper, the discussion of elderly mobility is guided by a *life-course* perspective, focusing on critical life events such as retirement, declining health and the death of a spouse and their consequences. Also considered are some of the implications of current patterns of mobility for changing the spatial distribution of the elderly population and the resulting effects on regional and local government. With regard to both of these issues, empirical evidence is provided on current structure and recent changes, using data from the Census and national surveys in Canada.

Perspectives on Mobility

Mobility is defined as any change in permanent residence, whether this be a move within the same apartment building or across the country. However, it is usual to distinguish between short-distance moves, or *residential mobility* ("local movers"), which take place within a given labour market and longer-distance moves, or *migration ("migrants"),* between such markets. Residential mobility tends to be associated with adjustments in housing and living arrangements within local areas, while migration generally produces major disruptions in established patterns of daily activities and social networks.

The nature of mobility has been viewed in a number of different ways which have significant consequences for both social research and public policy. The traditional perspective, a cohort view, has considered aggregate mobility as a response to aging and to economic change. The peak period for mobility lies between the late teens and early thirties, associated with many individual responses to the pursuit of tertiary education, job market entry, marriage and childbearing (Figure 1). The likelihood of moving declines steadily during the subsequent years with perhaps a small increase around the time of retirement. This basic structure is stable over both time and space, having been observed in a number of developed countries.[1] However, the overall magnitude or level of mobility tends to fluctuate in response to both economic and demographic conditions. As the number of opportunities for 'adjustment' decreases, so does the level of mobility. Thus, mobility tends to be lower in times of recession or depression; it also falls for relatively large cohorts as the internal competition for opportunities increases.[2] Overall mobility has declined markedly since 1976 as a response both to the entry of the baby boom cohort into the labour market and increasingly tough economic times (Table 1). The mobility of the elderly has behaved similarly (Table 1), suggesting similar patterns of response, particularly to economic conditions.

Homeownership plays a central role in the cohort view of mobility. Not only does homeownership represent a desired and, hence, intrinsically stable state for many households, but the fiscal commitments and attachment to a community associated with ownership increase the generalized costs of moving. The overall result is that the relative likelihood of moving in any given year for a renter is consistently several times higher than for an owner-occupier. Given that elderly individuals overwhelmingly live in owner-occupied dwellings (68 percent of those over 65 in 1990), the total mobility rate for the elderly naturally will be lower than for those in their twenties and thirties.

Attempts to construct explanations of local mobility and migration have pursued somewhat different paths, although at the core of both explanations lies an evaluation of the benefits and costs of choosing between alternative outcomes at specific locations. This process is referred to by Wolpert as the comparison of *place utilities*.[3] Theories of local mobility owe much to the seminal work of Rossi who stated that the likelihood of moving depends on the magnitude of the gap between housing satisfaction and housing expectations.[4] The occurrence and size of this 'gap' is subject to change as a consequence of household circumstances, which shift relative to the characteristics of dwelling and neighbourhood. These household circumstances are induced by changes in family structure associated with both increases and decreases in numbers, by changes in resources and status aspirations, and by shifting health conditions requiring greater access to health and social services as well as unexpected events such as fire, flood and eviction. The outcome of the decision is then mediated by the availability (both real and perceived) of acceptable alternatives and the costs of acquiring such an alternative.

Although the need for such adjustments occurs less frequently among the elderly, they are nevertheless important. For the elderly, however, as Golant points out, the opportunities are often limited both because of financial constraints and because of their ability or inability to cope with real or perceived barriers in the physical environment.[5] In these circumstances, the elderly often find that they wish to move but are unable to do so.[6]

Explanations of migration have evolved largely in the context of human capital theory, which sets the long-run returns from moving to another location against both the returns from staying at the current location and the costs (mostly short-run) of moving.[7] In the working-age population, returns are derived primarily from wages and salaries associated with labour-force activity. The principles still apply to the elderly, although the perceived benefits are often psychological and social and are amortized over considerably shorter periods than for the younger population.

Migrations may be classified in terms of whether they are "on-going" or return migrations. On-going migrations involve the move to a new area and are made primarily by more affluent couples choosing destinations with high levels of amenity. Return migrations, which involve moving back to the region of birth or where considerable portions of one's life have been spent, tend to be associated with the need to be closer to social supports from kin and are more likely to be made by individuals who have lost a spouse or are in declining health.

The Life-Course View

Recent discussions of mobility have focused on the role of life events and their impact on movement behaviour during the individual *life-course*.[8] Moves reflect responses to the various demographic and economic events experienced

Table 1
Changing Mobility
1961-1981

Year	Total Population %Moved	Population Over 65 %Moved	%Migrants
1961	44.2	26.6	9.4
1971	500.0	31.5	12.6
1976	50.4	31.0	13.2
1981	48.6	26.2	10.8
1986	44.5	21.7	9.0

Source: Census of Canada, 1966-1981

Table 2
Reasons for Moving

Reason for moving	Age Groups 55-64	65-74	74+
Support	10.3	19.1	28.2
Amenity	7.8	10.5	8.8
Housing	29.3	27.9	27.4
Retirement	11.6	14.9	5.9
Separation/ Divorce /Spousal Death	6.9	6.3	8.7
Finances	9.6	9.4	6.9
Employment	8.5	0.9	1.0
All Other Reasons	15.9	11.0	13.2
Total	100	100	100

by an individual and, in particular, to the timing of these events in relation to each other. Thus, the likelihood of migrating is seen to be a function not only of the state of being unemployed or of being retired, but also of the length of time since the individual entered such a state.

With regard to the elderly, a theoretical literature has evolved which is centred on the developmental perspective on elderly relocation of Litwak and Longino.[9] They argue that the motivation and outcomes of moves by healthy individuals following on retirement are different from subsequent moves which reflect needs arising from declining health and the desire to be close to family and other sources of support. Litwak and Longino suggest that three types of moves occur among the elderly. The first is the amenity-oriented move that is frequently associated with retirement. Such moves, typified by relocation to cities such as Victoria or Niagara-on-the-Lake, as well as the high amenity regions of Florida and the American South-West, are primarily by healthy, married couples with above av-erage incomes.[10]

The second move occurs somewhat later and is associated with an increasing difficulty in performing instrumental activities of daily living (IADLs) such as shopping, preparing meals and doing housework. Since the presence of a spouse mediates such problems, the greatest impact arises when widowhood and instru-mental disability are combined.[11] Moves are undertaken to be closer to those who are in a position to provide help. Table 2 illustrates the increasing importance of 'moving for reasons of support' with increasing age among the elderly in Canada. In fact, for those over 75, the 'support' reason is more common than reasons related to adjustment to changing housing needs.

The third type of move reflects limited access to kin resources and involves the transfer from a primary dependence on kin to institutional care. While we do not have good data in Canada on the transition process, the rapid increase with age in the proportion of the population in institutions is notable. While only 2.3 percent of the population aged 65-69 lives in institutions, fully 35 percent of those over 85 are institutionalized and their characteristics must be included in any overall representation of that age group. Although there are not consistent data on the issue, it is also clear that a significant proportion of the institutionalized elderly in Canada are there because of a lack of a suitable support network at home, rather than because of a health condition which prevents them from living in the community.

Effective analysis of the links between declining health and mobility requires access to longitudinal data such as are provided by the American Longitudinal Study of Aging (LSOA).[12] With the same individuals interviewed every two years, the impact of a variety of events (e.g. loss of a spouse, accident or illness) on life choices, including mobility and institutionalization, can be assessed. In Canada, we have rich data sources linking health and disability and recent mobility at fixed points in time, but we lack longitudinal data.

The Redistributive Role of Migration

In addition to the importance of mobility in the lives of individuals, there are larger scale redistributive consequences of mobility. The specific pattern of flows into and out of a neighbourhood, city or region changes the social, economic and even political character of these areas. In this context it is as important to identify those who do not move as those who do move. When more affluent healthy married couples move from industrial or resource centres in Ontario to British Columbia, for example, those remaining behind tend to be less affluent, more likely to be widowed and in poorer health. The implication is that the tax and spending base of the origin communities are diminished, while the potential burden of the health and social service domain is increased. These distributional inequities arising from migration are also found in other developed countries.[13]

The phenomenon of return migration adds to this redistributional effect. Migrants who return to areas where they spent most of their lives (and where kin are often located) are more likely to be in poor health and to have been recently widowed. In particular, return migrants to Canada from Florida or the Sun Belt of the American South-West are often returning to the relative financial security of the Canadian health care system. The implication again is that regions reaping the benefits of a healthy and affluent elderly population are not necessarily the same as those which incur the burdens of an increasing proportion of service-dependent elderly.

The overall role of migration in producing changes in the distribution of the elderly population is complex. By far the largest contributor to increasing concentrations of the elderly at the regional and local level is *aging-in-place*,[14] followed by out-migration of the younger population. Only in a small number of areas does active net in-migration produce significant increases, and these comprise the primary amenity-attraction areas of Canada — British Columbia and Southern Ontario[15] (Bekkering, 1988).

In this context, the nature of redistributive processes within cities is important. Although the overall mobility of the elderly population is low, there has been a rapid increase in the proportion of the population over 65 located in the inner suburbs of our major cities in the last decade. These are the areas of major post-war growth and the children raised in these homes have often moved out, leaving parents who are approaching retirement in owner-occupied homes with no outstanding mortgage. There is little incentive to move and the population ages rapidly with strong implications for regional disparities in the demand for social services. In the next twenty years there will be dramatic increases in the elderly population in the suburban areas of our major cities, primarily as a function of

Figure 1: Percent Movers
by age age and sex, Canada 1971 and 1986.

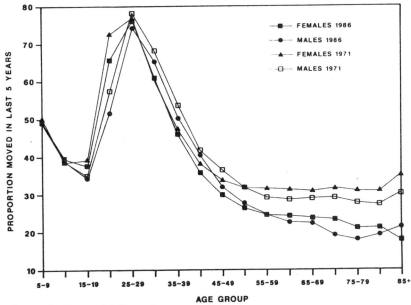

Figure 2: Percent Migrants
by age age and sex, Canada 1971 and 1986.

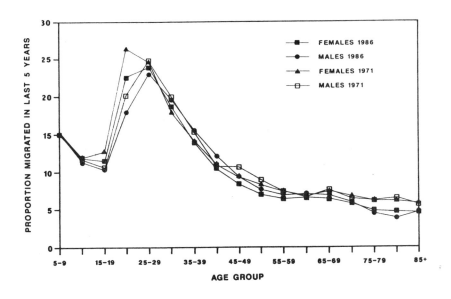

aging-in-place, together with the departure of younger members of the population.[16]

Post-War Mobility Experience In Canada

Figures 1 and 2 provide a succinct statement of both the overall age structure of mobility and changes over the past two decades. Although the overall structure is very stable, there are also important differentials.[17] A minor peak exists for migrants aged 65-69, although for total movers the peak is lower and comes somewhat later. The peak for migrants reflects amenity moves around the time of retirement while the later peak for total movers is indicative of a higher level of local moves responding to changing needs with regard to housing and social support.

Overall mobility has declined since 1971 but the decrease is particularly marked for local movers over 45, with the gap increasing for those over 70. The decline in migration propensity, although observable, is smaller and does not appear until after the age of 65. In part this pattern reflects changing economic conditions. It also reflects the significant outmigration from Quebec in the early seventies which affected the pre-retirement Anglophone population to a significant degree.[18] A third element in this change is the increase over the last twenty-five years in the proportion of the older population who live in owner-occupied housing, a shift which naturally lowers overall mobility. With more than three-quarters of the elderly owners having no mortgage, the operating costs of many dwellings are less than the costs of renting, particularly if little money is spent on maintenance. Elderly occupants of modest homes (i.e., those dwellings which may not yield large amounts of equity if sold) may become trapped in their homes as any acceptable alternative is too expensive. If this situation persists for many years, it also has strong negative implications for the quality of the housing stock, which is dependent on the level of maintenance.

Gender is an important dimension in mobility patterns. At young ages (15-30), males have consistently higher mobility and migration rates than females, a relation that has been observed since the early writings of Ravenstein in Britain.[19] Between the ages of 30 and 55, male rates are higher, while at older ages female rates, especially for local movers, are greater.[20] Since married couples move together, the differentials are entirely attributable to the movement behaviour among the single, widowed and divorced populations, particularly those who live alone. Since the latter group are more likely to move than married individuals, and females over 65 are two to three times as likely to live alone than males (Table 3), their higher mobility rate is really no surprise.

Clearly, marital status is a significant correlate of moving behaviour. Married individuals are much less likely to have moved in the previous five years than those who are single, widowed or divorced. However, part of the explanation for

Table 3
Living Alone by Age, Sex, and Community Size

Population Size	Proportion Living Alone			
	Males		Females	
	65-74	75+	65-74	75+
500,000	14.8	20.6	36.7	56.6
100,000-500,000	14.5	21.9	37.8	58.8
30,000-100,000	13.9	18.7	335.6	53.7
15,000-30,000	11.1	22.8	41.9	59.3
Small Urban Areas	14.2	18.5	37.6	55.9
Rural Areas	12.7	23.3	27.7	39.9

Source: Public Use Microdata Files, 1986 (Calculation by author).

Table 4
Elderly Migrants

Province	Aged 60-69 in 1981			Aged 70+ in 1981		
	Inmigrants	Outmigrants	Net	Inmigrants	Outmigrants	Net
Newfoundland	450	500	-50	250	350	100
P.E.I.	250	550	200	200	50	150
Nova Scotia	1400	1250	150	850	600	250
New Brunswick	1400	400	1000	850	650	200
Quebec	2450	7500	-5050	1200	5050	3850
Ontario	9450	8000	1450	6800	4400	2400
Manitoba	1500	22600	-1100	1350	2100	-750
Saskatchewan	1900	2250	-350	800	1550	-750
Alberta	3850	6900	-3050	3650	22750	900
B.C.	11300	4000	7300	4650	3000	1650
Yukon/N.W.T	750	750	0	50	150	-100

Note: Numbers represent individuals who lived in a different province in 1981 and 1986.
Source: Census of Canada, Public Use Microdata Files, 1986 (calculation by author).

this pattern is a function of the relation between marital status and homeownership. The more relevant question of the way in which the life events of divorce or loss of spouse themselves stimulate movement is difficult to assess. Crossman used the 1977-81 Quality of Life Surveys from York University to estimate the relation between several life events and mobility in Canada between 1977 and 1979 and between 1979 and 1981[21] for the population over 60. About 4.5 percent of owners and 7.5 percent of renters experienced a loss of spouse (either through death, divorce or separation) during each 2 year period. Approximately 40 percent of owners and 50 percent of renters experiencing these changes also moved during the same period, suggesting that these events are both highly influential in individual lives and, cumulatively, maintain a steady pressure on aggregate mobility.

Migration and Redistribution

Although the majority of moves by the elderly are local, migration is still of consequence. In the 1986 Census, approximately 60,000 Canadians over 65 had migrated interprovincially at least once over the previous five years. This is an underestimate of the total number of migrations during the period as many individuals move more than once. In a study that followed individuals aged 50-54 and 55-59 in 1971 through the period 1972-1983, Moore and Ball showed that while the probability of at least one interregional migration for both males and females during this period was only 0.04, the probability of a second migration, given that one had already been made, was 0.24.[22] In the great majority of the latter moves, the individual returned to the region he or she had left.

The magnitudes of flows between provinces naturally reflects the sizes of the origin and destination areas, with Ontario and Quebec being the largest generator of moves. British Columbia is still a disproportional recipient of elderly migration, especially among the younger elderly, as is evident in previous studies (Table 4).[23] Among the older elderly, Ontario and Alberta are also net gainers. However, provinces are crude units for measuring redistribution. Within provinces, there are additional foci. The attraction of high amenity areas with moderate climates such as Victoria, the Okanagan Valley, the Niagara peninsula and the Muskokas are well known. More subtle are the moves from rural areas to small towns and from metropolitan areas to smaller urban places.[24] Although the annual rates of migration are small, they are also selective with respect to demographic variables such as marital status and, more particularly, to those with higher incomes. The result, as stressed earlier, is a cumulative burden on less favoured communities, particularly if such communities are also experiencing a rapid outmigration of a younger, working age population.[25]

Central Issues in the Mobility of the Elderly

The following section addresses more specifically three of the most fundamental relationships linking elderly mobility and issues of concern for public policy. Litwak and Longino argue that retirement and declining health are central to the understanding of elderly mobility. While both events contribute significantly to patterns of migration, local mobility continues to reflect adjustments of the elderly to housing needs in later life.

Mobility and Retirement

Litwak and Longino identify retirement as a key event in the life of the elderly, which has strong associations with mobility.[26] While moves at this time are clearly not universal, the quantitative impact is significant. According to the *Survey on Aging and Independence* (1991),[27] 497,562 persons aged 55 to 64, 369,904 persons aged 65 to 74 and 173,955 persons aged 75 and over are estimated to have moved at least once between 1986 and 1991. When asked why they moved, about 12 percent of the responses provided among the population aged 55 to 64 and about 15 percent of the responses of the population aged 65 to 74 identify retirement as a reason for moving. In the population aged 75 and over, retirement is far less important as a reason for moving (Table 2).

For a select segment of the elderly population, mobility and retirement have been connected to particular types of moves. First, there is the move to amenity residential areas where the new dwelling is often a converted seasonal property. This is the group of elderly people who move to places like Vancouver Island, the Fraser and Okanagan Valleys in British Columbia, Niagara-on-the-Lake or the Muskoka and Kawartha Lakes areas of Ontario, and to a lesser extent to some of the small seaside communities in the Maritime provinces. Rosenberg and Halseth have noted that most of those who move to amenity residential areas are generally the young-old, the married, the "empty-nesters" and those who have higher education-levels and higher incomes than the comparison groups of permanent residents in their study areas.[28]

The second type of move is the seasonal migration to communities in the United States Sunbelt. Seasonal migrants to Florida are relatively young, usually married and economically well-off as compared with the general populations of non-migrants in the same age cohort. Tucker also reported that almost 75 percent of the respondents to their surveys own their dwellings in Florida and closer to 80 percent continue to own their dwellings in Canada.[29]

Because we do not have a good longitudinal data base for the Canadian population, a more critical analysis of the impacts of retirement is not possible. However, we know that those who make an 'amenity' move are more affluent, and that the income decline for many elderly individuals upon retirement is substantial and it can effect mobility in other ways. Those on fixed incomes have few choices

Table 5
Self Reported Health Status

Age	Health Status		in Good Health (%)
	Excellent/Good Health	Fair/Poor Health	
55-64	1642000	461000	78.1
65-74	1143000	471000	70.8
75+	5760000	291000	66.4

Source: 1991 Survey on Aging and Independence, Statistics Canada (calculations by author).

and the critical question relates to the continued affordability of the current dwelling, which is addressed below following a discussion of the impacts of health on mobility.

Mobility and Health

From a cohort perspective, the likelihood of having moved in the last five years among the elderly is consistently higher for those who are instrumentally disabled, with the gap becoming even more marked for those over 75 (Figure 3).[30] However, the specific links among mobility, health status, and support from formal and informal networks are complex. In the Survey *of Aging and Independence,* 78 percent of the population aged 55 to 64, 71 percent of the population aged 65 to 74 and 66 percent of the population aged 75 and over are estimated to be in excellent or good health. These proportions only vary slightly for those living alone in the three age cohorts (Table 5).

The proportion of movers citing a desire to be closer to sources of support increases rapidly with age, while housing adjustment reasons are always important (Table 2). As Connidis observes, relatively few older Canadians wish to move in with their children and will often prefer an institutionalized setting, but proximity to kin is important and moves to achieve this goal are often associated with declining health.[31]

As a factor in moving, however, support reasons rank second in the frequency with which they are mentioned for the population aged 55 to 64 and 65 to 74 and are mentioned slightly more often (ranking first) than housing reasons for the population aged 75 and over (Table 2). But among movers in every age cohort who gave support reasons as a factor in moving, the majority indicated that they were in excellent or good health. At first glance, these results would seem to indicate that the majority of the elderly population moves in anticipation of future health problems. A cautionary note is due, however, because the results may be,

Figure 3: Mobility of the Elderly, by age and disability — Canada, 1986

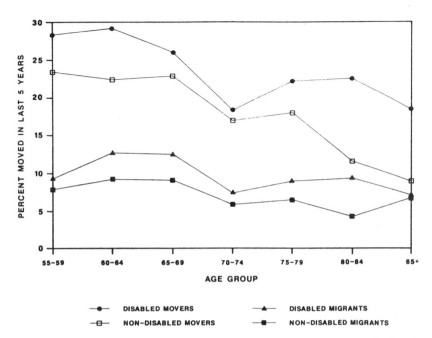

at least partially, an artifact of how the questions were originally asked and have been combined in this analysis. The support reasons include those who moved because of a decline in health of self or spouse/partner, as well as those who moved to receive support from a relative, to be close to family/friends and to be close to services. The problem is that there is no way to determine whether the respondent who indicates his or her health is excellent or good is referring to himself or herself or a spouse/partner in responding to the support reasons. Those who are responding because of a decline in their health or their spouse's/partner's are obviously moving as the result of health problems, not in anticipation of future health problems.

Regardless of the ambiguity surrounding whether elderly persons move in anticipation of future health problems or as a result of immediate health problems, what is clear is that moves are made much more often to receive care or support from family members and friends in contrast to formal service providers. Care and support are also much more likely to be the responsibility of family members and friends, even in institutional settings.[32] In quantitative terms it has been estimated that about 80 per cent of care to aged persons comes from informal sources, largely family.[33]

There are interesting geographical implications of moves that are made to seek support. Based on the *Survey on Aging and Independence,* the relative likelihood of having moved for this reason is significantly lower in rural areas than elsewhere and is highest in small towns. This is supportive of some of the earlier redistributive comments of Liaw and Kanaroglou,[34] and is also suggestive of a move from rural areas to nearby urban centres as the ability for independent living declines. This finding, if confirmed in more direct studies, has important implications for the planning of service delivery, since a focus of service provision on urban nodes rather than dispersed rural services might prove to be a more effective strategy.

Mobility and Housing Adjustments

As already reported above, as individuals move from pre-retirement to the old-old age category, they are less likely to live in family households and are more likely to live alone. They are also less likely to live in their own home and are more likely to live in collective dwellings. In 1986, only 9 percent of males and 15 percent of females aged 55 to 64 lived alone, but 17 percent of males and 38 percent of females aged 75 and over lived alone. Only 2 percent of males and 1 percent of females aged 55 to 64 lived in collective dwellings, but 12 percent of males and 20 percent of females aged 75 and over lived in collective dwellings.[35]

In 1988, the percentage of the population aged 65 and over who owned their own home without a mortgage (54.7 percent) is not much different from the population aged 55 to 64 (53.2 percent). The percentage of the population aged 65 and over who owned a home with a mortgage is much lower (8.8 percent) compared to those aged 55 to 64 (23.5 percent). The percentage of the population aged 65 and over who rented, however, is much higher (33.6 percent) compared to the population aged 55 to 64 (23.3 percent).[36] This pattern, which at first glance might appear to be paradoxical, can be explained by those persons aged 65 and over who were homeowners prior to retirement, who either give up their homes voluntarily or are required to give up their homes because they can no longer afford them after retirement. It is likely that the former group is made up mainly of homeowners without mortgages, whereas the latter group is made up of homeowners with mortgages or those who no longer can afford the upkeep of their homes even though they do not have mortgages.

Within the more affluent group of elderly, the rise of condominium ownership, particularly in large cities, has been important.[37] Condominiums are attractive in terms of size, security and the fact that responsibilities for maintenance are transferred to the management of the condominium. They have become a viable option for many older individuals, especially women, who have sufficient financial resources (often from the sale of a previous dwelling). While only about three percent of the total housing stock in Canada consists of condominiums, their role in the lives of the urban elderly has expanded rapidly and has encouraged relocation from larger units in the suburbs to more central locations.

The condominium solution is viable for only a small minority of the elderly. For most, retirement brings some increased financial stress. Studies in Canada and the United States have demonstrated that housing and its upkeep are a financial burden for significant proportions of the elderly population, regardless of whether they are renters or homeowners in the respective countries.[38] Brink reported that 28.7 percent of Canada's elderly home owners spent more than 25 percent of their income on shelter expenditures and among renters 47.1 percent spent more than 25 percent of their incomes on shelter expenditures. She also estimated that 24 percent of renter households with heads aged 65 to 69 and 32 percent of renter households with heads aged 70 and over are unable to afford adequate, uncrowded housing without paying more than 30 percent of their gross income.

It should come as no surprise then that in the *Survey on Aging and Independence* (1991), housing issues are given most often as the reason for moving among those aged 55 to 64 and those aged 65 to 74.[39] But even among the respondents aged 75 and over, housing issues are cited almost as often as support issues as a reason for moving (see Table 2). When the housing issues are examined individually, most of the responses are that the individual's previous home was too big or too small. Very few respondents in any age group indicated that they were forced to leave their previous residence, but financial reasons ranked fourth in frequency for those aged 55 to 64 and 65 to 74 as reasons for moving. What cannot be assessed, however, is whether there is a direct correlation between financial reasons and housing reasons.

It is also not clear how death of a spouse, separation or divorce are related to housing and financial reasons for moving. As the result of these life course events, elderly women, in particular, often have to make housing and financial adjustments. They might, however, indicate that their reasons for moving are financial or because they no longer need a large house, not directly associating their move with a life course event which precipitated their financial problems and subsequent moves.

Conclusions

To date, there have been two general approaches to the study of elderly mobility and migration. First, the more general theories of mobility and migration, based on notions of place utility and human capital, have some utility in understanding the patterns of moves by Canada's elderly population since the 1950s. In general, studies based on this tradition find that the overall mobility rates of the elderly population are lower than those for the working age population. Within this elderly population, women, because they are much more likely to be single, widowed, divorced or separated have much higher mobility rates than men. Moreover, most migration flows among the elderly have been from Ontario and Quebec, with British Columbia being the major recipient.

In contrast, the theoretical literature that views elderly relocation from a developmental perspective appears to provide a broader framework for understanding the complex motives and outcomes of moves by the various age cohorts that make up the elderly population. Research within this perspective shows that the main reasons that the elderly population move are to adjust their level of housing consumption and to gain greater access to support and care networks. Underlying these reasons are a set of secondary reasons linked to retirement — the desire to live in high recreational-amenity areas, financial issues, and life course events. These secondary reasons for moving are much more relevant to those aged 55 to 64 and 65 to 74 than they are to those aged 75 and over. Among this latter group, the need to gain greater access to support and care networks and making adjustments in housing consumption overwhelm all other reasons for moving.

There is a distinct geography to the movement of the elderly population, and its implications are that some communities find themselves with relatively large and growing elderly populations, while others find themselves with relatively smaller and slower growing elderly populations. Overall, aging-in-place has resulted in the proportion of the population over 65 increasing everywhere; however, selective migration by both young and old produces inequities in the distribution of relative concentration, in the need for health care and social services, and in the affluence of the local elderly population.

The implications of the distinct geography of the mobility of the elderly population in Canada is that a growing number of local governments may find themselves under increasing pressure "to deliver more services and new forms of housing for the elderly, but their ability to do so will be constrained by the limits on their sources of revenue".[40] In particular, these pressures are likely to increase in those communities where the elderly population is growing relative to younger segments of the population. In some of these communities, this is likely to lead to highly divisive inter-generational debates over local government expenditures.

In summary, many of the conclusions of research in this area are speculative because of the constraints which have been imposed on researchers intent on understanding the links among mobility, migration, housing, services and health status among Canada's elderly population.

Chief among these constraints is the lack of attention paid to the design of questions that measure differences in the mobility and migration experiences of Canadians of all ages, and the absence of longitudinal data to answer questions about the role mobility and migration play in economic and social adjustments as people age. With the growth in Canada's elderly population as we move into the next century, the importance of understanding the role that mobility and migration play will become increasingly crucial in the effective planning of housing, health and social services to maintain independent living.

Notes

1. Rogers, A. (1988), "Age patterns of elderly migration: an international comparison", *Demography*, 25,3,3,55-70.

2. Easterlin, R. (1980), *Birth and fortune*, New York: Basic Books, and Rogerson, P. (1987), "Changes in U.S. national mobility levels", *The Professional Geographer*, 39:344-50.

3. Wolpert, J. (1965), "Behavioural aspects of the decision to migrate", *Papers of the Regional Science Association, 15:* 159-69.

4. Rossi, P.H. (1955), *Why families move*, Glencoe: Free Press.

5. Golant, S.M. (1992), *Housing America's elderly*, Newbury Park: Sage.

6. Moore, E.G. (1989), "Mobility intention and subsequent relocation", *Urban Geography*, 7:497-514.

7. Shaw, R.P. (1985), *Intermetropolitan migration in Canada: changing determinants over three decades*, Toronto: NC Press.

8. Mayer, K.U. and N.B.Tuma (1990), *Event history analysis in life course research*, Madison: University of Wisconsin Press.

9. Litwak, E. and C.F. Longino (1987), "Migration patterns among the elderly: a developmental perspective", *The Gerontologist*, 27:266-72.

10. Speare, A. and J.W.Meyer (1988), "Types of elderly residential mobility and their determinants", *Journal of Gerontology*, 43,3,S74-81.

11. Longino, C.F., D.J.Jackson, R.S.Zimmerman and J.E.Bradsher, "The second move: health and geographic mobility", *Journal of Gerontology: Social Sciences*, 1991, 46,4, S218-224.

12. Crimmins, E. and Y. Saito (1990), "Getting better and getting worse: transitions in functional status among older Americans", paper presented at the Annual Meetings of the Population Association of America, Toronto.

13. Biggar, J.C. (1980), "Who moved among the elderly, 1965 to 1970", *Research on Aging, 2:73-91.*

14. Morrison, P. (1992), "Is 'Aging in Place' a blueprint for the future?", annual lecture on New Directions in Population Geography, Annual Meetings of the Association of American Geographers, San Diego.

15. Bekkering, M. H. (1990), *Patterns of change in the spatial distribution of the elderly in Canada, 1966 to 1986*, unpublished Master's thesis, Department of Geography, Queen's University.

16. Rosenberg, M.W., E.G. Moore and S. Ball (1989) "Components of change in the spatial distribution of the elderly population in Ontario, 1976-1986," *The Canadian Geographer*. Vol. 33, No. 3, pp. 218-229.

17. Measurement of mobility in the Census and many related surveys identifies individuals who lived somewhere else five years before. The resulting rates underestimate total mobility as individuals may move more than once in five years. On an annual basis about 7 percent of movers and 20 percent of renters will move.

18. Beaujot, R. (1991), *Population change in Canada*, Toronto: McClelland and Stewart.

19. Ravenstein, E. (1889), "The laws of migration", *Journal of the Royal Statistical Society*, 52:241-301.

20. Liaw, K. and D.N.Nagnur (1985), "Characterization of metropolitan and nonmetropolitan outmigration schedules of the Canadian population system, 1971-76", *Canadian Studies in Population,* 12:81-102.

21. Crossman, S. (1988), *Impacts of life events on residential mobility,* unpublished M.A. thesis, Department of Geography, Queen's University.

22. Moore, E.G. and S.B.Ball (1988), "Interprovincial migration of the pre-retirement elderly in Canada 1972-83: an exploration of the 10 percent taxfiler file", paper presented at the annual meetings of the Western Regional Science Association, Napa, California.

23. Northcott, H.C. (1988), *Changing residence: the geographic mobility of elderly Canadians,* Toronto: Butterworths.

24. Liaw, K. and P. Kanaroglou (1986), "Metropolitan outmigration patterns of the elderly in Canada: 1971-76", *Research in Aging,* 8: 201-31.

25. Rosenberg, M.W., and E.G. Moore (1990) "The elderly, economic dependency, and local government revenues and expenditures," *Environment and Planning C: Government and Policy.* Vol. 8,pp. 149-165.

26. Litwak and Longino, *op cit.*

27. The *Survey of Aging and Independence* was undertaken in 1991 by Statistics Canada. It comprises a sample of 10,000 individuals over the age of 55 who are living in noninstitutional settings within the community.

28. Rosenberg, M.W. and G. Halseth (1993) *Recreational home conversion in Canada.* Ottawa: Canada Mortgage and Housing Corporation.

29. Tucker, R.D., L.C. Mullins, F. Beland, C.F. Longino, Jr., and V.W. Marshall (1992) "Older Canadians in Florida: a comparison of anglophone and francophone seasonal migrants," *Canadian Journal on Aging.* Vol. 11, No. 3, pp. 281-297.

30. The *Health and Activity Limitation Survey is* one of the largest surveys undertaken by Statistics Canada. Undertaken as a post-censal survey in 1986 and 1987, it sampled both the residential and institutional population of adults and children. The sample used responses to a screening question in the 1986 Census of Canada to select 78,000 individuals who said they experienced difficulties with activities of daily living and 78,000 who said they did not. Questions addressed detailed characterizations of the performance of tasks associated with ADLs, the nature of support needed and utilized, and difficulties associated with housing, education, employment, transportation and recreation.

31. Connidis, I. (1983) "Living arrangement choices of older residents: assessing quantitative results with qualitative data", *Canadian Journal of Sociology,* 8:359-75.

32. These findings are based on two studies using the *Health and Limitation Survey* (1991): Moore, E.G., and M.W. Rosenberg (1991) *Disabled adults in Ontario institutions.* Kingston, Ontario: Queen's University, Department of Geography; and Moore, E.G., S.O. Burke, and M.W. Rosenberg (1990) *The disabled adult residential population.* Kingston, Ontario: Queen's University, Department of Geography.

33. Chappell, N.L., L.A. Strain, and A.A. Blandford (1986) *Aging and health care: a social perspective.* Toronto: Holt, Rinehart and Winston.

34. Liaw, K. and P. Kanaroglou (1986), op *cit.*

35. Statistics Canada (1990), *A Portrait of Seniors in Canada,* Ottawa: Supply and Services, pp. 18 and 19.

36. Statistics Canada (1990) *A Portrait of Seniors in Canada.* Ottawa: Supply and Services.

37. Skaburskis, A. (1988), "The nature of Canadian condominium submarkets and their effect on the evolving urban spatial structure", *Urban Studies,* 25: 109-123.

38. Brink, S. (1984), *Shelter and Policy Options to House the Elderly.* Ottawa: Planning Division, Canada Mortgage and Housing Corporation; and Struyk, R.J., M.A. Turner, and M. Ueno (1988) *Future U.S. housing policy.* Washington, D.C.: Urban Institute Press.

39. The analysis of movers/stayers and reasons for moving is based on Questions H.13 and H.14 where individuals were asked, H.13, "Have you moved in the past 5 years, that is since September 1986?" and H.14, "What were the reasons for this move?" Respondents were instructed to mark all the categories that apply and were given a list of 10 preselected reasons plus an open-ended category. The open-ended category was then recoded as an additional 12 separate reasons and one catch-all category. In our analysis, we aggregate the 23 codes in the database into 8 groups of reasons.

40. Rosenberg, M.W., and E.G. Moore (1990), op *cit., p.* 163.

Design of Institutions: Cognitive Functioning and Social Interactions of the Aged Resident*

BRENDAN GAIL RULE, DORIS L. MILKE, ALLEN R. DOBBS

Increasing numbers of older people require long-term care in institutions. The physical setting has long-range effects on the social activities, cognitive functioning, and physical well-being of the residents (see reviews by Lawton, 1980: Reizenstein, 1981). Although attention to the needs of the users should be paramount in the design and alteration of facilities, criteria are often based on visual aesthetics, ease of upkeep, or the wishes of corporate owners, rather than on the functional needs of the residents (Andreasen, 1985).

The popular press, caregiving journals, and manuals impart recommendations regarding the height of public telephones and handrails, architectural advice on corridor design and room plans, and design features intended to maintain self-care skills. The need for such information about physical features is substantial, but these features constitute only a limited subset of the design features that determine the functional utility of a living space. Moreover, although administrators, man-

* Reprinted with permission from *Journal of Applied Gerontology* 11 (4), 1992

agement, and caregiving staff may use informed guesses to identify problems and pose solutions, there is a data base in research from which to build.

Our purpose is to review the literature that bears on how physical facilities can accommodate, to a greater or lesser extent, the sensory, cognitive, and social deficits that occur in older adults. In addition, we review special issues in the design of facilities for demented individuals. Finally, we offer conclusions with regard to research and applied problems.

Spatial Deficits

Spatial abilities mediate a person's contact with, and responses to, the physical environment. Unfortunately, spatial skills decline with age (Kirasic & Allen, 1985; Ohta & Kirasic, 1983). Walsh, Krauss, and Regnier (1981) have shown that those over 55 years of age with poor cognitive spatial abilities are disadvantaged in the use of the facilities in their community and have poor environmental knowledge of them. Moreover, the average institutional resident has difficulty maintaining spatial orientation within the typical institution. Weber, Brown, and Weldon (1978) demonstrate the wayfinding deficit of the normal elderly person. Nursing home residents (aged 72-93), despite having adequate vision and being cognitively alert, had very poor memory for spatial locations within the nursing home compared to younger people given only a 40-minute tour. Although accuracy was correlated negatively with age, it was not correlated with length of stay. Similarly, Herman and Bruce (1981) found that although elderly nursing home residents accurately recognized and placed locations along the central corridor, their accuracy decreased substantially with distance from it. Residents' poor knowledge of their nursing home suggested that they did not use the available space frequently enough to become familiar with the institution, and consequently got lost, or that they did not use the space because they were afraid of getting lost.

Several features of an institution that exacerbate spatial deficits can be avoided or altered. Endless corridors with myriad doors, a lack of windows, or a lack of access to windows often found in institutions can be avoided in designing the facility (Baltes & Brim, 1984; Sivadon, 1970; Spivack, 1967; Zimring, 1981). Signage within the building is frequently created post hoc, hand-lettered and awkwardly placed, rather than carefully planned, boldly printed, and saliently located. Geriatric facilities could benefit from Chapman, Grant and Simmons' (1986) review of research on institutional design with respect to wayfinding issues (numbering floors, selecting terms to use on signs, spacing signs, using colored lights, banners, and "you-are-here" maps that are aligned properly with the direction in the environment). They suggest that environmental cues such as plants, works of art, and furniture provide useful information about the location for wayfinders.

Landmarks are often serendipitous rather than planned. Landmarks should be clearly identifiable; have cultural, geographic, or religious meaning; and be distinctive in relation to their surroundings (Hiatt, 1980). Landmarks also should be adjusted to compensate for the deficits of the elderly person. For example, because many older people may look downward while walking (Hiatt, 1980), name plates in institutions should be put at their gaze level (Lawton, 1970a). Multiple cues are important (Schiff, 1982; Schwartz, 1975) to aid in wayfinding and locomotion. Provision of signs, special lighting, and texture cues used on floors, walls, and railings could advise the elderly resident of main routes, warn of hazards, and reduce general ambiguity.

Familiarity can compensate for poor spatial memory, as illustrated by the better route planning of elderly women relative to younger ones in a supermarket shopping task (cited in Kirasic & Allen, 1985). In extrapolating to an institutional environment, special attention should be given to newcomers to familiarize them with the setting. Familiarization should continue until the newcomer has demonstrated competence in the environment, and familiarization should be reinstituted when individuals are relocated within a facility. At least one technique has been investigated to improve orientation and wayfinding of older people in a new environment. Hunt and Roll (1987) found that confidence and efficient learning were promoted by a simulation comparable to that of an actual site visit to an unfamiliar building.

Sensory Changes
Changes in sight, hearing, balance, haptic senses, and mobility reduce the extent of elderly persons' experience with any new environment (Pastalan, 1979). Pastalan, Mautz, and Merrill (1973) sensitized students by using mechanical appliances and masking devices to simulate the environmental experiences of the elderly adult. The students navigated in a dwelling unit, a multipurpose center, and a shopping center. Among their reported problems were glare, color fading in the blue-green spectrum, edges, contouring, unstable boundaries, and depth perception as well as auditory, olfactory, and tactile declines.

Changes in vision such as yellowing and thickening of the lens, degrading of retinal image, reduced light to the retina, increased sensitivity to glare, and altered color perception underlie many recommendations in design (Quayhagen & Quayhagen, 1988). Given the older person's sensitivity to glare, lighting should be uniform and indirect. Shiny waxed floors present serious glare problems. Carpeting rather than vinyl is preferable to avoid glare problems as well as to reduce noise. Incontinence of the elderly resident, however, may present problems with regard to sanitation when carpets are used (Cheek, Maxwell, & Wiseman, 1971; Willmott, 1986). Nonglare wax is another solution for this problem and perhaps more appropriate for wheelchairs and those who shuffle. These are just a few examples of relevant design features that would promote accommodation to sensory changes in aging. Unfortunately, few studies directly assess the impact of such factors on acceptability to older people or on their actual behavior in environments incorporating such design changes.

Despite some mixed findings on the ability of older people to discriminate various colors (Standford & Pollack, 1984), color coding has been used to facilitate the wayfinding of even demented residents (Droubay, 1964). Unfortunately, color coding of floors or wings is seldom used effectively and often when it is used, the choice of colors may defeat the purpose of the changes. For example, many elderly persons cannot distinguish between the pale values of most colors (especially in the blue-green range) and even the strong values of others (Fozard, Wolf, Bell, McFarland, & Podolsky, 1977; Haitt, 1980, 1981; Horowitz & Wilner, 1980). Red, orange, and yellow with good illumination would be most effective.

Other visual losses influence orientation. Because elderly persons lose the ability to differentiate objects from their background (Pastalan, 1982), context is very important. Dark stripes on a pale floor may be perceived as "holes" (Hiatt, 1980) and, hence, are barriers to free locomotion. Depth perception and edge perception are altered so that people have difficulty in distinguishing edges of walls from the floor. The wrap-around-the-walls style of floor coverings often chosen by interior designers may especially provide difficulty to the elderly viewer. This style should be avoided, with preference given to floor coverings that clearly demonstrate the floor from the wall.

Many impairments in hearing develop as people age (Abend & Chen, 1985). Acuity is lower on the average, especially in the higher-frequency ranges. Hearing acuity decreases about one decibel per year after the age of 65. Moreover, because they cannot separate signal from noise, older people have difficulty in noisy environments. These deficiencies not only impair social interaction and have safety implications, but they may also increase confusion and disorientation. Abend and Chen (1985) recommend that effective standards be developed for compensating hearing loss. Moreover, acoustic walls would help diminish unwanted noise in the environment.

Social Behavior

Older people experience social deficits either by voluntary social disengagement as an adaptation strategy or by involuntary reductions in social interactions (Lawton, 1970b). Some authors (Lawton, 1970b; Pastalan, 1979) suggest that institutionalization leads to withdrawal as a substitute for loss of privacy. Appropriate physical structures, however, can redress low rates of social interaction (McClannahan & Risley, 1975; Snyder, 1980).

Physical barriers or distances directly affect the probability of social contacts (e.g., Friedman, 1966; for a review, see Lawton, 1970b). Increased physical distance even between friends in a building or within a dayroom reduces interaction and the initiation of contact. Lawton (1970b) reports that circular arrangements of bedrooms around the nursing station and a large central living space promote social interaction between staff and residents and among residents themselves. The Osmond plan (Osmond, 1957) divides open space to provide choices of private, small group, or public spaces (e.g., floorplans in Liebowitz, Lawton & Waldman, 1979).

Needs for privacy that are unsatisfied may result in territorial behaviour. Lipman (1968) found that residents and staff both rigidly maintained the territorial seating arrangements that residents had negotiated over time. Considerable verbal invective and physical attacks occurred to defend habitually-used chairs. This territorial behavior in typical side-by-side seating suggests that these arrangements permit a kind of privacy in public areas. Lipman found that territorial boundaries of patient groups appeared to be related to physical factors such as the positions of doors, windows, the furniture, or the shapes of rooms. Spatial divisions were used by residents as social barriers to divide people according to gender, social strata, and cognitive alertness.

Providing a patient with personal space may be important. Ittelson, Proshansky, and Rivlin (1970) found more social behavior in single than in multiple-bed rooms. The single-room occupant used the room as a home, whereas those sharing a room used it as a retreat, by rotating occupancy. Even minimal physical adjustments can have a marked affect on behavior. Nelson and Paluck (1980) and Wilmott (1986) revealed that simple demarcation of territorial boundaries by taping off areas in semiprivate rooms resulted in more sociability and decreased maladjustment. In contrast, those with multiple functional and social losses expressed a preference for an open ward to any type of room accommodation (Kayser-Jones, 1986). These differing results may not be inconsistent, but rather may emphasize the need for a more concerted effort to identify the match between the type of patient and privacy needs.

Spatial arrangements of furniture should promote social interactions, while not enforcing too intense a level of interaction. In their classic study, Sommer and Ross (1958) showed that social interaction increased among pairs, but not among larger groups of geriatric residents after furniture rearrangements had been made. However, Peterson, Knapp, Rosen, and Pither (1977) found that furniture rearrangement increased only the incidence of talking but none of the 14 other behaviors observed. Lawton (1970b) discussed the advantages of sociopetal furniture arrangements in which chairs face each other rather than being arranged in the side-by-side line-ups characteristic of bus stations and airports. The former increases social interactions.

Where furniture is clustered may be as important as its arrangement. Snyder (1980) found that in two of three homes studied, fewer than a fifth of the chairs in any dayroom or lounge were used. Designated social areas were not necessarily an inducement to conversation. Instead, the popular chairs were those with a view, precipitating conversations about observed events (e.g. views from a window, arrivals and departures, sounds, strong odors, and unconventional resident behavior). Bakos, Bozic, Chapin, and Neuman (1980) found that social interactions improved for those who had been randomly selected to make decisions about rearranging and remodelling dayrooms. This may occur because they were given a job to do or because they subsequently used the new arrangement, which promoted social interaction.

The provocative and potentially important results in this area invite more thorough research. Despite Lindsley's (1964) plea for direct observation and measurement of behavior of elderly people, few researchers have done so.

Facilities for Dementia Patients

Dementia is one of the leading reasons for institutional placement. Because a minimum of 60% of elderly people in most institutions suffer from some degree of dementia and the segment of the population at greatest risk for dementia is growing most rapidly, matters pertaining to the care of the demented elderly person are pressing ones (Brody, Lawton, & Leibowitz, 1984; Rovner & Rabins, 1985). Appropriate design of facilities will depend on whether demented people have special characteristics and needs.

The sensory capabilities of Alzheimer patients decline similarly to those of nondemented people of their age; hence, the same design considerations are relevant for managing their perceptual deficits. Because spatial impairment is greater, however, in the demented person than in normal elderly persons, even more attention should be given to selecting demonstrably salient cues to reduce the demented residents' disorientation and improve their wayfinding.

Although nursing home patients with mild to moderate dementia may be especially susceptible to spatial confusions (Howell, 1982), there is evidence that they can learn some basic routes when some effort is made to teach them how to use the cues (Droubay, 1964; Hanley, 1981). Because such techniques could assist with relocating mentally competent older people and could lead to signage systems to reinforce environmental learning, further research is crucial.

The demented person is viewed to be aggressive, to wander, to get lost, to seek attention, to be verbally incoherent, to trespass into other peoples' rooms, to interfere with others' possessions, and to be offensive in habits (Haugen, 1985; Pynoos & Stacey, 1986). The lore among caregivers (Bartol, 1979; Hoffman, Platt, Barry, & Hamill, 1985; Moos, 1976) emphasizes the demented persons' lack of communication skills, asocial nature, gathering behaviors, and wandering.

Systematic observational studies suggest that this characterization does not represent the typical behaviors of residents. Observers have documented that the demented residents spend most of their time doing nothing (Gottesman & Bourestom, 1974; Lawton, 1981; McClannahan & Risley, 1975) and spend little time

(10%) in their own rooms (cf. Stephens & Willems, 1979). Compared to nondemented residents, the demented spent more time in their lounge and were seldom away from their own ward (Lawton, 1981). Non-demented residents spent two thirds of their time in their lounge (Milke, Dobbs, Rule, & Milke, 1987). Milke et al. (1987) found that residents with dementia of the Alzheimer's type were silent people who spent one third of each day inactively sitting or standing. They rarely trespassed in private bedrooms in other wings and rarely absconded. Their communications were as often appropriate as inappropriate. Attention seeking and aggression seldom occurred. Although the data must be verified by further study, they suggest that in planning the residential environment, the greater use of lounges by demented residents and greater use of bedrooms by non-demented residents should be accommodated.

Cornbelth's (1977) finding, that wanderers improved their gait when provided with a protected walking area, has resulted in the provision of such walking areas for demented persons (e.g., Peppard, 1986). Cornbelth also showed that non-wanderers benefited more by an open ward, apparently walking more when given more choice in their routes. Designs that benefit wanderers, however, may not be appropriate for non-wanderers.

The impact of the physical structure on the social interaction of demented persons has been assessed in very few studies. Lawton and his colleagues (Fulcomer, Kleban, & Lawton, 1979 cited in Lawton, 1980; Lawton, Liebowitz, & Charon, 1970) found that improving the facility had some unexpected and unwanted effects. After a move from a traditional institution in to an Osmond-plan building there was no indication of change in the basic pathology. Both mental status and functional health declined significantly over an 18-month period, whereas, everyday behavior such as participation in activities and social behavior did not change. "Of 54 behaviors that could be classified as having a desirable-undesirable dimension, only one showed a significant decline, 39 remained the same, and 14 showed a significant improvement" (Lawton, 1980, p.131). An undesirable decrease in patient-care activities by staff occurred, possibly because residents were readily visible from the nursing station (Lawton, Fulcomer, & Kleban, 1984). Lawton et al. (1970) remodeled a ward, giving more private space to residents with an open social space visible from the nursing station. Again, the residents' increased visibility was related to a decrease in staff-resident interaction. There was no change in levels of patient interaction after remodelling.

Both studies had problems with subject attrition. In the former, 79 of 135 patients were lost through transfer or death, and in the latter, only 1 of 9 patients survived to be moved into the renovated ward. Neither study can be considered a definitive test of the improvements done, although both suggest that easy surveillance of patients by staff may be a design criterion to be reconsidered (Lawton, 1970a).

Integration Versus Segregation

A major controversy concerns whether demented patients should be segregated on the basis of the degree of mental impairment or integrated with the non-demented patients (Moos & Lemke, 1984). Presumably non-demented residents would provide stimulation for the demented residents, whereas the latter would provide an opportunity for the nonconfused people to accept responsibility in caring for the demented people (Lipman & Slater, 1979).

The advantages of integrated homes may be more theoretical than actual. In studies of a number of homes, Meacher (1972) and Snyder (1980) found that demented patients were segregated by staff and ostracized by nondemented residents even when the home was integrated. Harris, Lipman, and Slater (1977), similarly found that the residents of different mental competencies were segregated from one another in sitting spaces in all of the homes they studied. Lipman and Slater (1977) found that the confused residents were disadvantaged by their non-demented counterparts, who occupied the desirable seats and locations. Moreover, according to qualitative reports, nursing personnel say that the more intact people become very anxious when forced into close proximity with the senile residents, and only 15% of the residents' relatives favor integration (Lawton, 1981). In a review of the problems in mixed settings, Pynoos and Stacey (1986) noted that even though non-demented residents express tolerance and sympathy for demented people, they agree that the patients should be segregated.

Pairing demented and nondemented residents had deleterious effects on the mentally competent people (Wiltzius, Gambert, & Duthie, 1981). The competent people expressed depression, loneliness, and insecurity over having a confused roommate. Caregivers' responses to the pairing of demented and nondemented people is apt to be a litany of the problems that some have called "cruel and unusual punishment" of the rational residents (Ablowitz, 1983; Gang & Ackerman, 1983).

Recently, Benson, Cameron, Humbach, Servino, and Gambert (1987) assessed residents admitted to a specially designated dementia unit prior to admission, as well as at 4 and 12 months postadmission. The patients showed increased levels of functioning in mental and emotional status as well as in basic functions of daily living. Although several other authors (Gutman, 1989; MacKay, 1976; Prinsley, 1973; Rabins, 1986) have outlined the advantages and problems of establishing dementia units in nursing homes, few empirical evaluations have been done.

Because of the recognition of unique needs of Alzheimer patients, special care units are increasing (Calkins, 1987). In their review of policy manuals and published and unpublished reports describing special care units, Ohta and Ohta (1988) describe considerable heterogeneity in philosophy, focus of patient care, environmental design, and therapeutic approach. There has been no assessment of the value or problems associated with the differences, nor with the integration versus segregation issue (Gutman, 1989; Ohta and Ohta (1988). Given the importance of this issue, it is evident that systematic research must be undertaken to evaluate the question. Observations, interviews, and behavioral measures of staff and demented and nondemented residents are required to document the qualitative and preliminary data on mixed versus segregated facilities. Despite the difficulty in achieving rigorous experimental designs with random assignment to groups and using control groups, (Ohta & Ohta, 1988), there is much to be gained through systematic descriptions that can provide a more informed knowledge base for making decisions about programs and design of institutions for the older adult. The answer may be that either integrated or special care facilities are appropriate, depending on the programs and care plans implemented within the facility. Ascertaining how an integrated facility can be functionally optimal is important, given that special care units may not be feasible, such as in rural settings.

Conclusion

Lawton's conclusion in his 1981 review that not much systematic information is available about institutional design holds true at least 9 years later. Our review shows that, with the exception of the information about sensory changes in aging, the soundness of our knowledge base is challenged by the lack of systematic research on most issues. There is an abundance of speculation from which to develop testable hypotheses and there are now methods (Milke et al., 1987) and statistical analyses (e.g., Jarvik, 1982) to provide solid empirical tests of those hypotheses.

The paucity of research in this area shows that conclusions cannot be drawn with confidence. Moreover, the methodology in the extant research begs for more rigor and more sophisticated statistical procedures. Because decisions having financial and humane consequences are being made daily, it is hoped that the press for firm information will stimulate research in this area.

Although systematic evaluations of environmental changes are necessary, sensitization to the current state of the literature should enable architects, psychologists, sociologists, and gerontologists to attempt changes in the design of facilities for the elderly population. Analysis of each particular setting with knowledge of what is known in this area should promote more adequate functional designs until such systematic evaluations are available

References

Abend, A & Chen, A. (1985). Developing residential design statements for the hearing-impaired elderly. *Environment and Behavior, 17,* 475-500.

Ablowitz, M. (1983). Letter to the editor. *Journal of the American Geriatrics Society, 31,* 627.

Andreasen, M.E.K. (1985). Make a safe environment by design. *Journal of Gerontological Nursing, 11,* 18-22.

Bakos, M., Bozic, R., Chapin, D., & Newman, S. (1980). Effects of environmental changes on elderly residents' behavior. *Hospital and Community Psychiatry, 34,* 677-682.

Baltes, P.B. & Brim, O.G., Jr. (Eds.). (1984). *Life-span development and behavior.* New York: Academic Press.

Bartol, M.A. (1979). Nonverbal communication in patients with Alzheimer's disease. *Journal of Gerontological Nursing, 5,* 21-31.

Benson, D.M., Cameron, D., Humbach, E., Servino, L., & Gambert, S.R. (1987). Establishment and impact of a dementia unit within the nursing home. *Journal of the American Geriatrics Society, 35,* 319-323.

Brody, E.M., Lawton, M.P., & Liebowitz, B. (1984). Senile dementia: Public policy and adequate institutional care. *American Journal of Public Health, 74,* 1381-1383.

Calkins, M.P. (1987). Designing special care units: A systematic approach. *American Journal of Alzheimer's Care and Research, 2,* 30-34.

Champman, J. R., Grant, M.A., & Simmons, D.A. (1986). *Design that cares.* Owings Mills, MD: National Health Publishing.

Cheek, F.W., Maxwell, R., & Weisman, R. (1971). Carpeting the ward: An exploratory study in environmental psychiatry. *Mental Hygiene, 55,* 109-118.

Cornbleth, T. (1977). Effects of a protected hospital ward area on wandering and nonwandering geriatric patients. *Journal of Gerontology, 32,* 573-577.

Droubay, E.H. (1964). Blue is for bathrooms. Colors guide geriatric patients. *Mental Hospitals, 15,* 386-390.

Fozard, J.L., Wolf, E., Bell, B., McFarland, R.A., & Podolsky, S. (1977). Visual perception and communication. In J.E. Birren & K.W. Schaie (Eds.), *Handbook of the psychology of aging* (pp. 497-534). New York: Van Nostrand Reinhold.

Friedman, E.P. (1966) Spatial proximity and social interaction in a home for the aged. *Journal of Gerontology, 21,* 566-570.

Gang, R., & Ackerman, J.O. (1983). Letter to the editor. *Journal of the American Geriatrics Society, 31,* 627-628.

Gottesman, L.E., & Gourestom, N.C. (1974). Why nursing homes do what they do. *The Gerontologist, 14,* 501-506.

Gutman, G.M. (1989). *Dementia patients in institutions: A review of recommendations and research concerning their design, staffing and programming needs (Report prepared* for the Pacific Health Care Society, the Gerontology Research Centre). Burnaby, BC: Simon Fraser University Press.

Hanley, I.G. (1981). The use of signposts and active training to modify ward disorientation in elderly patients. *Journal of Behavioral Therapy and Experimental Psychiatry, 12,* 241-247.

Harris, H., Lipman, A., & Slater, R. (1977). Architectural design: The spatial location and interactions of old people. *Gerontology, 23,* 390-400.

Haugen, P.K. (1985). Behavior of patients with dementia. *Danish Medical Bulletin, 32,* 62-65.

Herman, J.F. & Bruce, P.R. (1981). Spatial knowledge of ambulatory and wheelchair-confined nursing home residents. *Experimental Aging Research, 9,* 83-85.

Hiatt, L.G. (1980). Disorientation is more than just a state of mind. *Nursing Homes, 29 (4),* 30-36.

Hiatt, L.G. (1981). The color and use of color in environments for older people. *Nursing Homes, 30,* 18-22.

Hoffman, S.B., Platt, C.A., Barry, K.E., & Hamill, L.A. (1985). When language fails: Nonverbal communication abilities of the demented. In J.T. Hutton & A.D. Kenny (Eds.), *Senile dementia of the Alzheimer type (pp. 49-64). New York: Liss.*

Horowitz, M.J., & Wilner, N. (1980). Life events, stress, and coping. In L.W. Poon (Ed.), *Aging in the 1980s (pp. 363-374). Washington, DC: American Psychological Association.*

Howell, S.C. (1982). Built space, the mystery variable in health and aging. In A. Baum & J.E. Singer (Eds.), Advances in environmental psychology (pp. 31-47). Hillsdale, NJ: Lawrence Erlbaum.

Hunt, M.E., & Roll, M.K. (1987). Simulation in familiarizing older people with an unknown building. *The Gerontologist, 27,* 169-175.

Ittelson, W.H., Proshansky, H.M., & Rivlin, L.G. (1970). Bedroom size and social interaction of the psychiatic ward. *Environment and Behavior, 2,* 255-270.

Jarvik, L. (1982). Research on dementia: The philothermal response. *Psychiatric Clinics of North America, 5,* 87-88.

Kayser-Jones, J.S. (1986). Open-ward accommodations in a long-term care facility: The elderly's point of view. *The Gerontologist, 26,* 63-69.

Kirasic, K.C., & Allen, G.L. (1985) Aging, spatial performance and spatial competence. In N. Charness (Ed.), *Aging and human performance* (pp. 191-223). Chichester, England: Wiley.

Lawton, M.P. (1970a). Planner's notebook: Planning environments for older people. *Journal of the American Institute of Planners, 36,* 124-129.

Lawton, M.P. (1970b). Public behavior of older people in congregate housing. In J. Archea & C. Eastman (Eds.), *EDRA Two: Proceedings of the second annual Environmental Design Research Association conference, October, 1970, Pittsburgh, Pennsylvania* (pp. 372-380). Sourdsburg, PA: Dowden, Hutchinson, & Ross.

Lawton, M.P. (1980). *Environment and aging.* Monterery, CA: Brooks/Cole.

Lawton, M.P. (1981). Sensory deprivation and the effect of the environment on management of the patient with senile dementia. In N.E. Miller & G.D. Cohen (Eds.), *Clinical aspects of Alzheimer's disease and senile dementia (Aging)* (Vol. 15, pp. 227-251). New York: Raven.

Lawton, M.P., Fulcomer, M., & Kleban, M.H. (1984). Architecture for the mentally impaired elderly. *Environment and Behavior, 16,* 730-757.

Lawton, M.P., Liebowitz, M.S.W., & Charon, H. (1970). Physical structure and the behavior of senile patients following ward remodeling. *Aging and Human Development, 1,* 231-239.

Liebowitz, B., Lawton, M.P., & Waldman, A. (1979). Evaluation: Designing for confused elderly people. *American Institute of Architects Journal, 68,* 59-61.

Lindsley, O.R. (1964). Geriatric behavioral prosthetics. In R. Kastenbaum (Ed.), *New thoughts on old age* (pp. 41-60). New York: Springer.

Lipman, A. (1968). Some problems of direct observation in architectural social research. *Architects' Journal Information Library, 147,* 1349-1356.

Lipman, A. & Slater, R. (1977). Status and spatial appropriation in eight homes for old people. *The Gerontologist, 17,* 250-255.

Lipman, A. & Slater, R. (1979). Homes for old people: Towards a positive environment. In D.V. Canter & S. Canter (Eds.), *Designing for therapeutic environments* (pp. 277-308). Chichester, England: Wiley.

MacKay, D.B. (1976). The effect of spatial stimuli on the estimation of cognitive maps. *Geographical Analysis, 8,* 439-451.

McClannahan, L.E. & Risley, T.R. (1975). Design of living environments for nursing-home residents: Increasing participation in recreation activities. *Journal of Applied Behavior Analysis, 8,* 261-268.

Meacher, M. (1972). *Taken for a ride.* London: Longman.

Milke, D.L. Dobbs, A.R., Rule, B.G., & Milke, A.L. (1987). The use of space by Alzheimer disease patients in a nursing home. *Canadian Psychology, 28(2A),* 415. [abstract]

Moos, R.H. (1976). *The human context: Environmental determinants of behavior.* New York: Wiley.

Moos, R.H. & Lemke, S. (1984). Supportive residential settings for older people. In I. Altman, M.P. Lawton, & J.F. Wohlwell (Eds.), *Human behavior and environment: Advances in theory and research: Vol. 7, Elderly people and the environment* (pp. 159-190). New York: Plenum.

Nelson, M.N. & Paluck, R.J. (1980). Territorial markings, self-concept and mental status of institutionalized elderly. *The Gerontologist, 20,* 96-98.

Ohta, R.J., & Kirasic, K.C. (1983). The investigation of environmental learning in the elderly. In G.D. Rowles & R.J. Ohta (Eds.), *Aging and milieu: Environmental perspectives on growing old* (pp. 83-95). New York: Academic Press.

Ohta, R.J. & Ohta, B.M. (1988). Special units for Alzheimer disease patients: A critical look. *The Gerontologist, 28,* 803-808.

Osmond, H. (1957). Function as the basis of psychiatric ward design. *Mental Hospitals, 8,* 23-32.

Pastalan, L.A. (1979). Negotiating the environment. In T.O. Byarts, S.C. Howell, & L.A. Pastalan (Eds.), *Environmenal context of aging: Lifestyles, environmental quality and living arrangements* (pp. 103-126). New York: Garland.

Pastalan, L.A. (1982). Research in environment and aging: An alternative to theory. In M.P. Lawton, P.G. Windley, & T.O. Byerts (Eds.), *Aging and the environment* (pp. 122-177). New York: Springer.

Pastalan, L.A., Mautz, R.K., II. & Merrill, J. (1973). The simulation of age related sensory losses: A new approach to the study of environmental barriers. In W.F.E. Preiser (Ed.), *Environmental design research* (Vol. 1, pp. 383-391). Stroudsberg, PA: Dowden, Hutchinson, & Ross.

Peppard, N.R. (1986, May). Effective design of special care units. *Provider,* pp. 14-17.

Peterson, R.F., Knapp, T.J., Rosen, J.C., & Pther, B.F. (1977). The effects of furniture arrangements on the behavior of geriatric patients. *Behavior Therapy, 8,* 464-467.

Prinsley, D.M. (1973). Psychogeriatric ward for mentally disturbed elderly patients. *British Medical Journal, 15,* 574-577.

Pynoos, J., & Stacey, C.A. (1986). Specialized facilities for senile dementia patients. In M.L.M. Gilhooly, S.H. Zarit, & J.E. Birren (Eds.), *The dementias: Policy and management* (pp. 111-130). Englewood Cliffs, NJ: Prentice-Hall.

Quayhagen, M.P. & Quayhagen, M. (1988). Alzheimer's stress: Coping with the caregiving role. *The Gerontologist, 28,* 391-396.

Rabins, P. (1986). Establishing Alzheimer's disease units in nursing homes: Pros and cons. *Hospital and Community Psychiatry, 37,* 120-121.

Reizenstein, J.E. (1981). Hospital design and human behavior: A review of the recent literature. In A. Baum & J.E. Singer (Eds.), *Advances in environmental psychology: Vol. 4, Environmental Health* (pp. 137-169). Hillsdale NJ: Lawrence Erlbaum.

Rovner, B.U., & Rabins, P.V. (1985). Mental illness among nursing home patients. *Hospital and Community Psychiatry, 36,* 119-128.

Schiff, M.R. (1982). Environmental design. Helping residents find their way. *Ontario Association of Homes for the Aged, 18,* 7-8.

Schwartz, A.N. (1975). Planning micro-environments for the aged. In D.S. Woodruff & J.E. Birren (Eds.), *Aging: Scientific perspectives and social issues* (pp. 279-294). New York: Van Nostrand.

Sivadon, P. (1970). Space as experienced: Therapeutic implications. In H.M. Proshansky, W.H. Ittleson, & L.G. Rivlin (Eds.), *Environmental psychology: Man and his physical setting* (pp. 409-419). New York: Holt, Rinehart & Winston.

Snyder, L.H. (1980) An exploratory study of patterns of social interaction, organization, and facility design in three nursing homes. In J. Hendricks (Ed.), *Institutionalization and alternative futures* (pp. 66-80). Farmingdale, NY: Baywood.

Sommer, R., & Ross, H. (1958). Social interaction on a geriatrics ward. *International Journal of Social Psychiatry, 18,* 21-30.

Standford, T., & Pollack, R.H. (1984). Configuration color vision tests: The interaction between aging and the complexity of figure-ground segregation. *Journal of Gerontology, 39,* 568-571.

Stephens, M.P. & Willems, E.P. (1979). Everyday behavior of older persons in institutional housing: Some implications for design. In A.D. Seidal & S. Danford (Eds.), *Environmental design: Research theory and application* (pp. 344-348). Washington, DC: Environmental Design Research Association.

Walsh, D.A., Krauss, I.K., & Regnier, V.A. (1981). Spatial ability, environmental knowledge, and environmental use: The elderly. In L. Liben, A. Patterson, & N. Newcombe (Eds.). *Spatial representation and behavior across the life span* (pp. 321-357). New York: Academic Press.

Weber, R.J., Brown, L.T., & Weldon, J.K. (1978). Cognitive maps of environmental knowledge and preference in nursing home patients. *Experimental Aging Research, 4,* 157-174.

Willmott, M. (1986). The effect of a vinyl floor surface and a carpeted floor surface upon walking in elderly hospital in-patients. *Age and Aging, 15,* 119-120.

Wiltzius, F., Gambert, S.R., & Duthie, E.H. (1981). Importance of resident placement within a skilled nursing facility. *Journal of the American Geriatrics Society, 29,* 418-421.

Zimring, C. (1981). Stress and the designed environment. *Journal of Social Issues, 27,* 145-171.

Brendan Gail Rule, Ph.D., was a Professor of Psychology at the University of Alberta and Director of the Centre for Gerontology. Just prior to her untimely death, she was awarded the G. Kaplan Award for Excellence in Research based on her past work on aggression and more recent research on cognitive changes associated with aging.

Doris L. Milke, Ph.D., is currently in the research division of the Long Term Care Branch of the Alberta Government, consulting on environmental design and related issues. Her research focuses on wandering in dementia patients.

Allen R. Dobbs, Ph.D., is the current Director of the Centre for Gerontology at the University of Alberta and Director of the Neurocognitive Research Program at the Edmonton General Hospital. His research concerns memory and cognitive deficits associated with Alzheimer's disease, behavioral manifestations of these cognitive deficits, and implications for environmental design.

AUTHORS' NOTE:
Grants from the Alberta Senior Citizen's Secretariat and the Social Sciences and Humanities Research Council partially supported this work.

Technology and Aging

NEENA CHAPPELL

A Growing Interest

The technological society is usually imaged by sophisticated robots, spaceships, and curative medical inventions. While high tech is part of technology and aging, low tech and rehabilitative or assistive devices are frequently the concern in gerontology.

Technology in the field of health and aging has been defined as devices or systems which assist in achieving and maintaining an independent lifestyle.[1] Technology can be differentiated in several ways. Paul Haber, for example, distinguishes three levels.[2] High technology uses physical and chemical principles to report and define information on the state of health of the elderly (included here would be ultra-sound equipment, magnetic resonance imagers, etc.). Middle technology uses advanced principles in every-day equipment around the home, like the television and stereo. Low technology includes devices such as furniture, doors, cabinets, stairs, bathroom appliances, heating utensils, flatware, cooking utensils, and clothing. Much of the interest in aging revolves around the use and adoption of low technology to enhance safety and the quality of life.

Technology can increase the function of an individual (for example, by means of a joint replacement) or it can affect a person's independence through modification of one's environment. Grab bars, wheelchair ramps, and one-story houses are examples of environmental features which can enhance independence. One can also distinguish between technologies which help to manage disability (such as wheelchairs and grab bars), those which prevent accidents and injuries (footwear design and flooring), and those which promote and maintain independence (such as aspects of architectural design). In addition, the home environment can be divided into the physical environment (kitchen, hallways, doors, etc.) and the technology within it (monitors, appliances, furniture).

For some time, individual manufacturers and retailers have been involved in technological inventions and innovations for an aging population; until very recently, however, there has been no visible national effort in Canada in this area. Several recent events suggest that technology in relation to aging is now becoming a major area for development across the country. For example, the federal and Manitoba governments each contributed to a new aging and rehabilitation product development centre (known as ARCOR) which became operational in 1990. This non-profit, non-governmental agency is located in Winnipeg with a mandate to develop products, primarily in conjunction with business, which are marketed to an aging society. The Seniors Independence Program (SIP) has funded research at the University of Waterloo to catalogue and evaluate a variety of assistive devices for seniors. Ontario opened the Window on Technology Centre in 1990, a community-based resource centre for technology display and training.

Other examples include a federal Network of Centres of Excellence which is working with seniors to identify needs which could be met through product development in the private sector. This project is based at the University of Manitoba. The Centre for Studies in Aging at Sunnybrook Health Sciences Centre in Toronto has expanded its research in this area. Three main areas in which research is being conducted include the mechanics and predictors of falling to assist in the design of technologies to prevent falling (including floor surfaces, grab bars and lighting); assistive devices related to mobility, including lifts, transfers and seating; and cognitive dysfunction. These examples illustrate the new recognition of and interest in the area of technology and aging in Canada.

One of the major reasons for interest in this area is that the use of technology can help disabled seniors and those with deteriorating health to live independently. Here the interest is more with middle and low technology (i.e. assistive devices and appropriate environments), although high technology can be important in the diagnosis and treatment of various forms of diseases.

Examples of technological products currently in general use in Canada include electronic emergency response systems and automatic shut-off mechanisms for appliances. Many products, however, are not readily affordable or at least not readily available at affordable prices. A summary of functional impairments, their consequences, and the available technology is provided in Table 1. Reprinted from the report on *Technology for the Elderly* of the Metropolitan Toronto District Health Council, this table provides a useful overview of the types of technologies that are currently available.[3]

TABLE 1

Functional Impairments, Consequences and Available Technology

	Further Consequences	Present Technology
Functional Impairment with Mobility - inability to: walk, climb stairs, stand for long periods, bend	- difficulties moving around home, entering or leaving home, therefore no access to shopping, recreation, transportation, driving, participation in fitness/exercise/sports - difficulty getting in and out of bed, turning in bed - difficulty getting up from sitting position and using bathroom - general increased risk of accidents, falls - difficulties in dressing, grooming, food preparation, feeding, carrying groceries, using telephone, picking up small objects - emotional and social problems	- lightweight wheelchair, power wheelchair, scooters, special controls for power chairs, i.e. head controls sip and puff, touch control systems, voice control wheelchair, van lifts, zero effort, steering for vans, SMART house, stair glides and elevator, improved artificial limbs, bionic limbs, porchlifts, improved access to transit, personal function aids, bathing, toileting, transfer aids
Sensory Impairment - Vision - inability to see clearly, perceive colours, depth, inability to see peripherally	- unable to read for pleasure, business, safety - impaired ability to enjoy previous activities, i.e. T.V., movies, artwork, nature, sports, theatre work and volunteer work - difficulty recognizing family and friends - difficulty using public transit - difficulty with personal grooming, awareness of health problems - safety concerns with medications, food preparation (insects or mould), driving, walking, walking alone or in new areas, reading maps, street signs - emotional and social problems	- glasses/contact lenses, large-print books, audible signals in transit, elevators, laser cane, low vision aids, environmental design, i.e. street signs lit, tactile cues, medical technology i.e. implants, surgery
Sensory Impairment - Hearing - inability to understand spoken word (personal, T.V., radio, etc.), environmental noise (car horns, warning sounds, fire, police), household noise (timers, fire alarm, telephone, doorbell, door and windows being opened), public events (speeches, religious meetings, cultural events, sports)	- lack of safety in home and outside - insecurity in dealing with business concerns - may appear confused or less intelligent - inability to sustain previous activities and relationships - emotional and social problems	- hearing aids, whistling kettles, food timers, answering machines, hearing aid-compatible phones, wake-up and signalling devices, aids to hear conversations, lectures and television, hand-held hearing aids, close-captioning tele-communications devices

TABLE 1 (continued)

Functional Impairments, Consequences and Available Technology

	Further Consequences	Present Technology
Sensory Impairment - inability to pick up coins, needles, papers, etc., distinguish fabrics, surfaces, open packages, letters, fasten buttons, zippers, snaps, broaches, etc., tie bows, laces, string, react to temperature changes, sharp surfaces, react to odours, taste	- difficulties handling day-to-day activities, i.e. tidying, picking up dropped objects (safety hazard), handling money - inappropriate dressing and grooming - burns, cuts, body odours, food poisoning, high salt intake, high sugar intake, poor appetite	- reaching aids, magnetic aids, fire alarms, improved thermostat controls warning if temperature is too high or too low, smoke detectors, heat detectors and alarms for existing stoves and appliances, infrared elements
Cognitive Impairment - inability to comprehend, remember, communicate thoughts, feelings, needs - inability to concentrate - inability to interpret sensory input	- inability to participate in previous activities at home, with family and society in business, culture and recreation pursuits - inability to care for self - danger to self and family and others, i.e. wandering, driving, cannot express pain or need for health care - increased vulnerability to crime, being taken advantage of - emotional and social problems	- memory aids, alarm systems, SMART house - drug-dispensing aids
Communication Impairment - loss or impairment of speech (meetings, cultural events, sports)	- cannot express needs, feelings, thoughts - cannot participate in family, social activities, business/work/volunteer work - Activities of Daily Living are impaired, shopping, asking for advice/help/information, talking on telephone - fear of danger from lack of communication - emotional and social problems	- communication board, special telephone, teletype communication - voice amplifiers - voice synthesizers - miniature printers/display boards - personal computers
Incontinence - loss or impairment in voluntary control of bladder and/or bowel	- skin breakdown, bladder infections, bladder stones, odour, discomfort, constipation - emotional and social problems	- disposable pants, pads - catheters, condom drainage - external clamp (male), pessary (female) - electrical stimulator - ultrasonic sensor (experimental) - biofeedback and bladder retraining

Source: Report on Technology for the Elderly, Metropolitan Toronto District Health Council, 1988.

Increased Need

The need for assistance increases with age. Table 2 shows the percentage of seniors by age requiring assistance with selected daily tasks. Of the six tasks listed, most require assistance with heavy housework, ranging from 63 percent among those age 65-74 through to 86 percent among those age 85 and over. Many also need assistance with shopping — 29 percent of those age 65-74; 43 percent of those age 75-84; and 71 percent of those age 85 and over. Those with disabilities may or may not be housebound. The Canadian Health and Disability Survey reports that 3.7 percent of the Canadian population over the age of 65 are housebound.[4] This represents 9.5 percent of seniors who are disabled.

TABLE 2

**Percentage of Seniors Requiring Assistance
with Selected Daily Tasks by Age**

	Age		
Daily Task	**65-74**	**75-84**	**85+**
	%	%	%
Meal preparation	16	23	46
Shopping	29	43	71
Housework	30	41	62
Heavy housework	63	74	86
Personal finances	18	29	55
Personal care	12	15	31

Source: HALS Report, August, 1990.

Not all of those who are disabled use assistive technological aids. Some may not use assistance, some may use personal help, some may use technical aids, and some may use a combination of each of the above. George Abrahamsohn, in Table 3, reports the use of technical aids and personal help for selected activities of daily living.[5] As Table 3 shows, the same proportion (14 percent) use technical aids and personal help for assistance with bathing. However, far more use technical aids than personal help for in-home mobility (21 percent vs. 3 percent). Similarly, many more use technical aids for transfers in and out of bed than use personal assistance (14 percent vs. 5 percent). However, many more have personal help with dressing than use technical aids (15 percent vs. 1 percent). Whether individuals choose personal assistance when technical aids are available at affordable prices is not known. We know very little about the characteristics of those who prefer technical aids over personal assistance; neither do we know in which need-areas technical aids are preferred, nor the optimal mix of technical aids and personal assistance for maintaining independence while also maintaining personal ties. Under what circumstances will a person reject the use of an aid? When will they embrace it? These questions include the broader issues of personal choice, autonomy, and dignity.

TABLE 3

Use of Technology vs. Personal Assistance
for Selected Activities of Daily Living

	Technical Aids	Personal Help
	%	%
In-home mobility	21	3
Bathing	14	14
Transfer in/out of bed	14	5
Toileting	10	4
Dressing	1	15
Eating	0	5

Source: Abrahamsohn, 1991 (derived from C.L. Macken, "A Profile of Functionally Impaired Elderly Persons Living in the Community," *Health Care Financing Review* 7 (1986), 33-49.

While the numbers of people who are elderly are growing, we do not know whether we can expect more or less disability among seniors in the future. James F. Fries's famous hypothesis about the triangulation of morbidity argues that disability and disease will be postponed until the end of life. However, this has not yet been confirmed empirically.[6] So far, there has not been a noticeable decrease in disability among those who are elderly. Furthermore, the young disabled, who are now living longer, represent a group frequently requiring assistance. That is, we can expect as much, if not more, disability in old age in the future as we see now.

Given such potential for increased need, it is surprising that there is no national standardized body which assesses the safety of products for the entire country. At the present time companies who wish to market various products, particularly health care products, must have them approved in each of the provinces. There is no system for delivering technology across the country; rather, there are a number of different local and provincially funded agencies which work with professionals, assessment centres, and commercial enterprises involved in manufacturing and distributing products to the public. The several players within the system include the manufacturers of technology; the research and development centres which innovate new technology; the funders, whether they be private or public; the providers who supply the technology; the authorizers, who are typically health care professionals ensuring that the technology is appropriate; and ultimately the consumers. All are involved with technological use but there is no coordination of their efforts.

A variety of assistive devices are now on the market for seniors and other disabled persons. However, without a centralized dissemination point where an individual can learn what is available for which disabilities, many older persons and their care-givers are unaware of the devices which exist or how they can obtain them. A general lack of awareness of the many products on the market, not only among consumers but also among health care professionals, is also a problem. Looking at one specific area, William F. Forbes *et al.* report that hearing impairment increases with age. Men are also more likely to be hearing impaired than women, the non-married and those residing in rural areas.[7] These researchers report substantial unmet need. That is, many persons who use an assistive device for hearing still report a need, while others who report a need do not use devices. If those in need do not know products are available, or do not know how to find out about them or where to purchase them, these products cannot contribute to their independence or quality of life.

The meeting of unmet needs through technological development is an area in which little research has been conducted. The assumption is that technological development will facilitate independence. Related questions are seldom asked. Will technological development create dependency? Under what circumstances are certain technologies isolating? Who should assess who can benefit from the device and, if it is a retail outlet, is it the needs of consumers which will be given priority? Where is one to obtain advice and staff for follow-up, maintenance, and servicing?

Technology is sometimes expensive. Virtually all provinces have programs which will cover all or part of the cost of approved assistive devices. However, as the report on *Technology for the Elderly* of the Metropolitan Toronto District Health Council notes, these programs were initiated to assist young people and their families with the high cost of medically necessary devices.[8] Devices appropriate to the elderly are therefore not always included. The question of which assistive devices for independent living will be covered by these programs has not yet been answered. Many aids for living, such as lift and transfer devices and batteries for electric chairs, are frequently not covered by these programs.

In Canada the system buys very little, but for equipment which *is* covered only a functional diagnosis is required; that is, documentation that a disability exists and not a medical diagnosis. Seniors pay 25 percent of the cost of covered equipment. Some provinces cover more equipment than is mandated federally; however, some do not, so that portability across provinces is not assured. Furthermore, programs provide durable medical equipment (defined as equipment which serves a medical purpose, that can be used later by other patients, and is of no use to persons who are well), but not assistive devices that promote function and safety.[9]

Technological products need not be beneficial only for the disabled senior, or only for seniors. Remote controls for television sets and safety alarm systems, like other electrical appliances, can be important features enjoyed by the well elderly in addition to those who are younger. This broader market can lower the cost per unit and can help avoid stigmatization of the elderly. Technologies, in other words, can be appropriate, desirable, and beneficial even though they do not fall into the classification of rehabilitation aids.

What is inescapable is that more and more people are living to old age, a time when the need for assistance is likely to increase. Furthermore, there is no conclusive evidence that future cohorts of elders will experience less illness or disability. Yet we know little about the choice of technical aids and there is no national standardized body to assist the consumer or their care-giver in this regard. Few technical aids are covered in federal or provincial programs, and those that are charge a percentage of the cost to the consumer.

Seniors – An Untapped Market

As seniors increase in numbers, businesses are beginning to view them as an attractive market for their products, and gerontologists are turning more attention to persuading the business sector that seniors constitute a growing, yet relatively untapped market. This is particularly so for the community-living elderly (this institutional sector represents a mature market where products are well-developed). Manufacturing, marketing and retail sectors are all potential beneficiaries of this emerging economic market. Research points to the growing numbers of seniors as a vast market, to the fact that their financial resources are greater than previously assumed, and to their receptivity to various products as greater than many realized.

Part of the interest in the seniors market stems from an increase in this segment of the population. In 1976 in Canada there were approximately two million individuals aged 65 and over and by the year 1990 there were three million. By the year 2031 there will be close to eight million. Those aged 75 and over are increasing particularly rapidly (there were 3/4 of a million in 1976, 1.25 million in 1990 and a projected four million in the year 2031).[10] This expanding market will reach its peak around 2020 when the baby-boom generation becomes elderly. It is also important to note that the majority of seniors live in the community, not in long-term institutional care. In 1986, 6.7 percent of seniors lived in long-term care institutions while 93.3 percent lived in the community. This is particularly relevant to this discussion of the market since we know the long-term institutional sector is a mature market. Those living in the community represent a still relatively undeveloped market. There are many products which could be developed for these consumers.

Not only is the number of elderly consumers increasing, but there are reasons to believe this age group has more money available for spending than has traditionally been thought. As noted by Caroline Tynan and Jennifer L. Drayton, seniors have a higher level of disposable income than their total income level may indicate.[11] They are more likely than younger adults to have accumulated savings and assets, and to be without long-term debt and dependants to support. In other words, fewer responsibilities and obligations than younger individuals can leave seniors with a higher percentage of their total income for discretionary spending. In addition, there are sources of "extra income" from various benefits, such as tax exemptions, social security payments, income from assets, local property tax reductions, discounts on food, transportation and drugs.[12]

TABLE 4

**Percentage Reporting Income from Selected Sources
by Age and Sex, 1988**

Source	Total Population*		Males	
		65-69	**70-74**	**75+**
Bank Interest	42%	71%	77%	81%
Bond Interest	15	26	28	33
Taxable Dividends	10	13	13	14
Annuities	2	11	18	13
Capital Gains	5	7	6	6
Source	**Total Population***		**Females**	
		65-69	**70-74**	**75+**
Bank Interest	40%	75%	78%	83%
Bond Interest	19	35	36	37
Taxable Dividends	7	14	16	18
Annuities	2	11	14	10
Capital Gains	3	5	6	6

Source: National Advisory Council on Aging, *The Economic Situation of Seniors,* Cat #H71-3/14-1991E.

* Total population includes all tax filers.

Furthermore, poverty is less widespread than was previously the case among this age group. The earlier image, which equated old age with poverty, is not necessarily true today. The percentage of seniors who are classed as having low income has been decreasing much faster than for the remainder of the population. In 1980, 11 percent of households with heads less than age 65 could be considered poor, whereas the comparable figure was 13 percent for households with a head age 65 and over. The figures for 1989 were 10 percent and 6 percent respectively. For unattached individuals, 30 percent of non-seniors lived in poverty in 1980, whereas 62 percent of seniors lived in poverty. In 1989 the figures were 28 percent and 38 percent, respectively.

Seniors are also much more likely to report income from bank interest, bond interest, and annuities and somewhat more likely to report income from taxable dividends than is true of the total population. As Table 5 shows, seniors have a greater wealth or net worth than the remainder of the population. This table also indicates that there is much less indebtedness when one is older than when one is younger. Finally, Table 5c shows that seniors are more likely to own a home, and are much more likely to own a home that is mortgage-free than is true of other individuals. That is, significant proportions of seniors have considerable disposable income, and frequently more than younger adults.

TABLE 5

Wealth and Indebtedness

A) Measure of Wealth for Selected Populations, 1984*

	Families**		Unattached Individuals**	
	All	Head 65+	All	65+
Wealth	$104,222	$131,005	$38,148	$52,185

Source: National Advisory Council on Aging, *The Economic Situation of Seniors*, Cat #H71-3/14-1991E.

B) Incidence of Selected Sources of Indebtedness by Age and Household Type, 1984

Debt Type	All	Head 65+	All	65+
Consumer	61%	29%	40%	14%
Other Personal	15	6	12	2
Mortgage	38	7	8	3
Total in Debt	73	34	49	17

Source: National Advisory Council on Aging, *The Economic Situation of Seniors*, Cat #H71-3/14-1991E.

C) Percent Owning Their Own Home, With or Without Mortgage, By Age and Household Type, 1984

Year	Families**		Unattached Individuals**	
	All	Head 65+	All	65+
Without Mortgage	34%	72%	19%	38%
With Mortgage	37	8	8	3
Total	71	80	27	41

Source: National Advisory Council on Aging, *The Economic Situation of Seniors*, Cat #H71-3/14-1991E.

* Measure of wealth is the combined net worth of the family or individual.
** Families are groups of individuals living in the same household and related. Unattached individuals are all those, 15 and over, who live alone or with other non-relations.

Buying Behaviour

We also know something about the buying behaviour of Canadian seniors. Seniors are just as likely to buy items such as refrigerators, freezers, air conditioners, smoke detectors, vacation homes, telephones, radios, and televisions as are other Canadians. However, there are some differences which occur with age. At the present time, elders are less likely to possess recent high technology products such as compact disc players and video recorders. They are also less likely to have recreational equipment products such as gas barbecues, tents, snowmobiles, motorcycles, bicycles and skis.[13] Whether it is the particular cohort of seniors today who are less receptive to new technology or whether this is an age-related phenomenon is not known. The literature which is available (most frequently from the United States) is fairly consistent in concluding that seniors have both the ability and desire to adapt to and to utilize new technology effectively.

Merry Lee Eilers studied a sample of seniors in a computer education program and concluded seniors actively adapt to technology and concomitant social change.[14] Troy Festervand and Margaret Wylde argue that, while seniors have to be given more time to take in new instructions, they can effectively use and enjoy new technological devices.[15] Dennis La Buda believes that future cohorts of seniors will be more open to technological change as it has been more a part of their early years.[16] Interestingly, Glynis Breakwell and Chris Fife-Schaw conclude that while many older adults felt unable and/or unwilling to master aspects of new technology, many nevertheless were using automatic cash dispensers, remote control TVs, and video recorders.[17] They did not express an interest in learning the principles underlying their functioning; rather, learning enough to operate the devices was sufficient.

The elderly are a heterogeneous group. They buy a variety of products. However, there is a scarcity of social science research in Canada on seniors as potential consumers. Most research has been completed in the United States. All the available literature suggests that older age groups are not a homogeneous market.[18] High technology products are more sought after in urban areas than in rural areas. In terms of recreation (see Table 6), fewer seniors participate in all categories than do the total population. Only when package travel tours and reading material are compared are the percentages comparable. Indeed, virtually all seniors like to read. The next highest percentage is reported for recreational equipment and services, followed by spectator entertainment and performances.

TABLE 6

Percentage Reporting Spending on Selected Recreation, 1986

	Couples, Head 65+	All*
Recreational Equipment and Services	66%	83%
Home Entertainment Equipment and Sales	45	76
Spectator Entertainment Performance	64	82
Recreational Facilities	39	64
Package Travel Tours	12	11
Reading Material	94	93
Education	9	44

Source: National Advisory Council on Aging, *The Economic Situation of Seniors*, Cat #H71-3/14-1991E.

* This category includes all families and unattached individuals. Families are groups of individuals living in the same household and related. Unattached individuals are all those, 15 and over, who live alone or with other non-relations.

Diversity among seniors extends to their reactions to advertising. Research by Brian Davis suggests that some are accepting and unquestioning of advertising whereas others are skeptical.[19] Some rely more on formal sources of information, such as advertising, whereas others rely on more informal sources, such as friends and neighbours. There is also some evidence to suggest that seniors' preference for newspapers is being replaced by a preference for television, particularly as more news-oriented programs are available in this medium. They prefer information content rather than entertainment. Heterogeneity, of course, means that advertising should target particular segments of the elderly population.

The available literature is also consistent in the message that, when businesses are trying to sell their products to seniors, they should be careful not to stigmatize seniors as different and less valued than others. They should convey the message that seniors are valued as shoppers.[20] We do not know whether seniors like to be separated out as different from other adults or prefer to be treated as similar. Previous assumptions that older people do not identify with their own age segment are now being questioned. It could be that if they were treated as different, but positively and with appropriate recognition of value, they would not mind being separated out.

Summary and Conclusions

A major interest in technology for seniors is its capability to enhance their independence. With age comes increased disability and, therefore, increased potential for the use of technology. Ironically, as one's need for technological assistance increases, the ability to use it can simultaneously decrease. Nevertheless, technological development offers the potential of independence when health fails. Despite increasing recognition of the need for technological devices as Canadian society ages, there still is no national standardized body for assessing the safety of products. Similarly, there is no centralized source of information for seniors, their families, and/or their care-givers to find out what products are available or how to purchase them.

With technological advances, many opportunities are open to the individual which were not available in the past. However, with them come ethical dilemmas about their use, dilemmas which may not have been foreseen in their development. The questions which are currently being asked and answered about the use of technology relate to life-saving scenarios. Society is developing the consensus that where the individual is cognitively intact, and does not wish to have life-sustaining technology, that is his or her choice.

Other questions tend not to be asked. These are questions which have to do with ethical dilemmas that arise with the use of technology. For example, when is the use of technology advisable? If a disabled senior is finding it very difficult to be personally mobile even with the use of a walker, and it is clear that an electric wheelchair would assist, is this necessarily the best thing? When one chooses to switch to the electric wheelchair, that individual will probably lose all personal mobility, even with a walker. As another example, consider the use of technology for health monitoring; it is frequently discussed as saving both the time and salaries of sending nurses out to the home. However, we do not know the effect of taking this social contact away from seniors. This type of monitoring should be implemented while ensuring social contact through other means. Should those requiring assistive devices have their choice of devices available or, if the state is paying, should they necessarily have only one model because of economic efficiency? And when do monitoring devices become an invasion of privacy?

Even though we frequently associate technological devices with disability, all of us use technology in our lives on a day-to-day basis. Seniors, however, represent a growing and as yet a relatively untapped market, one which includes both disabled and well persons. Although research is not abundant in this area, we know that seniors do use technology and have the ability when motivated to learn to use new technologies. Like all others, however, seniors represent a heterogeneous group; thus one needs to understand which seniors are interested in what types of technologies rather than simply classifying them all as old people. As the baby-boom generation ages, seniors will undoubtedly receive much more attention from all aspects of the business sector. As their value as a large market is recognized, no doubt much of the stigma still attached to old age will decrease. It will be interesting to see if at that time the stigma associated with the use of those assistive devices classed as rehabilitation aids will decrease. One can even speculate about a time when robotic limbs and motorized personal mobility devices will be a status symbol rather than the sign of a handicap. As young children today sometimes cry because they want a ride on the wheelchair or envy the use of a robotic arm, one day seniors with advanced technological devices may be envied. But while technology offers many promises (such as increasing the literacy rate, talking visual books, electronic libraries, etc.), it brings with it the responsibility to use these devices in a wise way.

The area of technology and aging is receiving increased research interest in Canada, but it is an area where much more research remains to be done. As Canada's population ages, we can expect greater recognition of this area and subsequent research attention devoted to it. As the research results grow, so too will the list of innovative and exciting questions and issues to be explored. We look forward to investigating the circumstances under which technology can enhance independence while at the same time enabling or facilitating social ties. We look forward to a time when we can advise disabled seniors when they should switch from their walkers to their electric wheelchairs, not to encourage dependence but to enhance their personal mobility. We look forward most of all to learning from seniors themselves which technologies will benefit them most.

NOTES

1. Metropolitan Toronto District Health Council, *Technology for the Elderly* (Toronto: Metropolitan Toronto District Health Council, 1988).
2. Paul A.L. Haber, "Technology, Environments, and the Process of Aging," *International Journal of Technology and Aging* 1 (1988), 5-8.
3. Metro. Toronto Dist. Health Council, 1988.

4. Statistics Canada, *Highlights from the Canadian Health and Disability Survey 1983-1984*, Catalogue 82-563E (Ottawa: Minister of Supply and Services, 1984).

5. George Abrahamsohn, "Technology and Aging" (North York: Information Services and Applied Technology Division, Ontario Ministry of Community and Social Services, 1991), presentation for a pre-conference workshop, Canadian Association on Gerontology meeting.

6. James F. Fries, "Aging, Natural Death, and the Compression of Morbidity," *New England Journal of Medicine* 303 (1980), 130-36. And Kyriakos S. Markides, "Trends in the Health of the Elderly in Western Societies" (Galveston, Texas: Department of Preventive Medicine and Community Health, University of Texas Medical Branch, 1990), paper presented at the annual meeting of the International Sociological Association, World Congress, Madrid, Spain.

7. William F. Forbes, Duveen Sturgeon, L.M. Hayward and N. Agwani, "Hearing Impairment in the Elderly — An Integrated Approach to the Appropriate Provision of Assistive Listening Devices" (unpublished).

8. Metro. Toronto Dist. Health Council, 1988, *op. cit.*

9. Ron Stone, "Comparison of Service Delivery Systems for Assistive Technologies: Canada, Sweden, USA" (Washington: School of Occupational and Physical Therapy, University of Puget Sound, 1991), paper presented at the annual meeting of the Gerontological Society of America, San Francisco, California.

10. Statistics Canada, *Population Projections for Canada, Provinces, and Territories*, Cat. #91-520 (Ottawa: Minister of Supply and Services, 1986).

11. A. Caroline Tynan and Jennifer L. Drayton, "The Neglect of the Older Consumer," *Journal of Consumer Studies and Home Economics* 12 (1988), 159-71.

12. Ellen Day, Brian Davis, Rhonda Dove and Warren French, "Reaching the Senior Citizen Market(s)," *Journal of Advertising Research* 27, 6 (1988), 23-30. Betsy D. Gelb, "Discovering the 65+ Consumer," *Business Horizons Review* May/June (1982a), 42-46. David Lees, "Golden Opportunities," *Canadian Business* May (1987).

13. Statistics Canada, *Household Facilities by Income and Other Characteristics*, Cat. #13-218 (Ottawa: Minister of Supply and Services, 1989).

14. Merry Lee Eilers, "Older Adults and Computer Education: 'Not to Have the World Close a Door,'" *International Journal of Aging and Technology* 2 (1989), 56-76.

15. Troy A. Festervand and Margaret A. Wylde, "The Marketing of Technology to Older Adults," *International Journal of Aging and Technology* 1 (1988), 156-62.

16. Dennis R. La Buda, "Education, Leisure and Older Persons: Implications for Smart House Design," *International Journal of Technology and Aging* 1 (1988), 31-48.

17. Glynis M. Breakwell and Chris Fife-Schaw, "Ageing and the Impact of New Technology," *Social Behaviour* 3 (1988), 119-30.

18. Day *et al., ibid.* Patricia Sorce, Philip R. Tyler and Lynetter M. Loomis, "Lifestyles of Older Americans," *The Journal of Consumer Marketing* 6, 3 (1989), 53-63. Jeffrey G. Towle and Claude R. Martin, "The Elderly Consumer: One Segment or Many?" in *Advances in Consumer Research,* ed. Beverlee Anderson (Assoc. for Consumer Research, 1976), 463-68.

19. Brian Davis, "An Empirical Investigation of Elderly Consumer Market Segments Based on Information Usage and Advertising Attitudes" (Georgia: University of Georgia, 1985), Ph.D. dissertation.

20. Hale N. Tongren, "Determinant Behaviour Characteristics of Older Consumers," *The Journal of Consumer Affairs* 22, 1 (1988), 136-57. Gelb, 1982a, *ibid.* Betsy D. Gelb, "Exploring the Grey Market Segment," *MUS Business Topics* Spring (1982b), 41-46.

Neena L. Chappell was founding director of the Centre on Aging at the University of Manitoba and is first director of the Centre on Aging at the University of Victoria, British Columbia. She has researched and published extensively in the areas of informal and formal support for seniors, factors affecting their independence, and social policy.

Population Aging in the Canadian Labour Force: Changes and Challenges

DAVID K. FOOT AND KEVIN J. GIBSON

Introduction

The challenges faced by Canadian labour markets over the 1960s, 1970s and 1980s have been phenomenal. Over this entire period, labour force growth in Canada has been unmatched in any other Western industrialized economy. Charles R. Bean, Richard Layard and Stephen Nickell summarize the labour force average growth rates for countries in the Organization for Economic Cooperation and Development (OECD) over the period 1961-84.[1] For the decade 1961-71, Canada's annual average growth rate of 2.8 percent was matched by only Australia, with New Zealand the only other country with labour force growth in excess of two percent. Labour force growth in Canada increased over the 1970s to annual rates in excess of three percent. This was totally unmatched, the closest countries being the United States and, to a lesser extent, Australia. Even though Canadian labour force growth slowed significantly over the 1980s, it still remained above other OECD countries.

This period of unmatched, sustained labour force growth in Canada can be attributed to two complementary forces: a substantial baby-boom generation that entered the labour force over the period, and considerable increases in labour force participation rates, especially by females. These historical factors are documented and discussed in the following section.

Not surprisingly, this sustained labour force growth placed upward pressures on unemployment rates in Canada over much of the period. Yet Canada did not experience the highest unemployment rate among OECD countries. For example, Canada's average unemployment rate of 9.4 percent over 1980-1983, which included a severe recession, was exceeded by Spain, Belgium, the United Kingdom, Denmark, the Netherlands and Ireland.[2] This reflects the fact that employment growth was significantly lower in these countries and highlights the substantial employment growth generated by the Canadian economy over this period, which prevented unemployment rates going higher.

Can these trends be expected to continue into the future, or does the recent experience of substantially lower labour force growth signal new trends for the Canadian economy? The analysis presented in this paper suggests the latter. By the 1980s the baby-boom generation in Canada reached their twenties and thirties and, hence, were all of labour force age. The age cohorts entering the labour force over the 1990s are much smaller, which can be expected to lead to lower labour force growth over this period. These projections for the 1990s are briefly reviewed in a subsequent section of the paper. As a consequence of slowing labour force growth, the demographic pressures on unemployment rates will be reversed, but new challenges in Canadian labour markets will arise as a result of the slowing labour force growth and the aging of the labour force. These challenges will centre around developing labour market inflexibilities and reduced promotional prospects as the baby-boom generation "clogs up" the labour force. The result may well be changing organizational structures, attitudes, and practices, as management and labour confront, or are confronted by, these developments. These issues are explored in the final section of the paper. The paper concludes with a summary of the main findings.

The 1970s and 1980s: An Overview

The 1980s could be described as a transitional decade for labour force growth in Canada — a transition from the rapid growth of the 1970s to the projected slower growth of the 1990s. Over the 1971-81 period, the Canadian labour force grew at an average annual rate of over three percent, two-thirds of which was attributable to source population (15 years and over) growth and the remaining one-third to increases in participation rates.

By contrast labour force growth over the subsequent decade (1981-91) averaged less than half that of the previous decade. This noticeable decline over the 1980s was shared equally between the two components. Source population growth, which had exceeded two percent per annum for three decades, slowed to an average annual 1.2 percent, due primarily to the much smaller cohorts following the baby-boom generation entering the Canadian labour force. At the same time, participation rate growth slowed from an average annual 1.1 percent over 1971-81 to 0.2 percent over 1981-91, reflecting in part the effects of the economic recessions experienced by the Canadian economy over the early 1980s and early 1990s.

TABLE 1

Components of Labour Force Growth
Canada, 1971-1991

	1971	Level[1] 1981	1991	Growth[2] (% p.a.) 71-81	81-91
Total:					
Source Population	14.872	18.368	20.746	2.1	1.2
Participation Rate (%)	58.1	64.8	66.3	1.1	0.2
Labour Force	8.639	11.899	13.757	3.2	1.5
Employment	8.104	11.001	12.340	3.1	1.2
Unemployment	0.535	0.898	1.417	5.3	4.7
Unemployment Rate (%)	6.2	7.5	10.3	1.9	3.2
Males:					
Source Population	7.329	8.994	10.117	2.1	1.2
Participation Rate (%)	77.3	78.1	74.8	0.1	-0.5
Labour Force	5.667	7.051	7.569	2.2	0.7
Employment	5.329	6.556	6.751	2.1	0.3
Unemployment	0.338	0.494	0.817	3.9	5.2
Unemployment Rate (%)	6.0	7.0	10.8	1.5	4.4
Females:					
Source Population	7.543	9.374	10.629	2.2	1.3
Participation Rate (%)	39.4	51.7	58.2	2.8	1.2
Labour Force	2.972	4.851	6.188	5.0	2.5
Employment	2.775	4.447	5.589	4.8	2.3
Unemployment	0.197	0.404	0.599	7.4	4.0
Unemployment Rate (%)	6.6	8.3	9.7	2.3	1.6

Notes:　[1]All levels in millions of persons unless otherwise indicated.
　　　　[2]Average annual rate of growth.
Source:　Statistics Canada, Historical Labour Force Statistics, 1991.

The recessions also contributed to a significant decline in employment growth over the 1980s compared to the 1970s. This resulted in increased unemployment rates which reached double-digit levels. By 1991 there were over 1.4 million persons unemployed, nearly 60 percent more than a decade earlier and 165 percent more than two decades earlier.

It is interesting to note that, given decreasing labour force growth, Canada could have sustained a decline in employment growth over the early 1980s without experiencing an increase in unemployment rates. This hypothetical scenario would have resulted from a decline in employment growth from the average annual 3.1 percent during the 1970s to around 1.5 percent over the 1980s, which would have absorbed sufficient new labour force entrants over the period to keep unemployment rates unchanged. As it was, however, employment growth declined even further to an average 1.1 percent, thus precipitating the increase in unemployment rates. In this sense, therefore, the economic recessions, and not demographic developments, contributed to the rise in unemployment rates in Canada over the 1980s compared to the 1970s.

These demographic developments were very similar for both males and females over the period. Yet, comparable data for males and females show that labour force growth for females far exceeded that of males throughout the period. The reason for this differing performance is apparent from these data. Whereas both groups experienced very similar source population growth over the period, they developed dramatically different participation rate behaviour, with overall rates for males actually declining over the period while rates for females continued to rise, although at a decreasing rate. This resulted in labour force growth for females averaging 2.5 percent over the 1980s (down from 5.0 percent over the 1970s) far exceeding the 0.7 percent for males (down from 2.2 percent over the 1970s). As a consequence, the proportion of females in the Canadian labour force increased from 34.4 percent in 1971 to 45 percent in 1991, with a corresponding decline in the male share.

Perhaps surprisingly, however, this did not result in increased unemployment rates for females. In fact, the data show that the ratio of female unemployment rates to male unemployment rates has reversed over the 1980s. By 1991 the unemployment rate for females was below the unemployment rate for males, thus reversing the position that had been prevalent at the beginning of the decade. Moreover, this trend took place in spite of increasing pressures for pay equity for females, which would tend to raise their relative wage. Hence, from an economic viewpoint, the relative demand for their services was lowered.

Many reasons can be posited for this labour market development. Two are considered below, but others are certainly possible. First, an increasing proportion of Canadian employment has been part-time employment. Again, labour force survey data show that of the 0.537 million new part-time jobs created over the 1980s, 65 percent were filled by females; that is, females captured an increasing share of the more rapidly growing employment source (3.1 percent compared to 0.8 percent annual growth for full-time employment). While it might be argued that part-time employment is not equivalent to full-time employment, this does nonetheless explain how the rapid explosion of females in the Canadian labour force over the 1980s did not lead to a relative increase in the female unemployment rate.

Second, the Canadian labour force is gradually becoming better educated. According to labour force survey data, 32.5 percent of the labour force had at least some post-secondary education in 1975, while 33.4 percent of the employed had the same educational attainment, thus lending support to the hypothesis that more education improves the chances of employment. On average females were more highly educated, with 33.6 percent of the labour force and 34.5 percent of those employed having some post-secondary education. The corresponding figures for males were 31.9 and 32.7 percent, respectively. Over the remainder of the 1970s these percentages fell as the remainder of the baby-boom generation entered the labour force. Then, during the 1980s the trend was reversed. Consequently, over the decade, employment has gradually moved towards more highly educated positions and females have been better able to capture these positions. Of the 0.823 million new "higher education" jobs created over the 1980s, almost 61 percent were filled by females; that is, females were better positioned to capitalize on the increasing educational requirements of new jobs. This also helps to explain why female unemployment rates decreased relative to male rates over the decade.

TABLE 2

**Source Population and Unemployment Rates
by Age, 1971-1991**

		Level[1]		Growth[2] (% p.a.)	
	1971	1981	1991	71-81	81-91
I. Source Population					
15-24	3.927	4.537	3.725	1.4	-1.9
25-54	7.572	9.520	11.790	2.3	2.2
55+	3.374	4.311	5.231	2.5	1.9
II. Unemployment Rate (%)					
15-24	11.1	13.2	16.2	1.7	2.1
25-54	4.5	5.8	9.2	2.6	4.7
55+	4.5	4.0	7.6	-1.2	6.6

Notes: [1]All levels in millions of persons unless otherwise indicated.
              [2]Average annual rate of growth.
Source: Statistics Canada, Historical Labour Force Statistics, 1991.

The aggregate trends also reflect considerable changes in the age composition of the Canadian labour force over the period. Table 2 summarizes the age composition of the labour force source population. The aggregate trends clearly reflect the effects of the baby-boom generation on the Canadian labour force. In Canada the baby-boom generation comprises the twenty-year generation with birth years between 1947 and 1966, with a peak at birth year 1961. By 1971 those in the first ten years of the boomers became of labour force age. Over the 1970s the second ten-year cohort of boomers became of labour force age. This explains the rapid growth in source population over these decades. Then, over the 1980s, the subsequent smaller cohorts of the "baby-bust" generation entered the Canadian labour force. As well, the youth age-group (aged 15 to 24 years) began to shrink, so much so that by 1991 there were 200,000 fewer youths in the source population than 20 years earlier.

This movement of the baby-boom generation through the labour force age-groups is reflected in the median age of the source population, which declined during the 1970s and then started to rise in the 1980s. By 1991 the median age of the source population had reached almost 40 years. As a postscript to these demographic developments, it is interesting to note the above-average growth in the senior (55 years and over) population in the 1970s, which is also often taken as an indicator of an aging population. Over the 1980s this growth slowed since the small group born in the depression years of the 1930s entered this age group. But, this does not mean that aging did not continue. However, since very few of these persons are actually in the Canadian labour force, this indicator is of limited use in the current context.

These demographic developments were reflected in unemployment rates over the decade. The 1970s witnessed a noticeable increase in youth unemployment rates, from 11.1 percent in 1971 to a peak of 19.8 percent in 1983. This latter figure reflected the effects of the economic recession in Canada at the time. Aggregate unemployment rates jumped to double-digit levels and peaked at 11.8 percent in 1983. David K. Foot and Jeanne C. Li have argued that youth unemployment rates relative to the aggregate unemployment rate started to decline before the onslaught of the economic recession and that, in fact, the youth fared relatively well over the recession.[3] A comparison of the youth unemployment rates to the unemployment rates for 25 to 54 year olds shows the ratio falling from 2.47 in 1971 to 1.75 by 1991. In essence, some of the unemployment is moving with the baby-boom generation into the older worker age-groups.

The more rapid growth in the unemployment rates among older workers became an issue of concern to policy makers in Canada over the 1980s. This occurred in large part because of the entry of the baby-boom generation into these age groups over the 1980s, which was accompanied by significant organizational restructuring, especially toward the end of the decade. It is unlikely that these trends will be reversed over the 1990s. The Canadian labour force will continue to age over the 1990s and concern for the employment prospects of older workers is likely to remain an important policy issue (see below).

In summary, by 1991 the Canadian labour force totalled 13.757 million persons of which 7.569 million (or 55 percent) were male and 6.188 million (or 45 percent) were female. A review of labour market developments in Canada over the 1970s and 1980s shows that some new trends have been established in the 1980s. In particular:

• The baby-boom generation has been completely absorbed into the Canadian labour force.

• Source population growth is slowing noticeably for both males and females.

• The median age of the Canadian labour force is now increasing.

- Female participation rates have continued to increase, while male participation rates have decreased over the 1980s.
- There is an increasing share of females in the labour force.
- Unemployment rates have reflected these demographic developments, although they have been partially offset for some groups, such as youths and females, by the changing structure of employment.
- Unemployment amongst older workers emerged as a major policy issue of the 1980s.

The 1980s can be viewed as a transitional decade between the rapid labour force growth of the 1980s and the projected slower growth of the 1990s. The next section reviews information available for the 1990s.

The 1990s: An Overview

The historical trends provide the foundation for an assessment of likely future labour market developments in Canada. Of particular interest is whether the past trends can provide a guide to the future and to what extent modifications are likely. These issues are briefly reviewed in this section, while the following section explores some of the implications of these empirical findings.

A number of authors projected the likely decline in labour force growth over the 1980s and beyond.[4] This trend now seems to be well established, with the slow growth over the 1980s clearly documented. Since labour force growth is the sum of source population and participation rate growth, realization of further declines in source population growth will be automatically translated into slower labour force growth.

Population projections by Statistics Canada show source population (15 years and over) maintaining an annual growth of 1.2 percent over the 1991-2001 period, with immigration levels averaging 200,000 per annum or declining to 1 percent, with immigration levels averaging 140,000 per annum.[5] Over the 1980s annual immigration levels averaged almost 133,000 per annum, suggesting that perhaps the lower projection might be more accurate. However, immigration increased over the decade, averaging 102,200 over the first half of the decade and 163,500 over the second half. Moreover, the federal government announced intentions to raise immigration levels towards 250,000 by the mid-1990s. These figures suggest that the higher projection might be more likely. But, whatever the actual immigration intake, it seems clear from these projections that there will not be a return to the labour force growth of the 1970s and that there may well be a further decline in the slower labour force growth experienced over the 1980s.

This outcome is even more likely because, increasingly, in an aging population, labour force source population growth rates are influenced by the continued above-average growth of the older (65 years and over) population who are largely unavailable to the labour force. Consequently, examination of growth projections for the 15 to 64 years age group indicates even slower labour force growth and suggests further declines of up to 0.2 percent per annum; that is, the reduced source population growth of the 1980s could be further reduced over the 1990s. Without any other labour market developments this would reduce annual labour force growth to around one percent or less over the 1990s, a dramatic reduction from the three percent experienced over the 1960s and 1970s, and a slight reduction over the 1.4 percent experienced over the 1980s.

These developments can be attributed to the decline in fertility rates over the 1960s and 1970s, resulting in a baby-bust generation that constitutes the domestic labour market entrants over the 1990s. Only towards the end of the 1990s will the children of the baby-boom generation (the baby-boom echo generation) who were born over the 1980s provide a modest respite to this downward trend. It is apparent that even noticeable changes in fertility rates will not affect these projections over the 1990s, since these labour market entrants are already born.

Similarly, as indicated above, the projections can be shown to be relatively insensitive to large changes in immigration levels. For example, the above calculations indicate that a sustained increase in immigration levels by 60,000 persons a year increases average source population growth by 0.2 percent per annum over the 1990s. Changes in the composition of immigration (e.g. towards more labour market entrants) would of course affect these calculations, but not substantially. Over the 1980s approximately 48.1 percent of the immigrants were expected to enter the labour force, up from 45.6 percent a decade earlier. Even a return to the average 51.4 percent of the 1960s would supplement the labour force by no more than about 8,000 additional labour market entrants, which is negligible growth in a labour force of around 14 million persons. At the margin, however, this could be a useful source of future labour market flexibility.

The inevitable aging of the baby-boom generation will lead to further aging of the Canadian labour force. Historically, the median age of the Canadian population reached its lowest point of 25.5 years in 1966. This was reflected approximately 12 years later in a median of 36.5 years in the source population, and a median of 33.6 in 1980 in the Canadian labour force. Thereafter, the Canadian labour force has been gradually aging.

This aging process can be expected to continue. Statistics Canada projections suggest that the source population will age on average approximately 3.2 years (or eight percent) over the final decade of the twentieth century.[6] This is a significant increase. To calculate the impact on the labour force it is necessary to take account of the participation rate structure. These calculations, which largely exclude the influence of the burgeoning senior population, suggest that the median age of the labour force will increase from 36.2 years to 38.8 years over the same period. This increase of 2.6 years is up from 2.5 years over the previous decade and suggests not only a continuation but also an increase in the pace of aging of the Canadian labour force over the 1990s.

This aging has been a new development over the 1980s and the accelerated pace of labour force aging is likely to have important implications in the 1990s and beyond. The following section explores some of these implications.

The Future: Implications

The Canadian labour force has undergone some dramatic changes over the 1970s and 1980s. The nature of the changes and the associated labour market challenges are now gradually emerging. Slowing source population growth and increasing average age are the dominant and most certain features of Canada's future labour force. These have far-reaching implications with respect to the successful utilization of this essential national resource.

In 1981 there were over three million youth in the Canadian labour market (25.8 percent of the labour force). Over the 1960s, and especially the 1970s, the challenges for the labour market primarily centred on job creation and on the successful absorption of the massive baby-boom generation into the Canadian labour force without "undue" pressures on unemployment rates. This was largely accomplished by the mid-1980s.

By 1991 the number of youth (15 to 24 years) had fallen by 575,000 persons and their share of the labour force had dropped to 18.2 percent. This trend will continue into the 1990s. By the mid-1990s, if participation rates do not change, the total could well drop another 16,500 persons. Thereafter, the baby-boom echo generation enters the Canadian labour force and, supplemented by immigration, youth numbers gradually increase over the second half of the 1990s. However, at unchanged participation rates, by 2001 the number will barely reach the 1990 level and they will represent 17 percent of the Canadian labour force. This means that organizations will be faced with relatively fewer younger people from which to recruit for their entry-level positions.

There are a number of labour market implications resulting from the "lack of new blood" in organizations. Traditionally, entry-level positions in an organization are filled by new, or at least young, labour market participants. These persons are presumed to be the most flexible with respect to location and occupation. They possess up-to-date labour market skills and they do not have a work history tying them to any particular organization or occupation. More-over, they are not already part of an organization's bureaucracy and culture and, hence, represent resources that can be deployed in the most efficient manner without disruptive costs to both employer and employee. At the margin they are by far the most adaptable resource available to an organization and their deployment facilitates growth in an ever-changing marketplace. But without this flexibility, what are the alternative options available to organizations in the 1990s?

The first baby boomers, born in 1947, reached age 45 in 1992. Over the 1990s, there will be a dramatic increase in the numbers of workers in the "second half" of their working lives. These individuals are likely to experience reduced promotional opportunities. Nathan Keyfitz has demonstrated that reduced rates of population growth can negatively affect the prospects for advancement of individual members of the population.[7] Frank T. Denton and Byron G. Spencer extended the Keyfitz framework to include labour force participation rates.[8] Drawing on Canadian experience and using computer simulation experiments, they confirmed that promotion prospects are positively related to the rate of population growth and to the age of retirement, and negatively related to population aging and the age of labour force entrance. They showed that the estimated age that divided the labour force of those aged 20 to 64 years into equal parts increased by 1.7 years between 1951 and 1966, and then fell by 3.6 years over the subsequent decade. With respect to the future, they conclude that the pattern that emerges is of an increase from 1981-2011 and a small decline thereafter. The effect is especially pronounced in the 1991-2001 decade when the relevant age increases by 3.2 years, as a result of the baby-boom generation reaching middle age. Moreover, they show that their conclusions are insensitive to alternative population projections, including variations in immigration levels. Therefore, to the extent that age matters in promotion prospects, the baby boom suffers some disadvantage as a result of its size.

To the extent that promotion prospects are considerably weakened by population aging, there may be increased discontent in the Canadian labour force in the years ahead. This discontent may make the effective utilization of existing resources more difficult; it could facilitate such redeployment, as employees move in an attempt to seek new challenges. Organizations will have to adapt and respond to this new labour market environment.

Building on the work of Michael J. Driver, David K. Foot and Rosemary A. Venne provide a useful framework in which to consider appropriate individual and organizational responses to these changing labour market conditions.[9] By drawing on both personnel and organization behaviour literature, they establish a link between employee career paths and organizational structures and cultures.

For the employee four different career concepts are identified. Each concept offers a widely held and subjectively valid view of the meaning of a career. The steady-state career concept defines a career as a vocation or calling and, hence, as a lifelong occupation. The linear career concept is, perhaps, the most familiar. Here, success requires continued vertical movement. The spiral career concept mixes lateral with vertical moves, and is characterized by major occupational changes over a working lifetime. Finally, the transitory career concept represents a pattern of inconsistency, where occupational changes are frequent and there is no attempt to seek vertical moves.

By drawing on organization behaviour literature, one can link each career concept to specific organizational structures, reward systems or cultures. Steady-state career organizations are flat with numerous specialized departments (such as universities). There is little mobility and rewards focus on security items such as tenure and benefits. Economic rewards parallel longevity and professional competence, not just managerial level. Training must be encouraged as obsolescence is very threatening (hence, the sabbatical leave). The linear career organization is a tall pyramid with many pay levels providing the opportunity for upward mobility. The key reward is promotion, although recognition and power are associated rewards. The spiral career organization has been more evident outside North America. Vertical hierarchy is kept to a minimum and movement is mainly lateral as projects change. Rewards are based on breadth of competence, rather than on current output, and education in new areas of interest or new types of assignment is encouraged. Re-education and retraining are essential in this type of organization. Transitory career organizations are ephemeral. Employees avoid fixed roles; temporary teams are used as the major organizational structure. Rewards emphasize variety and flexibility, with tolerance for unusual work habits and the opportunity for time off between assignments.

In North America most employees, managers and organizations define careers as a linear progression in a tall pyramid structure. Driver's basic premise is that this concept will experience great difficulty in the years ahead as the baby-boom generation saturates middle-management positions.[10] Moreover, this trend may be intensified by slower economic growth, which retards new openings, and by the movement towards non-mandatory retirement, which can block the routes to upper management. Driver views North American society as "headed toward a vast encampment of plateaued, frustrated linears who refuse to change."[11] His solution is a change in career concepts, with attendant changes in organizational structures and cultures.

Foot and Venne take the argument further.[12] They suggest that the tall pyramidal organizational structure is dependent on a pyramidal age structure of the labour force. Up to the 1980s the Canadian labour force displayed a pyramidal age structure, thus supporting tall pyramidal organizational structures and the associated linear career concept. But over the 1980s, as the baby-boom generation aged and as new entrants were drawn from the smaller cohorts of the baby-bust generation, the labour force "pyramid" began to narrow at the base and widen at the girth. As a result, over the 1980s the tall pyramidal organizational structure came under increasing pressure and flattening corporate structures came into vogue. This implicitly fostered an increase in the importance of the spiral career path and a decrease in importance of the linear career path, although there appears to have been little recognition by both employers and employees that this occurred.

In order to make this transition successfully, employers will need to adopt models of adult career development, which assume that transitions in work life may occur a number of times throughout a career.[13] This is the characteristic of a spiral career path. Re-education and retraining become a lifelong process and an essential part of the culture and rewards of the flattened organization.

A number of changes must occur before models of adult career development become accepted. First, the Economic Council of Canada notes that, in general, investment by Canadian industry in the development of human resources is inadequate.[14] Currently, private firms spend approximately $1.4 billion on training in Canada. On a per-employee basis, this represents less than half of what the private sector spends in the United States. West German employers spend four times as much — about 1.2 percent of GNP compared to 0.3 percent in Canada.[15] Also, nearly 60 percent of Canadian workers received less than one week's training in the previous two years, and more than half of all unskilled workers — who presumably need training the most — received none at all.[16]

The spiral career emphasizes lateral mobility and, hence, the need for general skills that are transportable across occupations. Employers are especially unlikely to offer general skills training to their employees. The hierarchical nature of organizations encourages specific rather than general skill training because specific skills increase an individual's productivity within a particular job, while general skills increase an individual's productivity across jobs. The problem with a general program of skills training is that it also increases a worker's mobility across firms. Yet, the skills demanded in the modern workplace are generic and portable. The ability to read blueprints, to use computers, to analyze and solve problems, or to work effectively within productive teams are far more easily transferred to other workplaces than knowing how to operate a particular drill press in a particular factory. The Ontario Premier's Council Survey found that a major disincentive for employers to increase their training effort is a fear that the skilled workers they train will be "poached" by other firms.[17] The poaching issue is part of the larger "free rider" problem, whereby those firms unwilling to invest in training take advantage of others who do.

Second, employers will need to rethink their attitudes toward the provision of training to older workers (especially general skills training). Employers are reluctant to train older workers, often noting that "training costs are high," that "younger workers are easier to train," that "younger workers are more comfortable with new technology," and that "younger workers provide a greater return on training investment because of longer tenure with the organization."[18] The arguments for not training older workers becomes important if it is perceived that most older individuals are not capable learners and that, even if they are successfully trained, their expected tenure with the organization is too limited to realize an acceptable return on the training investment. Previous research, however, has consistently shown that the average decline in psychological competence is typically of small magnitude until the seventies. In addition, the proportion of individuals who maintain their level of functioning on specific abilities is quite high. K. Warner Schaie for example, provides evidence that, depending upon the age group, from 60 to 85 percent of older individuals remain stable or improve on specific abilities.[19] The incidence of significant decrement was quite limited until age 60, and affected less than one-third of the participants until age 74. Even by age 81 only between 30 and 40 percent of the participants were affected.

Consistent with the evidence on psychological competence, effective training programs provide substantial benefits for the older adult.[20] Further, while older adults searching for employment may have a shorter working life, their expected tenure with the company training them is often as long as that of younger job hunters.[21] In addition, the relevant comparison is not years of remaining employment but years expected with the training firm in relation to the expected life of the training being acquired. Steven H. Sandell and Stephen E. Baldwin suggest that to the extent that turnover rates are higher for younger workers, it is possible that firms can expect to receive more years of upgraded service from older employees than from younger employees.[22]

Third, organizations can expect to feel increased pressure from government and society to assume a greater role in the retraining and reintegration of older unemployed and marginally skilled workers.[23] The economic and social costs of unemployment are extremely high. In 1991 over $17.5 billion were paid out in unemployment insurance (UI) benefits. These payments, however, reflect only a fraction of the total costs of unemployment. Additional costs include the waste of economic resources, monies paid out to older workers who have exhausted UI benefits and/or are receiving financial support from other forms of assistance (e.g., Program for Older Worker Adjustment), and the hardship and strain that are placed on individuals and their families.

A striking aspect of unemployment is the particular case of the long-term unemployed. The hardest hit by long-term unemployment are older workers over 45 years. These workers experienced the longest spells of unemployment during the 1981-82 recession, and during the subsequent recovery their rate of long-term unemployment continued to rise. In 1976 the average duration of unemployment for workers aged 45 and over was 18.5 weeks; by 1989 the average duration of unemployment had risen to 25.8 weeks.[24]

One factor that has led to increasingly long periods of unemployment for older workers is structural change in the economy. By 1988, 71 percent of Canadians were employed in the service sector and nearly 90 percent of the job growth in Canada since 1967 has taken place in this service sector.[25] Manufacturing industries, by contrast, accounted for one-third of the increase in unemployment in Canada between 1979 and 1984 and nearly every indicator suggests that these industries will continue to decline. The importance of industry growth and decline for occupational-age profiles is that contracting segments of occupations tend to have an older age structure, while expanding segments have a younger age distribution.[26] Contracting industries reduce personnel through layoff (which usually proceeds in reverse order of seniority) and by not replacing voluntary retirees. In each case the effect is to create an older work force. Expanding industries, in comparison, hire disproportionately from among new entrants to the labour market.

Older workers are disproportionately employed in the goods sector and these industries are declining. Older displaced workers are therefore more likely than younger workers to need to shift firms or industries in order to find new employment. Miles Corak argues that an unemployed individual will be able to find work more quickly with a firm in the same industrial sector than in a different sector.[27] The outcome of this is that an older worker is just as likely as a younger worker to be recalled by his or her former employer. Since the firm has already made its training investment in the worker, there is no reason to treat older workers any differently than younger workers. An older worker who must change firms or industries, however, faces a longer unemployment duration than a younger worker.

The economic recessions of the early 1980s and 1990s forced many organizations in Canada to streamline their operations through downsizing. If this was accomplished by eliminating levels in the organization, then it could be viewed as consistent with a flattening organizational structure. However, if it was achieved by eliminating employees within the existing hierarchical structure, it is not consistent with organizational flattening. But whatever the method, this response is unlikely to be appropriate when assessed against the future trends of the Canadian labour market.

The chief vehicle for achieving downsizing was to adopt a program of early retirement.[28] Given the projected labour market developments, employers will need to rethink carefully this policy toward early retirement. Early retirement may provide temporary relief in recessionary climates, but may prove disastrous in a climate of economic growth and labour force shortages, especially at entry levels. Under these conditions it might well be necessary to retain and perhaps attract older workers.

In order to retain these workers, employers will need to develop and implement innovative programs and remunerative packages that provide the appropriate incentives for continued participation. Research in industrial gerontology has pointed to six different job arrangements that can be used to accommodate effectively the work needs and preferences of middle-aged and older workers.[29] These arrangements fall within two broad categories: part-time work schedules, and job modifications for full-time older employees. Part-time work schedules include job sharing, phased retirement, and reemployment of retirees. Job modifications for full-time older employees include job redesign, job transfer and job retraining. The most frequently cited advantage of flexible work schedules is the ability of management to attract skilled older workers to their organizations and to retain productive retirement-age workers.[30] This could also ameliorate the long unemployment durations for older workers.

There may also be a need to challenge the attitudes of older workers. There is evidence that, over the past two decades, as retirement and the role of the retiree have become increasingly acceptable, if not valued, in our society, the work ethic has weakened and leisure values have begun to take precedence.[31] In addition, older workers who are in a financial position to retire early are often those workers who are the most valuable to the organization, such as those in the managerial and skilled trades occupations.

Governments can employ a number of mechanisms to improve the functioning of the future Canadian labour market (and lower the dependency ratio). These include increasing labour force participation among older workers, reducing discrimination in the hiring and paying of older workers, increasing incentives for remaining in the labour force, eliminating mandatory retirement, and redesigning pension benefits.[32] It will be necessary for governments to seek the assistance of the private sector in order to accomplish the goal of re-integrating the older worker into the labour force. It is critically important, therefore, to determine the degree to which both management and labour will cooperate in the achievement of these goals. With the inevitable aging of the Canadian labour force it is essential that these issues receive increased priority on the policy agenda of the 1990s, if Canada as a country is, efficiently and humanely, to utilize its biggest resource — namely, its labour force.

NOTES

1. Bean, C.R., Layard, P.R.G., and Nickel, S.J., "The rise in unemployment: A multicountry study," *Economics* 53, 210 (1986), 15-22.

2. *Ibid.*

3. Foot, D.K. and Li, J.C., "Youth unemployment in Canada: A misplaced priority?" *Canadian Public Policy* 12, 3 (1986), 499-506.

4. Denton, F.T., Feaver, C.H., and Spencer, B.G., *The Future Population and Labour Force of Canada: Projections to the Year 2051* (Ottawa: Economic Council of Canada, 1980). Foot, D.K., *Canada's Population Outlook: Demographic Futures and Economic Challenges* (Toronto: J. Lorimer & Co, 1982); and Foot, D.K. "The impacts of population growth and aging on the future Canadian labour force," in *Canadian Labour Markets in the 1980s* (Kingston: Queen's University, Industrial Relations Centre, 1983), 50-64.

5. Statistics Canada, *Population Projections for Canada, Provinces and Territories* (Ottawa: Statistics Canada, 1990).

6. *Ibid.*

7. Keyfitz, N., "Individual mobility in a stationary population," *Population Studies* 27, 2 (1973), 335-52.

8. Denton, F.T. and Spencer, B.G., *Age Structure and Rate of Promotion in the Canadian Working Population* (Hamilton: McMaster University, Faculty of Social Sciences, 1987).

9. Foot, D.K. and Venne, R.A., "Population, pyramids and promotional prospects," *Canadian Public Policy* 16, 4 (1990), 387-98. Driver, M.J., "Demographic and societal factors affecting the linear career crisis," *Canadian Journal of Administrative Studies* 2, 2 (1985), 245-63.

10. *Ibid.*

11. *Ibid.*, 260.

12. Foot and Venne, "Population, pyramids and promotional prospects."

13. Sterns, H.L. and Patchett, M., "Technology and the aging adult: Career development and Training," in P.K. Robinson, J.E. Livingston, and J.E. Birren (Eds.), *Aging and Technological Advances* (New York: Plenum Press, 1984), 261-67.

14. Economic Council of Canada, *Good Jobs, Bad Jobs: Employment in the Service Economy* (Ottawa, 1990).

15. *Ibid.*

16. Ontario Premier's Council Report, *People and Skills in the New Global Economy* (Toronto: Queen's Printer of Ontario, 1990).

17. *Ibid.*

18. Gibson, K.J., Zerbe, W.J. and Franken, R.E., "The influence of rater and ratee age on judgments of work-related attributes," *Journal of Social Psychology*, in press; and Gibson, K.J., Zerbe, W.J. and Franken, R.E., "Employers perceptions of the reemployment barriers

faced by older workers: Assessing the accuracy of employers beliefs," *Industrial Relations* in press.

19. Schaie, K.W., "Variability in cognitive function in the elderly: Implications for societal participation," in A. Woodhead, M. Bender, and R. Leonard (Eds.), *Phenotypic Variation in Populations: Relevance to Risk Management* (New York: Plenum, 1988).

20. Willis, S.L. and Schaie, W., "Training the elderly on the ability factors of spatial orientation and inductive reasoning," *Psychology and Aging* 1 (1986), 239-47. Bornstein, J.M., "Retraining the older worker: Michigan's experience with Senior Employment Services," *Journal of Career Development* 13 (1986), 14-22.

21. Bluedorn, A.C., "A unified model of turnover from organizations," *Human Relations* 35 (1982), 135-53. Sandell, S.H. and Baldwin, S.E., "Older workers and employment shifts: Policy responses to displacement," in I. Bluestone, R.J.V. Montgomery, and J.D. Owen (Eds.), *The Aging of the American Work Force: Problems, Programs, Policies* (Michigan: Wayne State University Press, 1990).

22. Sandell *et. al., ibid.*

23. Canadian Labour Market and Productivity Centre, *Report of the CLMPC Task Forces on the Labour Force Development Strategy* (Ottawa: CLMPC, 1990).

24. Gera, S. and McMullen, K., "Unemployment in Canada: Issues, findings, and implications," in S. Gera (Ed.), *Canadian Unemployment: Lessons from the 80s and Challenges for the 90s* (Ottawa: Economic Council of Canada, 1991).

25. Canada Employment and Immigration Advisory Council, *Older Workers: An imminent crisis in the labour market* (Ottawa: Minister of Supply and Services, 1985). And Economic Council of Canada, 1990.

26. Chen, M.Y.T., *Are Older Workers Marginal Workers?* Paper presented to the Annual Meetings of the Canadian Sociology and Anthropology Association, Montreal, 1985. And Kaufman, D.L. and Spilerman, S., "The Age Structures of Occupations and Jobs," *American Journal of Sociology* 87 (1982), 827-51.

27. Corak, M., *Eligibiligy rules in the Canadian Job Strategy: Shifting the burden or targeting the assistance? Working Paper No. 8* (Ottawa: Economic Council of Canada, 1990).

28. Dennis, H., Ed., *Fourteen Steps in Managing an Aging Work Force* (Toronto: Lexington Books, 1988).

29. Paul, C.E., "A human resources management perspective on work alternatives for older Americans," in S. Sandell (Ed.), *The Problem Isn't Age: Work and Older Americans* (New York: Praeger, 1987).

30. I*bid.*

31. McDonald, P.L. and Wanner, R.A., *Retirement in Canada* (Toronto: Buttersworth, 1987).

32. I*bid.*

David K. Foot, Professor of Economics at the University of Toronto, received his Ph.D. in economics from Harvard University and specializes in the economic and policy implications of population aging. Kevin J. Gibson has a Ph.D. in industrial psychology from the University of Calgary and is currently a Post-Doctoral Fellow with CARNET: Canadian Aging Research Network at the University of Toronto.

The Youth Freeze and the Retirement Bulge: Older Workers and the Impending Labour Shortage

LYNN MCDONALD AND MERVIN Y.T.CHEN

I. Introduction

In the present climate of concern about Canada's global competitiveness, the retirement of the older worker has come under closer national scrutiny. Amidst widespread downsizing, significant layoffs and escalating unemployment, the emphasis has been on removing the older worker from the labour force through early retirement schemes and through upholding the principle of mandatory retirement.[1] However, long-term demographic trends in Canada, namely slowing source population growth and the increasing average age of workers, are likely to initiate a shift in focus away from early retirement. As Canada's workforce continues to grow more slowly and as the workforce itself ages, the contribution of older workers to the Canadian economy is likely to become more critical.[2] Instead of retiring early, older workers may be called upon to remain in the labour force, or attempts may be made to entice the early retired to return to the labour force.

The past two decades offer a striking picture of changes in the growth of the Canadian labour force. During the 1970s, the labour force increased by 3.2 percent annually; however, during the 1980s, labour force growth declined to 1.9 percent annually and is expected to continue to drop to below one percent in the 1990s.[3] This considerable decline can be attributed to two factors, the slowing down of source population growth (aged 15 years and over) and a falling-off of the growth of the participation rate in the labour force.

Source population growth, which was above two percent through the 1970s, slowed to 1.4 percent in the 1980s due, primarily, to the baby-bust generation that followed in the wake of the baby-boom generation (Table 1).[4] This decline contributed to the condition of fewer entry-level workers throughout the economy. In 1971, the 15 to 24 age group made up 26 percent of the labour force, but in the year 2,000 this age group is expected to make up 17 percent of the labour force.[5]

TABLE 1

Labour Force Source Population by Age, Canada, 1975-1990

Age Groups	Population (millions)				Average Growth (% p.a.)		
	1975	1980	1985	1990	1975-80	1980-85	1985-90
BOTH SEXES							
15-24	4.297	4.554	4.244	3.749	1.2	−1.4	−2.3
25-34	3.428	4.027	4.410	4.645	3.3	1.8	1.1
35-44	2.516	2.819	3.488	4.180	2.3	4.4	4.0
45-54	2.420	2.454	2.498	2.790	0.3	0.4	2.3
55-64	1.854	2.085	2.294	2.327	2.4	1.9	0.3
65+	1.808	2.115	2.437	2.811	3.2	2.9	3.1
Total	16.323	18.053	19.372	20.430	2.0	1.4	1.1

Source: Statistics Canada, *The Labour Force,* various issues and calculations by the authors.

At the same time, there has been a slowing down in the growth of the participation rate in the labour force. From 1969 to 1979 the average annual rate of 0.9 percent dropped to about 0.6 percent in the 1979-89 period, which is partially a reflection of the recession in 1981-82.[6] The biggest drops in participation rates between 1979 and 1989 were for men aged 55 to 64 (from 76.4 to 64.7 percent), and men aged 65 to 69 (from 24.4 to 17.9 percent). As in the entry process of younger workers, some of the decline in numbers of older workers is offset by countervailing processes.[7] Nevertheless, overall, there are decreases in the relative number of workers on both ends of the age distribution, a condition which foretells a possible labour shortage in the immediate future.

The aging of the workforce is more accurately depicted as the middle-aging of the labour force in the sense that the workforce is not dominated by those 55 years of age plus.[8] Nonetheless, the workforce is growing older, largely as a result of the aging of the unusually large baby-boom cohorts born between 1947 and 1966. The oldest of this group will become 53 years of age around the turn of the century, less than ten years from now. As well, the growing concentration of older workers in the 25-44 component of the labour force reflects the beginning of this impact. The proportion of workers in this age group increased from 42.9 percent in 1971 to 52.4 percent in 1986. The average age of the labour force has gone from 35.5 in 1979 to 36.3 in 1989 and will rise through the 1990s to 2011 with a small decline thereafter.[9]

The problems of an aging workforce and the decline in the youth generation have spawned a number of possible remedies. For example, David K. Foot (1986) has suggested that immigration policy in Canada be directed at younger age groups corresponding to the age range of the baby-bust generation (1967-1980).[10] The role of immigration as a source of labour market growth, however, may not be a popular policy in an economic downturn. Others have looked to the increased labour force participation of women, although the rate of that increase is expected to taper off.[11] In the same vein, "family-friendly" programs that reconcile the needs of women, work, and families have been proposed.[12] In light of advances in technology, another suggested remedy is sending work offshore electronically, a process already being used in Canada.[13] For example, data processing has been sent by satellite to the Caribbean Islands and some Asian countries. Some have suggested increasing the labour force participation rates of minority groups who experience high levels of unemployment.[14] Still, others have proposed the reintegration and the retention of the older worker in the labour force.[15]

The purpose of this paper is to examine this latter solution, the reintegration and retention of the older worker in the labour force, against the backdrop of the changing nature of work and retirement in Canada. That is, the shift in the economic structure will have important implications for matching older workers and jobs in the labour force. An examination of retirement patterns provides some clues as to who is most likely to be retained or attracted to rejoin the labour force, and by what processes. Section II considers changes in the industrial structure and the structure of occupations by providing information about the nature of available jobs, their location, and the skills required. The uneven distribution of employment offers some evidence as to the form work will take in the future and a consideration of unemployment assesses the possibilities of reintegrating the older worker into the labour force. Section III looks at retirement trends, the reasons for these trends, and their implications for retaining the older person in the labour force. The concluding section assesses the overall viability of reintegrating and retaining the older worker in the labour force.

It is recognized at the outset that the retention or reintegration of the older worker is a scenario that many, especially those currently in management positions, would find implausible. One of the more pressing problems at the moment is to redesign work organizations to accommodate the blocked careers of middle-aged baby-boomers who find that the pyramidal shape at the top of the organization does not provide a sufficient number of middle and upper-management positions to satisfy their aspirations.[16] Yet the current glut of middle-management candidates will surely be followed by a shortage as the baby-bust cohorts move through their careers.[17]

II. The Changing Nature of Work

The Changing Industrial Structure

In their attempt to explain the process of industrialization, Clark Kerr *et al.* (1962) point out that a typical pattern is a continuing reduction in the proportion of the labour force in the primary sector — that is, in agriculture, fishing, mining and logging — and a shift toward the industrial sector including manufacturing and construction.[18] At a later stage of industrial development, a further occupational shift occurs with an increasing proportion of the labour force moving into the tertiary sector which produces services (e.g. drycleaning) other than goods. As in all countries in the Organization for Economic Cooperation and Development (OECD) in the postwar period, the changes in Canada have followed the same patterns described above.[19] The general trend of development from 1901 to 1990 is represented in Table 2.

It is apparent that the major changes in the industrial divisions of the Canadian labour force over the last 90 years have been the steady decline in the primary industries, particularly agriculture, and the impressive rise in the service-producing industries, especially in the last 50 years. The changes in the secondary sector (e.g. manufacturing and construction) have been relatively moderate.

The shift of employment from goods-producing activities (including primary and secondary industries) to services began early in the century. Until the 1940s, however, the transition was gradual: the service sector's share of the total labour force rose from about 28 percent in 1911 to 39 percent in 1941. Since then, there has been a striking acceleration in the growth of the services sector. According to an Economic Council of Canada analysis, between 1967 and 1988 service employment increased at an annual average rate of 3.2 percent, compared with 0.9 percent in goods-producing industries. By 1988, 71 percent of Canadian workers were employed in the service sector. This rate of increase does not appear to be levelling off, since projections for 1993 place 73 percent of workers in the service sector.[20]

TABLE 2

Percentage Distribution of the Total Canadian Labour Force by Industry, 1901-1990

	Primary	**Secondary**	**Tertiary**	**Other**	**Total (1,000x)**
1901	45.0	26.8	28.1	–	1752
1911	39.5	27.1	33.4	–	2722
1921	36.6	26.5	36.9	–	3173
1931	32.6	17.3	39.0	11.1	3917
1941*	30.9	28.3	39.0	1.8	4447
1951	21.1	32.3	45.3	1.3	5286
1961	14.2	28.4	55.0	2.4	6471
1971	8.4	26.0	57.7	7.9	8627
1981	7.0	25.3	66.2	1.5	12004
1990	5.6	22.8	71.1	0.5	13681

* The census of 1941 reported a separate category of "labourers" who were not included in the primary sector. These are included in the total of the secondary sector – manufacturing and construction.

Sources: 1901-1981: calculated from Censuses of Canada of the respective years.

1990: calculated from Statistics Canada, *Labour Force Annual Averages*, 1990.

At the same time, service activity has been undergoing considerable change. The service sector includes a range of diverse industries that goes beyond the traditional services of retail trade, accommodation, food and beverages, amusement and recreation, and personal services such as drycleaning and funeral services. Because of this diversity, several researchers have developed finer-grained typologies to provide a realistic view of this sector.[21] For instance, the Economic Council of Canada (1991: 9) developed a typology that adds two subsectors to the traditional services in the service sector — dynamic services and non-market services. Dynamic services have four subdivisions which include transportation, communications and utilities; wholesale trade; finance, insurance and real estate; and business services. Non-market services include education services, health services, social services, and public administration.

Currently, the traditional, dynamic and non-market subsectors each comprise slightly less than one quarter of all employment and have had relatively similar job-creation performance, with annual growth rates around three percent. However, business services had the fastest rate of growth of any industry with average annual employment gains of 7.3 percent followed by the traditional services. These trends are predicted to continue in the medium term with a small dip in the dynamic subsectors' share of employment in commercial services and a small increase in the commercial services of traditional services. These trends provide a general indication as to where workers will be required in the immediate future.[22]

Over one-half of females and about one-third of males, aged 15 to 24, are overrepresented in the service sector, particularly in the traditional services and in clerical sales and service occupations.[23] This overrepresentation suggests that the traditional subsector will experience increased labour market pressures and will face a "youth squeeze" because it depends heavily on a diminishing supply of younger workers.[24]

Other notable features of the service sector include the fact that, on several measures of technological change (mainly computer technology), the service sector is ahead of the goods-producing sector and, within the service sector, the dynamic subsector exceeded all other industries in the last decade.[25] These changes will have some implications for skill levels required in the workplace. Information-based employment — that is, work primarily concerned with the creation and use of data and knowledge — is likely to be an important feature of many jobs, at least in the dynamic and non-market subsectors. As well, the dynamic services, especially business services, finance, insurance and real estate, tend to locate in larger metropolitan areas, a trend matched in the goods-producing industries. This trend points to a continuation of rural-urban differences in job opportunities.[26]

When the size of the firms in the goods-producing and service sectors are compared, there are no differences in that the service sector has more smaller firms, although those workers in traditional services are more likely to be in smaller firms. What is important is that in both sectors, employment growth in the 1980s has taken place primarily in small firms. And as several researchers have found, jobs in small firms are less likely to be unionized, are less likely to be covered by pension plans, and are more likely to be terminated by permanent layoff and to pay lower average wages. The fact that, on average, workers in the traditional subsector receive fewer intrinsic and extrinsic work rewards can be traced, in part, to the prevalence of small firms which may not be able to provide benefits to employees and to the failure of unions to organize workers in these industries.[27]

If such factors as fewer labour market entrants and a decreasing labour force participation rate are seen in conjunction with growth in the service sector of the economy, it is clear where labour shortages are to be expected and where older workers will be needed if they are to be used as part of the solution to the labour shortage problem. The service sector and its subsectors, all growing at equal rates, are likely to be the site of employment, probably in urban centres and smaller firms. While there is some indication that skilled labour will be required in light of the technological changes occurring in the service sector, an examination of the occupational structure and its shifts over time sheds more light on this issue.

The Changing Occupational Structure

Accompanying the changes in the industrial structure are two major occupational shifts. Table 3 presents the percentage distribution of the seven main occupational groupings for 1971, 1981, and 1986. While these figures cannot be directly compared with those in previous years due to changes in the occupational classification system in the Canadian census, two general trends are unmistakable. First, there is a continued decline in the proportions of total workers in farming and in resource extraction and processing. Second, there are increases in managerial and administrative, professional, and to a lesser extent clerical, sales, and service occupations. With few exceptions, this latter trend has been spread across both the goods-producing and services industries which appear to be converging in their occupational profiles.[28]

Looked at another way, those occupations that have contributed the most to overall employment growth (i.e. managerial and administrative, medical and health, sales and services), were responsible for almost all the net employment creation between 1981 and 1986. For example, managerial and administrative occupations alone accounted for one out of every three new jobs during this time frame.[29]

TABLE 3

Percentage Distribution of Total Labour Force by Occupation for Canada
1971, 1981, 1986, 1990

Occupations	1971*	1981*	1986*	1990**
All Occupations ('000)	8,627	12,004	12,870	13,681
Marginal & Administrative	4.3	6.8	7.9	12.4
Professional	12.7	15.0	16.0	16.5
Clerical	15.9	18.2	17.7	16.5
Sales	9.5	9.5	9.9	9.5
Service	11.2	11.9	12.7	13.4
Subtotal	53.6	61.4	64.2	68.3
Farming & Resource Extraction	7.7	5.9	5.7	4.8
Processing, Fabricating & Related	28.2	27.7	25.1	26.4
Other	10.5	5.0	5.0	0.5

Sources: * 1971-1986, adapted from Censuses of Canada, *Trends in Occupations and Industry*. Cat. 98-135.
** 1990, Calculated from Statistics Canada, *Labour Force Annual Averages*, 1990. Cat. 71-220.

When the age distribution of occupations is considered (Table 4), it is evident that the greatest concentration of the prime age group (25-44) is in management and administrative occupations and in professional occupations (over 60 percent in both groups). This pattern is not surprising, of course, since advancement to these positions takes years of achievement in a person's career. However, the sharp drop in workers aged 45 to 64 in these occupational groups indicates a considerable loss of experienced workers, primarily to early retirement.[30] This "retirement bulge" — a large fraction of persons reaching early retirement age — is likely to place pressure on the labour market to retain or hire older workers to fill the gap. In short, one of the more important groups of older workers to be targeted for retention or re-employment would be those skilled workers in the managerial, administrative, professional and technical occupations.

In fact, overall, the changes in the occupational structure suggest that the required skill content of jobs is on the rise although this is a subject of some debate. On the one hand, it has been argued that skill requirements are upgraded as a nation moves to an increasingly high-technology service economy and, on the other, that the effect of economic development is to de-skill work.[31] In a very recent analysis, using a variety of analytical approaches such as occupational-trait and self-report skill measures, the Economic Council concluded that there is indeed an upgrading of skills in the overall Canadian economy. This finding is consistent with a number of other Canadian studies.[32] For instance, using occupational-trait analysis which measures five dimensions of Canadian occupations (i.e. general educational development, vocational preparation, cognitive complexity, task diversity, responsibility), the Council found that, for all measures, the skills in the workforce were upgraded between 1971 and 1986. As an example, in 1986, 25.3 percent of the employed were in jobs requiring more than two years training, compared to 20.8 percent in 1971. An examination of the relative skill levels by industry suggests that a higher proportion of service-sector workers than goods-producing workers are in high-skill categories for the five dimensions, although there are increases overall. Within the service sector, the non-market services have the largest share of high-skilled jobs and traditional services, the highest proportion of low-skilled jobs.[33]

If broad occupational groups are organized into three skill levels, the share of high-skilled occupations (managerial, administrative, professional and technical) increased seven percentage points from 1971 to 1986. The low-skilled group (service occupations) increased its share, but only by about one percentage point, while the medium-skilled occupations (clerical, sales and blue collar occupations) decreased by about seven percentage points.[34]

Based on these data, there are clear indications that the widely discussed and pending labour shortage should not be taken as a blanket shortage of workers. Specifically, high-skilled workers will be in demand. Recalling that about two-thirds of workers in the service sector are in dynamic and non-market subsectors and only one-third are found in traditional services, which have a preponderance of low-skilled jobs, the demand for skilled workers will be more acute. This does not ignore the fact that there is a bifurcated skill distribution in the service sector. The "hamburger economy" is a source of rapid job growth and, given a dwindling pool of teenagers, older workers are already being employed in these jobs.[35] There will be room for the unskilled older worker, but whether such people will want low-paying, tenuous employment with no benefits remains to be seen.

In light of the need for skilled workers, it is notable that the post-war generation has produced a better educated and more highly skilled labour force, and as Blossom Wigdor and David K. Foot (1988) point out, the fastest growing age group in university enrolment in Canada is the over-40 age group.[36] It would seem, then, that the potential pool of older workers for the future labour force may meet some of the requirements for skill.

TABLE 4

Percentage Distribution of the Total Experienced Labour Force
by Occupation and Age Groups, for Canada, 1971, 1981 and 1986

Occupation		Total	15-24	Age Groups 25-44	45-64	65+
	(Year)			(%)		
TOTAL	1971	100.0	25.1	42.9	29.0	3.0
	1981	100.0	25.4	47.5	25.1	2.0
	1986	100.0	21.4	52.4	24.5	1.7
Managerial and	1971	100.0	7.5	50.0	40.0	2.5
administrative	1981	100.0	5.7	59.5	33.3	1.5
	1986	100.0	4.8	62.0	31.6	1.6
Professional	1971	100.0	23.2	52.3	22.5	1.9
	1981	100.0	16.1	61.4	21.1	1.4
	1986	100.0	13.1	63.6	21.9	1.4
Clerical	1971	100.0	34.6	39.1	24.5	1.8
	1981	100.0	32.6	45.9	20.4	1.1
	1986	100.0	25.8	52.9	20.3	1.0
Sales	1971	100.0	22.6	41.4	32.8	3.2
	1981	100.0	26.1	44.3	27.1	2.6
	1986	100.0	25.2	47.6	25.0	2.2
Service	1971	100.0	27.5	36.4	32.1	4.0
	1981	100.0	35.1	37.3	25.6	1.9
	1986	100.0	33.9	41.5	23.1	1.4
Farming and resource	1971	100.0	24.7	34.9	34.4	6.0
extraction	1981	100.0	26.2	38.5	29.4	5.9
	1986	100.0	22.9	41.8	28.7	6.5
Processing, fabricating	1971	100.0	21.2	47.1	30.0	1.7
and related	1981	100.0	24.5	48.2	26.5	0.9
	1986	100.0	18.7	53.9	26.6	0.8
Other	1971	100.0	30.7	36.9	25.9	6.5
	1981	100.0	32.6	33.1	26.3	8.0
	1986	100.0	31.0	41.5	23.3	4.2

Source: Statistics Canada, *Trends in Occupation and Industry, 1989.* Catalogue 98-135.

The Uneven Distribution of Employment

The uneven development of employment coincides with the shift of employment towards the service sector. One of the most fascinating trends in industrialized nations is the rise of nonstandard work. Nonstandard work, usually refers to part-time, short-term, temporary work and "own account" workers who have no employees other than themselves. In 1989 nonstandard employment represented 28 percent of all employment in that year. Over the past 15 years this form of employment has steadily risen from 23.7 percent in 1975, to 25.4 percent in 1980, to 27.9 percent in 1985. As well, nonstandard employment has accounted for 44 percent of all employment growth in the 1980s.[37] Part-time work, the largest component of nonstandard work, grew by 51 percent compared to 28.3 percent for full-time jobs. Short-term work only showed modest gains and employment in the temporary help industry increased about 2.5 times during the 1980s. Own account self-employment accounted for about 10 percent of the job growth between 1975 and 1989.[38]

In the aggregate, nonstandard work tends to be more prevalent in the service sector, where 36.3 percent of all jobs are nonstandard compared to 27.7 percent in goods-producing industries. Traditional services tend to have more nonstandard jobs with close to one-half of the jobs representing this form of work. Interestingly, the non-market subsector also includes about 30 percent of their employees in nonstandard jobs.[39] Women are overrepresented in the non-standard labour force because of the high proportion of women found in part-time work. As seen in Table 5 over 70 percent of part-time workers are women. And, as Table 5 also illustrates, most nonstandard work, and part-time work in particular, is overrepresented with youth. Overall, the incidence rate for non-standard work is high for youth, declines for the prime age categories, and rises again for workers between the ages of 55 and 69 years.[40]

TABLE 5

**Part-time Employment by Age and Sex,
Canada, 1975, 1980, 1985 and 1988**
(percent)

	15-24	25-44	45 and over
1975			
Both	46.7	30.1	23.4
Males	73.8	8.0	18.3
Females	34.8	39.7	25.6
1980			
Both	44.0	32.3	23.6
Males	72.2	9.2	18.6
Females	33.4	40.9	25.6
1985			
Both	42.5	35.3	22.2
Males	67.3	15.6	17.1
Females	32.9	43.0	24.1
1988			
Both	41.9	35.6	22.5
Males	68.5	14.8	16.7
Females	31.6	43.7	24.7

Source: Statistics Canada, *Labour Force Annual Averages*, 1975-1983; 1981-1988. Catalogue 71-529 Occasional.

Some economists have argued that nonstandard work represents a fundamental change in the structure of the economy. This change is likely to endure, and workers in these jobs should not be considered marginal. Keeping in mind that nonstandard employment now represents about three out of every ten jobs and is responsible for almost one-half of the net job growth over the past decade, it is quite likely that older workers will be needed in nonstandard jobs and that very likely they will be attracted to these types of jobs. In a study of part-time employment, Lynn McDonald and Richard Wanner found that among employed workers aged 55 to 64, 12.8 percent worked part-time in 1986 compared to 8.2 in 1976.[41] For those workers 65 and older, the figure increased from 26.9 percent in 1976 to 34.7 percent in 1986. What is more, 58.4 percent of the male workers and 63 percent of the female workers preferred this form of work. It appears that there is a convergence between the developments in the labour force and the preferences of older workers.

The flaw in this development is that many nonstandard jobs — indeed, almost one-half — are "bad" jobs as defined by the Economic Council of Canada.[42] "Bad" jobs are typically characterized by low pay, limited potential for career advancement, and limited access to employer-sponsored and public benefits. The latest General Social Survey found that workers in nonstandard jobs reported less job autonomy, more repetitive work, and lower skill requirements than did those in standard jobs.[43] Using census data, McDonald and Wanner found that, although part-time workers aged 55 to 64 had a level of education equal to their full-time colleagues, they were concentrated in jobs on the periphery of the economy that typically have less than optimal working conditions.[44] While this form of work is obviously an advantage to older workers since they prefer part-time work, the inferior conditions of nonstandard work will have to be addressed if more older workers are to be attracted to the labour force.

The Unequal Distribution of Unemployment

There is little doubt that over the last 15 years the youth unemployment rates have been anywhere between 3.5 percent to 8 percent higher than the aggregate rates and considerably higher than for those of the 35-44 and 45-54 age groups. At first glance, the possibility of the unemployed older worker as a source of labour seems insignificant. However, a closer look at current research suggests otherwise.

In the first instance, older workers tend to experience long-term unemployment as compared to their younger colleagues. For example, workers over age 45 experienced the longest spells of unemployment during the 1981-82 recession, and during the subsequent recovery and recessionary periods, the rate of their long-term unemployment continued to rise. In 1976 the average duration of unemployment for workers over age 45 was 18.5 weeks compared to 25.8 weeks in 1989.[45] As Miles Corak found, older workers — as compared to younger workers — are less likely to give up searching for employment, suggesting a high degree of motivation to work on the part of the older worker.[46]

In the second instance, there is some suggestion that retirement provides a respectable route out of the labour force, cushioning the stigma attached to being unemployed. McDonald and Wanner have compared the labour force experiences between 1981 and 1984 of displaced workers aged 55-64 with those aged 25-54 who lost their jobs. While over 65 percent of the younger workers had found another job by January 1986, just 39.1 percent of the older workers had located a job. Only a small proportion, 13.8 percent of the younger workers, had withdrawn from the labour force (i.e. were not employed or not seeking work) whereas a sizeable 41.4 percent of the 55-64 year-olds were no longer in the labour force. In a further analysis of the data, they found that the longer the unemployment of the older worker, the more likely they would consider themselves retired.[47] The researchers conclude that these workers were "discouraged" into retirement by the labour market conditions they faced. These are workers who, in all likelihood, would have preferred to continue to work; they therefore present opportunities for reintegration into the labour force given their involuntary retirement.

One of the problems of reintegrating the unemployed older worker is the mismatch between job requirements and skills. In fact, some have argued that the reason for the longer unemployment periods of older workers is a direct reflection of this problem. At the present time, the highest rates of unemployment are found in the goods-producing sectors and in the blue-collar occupations; that is, those involving manual work.[48] As an example, the unemployment rate for blue-collar occupations was 9.1 percent compared to 6.1 percent for white-collar occupations in 1989. In the same year, the rate of unemployment in the managerial and administrative category was 3.8 percent compared to 12.4 percent for construction.[49] As a result, those losing their jobs are found primarily in goods industries, typically in jobs with intermediate skills or less. Yet, virtually all of the employment gains in the past decade have been in service industries, most frequently in jobs with either high-skill levels, or very low-skill levels (traditional services) associated with low earnings.[50] If older workers are expected to be active in the labour force, policies that provide services to increase their competitiveness in the job market (training, placement assistance, and counselling) and job-creation programs (hiring subsidies, direct employment creation, promotion of self-employment) would be required. Regrettably, retraining the older worker is not likely to occur in the immediate future given current policies pertaining to the older unemployed worker. The only major federal program for older unemployed workers — the Program for Older Worker Adjustment (POWA) — is simply compensatory in nature and designed to bridge unemployment and retirement.

Some American economists have argued the obvious — that older workers with low levels of education and vocational training or obsolescent skills will be obliged to work in the low-skilled jobs formerly held by youth in the traditional subsector. They argue not only that older workers will be desperately wanted, but also that these jobs will offer a certain amount of flexibility in terms of part-time and part-year work, despite the drawbacks of low pay and inferior working conditions.[51] Faced with retirement or a low-paying, low-skill job, it is not entirely plausible that older workers will opt for this alternative unless conditions of work are changed.

To recapitulate, the major shifts in the economy indicate that the sector most likely to come under increased labour market pressures to expand employment to older workers is the service sector. The overall shift to high-skilled white-collar jobs across the entire economy presages the need for skilled older workers. The retirement bulge in administrative, managerial and professional categories targets specific occupations in which the need for skilled workers is likely to be more pronounced. At the same time, the youth freeze within the lower-tiered traditional services suggests that there will also be a shortfall of workers for a relatively smaller pool of low-skilled jobs.

Many of the unoccupied jobs will be found in smaller firms in urban areas, and they will probably reflect non-conventional work arrangements. Obstacles to employment result from the fact that a substantial proportion of nonstandard jobs, usually in small firms, offer inferior work conditions that may prove unattractive to older workers. That well over one-half of older workers prefer part-time work (the most common form of nonstandard work) may help to offset this concern. Unemployed older workers, who carry the burden of long-term unemployment, represent an untapped resource in terms of motivation to work and involuntary retirement. The obstacles in their path to employment can be eliminated by programs that increase their competitiveness in the labour market. An awareness of the nature and form of available jobs, their location, and the skills required in a future labour market is only half of the equation. Skilled labour shortages are matched by a seemingly unwilling labour force engaged in a stampede to early retirement.

TABLE 6

Labour Force Participation Rates for Age Groups 55-64 and 65 or over by Sex, 1946 to 1991

Year	Males 55-64	Males 65+	Females 55-64	Females 65+
1946		47.5		5.0
1947		44.9		5.7
1948		44.0		5.1
1949		42.9		4.7
1950		40.4		4.2
1951		37.9		4.1
1952		36.7		3.9
1953	86.5	34.8	12.9	3.6
1954	85.4	33.2	14.0	3.7
1955	86.1	32.3	14.7	3.9
1956	86.4	34.0	15.8	4.5
1957	87.2	34.1	18.2	5.0
1958	87.0	32.1	19.2	5.2
1959	86.8	31.0	20.1	5.2
1960	86.7	30.3	21.3	5.6
1961	86.8	29.3	23.2	5.9
1962	86.1	28.5	23.8	5.6
1963	85.9	26.4	24.6	5.9
1964	86.2	26.8	25.6	6.3
1965	86.4	26.3	27.0	6.0
1966	86.0	26.2	28.4	5.8
1967	85.8	24.7	28.6	5.9
1968	85.4	25.3	29.0	6.1
1969	85.3	23.5	30.2	5.5
1970	84.2	22.6	29.8	5.0
1971	83.3	20.0	30.9	5.1
1972	82.4	18.6	29.7	4.3
1973	81.2	18.1	31.0	4.4
1974	80.3	17.7	29.6	4.3
1975	79.4	17.2	30.8	4.4
1976	76.7	16.0	32.1	4.1
1977	76.6	15.5	32.2	4.2
1978	75.6	15.0	32.6	4.0
1979	70.9	16.2	27.9	3.7
1980	76.2	14.7	33.7	4.3
1981	69.6	15.2	28.8	4.0
1982	73.7	13.8	34.0	4.2
1983	70.8	12.9	33.8	4.1
1984	67.0	13.7	28.6	3.7
1985	70.2	12.3	33.8	4.2
1986	69.2	11.2	33.5	3.6
1987	66.4	11.8	34.9	3.6
1988	66.6	11.5	35.5	3.9
1989	64.7	11.1	35.3	3.5
1990	65.0	11.3	35.7	3.7
1991	62.6	11.3	35.7	3.5

Note: Figures for ages 55-64 are not available from 1946 to 1952. The 1978, 1986 and 1990 figures are for June.

Source: Statistics Canada, *Labour Research Paper No. 23; Historical Statistics of Canada; Labour Force Annual Averages,* 1987, 1988, 1989, 1991, Catalogues, 71-529, 71-220, 71-001.

III. Retirement
Retirement Patterns

Canadian workers want to retire before the expected norm of age 65.[52] Virtually all Canadian studies since the early 1970s have found that Canadians desire early retirement; such a desire remains unabated today.[53] Most recently, the 1989 General Social Survey found that, among employed Canadians, over two-fifths intend to retire before age 65, while about one-third do not know when they will retire. Only 14 percent state they will retire at age 65, seven percent do not plan to retire at all, and one percent want to retire after age 65. When age is considered, almost one-half of the baby-boomers indicated a desire to retire before age 65, a rather startling finding since they will constitute the pool from which potential older workers will be drawn.[54]

The preferences of Canadians have been supported by their actions when the precipitous decline in labour force participation rates are considered. Table 6 shows labour force participation rates for Canadian men and women from 1953 to 1991. Among the men, participation rates for those aged 55 to 64 years were stable until about 1965 when, until 1980, the rate began to decline annually. From 1980 onward, the rate has fluctuated, while the overall trend has been downward. The most recent available data indicates that as of 1991, 62.6 percent of the men in this age group remain in the labour force.[55] The trend for men over age 65 is even more dramatic; nearly half of the men in this age group were in the labour force in 1946, compared to just over 11 percent 40 years later.

The picture of Canadian women portrayed in Table 6 is somewhat different than the pattern for men. As is the case for all Canadian women, the labour force participation rates of women aged 55 to 64 began steadily growing in the 1950s. By 1969, about 30 percent of the women were either working or unemployed, and the rate has increased only marginally since then to 35.7 percent in 1991. Since it is well-documented that the labour force participation rates of all women have increased from the 1970s to the 1980s and that women retire earlier than men, it is reasonable to observe that the apparent stability for women is the result of two offsetting forces: an increasing propensity for women to engage in paid employment and an increasing tendency to retire early. The same might be said of the trend for women aged 65 and over. The percentage of women in this age category in the labour force has never exceeded 6.3 percent in the post-World War II period.

Withdrawal from the labour force is not always synonymous with being retired; however, when the retired population is examined directly, the trend to early retirement is confirmed. Analyzing data from the 1989 General Social Survey, Graham Lowe found that 63 percent of the retirees in Canada retired before reaching age 65, only 17 percent retired at age 65, and another 16 percent retired after age 65.[56]

Perhaps even more telling is the fact that the majority of Canadians are very satisfied with their retirement. Life after retirement may not be smooth sailing for everyone, but few people suffer adverse consequences as a result of the act of retiring.[57]

Therefore, just as a labour force shortage of entry-level workers looms on the horizon, substantial numbers of Canadians are exiting the labour force for ever-earlier retirement. And, if the preferences of the baby-boomers are any indication, the trend will be carried into the next century. In the following sections we consider exactly who is retiring, when they are retiring, and for what reasons. Our goal will be to assess what can be done, if anything, to stem the tide of workers into retirement.

Early Retirement

The enormous number of studies of early retirement in North America are consistent in identifying self-perceived health and unearned income from pensions and assets as the two most important predictors of early retirement. People in poor health tend to retire early as do those who can afford to retire early. Earlier studies of retirement placed more emphasis on the role of health in early retirement while studies in the 1980s found more support for the financial factors, the basic argument being that health is an *ex post facto* rationalization in the face of a strong work ethic.[58]

The Canadian evidence is far from conclusive, but most studies do indicate that health and potential retirement income influence the early retirement decision.[59] The only problem is that researchers are not clear which factor is more important for whom and in what context. There is some indication that health and unearned income seem to be more salient factors for men than for women and that public sector workers are more influenced by work-related stress and financial adequacy compared to poor health for men in the private sector.[60] Forty-two percent of primary blue-collar workers retire for health reasons compared to 11 percent of managerial, professional or technical workers.[61]

Although the precise role of health in influencing retirement behaviour is still debated, the health factor is important from another perspective. The unhealthy appear to self-select themselves into early retirement, leaving the more hardy in the labour force. In fact, Meredith Minkler inadvertently makes a case for this position. When the retired are compared on the health variable to those who continue to work, it is not unexpected that the retired report poorer health, since that is why so many retired in the first place.[62] In some ways, this eliminates concerns about the health of most older workers and helps to explain why absences from work are only slightly higher for older workers than for younger workers.[63] It also calls into question the need for aggressive monitoring and evaluation of older workers by employers which some deem will be necessary with the removal of mandatory retirement.[64]

If early retirement is related to having an adequate income, this indicates that additional remuneration in the work place may not be a sufficiently strong incentive to entice all early retirees to maintain their attachment to the labour force. A recent Gallup survey for the American Association of Retired Persons reveals that the three most frequently cited reasons for working by persons over age 63 (past the early retirement norm of age 62) were that they enjoyed the job and the work, that work made them feel useful, and that work enabled them to contribute to society and help others.[65] Future jobs will have to be viewed by potential early retirees as a source of satisfaction that can compete with the perceived value of leisure pursuits. In some ways this bodes well for Canadians, if the American results pertain to the Canadian situation. Reported job satisfaction is as high or higher than national averages in the non-market and dynamic subsectors of the service sector for both standard and nonstandard work.[66]

These general findings mask, however, the heterogeneity found among retirees. An American study suggests that, at least among managerial, professional and technical workers, financial incentives might induce older workers, even those past age 65, to postpone retirement.[67] Nearly half of the respondents indicated that they would postpone retirement if the United States Social Security system were changed to abolish the earnings penalty on recipients aged 65 to 72 or to accord added benefits for years worked past age 65.

The retirement patterns of women in Canada have always been different from those of men. They have also been under-researched. The only clear factor related to women's early retirement is being married.[68] Marriage may provide opportunities for women to stop working because of the increased economic resources that result from the marital union. As the economic situation of women in the work place improves, it has been found that a married woman's decision to retire is influenced by her own wage level, social security entitlement, pension benefits and age, as well as by her spouse's wage level and his retirement status.[69] It might, therefore, be expected that, as women have more continuous employment histories and are thus more likely to qualify for early pension benefits, they will retire even earlier than they do at present. Moreover, if men continue to retire earlier, women who are influenced by their husband's retirement status may also retire early.

Another factor influencing women's early retirement is eldercare for a dependent elder. Eldercare responsibilities generally appear when workers are in their forties and fifties, the time when early retirement also becomes possible. The most recent data indicate that nine percent of care-givers for the frail elderly were lost to the labour force in 1990.[70]

The preponderance of women in the service sector in both high-skilled (health, education and welfare) and low-skilled jobs (retail trade and other consumer services) presents a difficult situation, if retention is the issue. It is doubtful that women will want to fill the labour market gap created by the shrinking youth cohort because these low-tiered service jobs have low status and low pay. By contrast, we know that only 30 percent of the education, health, and welfare industries offer nonstandard work which is preferred by women and which may become a more pressing need as family responsibilities force women into early retirement. Part-time work, part-year work, flextime, and perhaps job sharing will have to become more widespread in the high-skilled jobs if this source of labour is to be retained.

Individual preferences for early retirement have been strongly reinforced by structural factors, most notably the availability of public and private pensions. Studies of how the social security system influences retirement behaviour have generated a diverse array of findings in the United States. Most find that the timing of retirement appears to be affected by the eligibility requirements of the Social Security Act; in particular, sharp jumps take place at ages 62 and 65.[71] In Canada, several studies have shown that public pension benefits do influence the early retirement decision.[72]

Most recently, changes to the Canada and Quebec Pension Plans have demonstrated the powerful influence of pensions on early retirement. Implemented in 1966, with the addition of flexible retirement in 1984 (QPP) and 1987 (CPP), the plan permitted access to substantial benefits as early as age 60.[73] The response of Canadians was immediate and dramatic. In 1984, three out of every four persons receiving QPP retirement pensions were, for the first time, between the ages of 60 and 64. Two-thirds of new CPP beneficiaries in 1987 were aged 60 to 64.[74]

At the policy level, the potency of an adequate pension cannot be overlooked. If reducing early retirement is the goal, then public pension plans should be made less attractive, should be delayed, or should have some type of built-in disincentive. This, of course, is easier said than done. For example, simulations in the United States show that reductions in monthly benefits to the tune of 13 percent postpone retirement only by about a month.[75] In restructuring incentives, care has to be taken not to create undue hardship for those who are forced to retire early.[76] For example, blue-collar workers retire early primarily for health reasons that are frequently related to the physically demanding nature of such work.

There is also some evidence that private pension plans contribute to early retirement. For example, in 1989 over one-half of workers with employer-pension plans wanted to retire early, compared to one-third of those without such plans.[77] Employer-sponsored pension plans (RRPs) have grown and improved over the 1970s. Most notably, the availability of early retirement with and without reduction in benefits has increased. The proportion of RRP members, with an option to retire early on a reduced pension, grew from 87 percent in 1970 to 98 percent in 1989, while 77 percent of the members in 1989 could choose early retirement without employer approval, compared to 35 percent in 1970. In 1970 only 19 percent of members could retire early without reduced benefits, compared to almost 55 percent in 1989.[78] Pension formulas could be redesigned to create strong work incentives; in practice, however, this would be difficult, although not impossible.[79]

The other structural factor germane to the retention of the older worker is the occupational structure. There are occupation-specific retirement patterns, although much more research is required in this area. Looking beyond the blue-collar/white-collar distinction, men formerly employed in clerical, sales or service jobs are less likely than managerial/professional workers to retire early. The reverse holds true for women, as a much higher proportion of females in clerical, sales and service jobs retire before age 65.[80] The main reason for the findings for the men is that managers/professionals are more likely to be employed in large bureaucratic firms or government agencies with orderly career lines and mandatory retirement policies. Self-employment, known to be associated with late retirement, is also more pronounced among men in the clerical, sales, and service occupations.[81] Women, who are less likely to be self-employed in these occupations, probably leave as soon as it is financially feasible, given the substandard conditions of work. In support of this observation, one study found that women work into late retirement mainly because of financial hardship.[82]

Early retirement is a complicated issue, but there is room to manoeuvre if older workers are to be retained in the labour force. Older workers, both male and female, may be attracted by interesting and satisfying work in the high and medium-skilled non-market and dynamic subsectors. Public and private pension plans appear to increase early retirement, but reducing the amount of the pension may not be the issue as much as changing the timing of the benefit for select groups. A disincentive, such as raising the retirement age in the United States, deserves serious consideration. This change should be directed at the managerial/professional and technical occupations, where interest in continued work is expressed and losses are the most damaging to the economy. Delaying the retirement age for these workers and offering financial incentives for continued work may be effective. Women face different circumstances in both work and retirement as a result of family responsibilities. The increased availability of nonstandard work in non-market and dynamic services would be a logical impetus for these women to postpone early retirement. All the evidence suggests that women are not going to remain in or be attracted to the lower-tiered services. Far-reaching changes would have to be made to make these jobs more intrinsically and extrinsically worthwhile.

On-Time Retirement

What effect would the elimination of mandatory retirement have on the labour force participation rate of Canadians? There would be little or no effect. The extent of mandatory retirement in Canada is small. Earlier studies show that mandatory retirement, as a reason for retirement, is given by less than one percent of those under age 65, 17 percent of those age 65, and about 27 percent of those over age 65.[83] The abolishment of mandatory retirement in Manitoba and Quebec has shown that there have been no significant effects on labour force participation rates since the inception of the legislation.[84] The General Social Survey (1989) indicates that just over one-quarter of all individuals retired because of mandatory retirement.[85]

If compulsory retirement is not the major reason for "on-time retirement," what then are the other reasons? The answer is mainly speculative. However, mandatory retirement is, more often than not, linked to membership in a pension plan, so retirement at age 65 could reflect financial considerations. In one Canadian survey it has been reported that those who retired for compulsory reasons were more likely to be in receipt of a job-related pension.[86] What is important is that these jobs are usually the higher-status jobs. For example, C. Ciffin and J.K. Martin found that the main reason for retirement among managerial, professional and technical workers was compulsory retirement policies, with nearly 49 percent reporting it as a reason for retirement. Furthermore, support for mandatory retirement is inversely related to education and income.[87] This indicates that, while mandatory retirement may not have a large effect in the aggregate, its elimination may have an effect on the very occupations where workers are required. Mandatory retirement is within the purview of employers to change since it is part of the employee-employer contract.

In actual practice, mandatory retirement may not have a serious effect on participation rates in the aggregate, but the assumptions behind it do have an indirect effect because they fuel existing negative attitudes towards older workers.[88] The mandatory retirement debate has heated up in the wake of the recent Supreme Court's decisions which chose to support the concept of mandatory retirement. At the heart of this debate is the unavoidable assumption that older workers are unproductive as a result of the aging process, despite all the available evidence to the contrary.[89] There is a large body of research showing that on most measures older workers are just as productive as their younger counterparts. Studies in various work environments have shown that the connection between age and individual productivity is very weak and can be changed with the environment.[90] Age alone is not a sufficient criterion to decide on individual competency since there is such a wide variation in the rate at which people age. Although the abandonment of mandatory retirement is probably academic, the very attitudes underpinning the concept can serve as barriers to the employment of older workers and would need to be reversed. Eliminating mandatory retirement may help to soften these views.

Late Retirement

The reasons for late retirement are almost the exact opposite of the reasons for early retirement. Most studies confirm that there is little difference between the working retired (i.e. those who retire and then return to work) and those who simply continue to work past age 65. Both groups tend to be well-educated with upper-occupational status; they are married men and single women who enjoy reasonably good health and who are attached to their work. A large proportion of late retirees are self-employed probably because they are not subject to mandatory retirement provisions. There is also a greater propensity for recent immigrants from Third World countries to remain in the labour force after age 65.[91]

Though it seems to go against the evidence that it is upper-occupational status individuals who work beyond age 65, a number of studies have indicated that financial reasons often motivate the working retired and those who retire late.[92] Rachel Boaz showed that work during retirement by both men and women was a response to low or moderate levels of unearned income at the beginning of retirement. For men, it was also a response to a decrease in the real value of income during retirement. A comparable Canadian study supports these results. Canadian men and women who worked past age 65 did so out of financial need, but the need was greater among the women than among the men.[93] The reason was basically similar for immigrants who arrived in Canada after 1977. As newcomers they did not qualify for full pension benefits under Old Age Security and their country of origin did not have reciprocal pension agreements with Canada.

It is important to underscore the findings that those people who continue to work past age 65 have far more successful work histories than those who do not, making them an exceptional and valuable source of labour.[94] Reasonable wages and salaries should have a salutary effect on attracting and maintaining this group of skilled, older workers in the labour force.

This "claw-back" instituted by the federal government in 1989 may inadvertently sustain the trend to late retirement. The claw-back means that persons over 65 years of age, earning more than $50,000 a year, will have to pay back part or some portion of their Old Age Security pension. While this may appear just, the claw-back ceilings are not fully indexed to inflation. Therefore, the number of older persons subject to the claw-back will increase each year.[95] Indeed, it is estimated that persons who retire in 2019 with as little as $20,000 in annual income will have Old Age Security benefits reduced by the claw-back.[96]

This broad review of the retirement patterns of older Canadians and their reasons for retiring indicate that there are certain workers who might be potentially recruited back into the labour force or convinced to remain past normal retirement ages. All the data point to the need to retain those retirees from the managerial/professional and technical occupations who have the skills to offer, an attachment to their work, and the motivation to continue working voluntarily. Further, the conditions of work in these occupations are amenable to nonstandard work forms and would meet the need for job satisfaction and interest. Because these workers will be in high demand, the barriers to their employment such as mandatory retirement policies, the opportunity costs of skill up-grading, and the incentives to retire early found in most pension plans, may be reversed in these occupations once employers are confronted with labour shortages.

Those who retire late constitute a very important source of potential labour, especially in light of their successful work histories and upper occupational status. The challenge here will be to make the work available to them financially rewarding and to allow for employment on a part-time, part-year and seasonal basis. Policies that foster self-employment would be an additional incentive.

The retention of older women is only likely to occur in the non-market and dynamic service subsectors where women tend to be rewarded accordingly, where the work is interesting, and where job satisfaction is on a higher level. At the same time, if the trend towards early retirement can be reversed for some men, then there is a higher probability that women may curb their move into early retirement. In both instances, the family responsibilities of women will have to be recognized through special work programs if these women are to remain in the labour force. However, all the data indicate that women vacate the lower-echelon services as early as is financially feasible; thus, they are not likely to be the answer to the "youth freeze." The modifications that would have to be made to these low-skilled service jobs are just too encompassing to be practical or even financially possible, at least in the present economy.

From our perspective some workers should be retained; others, such as unneeded, unskilled and untrainable workers, many who are found in blue-collar occupations and low-level white-collar occupations, should be encouraged into early retirement. The question is how to design retirement policies that provide incentives for the latter to leave the labour force in financial comfort while at the same time providing incentives for the skilled to remain.

IV. Can Older Workers Fill the Identified Gap?

Labour shortages and the aging of the labour force will undoubtedly make the extension of working life an urgent matter for debate. We have examined the issue from the dual perspective of what the future labour market is likely to require in terms of labour shortages and what might be realistically possible to meet these needs, given the retirement patterns of older Canadians. Acknowledging that the issue is extremely complicated and that we have only touched on the more obvious factors, the forces for prolonging working life at least match the restraining forces.

The fact that older workers are healthy, vigorous and productive will encourage them to continue their attachment to the world of work. In the years ahead, the need for skilled workers in specific sectors of the economy will be roughly matched by the desire of these very workers to continue work and to postpone retirement. The jobs that will be available to these workers are likely to be interesting and satisfying because they will be "good" jobs located in the non-market and dynamic subsectors. Nonstandard work and work in small firms will be a plus for many of these potential workers in terms of flexibility because it is the kind of work they prefer. Furthermore, smaller and medium-sized firms will have less difficulty in adjusting to the accommodation of older workers than will entrenched bureaucracies. The expanding use of flextime, part-time work, and family support programs will allow workers to balance better work and family and may make it possible for older women, in particular, to continue working. Economic necessity, perhaps compounded by inflation, if not public policy (e.g. the claw-back), may induce employees to keep working or retirees to return to the labour force.

The forces restraining older persons from working in the labour force are many. The "bad" jobs found in traditional services are not likely to attract many older workers, especially women, who are overrepresented in these jobs. Once unemployed, older workers experience difficulties finding work in a reconfigured labour market because they lack the requisite skills. Unless they seek employment in the traditional subsector or upgrade their skills, they are likely to retire. This is exactly what current federal policy encourages (i.e. POWA). Retraining does not appear to be part of the national employment strategy; rather, the goal is to bridge the unemployed into early retirement. The fact that the majority of Canadians enjoy their retirement and want to retire early is a definite impediment to labour force attachment. Both public and private pension plans reinforce this general trend as does support for the concept of mandatory retirement. Negative stereotypes of older workers' lack of competency and productivity, held and encouraged by employers and unions, seem to die hard and will militate against the hiring of older workers. The current assumptions of the work place — that young people are the primary source of the vitality, dynamism and up-to-the-minute knowledge needed to run a successful enterprise — will continue to enhance these negative stereotypes.

The remedy of retaining and reintegrating the older worker to help assuage future labour force shortages is definitely within reach, but only barely. As we have seen, a number of obstacles will have to be overcome on the part of workers, employers, governments and unions. In some instances, the changes required are small and workable at the level of the firm; these include the introduction of part-time, flextime, and part-year work, the redesigning of jobs, better remuneration, and any number of programs that favour older workers' gradual transition into retirement. Unions will have to come to terms with the permanency of nonstandard work and recognize that it is not a threat to full-time work. Other changes will be slightly more daunting, such as the adjustment of federal and corporate pension policies, national educational and employment policies, and the values and attitudes of Canadians toward work in later life. Notwithstanding these obstacles, the demographic reality and the magnitude of the organizational and technological restructuring of the economy are likely to prevail, nudging Canada into the more effective use of the skills and experience of older workers. It requires no heroic assumptions to foresee that such planning must begin today.

NOTES

1. G. LaForest, The Hon. Mr. Justice McKinney v. University of Guelph. Ottawa, Supreme Court of Canada, December 6, 1990; Miles Corak, "Unemployment Comes of Age," in S. Gera, ed.,

Canadian Unemployment; Lessons for the 80s and Challenges for the 90s (Ottawa: Minister of Supply and Services, 1991).

2. Economic Council of Canada, *Employment in the Service Economy* (Ottawa: Minister of Supply and Services, 1991); M. Côté, "The Labour Force: into the '90s," *Perspectives on Labour and Income* 2 (Spring 1990), 8-16.

3. Côté, 9; David K. Foot, *Population Ageing and the Canadian Labour Force,* Discussion Paper on the Demographic Review, 87.A.5 (Ottawa: Institute for Public Policy, 1987); F.T. Denton, C.H. Feaver and B.G. Spencer, *The Future Population and Labour Force of Canada: Projections to the Year 2051* (Ottawa: Economic Council of Canada, 1980).

4. In Canada the baby-boom generation comprises those born during the high fertility period from post-World War II to the middle of the 1960s (1947-66). In the following period, fertility rates declined to below replacement levels resulting in a baby-bust generation (1967-80).

5. Harvey Krahn, "Quality of Work in the Service Sector," *General Social Survey Analysis Series* (Ottawa: Statistics Canada, 1992).

6. Côté, 9.

7. For example, the decreasing number of eligible entrants has been partially offset by the continued increase in the labour force participation rates of women. The decline in older workers has been compensated for by retirees returning to the labour force. Shelby Stewman, "Labour Market Opportunities for Middle-Aged and Older Workers," in Irving Bluestone, Rhonda J. Montgomery and John D. Owen, eds., *The Aging of the American Workforce* (Detroit: Wayne State University Press, 1990), 345-73.

8. John D. Owen, "An Aging Work Force? The Dog that didn't Bark," in Irving Bluestone, Rhonda J. Montgomery and John D. Owens, eds., *The Aging of the American Workforce,* 57-68.

9. Côté, 12; F.T. Denton and B.G. Spencer, "Population Aging, Labour Force Change and Promotion Prospects," *QSEP Research Report No. 30* (Hamilton: Faculty of Social Sciences, McMaster University, 1982), 9.

10. David K. Foot, "Population Ageing and Immigration Policy in Canada: Implications and prescriptions," *Population Working Paper No. 1* (Ottawa: Employment and Immigration, Canada, 1986).

11. The labour force participation rate for women is hypothesized to taper off in the near future for a number of reasons — women appear to be retiring earlier; increases in the labour force participation rates will have to occur just to maintain the current female share, and the growth in the female participation rate is likely to be slower as the rate approaches 100 percent. Côté, 10; P.L. McDonald and R.A. Wanner, *Retirement in Canada* (Toronto: Butterworths, 1990); David K. Foot, *Population Ageing and the Canadian Labour Force,* Discussion Paper on the Demographic Review, 7.

12. J.L. MacBride-King, *Work and Family; Employment Challenge of the '90s* (Compensation Research Centre: The Conference Board of Canada, 1990); W.B. Johnston and A.H. Packer, *Workforce 2000: Work and Workers for the 21st Century* (Indianapolis: Hudson Institute, Inc., 1987).

13. Personal communication with N. Charness, April, 1992.

14. Harry Bacas, "Desperately Seeking Workers," *Nation's Business* (February 1988), 16-23.

15. Economic Council of Canada, 165; Corak, 65-76; S.S. Rahman and S. Gera, "Long-Term Unemployment in Canada: Its Causes and Implications," in S. Gera, ed., *Canadian Unemployment: Lessons for the 80s and Challenges for the 90s*; Joseph A. Tindale, *Older Workers in an Aging Workforce* (Ottawa: National Advisory Council on Aging, 1991); G. Grenier, *Older Workers in an Aging Society: Trends, Theories and Policies* (Ottawa: Health and Welfare Canada, 1989).

16. David K. Foot and Rosemary A. Venne, "Population, Pyramids and Promotional Prospects," *Canadian Public Policy 18,* 4 (Dec. 1990), 387-98.

17. P.L. McDonald and R.A. Wanner, 123.

18. C. Kerr, J.T. Dunlop, F. Harbinson and C.A. Myers, eds., *Industrialization and Industrial Man* (1962; Hamonsworth: Penguin, 1973).

19. Mervin Y.T. Chen and Thomas G. Regan, *Work in the Changing Canadian Society* (Toronto: Butterworths, 1985).

20. Economic Council of Canada, *Good Jobs, Bad Jobs: Employment in the Service Economy*

(Ottawa: Minister of Supply and Services, 1990).

21. Krahn, 17-18; John Myles and Gail Fawcette, "Job Skills and the Service Economy," *Working Paper No. 4* (Ottawa: Economic Council of Canada, 1990); and J. Singelmann, *From Agriculture to Services* (Beverly Hills: Sage, 1978).

22. Economic Council of Canada, 52, 57-58.

23. Krahn, 31.

24. Peter B. Doeringer and David G. Terkla, "Business Necessity, Bridge Jobs and the Non-bureaucratic Firm," in Peter B. Doeringer, ed., *Bridges to Retirement: Older Workers in a Changing Labour Market* (Ithaca: ILR Press, 1990), 146-68.

25. Economic Council of Canada, 10-15.

26. *Ibid.,* 20-21.

27. Morissette, "Are Jobs in Large Firms Better Jobs?" *Perspectives on Labour and Income* 3 (Autumn 1991), 41-50. Krahn, 73, 137; Morissette, 41-43.

28. The growth in both goods and services is now concentrated among white-collar occupations. Technological change has been argued to be the major factor underlying the increasing concentration of goods sector growth in white-collar employment and the resulting convergence between the sectors in terms of occupational profiles. Economic Council of Canada, 32-53.

29. Economic Council of Canada, 90-91.

30. Earnest B. Akyeampong, "Older Workers in the Canadian Market," *The Labour Force* 43, 1 (Ottawa: Minister of Supply and Service, Nov. 1987).

31. Economic Council of Canada, 89-110; John Myles, "The Expanding Middle: Some Canadian Evidence on the Deskilling Debate," *Canadian Review of Sociology and Anthropology* 25, 3 (1988), 336-64; Johnson and Packer, 32-37; K. Spenner, "Deciphering Prometheus: Temporal Change in the Skill Level of Work," *American Sociological Review* 46 (1983), 824-37; D. Bell, *The Coming of Post-Industrial Society* (New York: Basic Books, 1973); H. Braverman, *Labor and Monoply Capital: The Degradation of Work in the Twentieth Century* (New York: Monthly Review Press, 1974).

32. John Myles and A. Hunter, "Formal Education and Initial Employment: Unravelling the Relationships between Schooling and Skills Over Time," *American Sociological Review* 53 (1988), 753-65.

33. Economic Council of Canada, 98-100.

34. *Ibid.,* 93-94.

35. B. Kuttner, "The Declining Middle," *The Atlantic Monthly* (July 1983), 60-72.

36. Côté, 12; Blossom Wigdor and David K. Foot, *The Over-Forty Society* (Toronto: James Lorimer and Co., 1988).

37. Economic Council of Canada, 81.

38. *Ibid.,* 72-81.

39. Krahn, 53.

40. Economic Council of Canada, 82.

41. P.L. McDonald and R.A. Wanner, "Part-time Work and the Older Worker in Canada," in B. Warme, K.L.P. Lundy and L.L. Lundy, *Working Part-Time: Risks and Opportunities* (New York: Praeger, 1992).

42. Economic Council of Canada, *Good Jobs, Bad Jobs,* 4.

43. Krahn, 107.

44. McDonald and Wanner, 196.

45. Rahman and Gera, 99.

46. Corak, 95.

47. P.L. McDonald and R.A. Wanner, *Retirement in Canada* (Toronto: Butterworths, 1990), 109-10; P.L. McDonald and R.A. Wanner, "Early Retirement Among Displaced Workers in Canada." Paper presented at the World Congress on Gerontology, Acapulco, Mexico, June, 1989.

48. Côté, 15; Economic Council of Canada, 64; Rahman and Gera, 110. Dave Gower, "Unemployment – Occupation Makes a Difference," *Perspectives on Labour and Income* 3 (Winter, 1991), 14-23.

49. Côté, 15.

50. Rahman and Gera, 110.

51. Doeringer and Terkla, 160-68.

52. There is considerable evidence that the determinants of early retirement, prior to age 65, on-time retirement at age 65, and late retirement after age 65, are different, as are the issues surrounding the determinants.

53. See P.L. McDonald and R.A. Wanner, *Retirement in Canada,* for an overview of these studies.

54. Graham S. Lowe, "Retirement Attitudes, Plans and Behaviour," *Perspectives on Work and Income* 3 (Autumn, 1991), 8-16.

55. C. Lindsay and M.S. Devereaux, "Canadians in the Pre-Retirement Years: A Profile of People Age 55-64," *Target Group Projects* (Ottawa: Ministry of Industry, Science and Technology, 1991).

56. Lowe, 14.

57. McDonald and Wanner, 81-95.

58. S. Ciffin and J. Martin, *Retirement in Canada: Summary Report* (Ottawa: Health and Welfare Canada, 1976); G.J. Bazzoli, "The Early Retirement Decision: New Empirical Evidence on the influence of Health," *The Journal of Human Resources* 20, 2 (1985), 214-34; F.J. Sammartino, "The Effects of Health on Retirement," *Social Security Bulletin* 50, 2 (1987), 31-47; O.S. Mitchell, "Pensions and Older Workers," in M.E. Borus, ed., *The Older Worker* (Madison: Industrial Relations Research Assoc., 1988), 151-68.

59. S. Ciffin, and J. Martin, *Retirement in Canada: When and Why People Retire* (Ottawa: Health and Welfare Canada, 1977); C. Kapsalis, "Pensions and the Work Decision," Paper presented at the annual meeting of the Canadian Economic Association, May, 1979; R. Baillargeon, "The Determinants of Early Retirement," *Canada's Mental Health* 303 (1982), 20-22.

60. P.L. McDonald and R.A. Wanner, "Socioeconomic Determinants of Early Retirement in Canada," *Canadian Journal on Aging* 3, 3 (1984), 105-16; Baillargeon, 20-22.

61. S. Ciffin and J. Martin, *Retirement in Canada: Summary Report.*

62. M. Minkler, "Research on the Health Effects of Retirement: An Uncertain Legacy," *Journal of Health and Social Behaviour* 22 (1981), 117-30.

63. Akyeampong, 87.

64. M. Gunderson and J. Pesando, "Eliminating Mandatory Retirement: Economics and Human Rights," *Canadian Public Policy* 6 (1980), 352-60.

65. United States Department of Labour, *Older Worker Task Force: Key Policy Issues for the Future* (Washington, D.C., June 1989).

66. Krahn, 132.

67. B. Rosen and T.H. Jerdee, *Older Employees: New Roles for Valid Resources* (Homewood, IL: Dow Jones-lrwin, 1985).

68. A.M. O'Rand and J.C. Henretta, "Delayed Career Entry, Industrial Pension Structure and Early Retirement in a Cohort of Unmarried Women," *American Sociological Review* 47 (1982), 365-73.

69. D. Galarneau, "Women Approaching Retirement," *Perspectives on Labour and Income* 3 (Autumn 1991), 28-39.

70. McBride-King, ix.

71. Peter B. Doeringer, *Turbulence in the American Workplace* (New York: Oxford University Press, 1991).

72. R.A. Wanner and P.L. McDonald, "Retirement, Public Pension Policy and Industrial Development: A Time Series Analysis," Paper presented at the annual meeting of the Canadian Sociology and Anthropology Association, Hamilton, Ontario, 1987. M. Gunderson and W.C. Riddell, *Labour Market Economics: Theory, Evidence and Policy in Canada* second edition (Toronto: McGraw-Hill Ryerson Ltd., 1988).

73. Health and Welfare Canada, *Monthly Statistics: Income Security Programs* (Jan-Dec., 1986), 8.

74. H. Frenken, "The Pension Carrot: Incentives to Early Retirement," *Perspectives on Labour and lncome* 3 (Autumn 1991), 18-27.

75. G.S. Fields and O.S. Mitchell, "Economic Determinants of the Optimal Retirement Age: An Empirical Investigation," *Journal of Human Resources* 19 (Spring 1984), 245-62; R.

Haveman, B. Wolfe and J. Warlick, "Labour Market Behaviour of Older Men: Estimates from a Trichotomous Choice Model," *Journal of Public Economics* 36 (1988), 153-75.

76. S. Bould, "Factors Influencing the Choice of Social Security Early Retirement Benefits," *Population Research and Policy Review* 5 (1986), 217-36.

77. Membership in employer-sponsored pension plans grew from about 19 percent of all Canadians 18 to 64 years of age in 1960 to 30 percent in 1980 and has remained stable since that time. Frenken, 22. Lowe, 15.

78. Frenken, 23.

79. J. Pesando and M. Gunderson, "Retirement Incentives Contained in Occupational Pension Plans and their Implication for the Mandatory Retirement Debate," *Canadian Journal of Economics* 21 (1988), 246-64.

80. Lowe, 13.

81. P.L. McDonald and R.A. Wanner, "Work Past Age 65 in Canada: A Socioeconomic Analysis," *Aging and Work* 5 (1982), 169-80.

82. *Ibid.,* 1980.

83. Gunderson and Pesando, 354.

84. F. Reid, "Economic Aspects of Mandatory Retirement: The Canadian Experience," *Industrial Relations* 43 (1) 1988, 101-14; Québec, Rapport triennial sur le efferts de la loi sur abolition de la retraite obligatoire (Québec: Ministere de la Main-d'oeuvre et de la sécurité du revenue, 1989).

85. Lowe, 14.

86. Ciffin and Martin, 52.

87. *Ibid.*, 20; Lowe, 9.

88. The recent rulings of the Supreme Court on mandatory retirement provide ample evidence of ageist attitudes to older workers. For example, one judgment ruled hospital policy reasonable on the grounds that "... older doctors are less able to contribute to hospitals' sophisticated practice." *Discovery,* "A Question of Discrimination," (Jan/Feb., 1989), 39; C. Bird and T. Fisher, "Thirty Years Later: Attitudes Towards the Employment of Older Workers," *Journal of Applied Psychology* 71 (1986), 515-17.

89. See for example, M. Doering, S.R. Rhodes and M. Schuster, *The Aging Worker* (Beverly Hills, CA: Sage, 1983); X. Gaullier, "The Management of Older Workers in a Flexible Career Cycle: The Case of France," *Ageing International* (Autumn/Winter 1986), 36-38; X. Gaullier, *La Deuxième Carrière: Ages, Emplois, Retraites* (Paris: Editions du Seuil, 1988).

90. N. Charness and E.A. Bosman, "Human Factors and Design for Older Adults," in J.E. Birren and K.W. Schaie, eds., *Handbook of Psychology of Aging,* second edition (San Diego: Academic Press Inc., 1990).

91. See P.L. McDonald and R.A. Wanner, *Retirement in Canada,* Chapter 4 for a review of the studies of late retirement.

92. R.F. Boaz, "Work as a Response to Low and Decreasing Real Income During Retirement," *Research on Aging* 9 (1987), 428-40; A. Fontana and J.H. Frey, "Post-Retirement Workers in the Labour Force," *Work and Occupation* 17 (1990), 355-61.

93. McDonald and Wanner, 179-80.

94. N. Morrow-Howell and J. Leon, "Life-Span determinants of work in retirement years," *Journal of Aging and Human Development* 27 (1988), 125-39.

95. National Council on Welfare, *Pension Reform* (Ottawa: National Council of Welfare, 1990).

96. M. Townson, "Pensions: Whose Responsible Anyway?" Keynote address presented at the annual meeting of the Canadian Association on Gerontology, Ottawa, Oct. 1989.

Lynn McDonald is an Associate Professor at the University of Toronto in the Faculty of Social Work. Mervin Y.T. Chen is a Professor of Sociology at Acadia University in Nova Scotia.

The Leisure Activities of the Elderly in New Brunswick

PIERRE OUELLETTE

According to Statistics Canada's Social Survey in 1986, people over the age of 65 had about eight hours of free time each day (Jones 1990, 29). At first blush, it would appear that the chunks of free time available to retired people allow them to lead full, enriching lives, the quality of which is raised in the process. The role of leisure in influencing personal well-being is an integral part of current retirement preparation sessions.

While Canadian interest in the potential of leisure as a factor in personal well-being has only recently been aroused, American researchers have devoted at least thirty years to the study (Kelly & Ross 1989, 47). Canadian research into leisure does not have such a long history. However, leisure studies programmes at Canadian universities have increased the amount of research in the field over the last few years. Since 1985, around ten studies into the leisure activities of the elderly have been done in New Brunswick alone.

The fact that New Brunswick has a significant Acadian community that is served by a thriving network of seniors' associations makes the province particularly suitable for the study of leisure among the elderly. Each of the two main linguistic groups lives and functions in its own language, has its own education system, and preserves its own distinct cultural heritage. Moreover, Aunger (1981, 15-18) sees these two main cultures as being made up of a number of smaller communities, each with a unique social structure based on its roots, traditional festivals, national symbols, etc.

Baudry (1966) describes the Acadians as a separate nation, martyrs to history. We recall briefly that after the Treaty of Utrecht in 1713, Acadians refused to swear allegiance to the British crown, as they were required to do. As punishment for their resistance, about 10,000 of them were deported, primarily to the American colonies, between 1755 and 1759. Between 1760 and 1800, many of them came back, often on foot, and set up home in the Maritimes, particularly in New Brunswick (Daigle 1982, 34-46; Thériault 1982, 47-55). In 1924, their epic story was immortalized by Longfellow in his famous "Evangeline, A Tale of Acadia," which was the touching story of two lovers who were separated by the deportation and who spent their lives trying to find each other again.

In order to compile a demographic profile of New Brunswick's elderly, it is useful first to take certain facts into account. According to the New Brunswick Senior Citizens' Bureau[1] (1992, 8-10, 15-21, 27-32, 48-53), the number of people aged 65 and over rose from 61,000 (9.0%) in 1976 to 78,700 (11.1%) in 1986. If this trend continues, the proportion of elderly people will reach 20% by 2021. In 1986, 57% of those 65 and over were women, mainly widows. Of those aged 90 and over, the proportion of married people was 40% for men and about 5% for women. Of the 17,620 older people living alone, nearly half of them were aged 65 or over, and 77% were women. English was the mother tongue of nearly 67% of them. Average personal income stood at just over $15,000 for men in 1989, and just over $10,000 for women. In 1986, 35,645 people aged 65 or over and living at home suffered from at least one physical handicap.

This article will give a summary of research conducted into the leisure activities of the elderly in New Brunswick. However, before embarking on the main points of our study, it will be helpful to those more unfamiliar with leisure studies to explain some of the definitions, theories, and the general thrust of the research that has been done up to now. So as to stay within the limitations of this paper, we will deal only with what is essential.[2]

Leisure—Definitions, Theories, Research

It is due in particular to the work of many respected authors—such as Thorstein Veblen, David Riesman, and Joffre Dumazedier—that leisure has been the subject of so many definitions and theories. Bammel and Bammel (1982, 132-139) list at least eight definitions and six theories of leisure currently in use. Three of these definitions are most widely employed.

A. Three significant definitions

Let us begin with the classical Aristotelian view. For this ancient Greek philosopher, leisure was all of the following: not having to work, a state of mind, an end in itself, and a way of developing the mind and the soul. For Aristotle, it was a thoughtful outlook which came close to a religious experience. In fact, Aristotle considered thought and music as the most refined forms of leisure.

Then, leisure was seen as a period of free time following work and upon fulfilment of various social obligations. This definition is especially accepted by researchers because it allows the notion of leisure to be quantified.

Finally, leisure is perceived to be a freely chosen and voluntarily accepted activity. Using this definition, leisure would become the generic term covering a range of recreational activities.

B. Theories of leisure and gerontology

Two theories are widely used to cover the relationship between work and leisure. On one hand, there is the theory of the compensation instinctively sought by a worker in order to build his/her leisure time, which is made up of the activities least compatible with that person's job. This is reminiscent of the famous image of the musician interested in history for relaxation, and of the historian becoming immersed in music so as to forget his historical work. On the other hand, the theory of generalization suggests integrating certain parts of one's job with leisure time. Consider, for example, manual labourers who do odd jobs in their spare time.

Two other theories of leisure are somewhat popular: the familiarity hypothesis and the theory of personal community. In the former, it is assumed that an individual acquires the habits necessary for social survival. The security obtained in this way appears more profitable than taking needless risks. In other words, leisure activities go along the same lines as the life experiences one is used to. As for the theory of personal community, it stresses the influence of the important people in one's circle of friends when choosing leisure activities.

Social gerontology suggests several additional theoretical approaches such as the activity theory, the disengagement theory, the continuity theory, the sub-culture theory, the personality theory, the age stratification model, etc.[3] Howe (1988, 448-463) shows that most of the studies of leisure among the elderly use the following theories: activity, disengagement, and continuity.

The activity theory holds that maintaining a high level of physical, social and intellectual activity upon retirement increases satisfaction with life. The disengagement theory, on the other hand, suggests that satisfaction comes from voluntarily reducing the number and the importance of the social roles held by the elderly person. The continuity theory holds that the smooth passage into the realities of old age comes from the uninterrupted pursuit of one's favourite pre-retirement activities after retirement.

C. American and Canadian research

We shall now look at the major areas of research in the U.S. and Canada into the leisure activities of the elderly.

1. The direction of American research

Howe (1988, 452-457) organizes American work in the area of leisure into four categories. The first deals particularly with the provision of programmes and recreation services. The second covers obstacles hindering participation. The third and fourth categories deal, respectively, with the time spent on leisure activities and with the theoretical constructs related to leisure participation.

Kelly and Ross (1989, 47-49) note that the study of leisure among the elderly has been dominated by two main issues: first, the relationship between age group and recreational activity, and second, the links between participation in leisure activities and gaining satisfaction from life.

For the first issue, it is clear that all the studies reveal that frequency of participation goes down as people get older. All the same, the fundamental difference between the various types of activity should not be ignored, nor should maintaining a high level of social interaction with family and friends.

Turning to the second issue, research reveals the link that exists between health, financial resources, and participation in leisure activities, and the satisfaction elderly people get from life.

Furthermore, Kelly and Ross (1989, 49-59) looked at four main research questions in the area of leisure among the elderly in terms of a personal resource index (e.g., income), different types of leisure activity and their relationship with life, motivating factors (e.g., family), and leisure as a factor in personal development and social identity. The results obtained suggest that the categorization of significant activities varies with respect to age cohorts, and contributes to defining a social identity stemming from leisure activities.

Finally, these authors propose a new seven-point research plan involving, among other things, not only the relationship between the type of activity and satisfaction with life at different times of life, but also the significance given to favourite and exceptional activities, according to aptitude and personal resources.

2. Some Canadian research

McPherson and Kozlik (1980, 114-120; 1987, 213-224) have listed the majority of Canadian studies profiling participation in terms of age group. The same authors have also done secondary analyses of participation in physical leisure activities based on data collected in a national survey.

These studies have shown that the older age cohorts seem less active in physical activity and that they take part in different recreational activities, at different levels, according to the age groups studied.

Each age group can be identified by varying participation rates depending on personal characteristics such as gender, education, and income. Although participation in physical activity is generally inversely proportional to age, it appears that, according to two national surveys conducted in 1976 and 1981, the percentage of elderly who are physically active rose from 30% to more than 50% over that period.

McPherson and Kozlik suggest two quite plausible explanations for this: first, the elderly are becoming involved in physical activity in greater numbers; second, the elderly that were polled more recently were more physically active in their youth and appear to value this type of activity in their later years. However, methodological difficulties, the need to use a firm conceptual framework, and the absence of any longitudinal studies prevent McPherson and Kozlik (1987, 225) from coming up with a definitive explanation for the decrease in physical activity with age. Nevertheless, they have what they consider three valid explanations stemming from the disengagement theory, the continuity theory, and the age stratification model.

After consulting most of the relevant Canadian and American studies, Delisle (1991, 135-144) identified the main trends that are likely to affect the supply and demand for leisure services for the elderly. Although the study was centred in Québec, the conclusions reached could be considered relatively applicable to the other provinces as well.

The author foresees a high demand for resources to organize physical activities, especially given the obvious advantages for those who participate. The elderly of the future will be better educated and will need better resources—this should see the demand for socio-cultural activities increase. Given that four per cent of elderly Canadians are pursuing studies of one kind or another, it is easy to predict an increase in future demand for education, either at the general interest or university level. In the area of social and tourism activities, new groups should be formed in line with tourism demands.

Lastly, in her study of aging in rural Québec, Keating (1991, 43) notes the difference in participation levels between the elderly in urban and rural areas. In particular, she remarks that the elderly in rural areas prefer leisure activities involving the family, the land, and their own age group and circle of friends.

Leisure activities of the elderly in New Brunswick: a collection of studies

This section will look at certain studies focussing on leisure activities of the elderly in New Brunswick, i.e., research articles, theses, and reports produced since 1985. These studies can be placed into six main categories: (a) the leisure activities of the members of seniors' clubs; (b) the activities of the members of the seniors' university in the south-east of the province; (c) the participation and satisfaction rates and the types of motivation; (d) the evaluation of physical ex-

Figure 1: Particpation in Six Activities by Level of Education

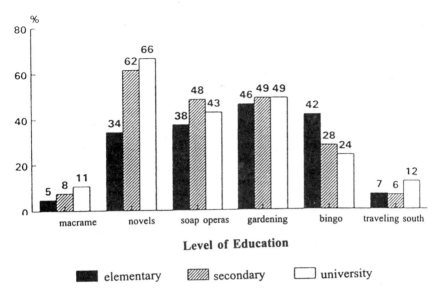

Level of Education

elementary   secondary   university

ercise programmes; (e) the effects of a leisure education workshop; and (f) the extent of interest in recreation.

A. The leisure activities of members of seniors' clubs

The first category, which deals with members of seniors' clubs, is subdivided further into five categories: (1) personal characteristics and leisure practices; (2) participation and interest: a multivariable approach; (3) the extent of travel activities among seniors' club members; (4) members of clubs on the Acadian peninsula; and (5) the leadership of club presidents.

In the first subdivision, personal characteristics and leisure practices, statistics illustrate in particular the extent of the variance in six specific activities with relation to variables such as age, gender, and socio-economic status. The data in these analyses came from a huge survey of 1,080 seniors' club members in New Brunswick. The questionnaire covered the interest and participation in 89 activities (Ouellette 1986, 259).

1. Personal characteristics and leisure practices

Current regulations allow club membership from the age of 50. However, the 50-60 age group represents only 12% while the 60-70 age group makes up 55% of club members. The 70-80 age group adds the remaining 33%.

Women represent 67% of the membership. Traditionally, seniors' clubs have always been frequented by women; nevertheless, the relatively small number of

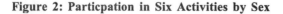

Figure 2: Particpation in Six Activities by Sex

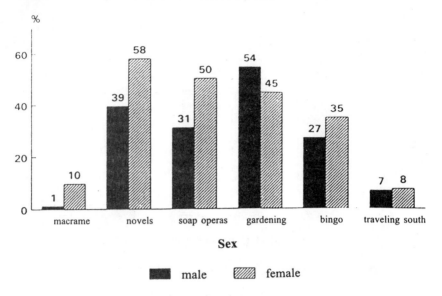

male members makes for some practical difficulties in certain activities, e.g. dance evenings.

The socio-economic makeup of the members has been measured using the socio-economic indices of Blishen and Roberts (1976, 71-79) and of Blishen and Carrol (1978, 352-371). These indices are calculated using the following three elements: educational level, occupational prestige, and income. Around 48% of club members scored between 30 and 60 points, considered here as average. There is an even distribution between francophones (48%) and anglophones (52%).

The ten most popular activities among the elderly are as follows: (1) church duties (88%); (2) reading newspapers (88%); (3) television news (84%); (4) talking with friends (82%); (5) listening to music on the radio (77%); (6) walking (74%); (7) having people visit (74%); (8) playing cards (73%); (9) listening to religious programmes (68%); and (10) the rosary (41%) among Catholics. The popularity of having visitors and talking with friends quashes the myth of the terrible isolation experienced by the elderly (Palmore 1980, 669-672). It is also interesting to note the popularity of walking—it is well known that access to transportation is a serious problem for the elderly (Ouellette, Vienneau & Thibeault 1990, 15, 18). It can be concluded that the popularity of walking is a practical necessity in many cases.

A study of participation rates in six everyday activities which show particular leisure trends, shows that reading novels (52%), watching soap operas (44%), and

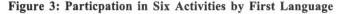

Figure 3: Particpation in Six Activities by First Language

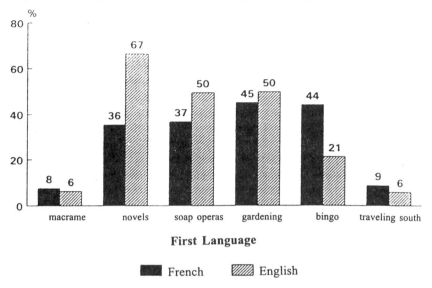

First Language

■ French ▨ English

gardening (48%) have average participation rates, whereas macramé (7%) and winter vacations in the sun (7%) have negligible participation rates. We must obviously take into account the seasonal nature of winter breaks in the south. We know informally that playing bingo is extremely popular among seniors' club members. Various public perceptions even indicate that it is the most popular activity. These beliefs notwithstanding, the participation rate for bingo is 32%.

While the popularity of activities varied according to certain personal characteristics, the amount of variation across different age groups was, on average, slight. The attraction of bingo and macramé decreases with age, but relatively little; for the 50-60, 60-70, and 70-80 age groups, the percentages are 38%, 33% and 28% respectively.

Macramé, reading, television serials, and bingo are more popular among women, while men prefer gardening. There are few notable gender differences in preferences for winter holidays in warm climates like Florida.

Participation rates vary with respect to the level of education of the elderly. As can be seen in Figure 2, those who have attended high school are more fond of television serials than those whose education stopped at the elementary level. Bingo is more likely to be played by the less educated, while reading appears more attractive to the elderly who went to high school and university. Elderly people who are former university students take more holidays in the south than those who attended only elementary or secondary school. This applies equally to macramé.

The less well-off on the socio-economic ladder are more inclined to be bingo players. Reading and southern vacations are activities more likely to be found among those who are on a higher socio-economic level. Also, those in a better economic position are more likely to watch television serials than those less fortunate. Anglophones read more and watch more television series, whereas francophones play more bingo and are more likely to take a winter holiday in the south.

The analyses presented above were conducted using one specific activity and one specific variable such as gender. This type of analysis is generally considered to be uni-variate, as opposed to multivariate. In the latter type of analysis, several variables are related to one another. Thus, an attempt is made to deal on the one hand with several groups of activities, and on the other with many demographic characteristics. This type of approach is increasingly common in the social sciences because of the complexity of the constructs under investigation. It is largely with this in mind, then, that two studies of the leisure pursuits of seniors' club members were undertaken (Ouellette 1986, 257-268; 1987, 1-20). This form of analysis goes by the name of "canonical analysis."

2. Participation and interest: a multivariate approach

As we have already noted, the sample comprised 1,080 elderly people who responded to a questionnaire with a total of 89 activities which, for the purposes of analysis, were divided into eight leisure activity categories: (a) civic, (b) intellectual, (c) artistic, (d) media-related, (e) physical, (f) social, (g) religious, and (h) travel-related.

The lowest participation rates were in the travel, artistic, and physical categories. Average rates were seen in the intellectual and civic categories, while the most popular leisure activities fell into the religious, social, and media-related groups.

More specifically, the study revealed that single or widowed anglophone women of a high socio-economic level prefer artistic, intellectual or media-related activities to physical ones. It will certainly come as no surprise to learn that francophone women participate in more religious activities. Finally, the study showed that a high socio-economic level, a younger age, good health, and participation in a "New Horizons" programme were conducive to activities in each of the eight categories.

The second part of the research, conducted using the same data, also looked at the relationship between two sets of variables, one being the same participation categories as above, while the other was a corresponding set of categories dealing with the leisure interest, aside from personal characteristics.

As a general rule, interest is proportional to participation. However, interest in a given activity does not necessarily translate into real participation. Constraints such as a lack of financial resources or transportation may hinder participation in recreational activities.

Without getting into great detail on canonical analyses, suffice it to say that at a statistical level, the results obtained clearly surpass those of the previous analysis. In fact, taking personal characteristics and interest in various types of leisure activity into account simultaneously allows for clearer prediction and explanation of the participation of members of seniors' clubs. More specifically, the most significant result shows the correlation between the religious tendencies of francophones and participation in religiously-based activities.

The second most important result shows that interest in artistic, intellectual, media-related and tourist activities, as well as a better level of education, a high socio-economic level, marriage, and being an anglophone, were all factors which led to greater participation in artistic, intellectual and media-related activities.

It is surprising to note that none of the other personal characteristics influenced, in any significant way, the other results stemming from the participation-interest relationship for specific types of activity. Therefore, the study stresses the need, in any leisure planning policy, to take into account not only the variables of leisure interests, but also personal characteristics.

3. Travel among seniors' club members

Travel features are one of the activities valued by seniors. To those who can afford it and who are healthy enough, travel offers obvious and varied benefits. Taking into account the number of short bus tours that exist, Leblanc (1986, 19-24) thought it relevant to look particularly at ten travel activities undertaken by seniors' club members. Note that Leblanc's data came from the same set of data used in the previous two studies.

The three most popular travel activities among the elderly are the following: (1) trips to visit friends or family in nearby towns and cities; (2) car trips; and (3) shopping trips to other towns and cities.

Some statistical analyses show that trips by car are favoured by men, whereas women would prefer organized bus tours and would take more shopping trips out of town. Anglophones travel more by car and go abroad more often. Francophones tend to visit more historical sites and travel to warmer climates like Florida. Married couples prefer organized bus trips, while widowed people are more inclined to visit family and friends who live nearby.

4. Seniors' clubs on the Acadian peninsula

In 1990, Robichaud (143-145, 176-190) conducted a study of 663 seniors' club members on the Acadian peninsula, in the north-east of New Brunswick. The aim of the study was to determine what factors affected the problem of continuing education among retirees. The data collected reflected personal characteristics, feelings about retirement, and the values and educational needs of the elderly.

Like clubs in other part of New Brunswick, women were in the majority, at around 65%. While 84% of the respondents considered themselves to be too old, they agreed on the importance of good health, family success, religion, and free time. For these seniors, further education—especially in an institutional setting—was of secondary importance. Since retiring, these club members had felt happy and fulfilled and had the distinct feeling of having had a successful life.

In this survey, the respondents were asked about the importance they would place on eleven values, both now and when they were 20. Their values for the present day ranked as follows: (1) family, (2) health, (3) friendship, (4) love, and (5) faith. However, as far as they could remember, they would have ranked the values as follows when they were 20: (1) work, (2) friendship, (3) faith, (4) family, and (5) love. Despite some only slight variations, we can see an increase in the importance placed on health and family during old age.

Also, it is particularly interesting to note that among the values of freedom, free time, and leisure (by definition three closely related concepts), there is an important shift in the priority given to them at the two age levels. At 20, freedom, free time, and leisure were ranked at around 67%, 60%, and 67% respectively, while at retirement, these figures rose to around 88%, 77% and 82% respectively. This shows the increasing importance of leisure in the lives of retired people.

In terms of attendance at their seniors' club, 66% regularly attend activities, except for the more educated among them. The main motivating factors are meeting people and making new friends. In addition, a total of 53% confirm that attending a club has changed certain aspects of their life for the better.

5. Leadership of club presidents

If there is one astonishing element to surface in a discussion of seniors' clubs, it must be the quality of the leaders. It is well known that the elderly are quite capable of organizing their club activities independently. In fact, the quality of club programmes can seldom be attributed to the intervention of social service professionals or leisure specialists.

Vienneau and Ouellette's study (1987, 100) supports this insofar as clubs are led by efficient seniors. However, leadership styles vary according to the seniors' mother tongue. Anglophone leaders find themselves at the helm of smaller clubs and administrative groups, and devote less time to club business. In such cases, the leadership style adopted is more open and is centred more on the needs of members. On the other hand, francophone leaders are in charge of larger clubs, which means they must devote more time to the running of club business.

B. Activities of members of the seniors' university of the south-east

There are around 150 seniors' universities in Europe, Australia, and North America. The first was founded in Toulouse, France, by Pierre Vellas in 1973. The goals, structures and activities of the universities are extremely varied as a result of their cultural milieux (Delisle 1991, 64-67).

Canada has around fifteen seniors' universities. The Seniors' University of the South-East (UTA) in Moncton, the second oldest in the country, is considered one of the most dynamic. Founded in 1977, UTA offers its members a process of educational development. It has, in the past, made a variety of educational and cultural services available to its elderly clientele. For example, the physical exercise programme, "Grouille ou rouille" (which loses much in its literal translation, "Be active or go rusty"), has met with great success, attracting nearly 800 people each week for physical exercise activities (Ouellette, Roussel & Schofield 1991, 5-7).

It was with members of the Moncton UTA that a study was considered to look at the relationship between personal characteristics, satisfaction, and participation in leisure activities (Ouellette, Nowlan & Ulmer 1987, 41-54).

Most of the 511 participants in the study were female, francophone, married, and of a low to average socio-economic status; a little more than half of them had been taking physical exercise courses for at least two years. The data show that those who were older, had more education, and were better off were more likely to participate in activities involving reading and popular entertainment, activities in organized groups, as well as intellectual and social activities. Furthermore, being male, having taken exercise courses for a long time, and expressing pleasure with leisure activities were all conducive to participation in the following five leisure categories: (1) physical, (2) parish-based, (3) organized group, (4) reading, and (5) popular entertainment. Finally, women, and those expressing a high degree of satisfaction with leisure activities, got involved more in social, parish-based, and group activities.

It is clear that physically active seniors are also active in other areas. We are faced, therefore, with a syndrome of generalized activity.

C. Leisure: participation, satisfaction, and styles of motivation

Losier (1991, 26-31) looked at various types of motivation among a group of 102 elderly people from Moncton, with relation to participation in, and satisfaction with, leisure activities.

The motivation scale had been prepared by Vallerand and O'Connor (1991, 226-228), following the self-determination theory of Deci and Ryan (1985, 43-112), which was based on three main elements: the determining factors, the types of motivation, and the consequences. The study in question was based on the following four motivation styles: intrinsic motivation, self-determined extrinsic motivation, non-self-determined extrinsic motivation, and amotivation.

It should be noted here that intrinsic motivation in an individual is demonstrated by the pleasure gained from a given activity, by a feeling of competence and self-determination, and by a sense of inner causality. In the case of self-determined extrinsic motivation, participation in an activity comes from reasons other than pleasure or interest. Participation in a certain activity could be motivated by the desire to make new acquaintances rather than by the pleasure derived from the activity itself—this would be self-determined extrinsic motivation. When an activity is performed for anticipated benefits, such as walking on the advice of a doctor, the motivation is categorized as non-self-determined extrinsic. The results of the study show that participation in leisure activities is linked to intrinsic motivation, self-determined extrinsic motivation, and a self-assessment of health. Leisure satisfaction is linked to intrinsic motivation and participation in leisure. Also, amotivation is linked very slightly to leisure satisfaction.

D. Evaluation of physical exercise programmes

Participation rates in physical activity among the elderly are generally low. Because of this, gerontologists—as well as civil servants—quickly sensed a need to vigorously promote the benefits of physical activity during old age. At the same time, seniors' groups created their own physical exercise programmes. In New Brunswick, two such programmes are worthy of comment: one at the Seniors' University of the South-East in Moncton, and the "Seniors' Pro-Action" programme in Edmundston.

These programmes were already subsidized by the provincial government and had been running for several years when the former Ministry of Tourism, Leisure, and Heritage ordered an evaluation of physical exercise programmes for the elderly, to include the two mentioned above. This evaluation, made available to Gionet, Couturier and Vienneau (1990, 12-16), was conducted by asking 1000 seniors to complete a lengthy questionnaire.

Energy, health, physical condition, and physical well-being were among the major motivating factors driving the elderly to participate in a structured programme of physical activity. Surprising as it may seem, staying slim and young-looking was not an issue. Persevering with the activity was put down to respect for the ability and the enthusiasm of the facilitators, acquiring healthy habits and an increased sense of well-being. These benefits were noted especially in the areas of joint movement, muscle strength, and stress management. Almost 32% of the participants said they had reduced their intake of medication as a result.

Those conducting the evaluation concluded that the programmes offered by the south-eastern UTA and Seniors' Pro-Action were highly effective, estimating that such programmes led to considerable health care savings for the province.

The establishment of a physical exercise programme across New Brunswick seemed, as a result, to be highly desirable.

E. Effects of a leisure education workshop

Going beyond the measurement of leisure participation and its motivating factors, we must consider the methods used to educate seniors in the leisure values proposed by the specialists. This involves exploring how the identification of leisure values can lead to changes in recreational behaviour. With this in mind, small group seminars have been set up to discuss such values, exploring themes such as time management and decision making. In order to assess the impact of a leisure education workshop on leisure motivation, participation, and satisfaction, 27 seniors participated in a two-day session in Moncton, conducted by seven facilitators (Ouellette 1988, 148-158). After comparing the various results of the study using a pre-test and a post-test, the researchers found that a workshop of this length could not have enough impact to noticeably change motivation and satisfaction levels. However, changes in participation levels were detected, including a drop in participation in organized group activities, and an increase in participation in religious activities, especially among women. The importance given to value identification in this workshop probably led participants to rethink certain aspects of their behaviour. The elderly must, therefore, be led to reassess their connection with certain associations and to draw their own conclusions, principally of their involvement is not based on intrinsic motivation. The women becoming more aware if the benefits they already gained from their religious activities, however, only led them to become more involved.

Although the size of the sample was relatively small in this study, and even with results that were less conclusive than expected, there is justification in doing another study with a tighter research plan and a workshop of greater length.

Conclusion

In the past, many people were reluctant to become involved with groups whose sole concern was the elderly. This resistance came, most likely, from the less than glowing image that society had of aging. Today, many of the myths surrounding old age have disappeared, leading to some increase in involvement. This is beneficial for many people; clubs make possible the establishment of new friendships, the launch of new recreation programmes, and involvement in a number of community events. If the quality of the leadership can be maintained, it would not be unrealistic to predict that these clubs could continue to contribute more to the personal and collective well-being of their members.

These clubs generally attract a membership composed, for the most part, of women and seniors of average socio-economic status. Members also show a certain interest in educational leisure activities, provided they are not within an institutional context. In addition to placing tremendous value on health, family life, and religion, they stress the importance of free time.

If the studies dealing with the range of seniors' club members' recreational behaviour patterns are examined, several conclusions emerge quite clearly. First, many of the results obtained are supported by studies conducted elsewhere. Nevertheless, it must be stressed that the major distinguishing factor of the New Brunswick studies is that of the two main linguistic groups. We recall, for example, that anglophones are more inclined towards car trips and foreign travel.

Religious and social activities, as well as those related to mass media, like reading newspapers, are extremely popular. Also, certain variables such as gender, age, socio-economic status, family situation, and linguistic group influence both participation and interest in certain activities or types of activity. Nevertheless, it is clearly recreational interest, as opposed to personal or demographic characteristics, that best determine leisure participation.

Concerned about maintaining their health and energy for as long as possible, seniors are increasingly becoming involved in physical activity. Structured physical exercise programmes are in particular demand. It is also interesting to note that those who participate in physical activity also tend to take part in other forms of leisure activity. This leads strongly to greater satisfaction with leisure activities.

Despite the currently healthy state of leisure participation, certain programmes must be set up in order to further expand available activities. Leisure education sessions appear to be desirable. However, these sessions will only be effective if they are of a reasonable length (around forty hours, for example) and particularly if they have realistic objectives. It would be ineffective to try to change negative attitudes towards leisure in just one evening. This example may seem a little odd, but most often that is the time allotted to the theme of leisure in many retirement preparation sessions.

It is probably useful to conclude with some directions for future research. First and foremost, it would be good to pay particular attention to the development of credible and appropriate measurement systems. Considering the predominantly rural nature of New Brunswick society and the presence there of two important linguistic groups, these two variables should play a greater role. The large number of intervention programmes created for the elderly and for researchers should be focused more specifically on evaluative research, particularly for assessing the effectiveness of physical exercise courses. Also, the increasing popularity of seniors' clubs and the factors motivating seniors to become involved in that sort of lifestyle should be the subject of more intensive research. Given the governmental priority placed on maintaining the independence of the elderly, it will be important to assess the role of leisure in maintaining and pursuing an active lifestyle. Finally, future studies should look at leisure practices of a more representative elderly population instead of smaller segments like seniors' clubs, seniors' universities, and residents of apartment buildings.

NOTES

1. This report includes statistics from both the New Brunswick Ministry of Health and Community Services and Statistics Canada.

2. For those who wish to expand their understanding of theories and definitions in leisure, here are some additional references: (Definitions): Murphy 1981, 13-79; (Theories): Goodale & Godbey 1988, 1-30; Kelly 1987, 1-41; Lanfant 1972, 62-196; Iso-Ahola 1980, 1-43, 183-271.

3. For a complete description of these and other theories, see McPherson 1990, 122-149; Roadburg 1985, 44-69.

References

Aunger, E. *In search of political stability: A comparative study of New Brunswick and Northern Ireland* (Montréal: McGill-Queen's Press, 1981).

Bammel, G. and L. Burrus-Bammel. *Leisure and human behavior* (Dubuque, IA: Wm. C. Brown, 1982).

Baudry, R. *Les Acadiens d'aujourd'hui: Rapport de recherche préparé pour la Commission royale d'enquête sur le bilinguisme et le biculturalisme* (Moncton, N.B: Auteur, 1966).

Blishen, B.R. and W.K. Carrol. "Sex differences in a socioeconomic index for occupations in Canada," *Canadian Review of Sociology and Anthropology* 15 (1978): 352-71.

Blishen, B.R. and A. Roberts. "A revised socioeconomic index for occupations in Canada," *Canadian Review of Sociology and Anthropology* 13 (1976): 71-79.

Bureau pour citoyens aînés. *Les citoyens aînés du Nouveau-Brunswick: Un rapport sociodémographique* (Fredericton, N.B.: Ministère de la santé et des services communautaires, Auteur, 1990).

Daigle, J. "Acadia, 1604-1763: An historical synthesis," *The Acadians of the maritimes,* Ed. J. Daigle. (Moncton: Centre d'études acadiennes, 1982), 17-46.

Deci, E.L. and R.M. Ryan. *Intrinsic motivation and self-determination in human behavior,* (New York: Plenum Press, 1985).

Delisle, M. *Un âge à dorer: Analyse des principales tendances permettant de caractériser l'offre et la demande de services de loisir destinés à la clientèle des personnes âgées* (Québec: Université Laval, Centre de recherche sur les services communautaires, 1991).

Gionet, N., H. Couturier et J.G. Vienneau. *Évaluation des programmes de conditionnement physique des citoyens aînés du Nouveau-Brunswick* (Moncton: Université de Moncton, Institut de leadership, École d'éducation physique et de loisir, 1990).

Goodale, T. and G. Godbey. *The evolution of leisure: Historical and philosophical perspective* (State College, PA: Venture, 1988).

Howe, C. "Selected social gerontology theories and older adult leisure involvement: A review of the literature," *The Journal of Applied Gerontology* 6 (1988): 448-63.

Iso-Ahola, S. *The social psychology of leisure and recreation* (Dubuque, IA: Wm. C. Brown, 1980).

Jones, M. "L'emploi du temps des personnes âgées," *Tendances sociales canadiennes* (été 1990): 28-29.

Keating, N. *Aging in rural Canada* (Toronto: Butterworths, 1991).

Kelly, J. *Freedom to be: A new sociology of leisure* (New York: MacMillan, 1987).

Kelly, J. and J. Ross. "Later-life leisure: Beginning a new agenda," *Leisure Sciences* 11 (1989): 47-49.

Lanfant, M.F. *Les théories du loisir: sociologies et idéologies* (Paris: Presses universitaires de France, 1972).

Leblanc, M. *Le tourisme chez les membres des clubs d'âge d'or du Nouveau-Brunswick* (Lyon: Université de Lyon II, 1986). Thèse de maîtrise non publiée.

Longfellow, H.W.O. *Evangeline: A tale of Acadia* (Chicago: A. Flanagan, 1924).

Losier, G. *Les styles motivationnels, la satisfaction et la participation dans les loisirs chez les personnes âgées* (Moncton: Université de Moncton, 1991). Thèse de maîtrise non publiée.

McPherson, B. *Aging as a social process (2nd ed.)* (Markham: Butterworths, 1990).

McPherson, B. and C. Kozlik. "Age patterns in leisure participation: The Canadian Case," *Aging in Canada: Social perspectives*. Ed. V.M. Marshall, 3rd ed. (Don Mills: Fitzhenry & Whiteside, 1987), 211-27.

McPherson, B. and C. Kozlik. "Canadian leisure patterns by age: Disengagement, continuity or ageism," *Aging in Canada: Social perspectives* Ed. V.M. Marshall, 113-22.

Murphy, J. *Concepts of leisure (2nd ed.)* (Englewood Cliffs, NJ: Prentice-Hall, 1981).

Ouellette, P. "Les effets d'un atelier d'éducation/counseling en loisir sur certaines variables chez les personnes âgées," *Canadian Journal on Aging* 7 (1988): 148-58.

Ouellette, P. *Les caractéristiques démographiques, l'intérêt et la participation au loisir des aîné(e)s* (Moncton: Université de Moncton, Centre d'études du vieillissement, 1991).

Ouellette, P. "The leisure participation and enjoyment patterns of French and English-speaking members of senior citizens' clubs in New Brunswick, Canada," *Canadian Journal on Aging* 5 (1986): 257-68.

Ouellette, P. "Personnes âgées à titre de participants," *Aging into the twenty-first century*. Ed. C. Blais (North York: Captus University, 1991), 102-08.

Ouellette, P., J. Nowlan et H. Ulmer. "Les loisirs des personnes âgées suivant des cours de conditionnement physique," *Revue de l'Université de Moncton* 20 (1987): 41-54.

Ouellette, P., H. Roussel et L. Schofield. *Rapport d'évaluation du projet Vieillir en santé de l'Université du 3e âge du sud-est du Nouveau-Brunswick* (Moncton: Université de Moncton, Centre d'études du vieillissement, 1991).

Ouellette, P., J.G. Vienneau et J. Thibault. *Vers l'élaboration d'une politique du loisir des aîné(e)s au Nouveau-Brunswick* (Moncton: Université de Moncton, Centre d'études du vieillissement, 1990).

Palmore, E. "The facts on aging quiz: A review of findings," *The Gerontologist* 20 (1980): 669-72.

Roadburg, A. *Aging: Retirement, leisure and work in Canada* (Toronto: Methuen, 1985).

Robichaud, V. *La personne retraitée et la problématique d'une éducation permanente aux derniers virages de la vie* (Grenoble: Université des sciences sociales de Grenoble, 1990). Thèse de doctorat non publiée.

Thériault, L. "Acadia, 1963-1978," *The Acadians of the Maritimes.* Ed. J. Daigle (Moncton: Centre d'études acadiennes, 1982), 47-86.

Vallerand, R.J. et B.P. O'Connor. "Construction et validation de l'échelle de motivation pour les personnes âgées (EMPA)," *Journal international de psychologie* 26 (1991): 219-40.

Vienneau, J.G. et P. Ouellette. "Le leadership chez les aîné(e)s des clubs d'âge d'or," *Canadian Journal on Aging* 6 (1987): 97-104.

Pierre Ouellette is an associate researcher at the Centre for Studies in Aging, and professor of leisure studies in the School of Physical Education and Leisure at the University of Moncton. His research focusses mainly on the recreational behaviour of the elderly.

Family Relationships and Support in Later Life

CAROLYN J. ROSENTHAL AND JAMES GLADSTONE

Introduction

Contemporary families, which are very different in structure and dynamics from families in the past, face unprecedented challenges as well as historically new opportunities. There is a persistent belief in North America that older people are abandoned by their families — neglected and, when they can no longer care for themselves, placed in institutions. This belief is, in fact, a myth. Rather, most older people are actively involved in supportive family relationships. Of course, the family relations of some older people are not completely harmonious. As is true for people of any age, the family relations of older adults consist of a mixture of positive and negative feelings and actions. The overall pattern, however, is one of mutual concern and involvement. While some older people are estranged from their children and thereby lend support to the belief in abandonment, these are relatively rare exceptions.

One misconception is that older people no longer belong to families once their children have grown up and married. Thus, it is helpful to begin by considering the question, "What is a family?" Families are formed by persons connected to one another either through biological ties or through the social tie of marriage. This definition implies several types of families. Social scientists have traditionally referred to nuclear families as those consisting of parents and children living together in one household. Individuals are typically members of two nuclear families — the one they are born into and the one they form when they marry and have children. Focusing on the nuclear family, however, diverts attention away from the fact that most children, after they marry and have children, continue to be actively involved with their parents and the family into which they were born.

It is important to recognize the diversity in Canadian families. Some people remain single throughout their lives, yet are actively involved in family relationships. Not all families include children. Not all families include two parents. And, not all families are formed through marriage. Moreover, lesbian and gay couples may form long-term unions that comprise families in social terms.

Changing Families

With respect to the impact of aging on family life, in many respects today's families sail in uncharted waters. Families have more members in older generations than they did in the past, and fewer members in younger generations. Because women typically outlive their husbands, the grandparent and great-grandparent generations often include mostly widows.

Since most people today live into old age, the duration of family ties is greater than in the past. Parents and children may now share as many as 50 years together.[1] Among persons born in 1910, only 16 percent of persons aged 50 had a surviving parent. Among persons born in 1930, this had increased to 49 percent, and among those born in 1960, 60 percent will have a surviving parent.[2] Marital ties, for those who remain married, also extend over a much greater length of time than in the past. The grandparent and grandchild relationship may extend well into the grandchild's adult years.

The longer duration of family ties has both positive and negative implications. On the positive side, there is increased potential for adults in families to form bonds that grow over time as a result of shared experiences and meanings. Moreover, the fact that there are fewer people in each generation may mean that family members have more opportunity to invest themselves in each of their kin relationships.[3] It is also noteworthy that, because of the sex difference in life expectancy, women experience longer duration of ties with children and grandchildren.

Two potentially negative aspects of the increased duration of family ties bear mention. First, where family relationships are conflict-ridden, this increased duration may simply prolong unhappy relationships. Second, increased duration means that a growing proportion of adults experience their parents' frailty and need for care.

The trend for women to work in the paid labour force is a social change that also affects older families. Because women are typically the major care-givers to family members, the potential for conflict between work and family responsibilities is of concern. Employment may constrain the ability of adult children to provide care to impaired elderly parents, although employment may also enhance care-giving; for example, by providing financial resources with which to purchase care. These issues are discussed in more detail in the section below on employment and care-giving.

Another social change is the significant increase in divorce. Divorce among today's elderly is unusual; in 1986, only 2.2 percent of older people were divorced.[4] Divorce in the "middle" generation (that is, among adult children) is much more common and affects older people in a variety of ways. They may be called on for help in providing money or a home, caring for grandchildren, or helping a non-custodial parent maintain contact with his or her children. Divorce may constrain the ability of a middle-aged daughter or son to provide social support to frail parents.

Family Relationships and Family Support in Later Life
Marital Relationships

Among Canadians aged 65 and older, over half (56 percent) are married.[5] While the likelihood of being married decreases over the course of later life, gender differences in marital status are quite dramatic. Among men, the percentage who are still married drops from 83 percent for men in their late sixties to 50 percent for men in their late eighties. Among women, the comparable percentages are 58 percent and 10 percent, respectively. Thus, most men have wives in later life but, once they enter their seventies, only a minority of women have husbands.

Researchers have been interested in how marriages change over time and in the quality of marriage in later life. In a study of the "endurance of love," Jane Traupmann and Elaine Hatfield distinguished between "passionate" love, "a state of intense absorption in another," and "companionate" love, "the affection we feel for those with whom our lives are deeply entwined."[6] Although they found a decline in both passionate and companionate love over time, they concluded that the decline was slight and that many couples enjoy intimate marital relationships in their later years. Some studies have tried to determine whether marital satisfaction diminishes over time, but findings have been somewhat conflicting. Most research indicates greater satisfaction expressed by the young and the old, and less by persons in middle age.[7]

How older couples divide responsibilities for household tasks may be related to marital satisfaction. Some studies have found that elderly couples who had less traditional or more equitable divisions of household responsibility reported greater marital satisfaction.[8] The complexity of this issue, however, is illustrated in a study by Jennifer Mason.[9] Not only were husbands and wives found to have gender-linked roles that did not appreciably change in later life, but wives felt ambivalent about changing to less traditional divisions of responsibility. Although they would have liked more help from their husbands, they wanted to be able to direct this assistance since they felt their domestic expertise was a source of control or power in the marital relationship.

Sometimes marital partners are on conflicting paths in terms of personal goals at particular life stages. Older men may turn towards their wives, wanting increased affiliation, at the same time that older women desire new roles outside the family.[10]

Retirement may have a positive or negative effect on the marital relationship. Most research has examined retirement among traditional couples; that is, a retiring male and a full-time homemaker. Among such couples, wives may experience a loss of personal freedom and autonomy with the increased presence of the retired husband.[11] However, most couples appear to negotiate changes in roles and establish new patterns of interdependence successfully.

Husbands and wives continue to provide support to each other in the later years, for example, by anticipating care should one of the partners become ill or by acting as a confidant.[12] There is also evidence, however, that marital exchanges of emotional support and health-related support decline somewhat over the course of late life.[13]

Widowhood

Most older Canadian women, but a minority of men, experience widowhood. This difference results from the joint impact of the sex difference in life expectancy and the social custom for women to marry men somewhat older than themselves. Among women aged 65-69, 30.1 percent are widowed, whereas only 6.5 percent of men in that age group are widowed. By age 75-79, 55.8 percent of women are widowed, compared to 16.3 percent of men.[14]

Widowhood is both an event — the loss of the spouse — and a process which extends over time. Widowhood has been deemed by those who have experienced it to have more profound effects than any other life event.[15] Initially, the widowed person experiences bereavement, a period characterized by intense grief, feelings of meaninglessness, apathy, disorganization of the widowed person's world, and identity confusion resulting from the loss of a central aspect of the self.[16] Over time, grief becomes less intense, the widowed person begins to reorganize and rebuild social relationships, and to construct a new identity as a single person.

Widowhood has a profound impact on social, emotional, physical and economic well-being. Widowed persons show higher rates of depression, mortality, and mental illness, although these effects lessen over time.[17] Being widowed, especially for women, is related to experiencing serious financial problems.[18] In Canada, almost half of unattached elderly women, most of whom are widows, are poor, although the proportion decreased somewhat during the 1980s.[19]

Children, especially daughters, are key figures in the support systems of the widowed elderly. Widowed elderly women have even more contact with their adult children than do married elderly women. Children are one of the preferred sources of support for advice, tangible help, or socio-emotional support.[20]

For widows, siblings may become important sources of social support. Widows appear to have more contact with siblings, to feel greater emotional closeness to siblings, and to show greater reliance on siblings for help with personal troubles than do married women.[21] The increased reliance on siblings is especially pronounced among widows who are childless or whose children are geographically distant.[22]

Remarriage

Among older people who become widowed, remarriage is relatively uncommon. Most elderly Canadians who have remarried have done so after age 65 and following widowhood rather than divorce.[23] This is so because divorce is very uncommon among the current elderly population. The central reason for remarriage among older people is a desire for companionship, as well as a desire to be useful and to feel that one is contributing to an intimate other's happiness. The success of remarriage is related to sharing common interests, receiving support or encouragement from friends and relatives, especially adult children, having adequate income, and not living in the home of one of the partners after remarriage, if she or he had been widowed.[24]

Men are much more likely than women to remarry in later life. They have more potential partners, partly because women outlive men and partly because it has been more socially acceptable for men to remarry persons younger than themselves. Remarriage may also be more attractive to men since they may find it more difficult to take care of the domestic aspects of life on their own. In contrast, women may value the independence that widowhood can bring, and not want to play, again, the role of nurse or care-giver at some point in the future.

Parent-Child Relationships

About 80 percent of Canadians aged 65 and over have at least one living child. Among older people who have children, a majority live in the same city as a child and the vast majority live within a 1-1/2 hour's drive.[25] Few older people share a household with a child, but this should not be interpreted as evidence of neglect by children. Most older people prefer to live near but not with a grown child. When asked where they would like to live if they could no longer live on their own, older people say they would prefer to move to a seniors' facility rather than live with a child.[26]

Supportive exchanges in the form of contact, emotional support, and tangible assistance characterize the relationships between older Canadians and their adult children. Between two-thirds and three-quarters of older parents see a child weekly or more often, and about half speak to a child on the telephone every day or two.[27] Some of this contact is likely associated with the provision of assistance. In general, older parents both give help to and receive help from their adult children. Emotional support is the most commonly exchanged type of help. Older people give more child care, financial assistance, and advice than they receive, while children give more practical assistance such as help with personal services, household chores, home repairs and personal care.[28] Even if help is not actually provided, one important aspect of support between parents and children is simply knowing that help will be there if it is needed.

Social class is associated with differences in parent-child relations. Working-class families tend to have less geographical mobility, meaning parents and children live somewhat closer to one another than is the case in middle-class families. This results, among other things, in more frequent face-to-face contact.[29] Working-class elderly persons receive more help from children than do middle-class elderly persons. Moreover, in working-class families, help tends to take the form of providing services, while in middle-class families help is provided through gifts or money. In working-class families, reciprocal exchange is more common than in middle-class families where the pattern is for help to flow downward, from older to younger generations.

Parent-child relations are also patterned by gender. Daughters are in greater contact with elderly parents and, as noted in a later section, are more likely than sons to become primary care-givers to an impaired elderly parent.[30] Women are central kin-keepers in maintaining family relations and the mother-daughter tie is the strongest intergenerational tie.[31]

Sibling Relationships

Among family relationships, the sibling relationship is distinctive because of the combined factors of long duration and shared early childhood family experiences. Because of the duration of relationships and the intimate sharing of childhood history, siblings provide connections to the past and can serve as "anchors" for personal identity and biography.

Most older people (80-85 percent) have a living sibling.[32] However, the number of surviving siblings drops sharply with age, with the result that the availability of siblings to provide support to very old people is somewhat limited.

Among those older people who have siblings, 29 percent of men and 52 percent of women see a sibling on a monthly basis or more often.[33] Contact by telephone is slightly more frequent. Single and childless elderly have more contact with siblings than do persons who have children or a spouse.[34] Even when siblings do not have direct contact with one another, the wider family network provides a basis for indirect contact through intermediaries. For example, parents serve as links between siblings, keeping them informed about each other. Ritual occasions such as holidays and birthdays also serve to keep siblings in contact.[35] While most older people do not turn to siblings for help, most feel that siblings would help if needed, implying that siblings provide a sense of security.[36]

Emotional closeness between siblings does not usually develop in later life. Rather, siblings who are close in late life tended to have been close as children.[37] However, emotional closeness is more common in early and late life, and less common in early and middle adulthood when siblings are more focused on their own spouses and children. In a study of Canadian widows, siblings, especially sisters, were found to be important sources of emotional support; half the widows in the study identified a sister as one of the three people to whom they felt closest.[38]

Grandparent-Grandchild Relationships

Despite a popular image of the snowy-haired grandmother, first-time grandmotherhood among Canadian women typically occurs around age 50.[39] Almost all (90 percent) older persons who have children also have one or more grandchildren.[40]

Older people see their grandchildren frequently. Contact remains high even when grandchildren are grown up. A Canadian study found that two-thirds of people over 70 saw an adult grandchild once a month or more, and one-third saw an adult grandchild as often as once a week.[41] As in so many aspects of family life, contact with grandchildren may vary by gender. One of the few studies to examine this issue found grandfathers had less contact than grandmothers.[42]

Grandparents and grandchildren exchange many types of support, though the amount of tangible assistance exchanged is low. Generally, grandparents bestow gifts, serve as babysitters, act as confidants and role models, pass down history and tradition, and have important symbolic functions in the family.[43] In addition, grandparents, who have been called the "family watchdogs," may keep a low profile in the family until they feel that their help is needed.[44] As well, grandparents are valuable resources to grandchildren during crises such as the death of a parent or divorce in the middle generation.[45] The adjustment of grandchildren to these events can be eased by grandparents who represent stability and continuity in their lives.

Grandchildren, in turn, act as companions to their grandparents, help to alleviate loneliness, and provide them with information about changing cultural values.[46] Grandparents may derive vicarious pleasure from the accomplishments of their grandchildren. Grandchildren may give their grandparents a sense of being young again, while grandparents may see their grandchildren as an extension of themselves and a continuation of their blood line.[47]

Generally, grandparenthood is considered to be a role with minimal rights and obligations. The ambiguity surrounding the grandparent role has prompted scholars to suggest that grandparents must negotiate their roles with grandchildren. The negotiation process actually begins not with the birth of the grandchild but with the arrival of the in-law child into the family and the relationship that is defined between the older parent (grandparent-to-be) and the new in-law child.[48] This process can have important implications for grandparents if the adult child's marriage ends and the in-law child receives custody of the grandchildren. Grandparents can be active participants in the negotiation process and can increase the likelihood of a satisfying result by recognizing the resources that they represent to the family.[49]

By contrast, great-grandparenthood is experienced by a minority of older

Canadians. One study of persons over 70 found that 23 percent of men and 38 percent of women had great-grandchildren.[50] Great-grandparenthood appears to be significant primarily for emotional and symbolic reasons, providing a sense of family renewal and continuity, and a marker of grandparents' longevity and survival.[51]

Family Relationships and Alternative Lifestyles

Very small minorities of older people have family lives that might be described as "alternative lifestyles." Specifically, the category refers to those who have never been married, are childless, or are gay or lesbian. Although relatively uncommon among the elderly of today, these situations may well become more common in the future. Changing behaviour with respect to marriage, having children, and sexual orientation among today's younger people will lead in the future to greater proportions of older people experiencing these "non-traditional" family lives.

The Never-Married Elderly

About 8 percent of elderly Canadians have remained single throughout their lives.[52] Although these people may not have spouses or children, this does not mean they have no family ties, or that they are particularly lonely or socially isolated.[53] While the never-married elderly are more concerned about loneliness than the married elderly, they are less so than persons who are widowed.[54]

The never-married develop different family patterns than the married; parents, aunts, uncles, siblings, nieces, and nephews have more central roles in their lives.[55] The never-married also have more contact with siblings than the separated or divorced elderly.[56] Note, however, that the pattern of substituting stronger relations with other kin for those with spouses and children may describe never-married older women rather than never-married older men, who receive less support and are more isolated from family members.[57]

The never-married also "compensate" for the lack of ties with spouses and children by forming stronger and more extensive ties with friends.[58] While the never-married elderly are less likely than the widowed and married elderly to visit with relatives, they are more likely than the married and no less likely than widows to get together with friends.[59]

Never-married persons may be advantaged in that they avoid the loss, bereavement, and disorganization of life that accompanies widowhood. Being single is a "way of life" that they have developed over many years of adulthood. The overall effect of lifelong singlehood includes having developed qualities of independence, self-reliance, and habituation to living alone.[60]

The Childless Elderly

Having children is socially valued in our society, especially among those persons who are currently in their later years. Moreover, research has documented the contributions children make to the lives of older people. One might conclude, therefore, that the 20 percent of older people who do not have children are disadvantaged and feel something is missing in their lives. In part, this may depend on whether childlessness was voluntary or involuntary.

A recent review of existing research, however, suggests that children are not necessary in order for older people to have a satisfying old age.[61] The childless elderly are no more socially isolated than those with children. Although those with children have more family visits and receive more support than those who are childless, both groups have similar levels of loneliness and life satisfaction.[62]

Gay and Lesbian Elderly

Very few studies have considered what it is like to be an older gay man or an aging lesbian woman, and there is almost no research on the family lives of older gays and lesbians. We speculate that many gays and lesbians maintain relationships with parents, siblings and siblings' children, and that as social acceptance of this lifestyle grows, these relationships will be easier to maintain than they may have been in the past. Moreover, gays and lesbians can form long-term intimate relationships which provide the kind of support experienced by married people.

What little research that does exist in this area suggests that, as in so many other aspects of aging, myths and stereotypes are not supported by available data. For example, one stereotype is that aging in the gay subculture is more difficult than in the general population because the gay subculture presumably values youthfulness. However, older heterosexual men are as likely as older gays to feel less positively about their physical appearance and to prefer younger sexual partners.[63] Therefore, it may be the factor of age rather than sexual orientation that is related to attitudes and behaviour.

Older gay men are not necessarily lonely, isolated, or unhappy in their later years.[64] Older gays are satisfied with their lives, and may be even more satisfied than older persons in the general population. Older gays have been found to be more self-accepting and to have less depression and psychosomatic symptoms than younger gays.[65] Moreover, greater social integration into the gay community, and specifically having a greater number of gay or lesbian friends, are associated with greater self-acceptance, less depression, and higher satisfaction with life.[66]

Some aspects of aging, such as the need for social and emotional support in old age, are the same for gays and lesbians as they are for heterosexuals. Similarly, health and income are the main factors influencing life satisfaction whether one is gay or heterosexual.[67]

There is even less research on older lesbians than there is on older gays. In one survey, a majority of older lesbian respondents described their mental health as good or excellent, and reported that they were very satisfied with their lives and felt positively about their own aging.[68] Older lesbians may have different lifestyles from those of older gay men. In particular, they are more likely to be in long-standing monogamous relationships. Older lesbians also appear to be less concerned about age-related changes in physical attractiveness than are older gay men.[69]

Family Support to the Frail and Impaired Elderly

As pointed out in earlier sections of this article, older people are involved in family relationships in which they both give and receive assistance, ranging from emotional support to more tangible types of help. However, should older people experience serious impairment and disability in late life, their need for help grows and their ability to provide help diminishes. In these circumstances, help may be thought of as changing from support to care-giving or caring.[70]

Impaired older persons typically need help in order to remain in the community (that is, outside an institution). The kind of help required may range from transportation and shopping, to housework and cooking, and to personal care such as bathing and feeding. The vast majority of such help comes not from the formal health and social service system, but from informal providers, especially family members.

Although much media attention has been given to the predicament of women who are simultaneously caring for older parents and their own young children (those labelled as members of the "sandwich generation"), most persons caring for highly impaired elderly are themselves middle-aged or young elderly persons whose children are grown up.[71] Spouses are much more likely than other family members to become "primary care-givers." Spouses usually provide the highest level of care over the longest period of time. Given the gender differences in life expectancy, it is typically wives who become care-givers to husbands. When older women experience serious health losses and require care, they are usually widowed and turn to children, especially daughters. While children provide extensive care, the level and duration are less than when care is provided by spouses. Siblings, friends and neighbours are much less involved (in terms of extensiveness and duration of care) as long-term care-givers to chronically ill elderly persons. Thus, the viability of family care depends on the types of relatives an older person has. This means that certain groups of elderly — for example, those who have never married and those who have never had children — are less likely to receive family care to any significant degree in late life.[72]

Overall, women provide the bulk of family care given to older persons. Substantial minorities of men, however, assume care-giving roles for wives and for impaired parents, especially if they do not have sisters.[73] Caring for an impaired elderly person can be very stressful. Some studies suggest that spouses find care-giving more stressful than children do, although this finding is not universally supported.[74] Wives who provide care experience greater depression and feelings of burden than do husbands.[75] Notwithstanding the stress associated with care-giving, individuals may also derive a sense of satisfaction or accomplishment from the services they provide.[76]

Care-givers usually try to keep the impaired elderly person in the community for as long as possible. When institutionalization does occur, family care-givers continue to be involved through visiting and providing care. Furthermore, the stress associated with care-giving may remain at a high level, even after the elderly family member has been moved to an institution.[77] A Canadian study found that wives in this situation enter a period of "quasi-widowhood."[78] Like widows, such older wives experienced elevated levels of depression, deteriorating health, and feelings of sadness, loneliness and loss, although they also felt relieved. Unlike widows, however, who have an opportunity to resolve their grief and rebuild their lives, these wives still had obligations and continuing involvement with their husbands.

Women's Employment and Care-giving

Although there is a growing trend for women to work in the paid labour force, this should not lead to the conclusion that employed daughters (or sons, for that matter) do not provide care to aging parents. Several Canadian studies demonstrate the involvement of employed men and women in providing help to older relatives. In one survey, 16 percent of employed men and women reported that they or someone in their household provided care or assistance to an elderly, disabled, or infirm family member.[79] An average of slightly over five hours per week was spent providing this assistance. In an Alberta survey, 42 percent of women and 35 percent of men who were employed full-time reported providing some degree of assistance to an elderly relative.[80] Narrowing the focus to help with personal care such as bathing and toileting (the type of care that indicates significant disability on the part of the elderly recipient), 10 percent reported providing such help. In a national Canadian study currently underway, preliminary results show that 12 percent of women and seven percent of men have provided help with these demanding personal-care activities "during the past six months." Larger percentages (29 percent of women and 39 percent of men) had provided one or more of the less demanding types of aid such as help with shopping, housework or finances.[81]

These figures show that employment does not prevent the provision of assistance to older relatives. Relatively small proportions of employed persons provide high levels of care to an impaired elderly person, but this in part reflects the fact that most elderly persons do not need this type of help. Those persons who simultaneously provide extensive care for an older relative while being employed can be especially subject to strain because of the multiple demands of work and family responsibilities.

One way of resolving the conflicting demands of work and eldercare is for the care-giver to leave the paid labour force. In the Alberta study, five percent of currently employed women said they had quit a job at some point in the past in order to care for an elderly person.[82] Another strategy might be to reduce the time and burden of care-giving by placing the elderly person in an institution. While institutionalization does not mean that families cease to provide care, it at least enables care-givers to gain control over the timing of their care activities.

Elder Abuse and Neglect

Although the great majority of elderly persons have positive, supportive relationships with other family members, a small percentage of elderly people are victims of elder abuse and neglect by their care-givers. Elder abuse has received a great deal of media attention in recent years. However the information that is conveyed may be inaccurate or misleading, in part because there has been very limited research and in part because so many different definitions of abuse have been used.

Not all abuse and neglect is perpetrated by a family member. However, because most elderly are cared for by family members, most abusers are related to their victims.[83] The abuser is, in many cases, the son or daughter or spouse of the elderly victim. Linda Phillips points out that some elder abuse is probably "spouse abuse grown old."[84]

Estimates of the incidence of elder abuse are limited because studies have used different definitions of abuse and have often used small, non-representative samples. The most rigorous Canadian study suggests that about four percent of older people living in the community have experienced some type of abuse or neglect over the years since their 65th birthday.[85] Material abuse was the most common type of abuse reported (2.5 percent), followed by chronic verbal aggression (1.4 percent), physical violence (0.5 percent) and neglect (0.4 percent).

Researchers have attempted to identify the factors which place an older person at risk for abuse. Some studies have identified such factors as being female, of advanced age, economically dependent on a care-giver, socially isolated, and physically or cognitively impaired as risk factors.[86] Other studies, however, have found that economic dependency and advanced age were unrelated to susceptibility to abuse.[87] After reviewing the existing research on elder abuse, P. Lynn McDonald and colleagues concluded that the profile of older persons who are abused is very similar to the profile of older persons who are not abused.[88]

Care-givers who are more likely to be abusers are those with an alcohol or drug problem, those with a cognitive impairment or mental illness, those experiencing personal economic difficulties, those who were abused as a child, and those who are socially isolated. Additional factors that may be associated with elder abuse include care-givers receiving minimal family support from others, overcrowding in the home, and marital or family conflict.[89] On the whole, however, predictors of abuse have yet to be confirmed in a definitive way. Most of the factors discussed are stress-related. Stress, however, does not appear to be a clear predictor of elder abuse since, while the majority of family care-givers experience stress, they do not abuse their elderly relatives.[90]

It is important to emphasize that elder abuse and neglect are serious problems, but also that they are experienced only by a small minority of older persons. There is no evidence that abuse of the elderly is increasing in terms of the percentage of victims. A misperception that elder abuse is more common than it was in the past may stem from the fact that there are greater numbers of elderly persons in the population, and therefore greater numbers of abused persons. Alternatively, increased reporting and media attention can increase the likelihood that an incident of elder abuse becomes public.

Conclusion

Most older Canadians are engaged in a variety of family relationships. These family ties include spouses, children, grandchildren, and siblings. The importance and supportiveness of specific relationships varies according to whether the older person is married, widowed, or has always been single. Whether the older person has children is also important. Persons who have followed paths that were somewhat unusual, such as never marrying, have family lives that are different from those of their more traditional peers.

While it is difficult to predict what family life will be like among tomorrow's elderly, it is no doubt safe to assume it will be different than today. At the same time, it is likely that older people will continue to have active family lives.

In the immediate future, childlessness will not be a major feature among the older population. Parents of the baby-boom generation will have ample numbers of children and grandchildren. Current declines in fertility, however, will mean that in the more distant future (by the year 2025) greater proportions of older people will be childless, suggesting that ties with siblings, other extended family members, and "fictive kin" will be more emphasized than they are today.[91] By the year 2025, not only will older people have fewer children than is the case today, but they will have fewer siblings and, indeed, a smaller pool of close relatives.

In the future, greater proportions of older people will have experienced alternative family lifestyles — married and childless, never-married, or gay or lesbian. As well, higher proportions of tomorrow's elderly will have experienced divorce. The family ties and social-support networks that these elderly will have built up over their adult lives will reflect their different histories.

The goal in this article has been to counter the myth that older people are uninvolved with or neglected by their families. However, we do not wish to go to the other extreme by implying that families are the best or only source of support for older people. In the present era, when the needs of the older population are growing and the government purse is shrinking, it might be tempting to declare that the care of the elderly should be the responsibility of the family. There are many reasons to resist such a declaration. One is that not all older people have family members who are available to provide care. Another is that "family care" usually means care provided by women; thus, policies that promote family care may result in perpetuating disadvantage and dependency among women. Moreover, family care is not necessarily what older people themselves prefer. Older people often find it very difficult to depend on family members for assistance and are torn between their experience of needing care and having to turn to children to meet this need.[92] Research tends to support the conclusion that, in our society, older people prefer to seek emotional support from children but to use other sources, often formal services, for tangible assistance.[93] These considerations suggest that in the near as well as the more distant future, government involvement in providing supportive services to older people, whether in conjunction with or independent of family care, will not only continue to be essential but may, in fact, serve to strengthen the family relationships of older people.

NOTES

Carolyn J. Rosenthal gratefully acknowledges the support of a Career Scientist Award, Ontario Ministry of Health, Health Research Personnel Development Program.

1. V.L. Bengtson, C.J. Rosenthal and L. Burton, "Families and Aging: Diversity and Heterogeneity," in R.H. Binstock and L. George, eds., *Handbook of Aging and the Social Sciences, 3rd Edition* (New York: Academic Press, 1990), 263-87.

2. E.M. Gee, "Demographic Change and Intergenerational Relations in Canadian Families: Findings and Social Policy Implications," *Canadian Public Policy* 16 (1990), 191-99.

3. Bengtson *et al.*, "Families and Aging."

4. I.A. Connidis, *Family Ties and Aging* (Toronto: Butterworths, 1989).

5. *Ibid.*, 9.

6. J. Traupmann and E. Hatfield, "Love and Its Effect on Mental and Physical Health," in R. Fogel, E. Hatfield, S. Kiesler and E. Shanas, eds., *Aging: Stability and Change in the Family* (New York: Academic, 1981), 253-74.

7. P. Yarrow, L. Marcus and M. MacLean, "Marriage and the Elderly: A Literature Review," *Canadian Journal of Social Work Education* 7 (1981), 65-69. E. Lupri and J. Frideres, "The Quality of Marriage and the Passage of Time: Marital Satisfaction Over the Life Course," *Canadian Journal of Sociology* 6, 3 (1981), 283-305.

8. P.M. Keith and R.B. Schafer, "Equity, Role Strains, and Depression Among Middle-Aged and Older Men and Women," in W. Peterson and J. Quadagno, eds., *Social Bonds in Later Life* (Beverly Hills: Sage, 1985), 37-49.

9. J. Mason, "A Bed of Roses? Women, Marriage and Inequality in Later Life," in P. Allatt, T. Keil, A. Bryman and B. Bytheway, eds., *Women and the Life Cycle. Transitions and Turning Points* (Houndsmills, Basingstoke, Hampshire: MacMillan, 1981), 90-105.

10. M. Zube, "Changing Behavior and Outlook of Aging Men and Women: Implications for Marriage in the Middle and Later Years," *Family Relations* 31, 1 (1982), 147-56.

11. N. Keating and P. Cole, "What Do I Do With Him 24 Hours a Day? Changes in the Housewife Role After Retirement," *The Gerontologist* 20, 1 (1980), 84-89.

12. B. Ingersoll-Dayton and T. Antonucci, "Reciprocal and Nonreciprocal Social Support: Contrasting Sides of Intimate Relationships," *Journal of Gerontology* 43, 3 (1988), S65-73.

13. C.E. Depner and B. Ingersoll-Dayton, "Conjugal Social Support: Patterns in Later Life," *Journal of Gerontology* 40, 6 (1985), 761-66.

14. A. Martin Matthews, *Widowhood in Later Life* (Toronto: Butterworths, 1991), 9.

15. A. Martin Matthews, "Canadian Research on Women as Widows: A Comparative Analysis of the State of the Art," *Resources for Feminist Research* 11 (1982), 227-30.

16. E.A. Bankoff, "Social Support and Adaptation to Widowhood," *Journal of Marriage and the Family* 45, 4 (1983), 827-39.

17. L.I. Pearlin and J.S. Johnson, "Marital Status, Life-Strains and Depression," American *Sociological Review* 42 (Oct. 1977), 704-15. W. Gove, "Sex, Marital Status and Psychiatric Treatment: A Research Note," *Social Forces* 58 (1979), 89-93.

18. Martin Matthews, *Widowhood in Later Life*, 86.

19. National Council of Welfare, *Poverty Profile 1988: A Report by the National Council of Welfare* (Ottawa: Minister of Supply and Services, 1988).

20. C.J. Rosenthal, "Aging and Intergenerational Relations in Canada," in V. Marshall, ed., *Aging in Canada: Social Perspectives,* Second Edition (Toronto: Fitzhenry and Whiteside, 1987), 311-42. Martin Matthews, *Widowhood in Later Life,* 71.

21. A. Martin Matthews, "Support Systems of Widows in Canada," in H. Lopata, ed., *Widows, Vol. 2, North America* (Durham, North Carolina: Duke University Press, 1987), 225-50.

22. S.L. O'Bryant, "Sibling Support and Older Widows' Well-Being," *Journal of Marriage and the Family* 50, 1 (1988), 173-83. C.L. Johnson and D.H. Catalano, "Childless Elderly and Their Family Supports," *The Gerontologist* 21, 6 (1981), 610-18.

23. T.K. Burch, "Remarriage of Older Canadians," *Research on Aging* 12, 4 (1990), 546-59.

24. Connidis, *Family Ties and Aging,* 36.

25. *Ibid.,* 46. Rosenthal, "Aging and Intergenerational Relations in Canada."

26. I. Connidis, "Living Arrangement Choices of Older Residents: Assessing Quantitative Results with Qualitative Data," *Canadian Journal of Sociology* 8, 4 (1983), 359-75.

27. Connidis, *Family Ties and Aging,* 46.

28. Rosenthal, "Aging and Intergenerational Relations in Canada."

29. D.J. Dewit, A.V. Wister and T.K. Burch, "Physical Distance and Social Contact Between Elders and Their Adult Children," *Research on Aging* 10, 1 (1988), 56-80. B.J. Gottlieb, "Informal Care Among the Elderly," in B.J. Gottlieb, *Social Support Strategies, Guidelines for Mental Health Practice* (Beverly Hills: Sage, 1981), 177-203.

30. Connidis, *Family Ties and Aging,* 47.

31. C.J. Rosenthal, "Kinkeeping in the Familial Division of Labor," *Journal of Marriage and the Family* 47, 4, 965-74.

32. Connidis, *Family Ties and Aging,* 13.

33. Rosenthal, "Aging and Intergenerational Relations in Canada."

34. Connidis, *Family Ties and Aging,* 84.

35. Rosenthal, "Kinkeeping in the Familial Division of Labor. C.J. Rosenthal and V.W. Marshall, "The Transmission of Family Ritual Behavior," *American Behavioral Scientist* 31, 6 (1988), 669-84.

36. V. Cicirelli, "The Role of Siblings as Family Caregivers," in W.J. Sauer and R.T. Coward, eds., *Social Support Networks and the Care of the Elderly* (New York: Springer, 1985), 93-107.

37. Connidis, *Family Ties and Aging,* 75.

38. A. Martin Matthews, "Widowhood as an Expectable Life Event," in V.W. Marshall, eds., *Aging in Canada: Social Perspectives,* second edition, 343-66.

39. E.M. Gee, "The Transition to Grandmotherhood: A Quantitative Study," *Canadian Journal on Aging* 10, 3 (1991), 254-70.

40. Connidis, *Family Ties and Aging,* 12.

41. Rosenthal, "Aging and Intergenerational Relations in Canada."

42. V.R. Kivett, "Grandfathers and Grandchildren: Patterns of Association, Helping, and Psychological Closeness," *Family Relations* 34, 4 (1985), 565-71.

43. V.L. Bengtson, "Diversity and Symbolism in Grandparental Roles," in V.L. Bengtson and J.F. Robertson, eds., *Grandparenthood* (Beverly Hills: Sage, 1985), 11-25.

44. L.E. Troll, "Grandparents: The Family Watchdogs," in T.H. Brubaker, ed., *Family Relationships in Later Life* (Beverly Hills: Sage, 1983), 63-74.

45. J.W. Gladstone, "Perceived Changes in Grandmother-Grandchild Relations Following a Child's Separation or Divorce," *The Gerontologist* 28, 1 (1988), 66-72.

46. W.J. Breslaw, "Even Unto the Fourth Generation," *The Gerontologist* 20, 4 (1980), 434-36.

47. C.L. Johnson, "A Cultural Analysis of the Grandmother," *Research on Aging* 5, 4 (1983), 547-67.

48. J. Sprey and S.H. Matthews, "Contemporary Grandparenthood: A Systemic Transition," *Annals of the American Academy of Political and Social Science* 464 (1982), 91-103.

49. J.W. Gladstone, "Grandmother-Grandchild Contact: The Mediating Influence of the Middle Generation Following Marriage Breakdown and Remarriage," *Canadian Journal on Aging* 8,

4 (1989), 355-65. J.W. Gladstone, "An Analysis of Changes in Grandparent-Grandchild Visitation Following an Adult Child's Remarriage," *Canadian Journal on Aging* 10, 2 (1991), 113-26.

50. Rosenthal, "Aging and Intergenerational Relations in Canada."

51. K.J. Dotka and M.E. Mertz, "The Meaning and Significance of Great-Grandparenthood," *The Gerontologist* 28, 2 (1988), 192-97.

52. Connidis, *Family Ties and Aging,* 9.

53. R.L. Rubenstein, "Never Married Elderly as a Social Type: Re-evaluating Some Images," *The Gerontologist* 27, 1 (1987), 108-13. D.E. Stull and A. Scarisbrick-Hauser, "Never Married Elderly," *Research on Aging* 11, 1 (1989), 124-39.

54. Rubenstein, "Never Married Elderly as a Social Type."

55. I. Connidis and L. Davies, "Confidants and Companions in Later Life: The Place of Family and Friends," *Journal of Gerontology: Social Sciences* 45, 4 (1990), S141-49.

56. L. Strain and B. Payne, "Social Networks and Patterns of Social Interaction Among Ever-Single and Separated/Divorced Elderly Canadians," *Canadian Journal on Aging* 11, 1 (1992), 31-53.

57. Connidis, *Family Ties and Aging,* 42.

58. A. Martin Matthews, "The Relationship Between Social Support and Morale: Comparisons of the Widowed and Never-Married in Later Life," *Canadian Journal of Community Mental Health* 10 (1991a), 47-63.

59. Stull and Scarisbrick-Hauser, "Never Married Elderly."

60. Johnson and Catalano, "Childless Elderly and Their Family Supports."

61. Connidis, *Family Ties and Aging,* 59.

62. *Ibid.,* 58. J. Rempel, "Childless Elderly: What Are They Missing?" *Journal of Marriage and the Family* 47, 2 (1985), 343-48.

63. H. Gray and P. Dressel, "Alternative Interpretations of Aging Among Gay Males," *The Gerontologist* 25, 1 (1985), 83-87. Lee, "Invisible Lives of Canada's Gray Gays," in V.W. Marshall, ed., *Aging in Canada*, second edition, 138-55.

64. R.M. Berger, *Gay and Gray* (Urbana, Illinois: University of Illinois Press, 1982). Gray and Dressel, "Alternative Interpretations of Aging," 83-87.

65. Berger, *Gay and Gray.*

66. *Ibid.* Lee, "Invisible Lives."

67. Lee, *ibid.*

68. R.M. Berger and J.J. Kelly, "Working with Homosexuals of the Older Population," *Social Casework* 67, 4 (1986), 203-10.

69. *Ibid.*

70. N.L. Chappell, *Social Support and Aging* (Toronto: Butterworths, 1992), 31.

71. *Ibid.,* 34. C.J. Rosenthal, S.H. Matthews and V.W. Marshall, "Is Parent Care Normative? The Experiences of a Sample of Middle-Aged Women," *Research on Aging* 11, 2 (1989), 244-60.

72. Johnson and Catalano, "Childless Elderly and Their Family Supports." Martin Matthews, "Relationship Between Social Support and Morale."

73. N.L. Chappell, "Living Arrangements and Sources of Caregiving," *Journal of Gerontology: Social Sciences* 46, 2 (1990), S51-58.

74. L. George and L.P. Gwyther, "Caregiver Well-Being: A Multidimensional Examination of Family Caregivers of Demented Adults," *The Gerontologist* 26, 3 (1986), 253-59. And S.H. Zarit, K.E. Reever and J. Bach-Peterson, "Relatives of the Impaired Elderly: Correlates of Feelings of Burden," *The Gerontologist* 20, 6 (1980), 649-55.

75. R.A. Pruchno and N.L. Resch, "Husbands and Wives as Caregivers: Antecedents of Depression and Burden," *The Gerontologist* 29, 2 (1989), 159-65.

76. A.K. Motenko, "The Frustrations, Gratifications, and Well-Being of Dementia Caregivers," *The Gerontologist* 29, 2 (1989), 166-72.

77. C.J. Rosenthal and P. Dawson, "Wives of Institutionalized Elderly Men: The First Stage of the Transition to Quasi-Widowhood," *Journal of Aging and Health* 3, 3 (1991), 315-34.

78. Rosenthal and Dawson, "Wives of Institutionalized Elderly Men."

79. J.L. MacBride-King, *Work and Family: Employment Challenge of the '90s* (Ottawa: The Conference Board of Canada, Report 59-90, 1990).

80. A.L. McKinnon, "Integrating Work and Family Responsibilities for Eldercare: Results of the 1991 Alberta Survey," paper presented at the 20th Annual Meeting of the Canadian Association on Gerontology, Toronto, October, 1991.

81. A. Martin Matthews and C.J. Rosenthal, "Structural Contexts of Work and Eldercare," paper presented at the 69th Annual Meeting of the American Orthopsychiatric Association, New York, May, 1992.

82. McKinnon, "Integrating Work and Family Responsibilities."

83. K. Pillemer and D. Finkelhor, "The Prevalence of Elder Abuse: A Random Sample Survey," *The Gerontologist* 28, 1 (1988), 51-57.

84. L.R. Phillips, "Theoretical Explanations of Elder Abuse: Competing Hypotheses and Unresolved Issues," in K.A. Pillemer and R.S. Wolf, eds., *Elder Abuse: Conflict in the Family* (Dover, Mass.: Auburn House, 1986), 197-217.

85. E. Podnieks, K. Pillemer, J. Nicholson, J. Shillington and A. Frizzell, *National Survey on Abuse of the Elderly in Canada: Preliminary Findings* (Toronto: Office of Research and Innovation, Ryerson Polytechnical Institute, 1989).

86. J.I. Kosberg, "Preventing Elder Abuse: Identification of High Risk Factors Prior to Placement Decisions," *The Gerontologist* 28, 1 (1988), 43-50. E. Rathbone-McCuan, "Elderly Victims of Family Violence and Neglect," *Social Casework* 61 (1980), 296-304.

87. Pillemer and Finkelhor, "The Prevalence of Elder Abuse."

88. P.L. McDonald, J.P. Hornick, G.B. Robertson and J.E. Wallace, *Elder Abuse and Neglect in Canada* (Toronto: Butterworths, 1991).

89. Kosberg, "Preventing Elder Abuse."

90. *Ibid.*

91. H. MacRae, "Fictive Kin as a Component of the Social Networks of Older People," *Research on Aging* 14, 2 (1992), 226-47.

92. Jane Aronson, "Older Women's Experiences of Needing Care," *Canadian Journal on Aging* 9, 3 (1990), 234-47.

93. Connidis, *Family Ties and Aging*, 92-99.

Carolyn J. Rosenthal is an Associate Professor in the Division of Occupational Therapy, University of Toronto, and a member of the University's Centre for Studies of Aging. James Gladstone is an Associate Professor in the School of Social Work, McMaster University.

Women's Sense of Responsibility for the Care of old People: "But Who Else Is Going to Do It?"*

JANE ARONSON

The bulk of the care of old people in North American society is provided informally — generally by families and, at that, by women relatives (Brody; 1985; Walker 1985). This division of care is subject to different interpretations. On one hand, it has been seen as the product of taken-for-granted ideas about gender and the responsibilities of the state (Cicirelli 1981; Moroney 1980). On the other hand, it has been seen as a consequence of a division of labor that obliges women to assume responsibility for others' needs, confines them to the private sphere, and constrains their access to resources and to independence (Finch 1984; Hooyman and Ryan 1987). The first approach assumes the unpaid labor of female relatives and points to social policies and interventions aimed at sustaining them in their caregiving obligations. The second defines women as a group with interests of their own and seeks ways of meeting the needs of old people without oppressing them or their female kin.

---

*Reprinted, with permission, from *Gender and Society*, 6 (1), March 1992

This article explores women's views in relation to these conflicting conceptualizations of obligation and responsibility. Building on the growing literature on women and caring and on a qualitative study of mothers and daughters who give and receive care, I consider how female caregivers think about the boundaries between formal (publicly provided) and informal care and between women and men in families. Examining women's experiences of the division of care can contribute to our understanding of the social processes that sustain the social organization of gender and the reproduction of women's disadvantage. Such examination also informs consideration of strategies for change and movement toward a more equitable division of caring labor.

The Current Pattern of Care of Old People

In Canada, as in comparable market economies such as the United States and the United Kingdom, the pattern of care of old people relies heavily on the taken-for-granted notion that families are "naturally" responsible for members' needs and welfare. Based on this assumption, publicly provided health and social services remain in the background, accounting for only about 10 to 15 percent of the total care of the elderly (Chappell, Strain, and Blandford, 1986; Lee 1985). Family or informal sources of care are seen as the first line of resort for old people, and formal services are introduced only when informal sources are deficient or seriously depleted (Twigg 1989).

In the current climate of economic recession, alternatives to expensive institutional care are favored, and care in the community is regarded as an inexpensive and attractive policy option (Health and Welfare Canada 1986). Subject to critical scrutiny, community care policies emerge as insubstantial initiatives that obscure the systematic deflection of responsibility from the public sphere to families and, within families, to women (Osterbusch et al. 1987; Walker 1985). They have been poorly funded and have rested on concepts of community and informal networks that erroneously imply an abundance of available and geographically concentrated social resources outside the formal service system (Bulmer 1987). These thrusts in public policy have been reinforced by a political rhetoric that exhorts conformity to traditional family values and womanly virtues (Eichler 1988, 412).

Uncovering the origins and costs to women of this pattern of caring has been an important focus of feminist critiques of social policy (Baines, Evans, and Neysmith 1991; Finch and Groves 1983). Research specifically on the experience of female family caregivers has provided us with knowledge of the sheer hard work of assisting an elderly relative with the tasks of daily living (G. Parker 1985), the complexity of the physical and emotional labor involved (Bowers 1987; Ungerson 1987), and the implications of caring that may jeopardize caregivers' own later economic independence (Finch and Groves 1980). Theoretical analyses located the origins of women's association with caring in the context of wider social, economic, and political forces and call attention to both the material and ideological character of struggles to enhance women's welfare (Finch and Groves 1983; Ungerson 1987). While efforts to secure specific benefits and services for caregivers may address women's immediate material concerns, more fundamental is the meaning and interpretation of women's needs (Finch 1984; Fraser 1989).

Alongside such critical analyses of the present structuring of care and of women's welfare, we are witnessing continuation of the resource constraints and associated belt-tightening political rhetoric that have characterized the later 1970s and the 1980s. In this context, notions of gender justice or entitlement to public support are not high on government agendas. Exploring women's own interpretations of their situations as caregivers in this contested and shifting context is crucial for understanding how the gender division of labor is sustained and how we can think about possibilities for change (Chafetz 1988).

Methodology

The data on which this exploration is based (carried out in Toronto in 1987 and 1988) are drawn from a qualitative study of women who identified themselves as relying on support of daughters or as feeling responsible for their mothers (Aronson 1988). This article focuses on the experiences of 28 women between the ages of 35 and 80 who identified themselves as key to their mothers' informal support systems. All thought they provided important emotional and moral support and, depending on their situations, provided a range of practical assistance: help with heavy shopping, cleaning, transportation and personal care, and information or support in linking their mothers with formal services.

Eighteen of the study subjects (aged 35-63) described their current feelings of responsibility toward their aging mothers, while the other 10 spoke retrospectively about assisting their mothers in the past. For 5 of this latter group (aged 59-74), these memories were very fresh, as their mothers had died within five years of the interview; the remaining 5 (aged 68-80) described more distant recollections of assisting their mothers. The inclusion of both retrospective and current accounts permits explorations of women's experiences of responsibility in the sweep of their whole lives, not just as bounded spans in midlife.

I located the 28 subjects in a snowball fashion from the membership of provincial associations of retired and working schoolteachers. I sought subjects who had worked outside the home and had some degree of economic independence to maximize the likelihood of finding respondents who questioned assumptions about women's primary association with home and family ties. Predictably, the resulting sample of teachers or former teachers was made up of mainly white Canadian-born women, none of whom was in serious financial hardship. This small sample is limited by social class, race, and employment history. The data are also confined to the context of the mother-daughter relationship — a pivotal channel of women's support to old people but certainly not the only one.

Choosing the subjects by virtue of an occupational affiliation, rather than by virtue of their identification as service recipients with problems, permits exploration of the *ordinary* processes for an elderly mother, rather than of particularly strained or critical caregiving situations. The circumstances of the 28 subjects' mothers were ordinary in that they mirrored the realities of the broader population of elderly women: Most were widows living alone experiencing a variety of chronic health conditions that led them to rely on others for assistance to varying degrees. Only 4 subjects described mothers who received substantial amounts of formal supportive services on an ongoing basis (Given universal health programs in Canada, most of these formal services were publicly provided; in two instances, subjects' mothers purchased minor additional services privately). Some mothers had episodes or illness that required hospitalization and short-term contacts with social services for help with household tasks or minor personal care. The majority engaged only in routine contact with family doctors. Otherwise, they managed by themselves and with informal help.

In unstructured interviews, women described their life histories, family contexts, and their thoughts and feelings about the care they gave and responsibility they felt for their mothers. They recalled the ways their mothers' needs and their own responses to them had emerged. With subjects' consent, interviews were taped and transcribed. So that quoted material can be understood in context, relevant aspects of the subjects' social situations (their ages, their paid and unpaid work, commitments, whether their caregiving was ongoing or in the past) are identified.

In analyzing subjects' accounts, I regarded their experiences as both individual descriptions of obligation and as what Smith (1986,7) terms "points of entry" into the wider social relations that shape the structured division of responsibility for caring labor. Exploring how forces beyond women's immediate worlds give form to their personal experiences draws on the work of theorists seeking to understand the entanglement of subjectivity with social structure and ideology. Prevailing ideologies provide images, vocabularies, and symbols that powerfully shape our thinking about ourselves and our social worlds, defining our conceptions of what is right or desirable and what is possible or thinkable (Smith 1987; Therborn 1980). This penetration of dominant ideology into our inner worlds is, typically, unnoticed. Thus, in her analysis of gender relations, Chafetz (1988) notes how the definitional processes undergirding women's systematic disadvantage are so successfully obscured as to seem inevitable. Their acceptance as natural and uncoercive is, she suggests, testament to their legitimacy and stability. In the present study, we can explore how structural realities (the availability of alternative sources of assistance) and ideological forces (prevailing ideas and norms about gender roles, family ties, responsibility for others) intersect and shape women's sense of obligation.

Analysis of the interview material is organized around three themes that emerged from the data: (1) women's experiences of the boundary between the responsibilities of public services and of families for their mothers' care; (2) women's accounts of the boundary between their responsibilities toward their mothers and those of the men in their families, specifically their brothers and husbands; and (3) inner tensions that women felt between acceptable and unacceptable degrees of responsibility that they were prepared to take on. Thus, the first two sections address the contextual constraints that shape women's obligations — the limits of public services and the limits of male family members; and the third focuses on women's internal limits, which emerged as a central theme of the study.

The Limits of Public Responsibility

At points when decisions about the allocation of public resources were required, the boundary between formal services and families' responsibilities were negotiated or explicitly articulated. Women experienced the structured limits of public responsibility in encounters with formal service providers (doctors, nurses, social workers).

For example, a 51-year-old woman described her mother's recent stay in an acute-care hospital, while waiting for a bed in a nursing home. Urged by her mother's doctor to take her home during the waiting period, the daughter did not feel that he took into account the limits of her capacity to take time from work to care for her mother:

> I always felt the doctor and social worker were suspicious. I always felt they thought we were going to *dump* her or...we didn't *care* about her. I didn't feel, you know, even though I have a feeling that social workers care about both sides...I didn't feel that.

Similarly, a 42-year-old subject, knowing how little time work and her children's care left her, recalled her frustration with hospital staff when she tried to ensure that her mother's discharge would be as smooth and secure as possible. Repeatedly unable to locate her mother's doctor, she finally met the head nurse:

> I said: "I want the doctor to *know* that I think this should be investigated for home care." Because if you don't *ask* for it, you don't get it.
>
> [Interviewer:] And the system responded or...
>
> A little grudgingly, a little grudgingly...I had to *fight* for it. I felt it should have been offered. I felt somebody should have been in there, talking to my mother and finding out what was her situation.

The absence of information and of an invitation to claim entitlement to services can be understood as a form of service rationing (Judge 1978; R.A. Parker 1967,

11), with formal care providers communicating the expectation that patients and families should fend for themselves. In response to the "grudging" response of service providers, this same respondent justified her demands at some length:

> In my case, for example, with full-time jobs and a family and children and a home to run, *we*'re under pressure too. I mean, not as badly, we could provide support, but there were *limits* — there really were limits...It sounds awful but my mother's been a Canadian citizen for umpteen years and I pay a hell of a lot of income tax every year, my husband pays a hell of a lot...and now and then, when we need some short-term help, I don't think it should be difficult to find.

Both she and the previously quoted respondent felt that service providers questioned the legitimacy of their positions and their affection for their mothers. The need for explanation suggests that the proper boundary between public and private responsibility for care had been violated and, further, that conventional daughterly behavior had been transgressed.

Respondents' contacts with their mothers' family doctors represented another critical meeting point between public and family obligations. Family doctors are a pivotal link in the formal health and social service system and are uniquely placed to legitimate or undermine old people's and family members' definitions of their needs and entitlements. A 53-year-old subject, worried by her mother's increasing confusion, noted:

> I need to be able to go to him and say, you know: "What are *we* going to do?" And I didn't have that with the other doctor.

Other respondents did not enjoy this sense of confidence in the shared assumption of responsibility. A 47-year-old subject felt that her mother's doctor prescribed sleeping pills carelessly and was worried about her mother's depression. After cleaning her mother's apartment and disposing of the accumulation of pills, she phoned him only to be told: "Well, mother's getting older, you know, and I can't be responsible for her behavior." The encounter confirmed the respondent's impression that doctors have little interest in old people and her sense that "I knew I was on my own."

Recognizing that she was "on her own" prompted this subject to resolve that she would not seek the help of the family doctor again — that she would manage her mother's situation without his help. This incident captures the distinction between "service rationing" and "consumer rationing" (Judge, 1978). The doctor's rebuff represents the declaration of the limits to his time and resources as a service provider. The subject's resolve represents her decision not to claim entitlement to publicly provided support in the future; her low expectations prompt her to ration herself and her mother out of consideration. Set in a wider context, this encounter can be understood as an instance of the intersection between the structural and ideological forces that shape women's sense of responsibility. The doctor's dismissive conduct constitutes a material limit to public responsibility for the elderly woman concerned. The subject's response suggests an internalization of the message and acceptance that, as her mother's daughter, she must indeed cope alone.

Women's experiences of the limits to public responsibility consisted less of the relatively hard-edged service rationing or material limits described above and more of a general consciousness of expectations about the locus of responsibility for old people. That public service limits existed at the level of perception more commonly than in actual experience of tested boundaries may be partly attributable to the nature of the sample; as noted above, subjects' mothers were not generally making heavy claims on services or resources. It is likely, however, that the norms and expectations at play and the resulting consumer rationing behavior stifle claims making and reduce demands on the public service system.

Subjects spoke at length about their awareness of the current pattern of care in which families are encouraged to look after their members' welfare with minimal public supports. Normative expectations about family obligations were so assumed as to be practically unnoticed. For example, a 45-year-old subject dealing with her mother's deteriorating health noted:

This is supposed to be a civilized society. I think it's our duty to do those things. And, uh, I don't think that most people...I think most people find it natural to do it.

However, when women moved beyond general assertions about family responsibilities into more particular consideration of the realities they faced, their feelings of responsibility emerged less as a matter of voluntary adherence to family values and more as a matter of necessity. The 41-year-old daughter of a recently widowed mother observed:

I definitely think that younger members in a family should feel the responsibility and should feel the need to see to it that the older person gets cared for. It isn't always possible to be the person — the caretaker. But I definitely think that the younger generation owes it to the older generation. Who else is going to do it?

Looking back, a 79-year-old respondent reflected on the pressure of necessity from both the giver's and the receiver's points of view. A generation before, she had provided her mother with a lot of support on an everyday basis and, while worrying that she gave her husband and children too little attention, felt that she had no choice in the matter. She observed:

I think children should be sympathetic...but I certainly don't think they should give up their youth and be *dominated* by a parent...I certainly don't. That becomes a worry when you're over 70. If anything should happen...I almost made my daughter promise, I said: "Please don't put me in a home."

I'm in that position where I just worry about the end of life. Who *is* going to...?

This recurring theme — Who *is* going to assume responsibility? (if not me for my mother or my daughter for me?) — draws attention to the absence of choice faced by most women as providers of care. Respondents articulated it most especially when they faced the possibility of their mothers' being unable to live independently and the specter of institutional forms of care arose. "But I'd never let my mother go into one of those places" was a common assertion, based partly on concerns about the poor quality of institutional care and partly on concern for their own and their mother's emotional well-being: "They don't treat people as human"; "I couldn't bear the guilt"; "She'd hate being ruled."

In summary, these perceptions — of the nature and availability of public services and of the obligations of families toward their elders — form part of the pattern of "constraints within which individuals conduct their own negotiations, restricting or expanding the range of alternatives available" (Finch, 1987, 162). These patterned constraints were also manifest in a more concrete form in subjects' experiences of the rationing practices of service providers and the more general context of scarcity in public resources.

The Limits of Men's Responsibility

Research indicates consistently that women rather than men are expected to assume responsibility for the care of elderly relatives and other dependents (Brody 1981; Bulmer 1987). The small amount of research that has compared women's and men's motivation to care for an elderly dependent reveals the powerful link between femininity and caring. While women express their motives in terms of duty and obligation, men speak of love. Women feel obliged and experience guilt, while men experience satisfaction at acting on a conscious choice (Ungerson 1987, 86). All the women who participated in the present research had brothers or husbands and offered insights into the way cultural images of gender and care unfold into their realities.

Subjects described both real and perceived limits to the brothers' and husbands' contributions to their mothers' care. Explicit lines of responsibility tended to be identified at times of crisis or rapid change in their mothers' circumstances. For example, a 53-year-old woman recalled exchanges with her brother after her father died:

I found out that my brother's attitude was: "I have my wife and family, you're single, you have no one to spend your money on, *you* look after mother." The attitude ever since has been: "Well, she needs the money, I'll send her $10 every so often." Whereas I was spending as much money as I could on a regular basis.

A 66-year-old respondent, whose mother had died five years prior to the interview, guiltily described how her mother's growing frailty and, finally, a fall had prompted her admission to a nursing home. For some years, she had gone to her mother's at least once a day while she was also teaching to support herself, her chronically ill husband, and their three children. After her mother's fall, she had contacted her brother, a physician, and asked him to get involved:

Joseph came down...looked at the nursing home, said: "Well, that's OK." Now, he could very well have taken my Mum...I think. But his practice was heavy at the time....He hardly ever visited.

Similarly, a woman in her late 40s described how she "kept an eye on" and assisted her frail mother, while her two brothers were uninvolved. The year before the interview, when the respondent herself had been ill, she recalled:

And at that point, after Thanksgiving, I did yell at my brothers...and they did go down and visit, you know...but none of them go down and clean or bring laundry.

Instances like these, in which brothers defined their limits or women made demands on their brothers to share responsibility for their mothers, were unusual. In general, respondents had integrated normative expectations of men and women in families. Thus, they thought it so obvious that daughters would "naturally" step in to assist their mothers as to be unremarkable — "I've never even thought about it before." While respondents noted such events as their mothers' widowhood or illness as precipitants of a greater sense of concern, the actual distribution of care — whether practical or emotional — was seldom discussed explicitly. They referred, rather, to unremarked, gradual processes that "just evolved" or "just worked out that way." That these incremental decisions passed largely unnoticed accords with Chafetz's (1988, 122) observation that the definitional processes that sustain the gender division of labor are obscure — hidden from view and, therefore, from debate and contention.

Typically, those normative expectations about gender and care came into view when women felt that they were not conforming to them. For example, several respondents felt uncomfortable that work responsibilities or distance resulted in their doing less for their mothers than did their brothers. Because of her husband's job, one woman in her late 50s had moved away from the small town where her mother and brother still lived. She spoke to her mother frequently and visited regularly but explained how guilty she felt that responsibility for day-to-day contact fell to her brother. Another respondent, separated from her husband, supporting two adolescent children, and taking night classes regretted that she could not help her mother with weekday tasks:

When she's going to the doctor, my brother's very good about it, but I guess it kind of bothers me — I guess it's kind of old-fashioned thinking on my part, too — that a woman would like another woman around when

she's going to the doctor...it's just impossible for me to be there, so I try
not to let it work on me at all.

More detailed study of such instances is needed to explore the complex interplay
of gendered expectations about family obligations and the forces that modify or
confirm them in actual practice (Finch and Mason 1990).

The crucial role of gender in determining expectations and the distribution of
responsibility within women's families emerged in their consideration of the roles
of their sisters-in-law and their husbands. Qureshi and Walker (1989, 130) articulated an empirically based hierarchy of obligations to elderly relatives in which
— after spouses and daughters — daughters-in-law were the next line of resort.
Respondents recognized this patterning; for example, the separated woman quoted
above observed:

I think we're lucky that all the wives who are involved are very good about
it, too. My brothers' wives are very pleasant and attentive to my mother...it's
the female element that counts.

In contrast, the commitment expected of sons-in-law (respondents' husbands)
was very small. Gender, rather than the kin tie of being a child-in-law, determined
their involvement. An older respondent recalled caring for her mother over a long
period. She remembered how guilty she felt at spending so much time away from
her husband. She noted, with gratitude, his tolerance: "He put up with more than
most men would." That husband's claims on their time and attention were greater
than their mothers' was a view expressed by many women — a view that left
them trying to balance and juggle commitments. A woman in her 30s explained
that her recent marriage coincided with her father's death and, as a result, her
mother's need for her attention:

So he [subject's husband] hasn't been that much of a support, especially
because I feel I can't say too much in a way because he gets annoyed if
I'm depressed, you know. If I'm on the phone, talking to my mother and
I get depressed, he'll tend to get annoyed with her...you know [laugh] I
have to be careful about that too.

These women's observations accord with others' findings that husbands actually share little in their wives' responsibilities to their mothers but were appreciated for the absence of their objections (Abel 1989).

Respondents identified two explanations for their lack of expectation of their
husbands' and brothers' sense of obligation: men's primary commitment to the
work world and men's relative lack of ability to anticipate and respond to their
mother's needs. A woman teaching full-time, in poor health, and feeling overex-
tended described her brother's lack of involvement with her frail mother. She
described him very protectively:

But, you see, he's in a different situation. He's head of a company. He's under a lot of pressure. He's inherited some of the problems my father had physically....So I'm not going to put a load of anything on him.

Another woman similarly absolved her brother from responsibility for their mother's care. She had cared for her mother through very difficult years in her own life but expected that her brother, a doctor, would do little because "his practice was heavy at the time."

The assumption that men's commitments to the paid workplace took precedence over women's led subjects to expect or demand little of brothers in terms of sharing responsibilities for their mother's care. The notion that men's work has primacy while women take on responsibility for dependents and adapt their employment accordingly is associated with traditional notions of the family wage and a rigid division of labor along gender lines (Rimmer 1983). The assumptions of the two women quoted above appear to be rooted in these traditional images, yet, ironically, neither conformed to this image of family life: The first was unmarried and supported herself, while the second was married and the sole support for her disabled husband and three children. Despite the material realities of these two women's lives and despite the fact that, as teachers, all the study subjects were or had been relatively advantaged in the labor market, the ideology that associates women with the private sphere and unpaid work was strikingly robust.

Also perpetuating women's obligation to care was their recognition that they were better at it than their brothers, especially in providing emotional and moral support. One woman, married and with small children, noted the differences between herself and her brother after their father died three years before the interview:

My brother, of course, was still not married so he was very supportive, too. But, you know, he's a male — he doesn't realize what *little* things...he's very good, but just doesn't think...just: "Oh, she'll be home with nobody there..." So, just a phone call even or: "I'll think I'll go and do my washing over there tonight — it'll be an excuse to go and I'll get something done in the meantime."

Another respondent remembered her surprise when her brother proposed that his family and hers plan a holiday in Europe the following year:

And I think I'm the only one that thought about mother — what's going to happen to *her* if all of us take off in the summer? It's not that I don't dearly want to go — and with them — but [sigh] I feel a responsibility towards her. And, you see, when I think of a trip in the summer, I don't think of it *with* them — or certainly not until after mother's gone. I was quite shocked and surprised.

Thus, respondents included their mothers in their thoughts about everyday activities and future plans. Their accounts accord with the notions of "protective" and "anticipatory" caregiving described by Bowers (1987) — forms of emotional labor aimed at minimizing their mothers' awareness of being dependent and at looking ahead to anticipate future possibilities and needs. Women had little expectation that their brothers would participate on equal terms in such processes.

Some respondents minded the limits to their brothers' engagement with their mothers. At a practical level, some noted that when their brothers did involve themselves in assisting their mothers, they did the "nice tasks." As a woman with a new teaching job and children of preschool age observed:

> I'm the one who's aware of the fact that she had to eat, you know...that she had to get food in the house or she can't eat. Whereas they...they'd probably enjoy more taking her out or something where they might buy her something...and sort of don't think of the everyday routine things.

Another respondent phoned her brother to ensure that he would step in for her at a time when she was ill. She expressed anger at having to prompt him at all, and then observed that he did visit and took flowers but would not think of helping their mother with necessary household tasks.

Some women were impatient at their brothers' inability to engage in the invisible emotional labor described above. Finding their brothers "thoughtless" and "self-absorbed," they felt very much alone with their concerns. Prompting their brothers into thoughtful behavior — as a means of protecting or affirming their mothers — became an extra responsibility for some. For example, a woman in her 50s described her brother with frustration:

> I have to boot him to remember to phone her — even on her birthday. Otherwise, I can't stand her sadness and moaning and groaning that she hasn't heard from him. So I usually phone a couple of days before Mum's birthday.

To summarize, women generally took for granted that daughters and daughters-in-law rather than sons or sons-in-law would respond to and anticipate their mothers' needs. While any questioning or resisting of this division was seldom translated into demands or action, subjects were aware that they bore "ultimate responsibility" (Saraceno 1987, 199) for thinking of and assisting their mothers.

Women Setting Limits

While only a few respondents tested of challenged the limits of public services and the limits of men, many were conscious of and minded the definitional processes that fixed responsibility for care on them. Margolis (1985) differentiates between challenges to accepted definitions in public contexts, in private arenas, and in unspoken reflection. Inner and private questioning are, she suggests, sometimes the antecedents of more public challenges to dominant meanings and claims for change, and all levels of questioning represent different facets of consciousness-changing processes. As she observes, "An audience can be as small as a single person thinking that definition she has previously taken for granted contradicts her experience" (1985, 341).

At a general level, women endorsed the prevailing definitions of families' and especially daughters' special ties and obligations to elderly mothers. However, the translation of these definitions into the particulars of their own lives was much more complex. A striking commonality in respondents' accounts of this complexity was their reference to setting limits on how they actually acted on their sense of obligation and responsibility. They spoke of setting limits in terms of physical space, finances, time, energy, and a hierarchy of commitments to others. For example:

If push came to shove, she would end up here [sharing respondent's home]. I'm hoping in some ways that she doesn't...because I think it'd be very difficult for her. I *know* it's going to be difficult for me (47-year-old subject, separated and working to support herself and two children).

I used to go over there every evening and stay. My husband really put up with a lot...he missed me and I cut down to five days a week (79-year-old respondent, looking back on caring for her confused and frail mother 20 years before).

She [mother] was out here quite a bit....I just had to draw the line...I couldn't, you know...Keeping an eye — they're teenagers, but sometimes I think they take more care than when they're younger, you know (47-year-old subject, working part-time, with two children).

Thus, women sought to "draw the line" between actions in relation to their mothers that they considered acceptable, desirable, or possible, and those that were not. Defining their boundaries in this way suggests resistance and self-definition in relation to forces perceived to be in some sense threatening or intrusive. Dominant definitions do not correspond with their experience. Such incongruence between personal experience and prevailing cultural meanings has been articulated by feminist scholars as a predictable feature of women's lives (Smith, 1979). Women confront a social world in which they have been precluded from contributing to dominant definitions of reality and therefore face the task of relieving the structured tensions between their realities and the social order.

To resolve the tensions in their situations as caregivers, women set limits on their responsibilities to their mothers. They sought to explain and justify these limits by using available legitimations to align their conduct with prevailing norms. For example, respondents referred to their competing commitments to their husbands and their children. An unmarried woman articulated these taken-for-granted justifications and the implied ordering of commitments:

From my point of view — I have no reason *not* to look after my mother. Like I have no responsibilities — there's just me and my job....I think it's much easier to be dedicated, and all the rest if you're not married — if you do have other responsibilities, your immediate family is first.

A few respondents explained their limits in terms of their capacities and defined their own terms; for example, a divorced woman of 51 teaching and taking university courses noted:

If they'd forced me into that [having her mother home from hospital], I would have had to stop my development of a second career, which is going to help *me* in my retirement....I would've had to stop, you know, a lot of things that interested me and...it would have interfered with my job to some degree, as well, so....it would have closed my life *down*, I think.

Raising these self-centered rather than other-centered concerns was difficult, as women recognized the "selfish" explanations for their limits were less legitimate than explanations related to work and family life. This recognition and the implied attunement to prevailing norms were articulated particularly candidly by a subject who had been recently divorced and was anxious to develop friendships and a new "life of her own."

Work is also a release. I would imagine the woman who's not working and is at home and doesn't have the other outlet and the other demands would find it sometimes overpowering. Like, I have my children too...and lots of excuses and justifications for why I can't do more.

While the now commonly used notion of "women in the middle" (Brody 1981) has provided a useful descriptive image of the competing commitments encountered by women, it also confirms women's place in the family sphere and in the realm of legitimate constraints on their capacities to respond to elderly parents. Thus, the woman quoted above consciously invoked legitimate explanations for her limits. The alternative explanation — that she was unwilling to forgo social and recreational activities that she enjoyed — was, she judged, unlikely to be deemed acceptable. She employed a vocabulary that aligned her with prevailing norms (Mills 1940) in order to sustain an image of caring, responsiveness and femininity.

Respondents noted their general reluctance to talk about their limits and their reasons for setting them. If they spoke of them at all, it was with women friends and never with their mothers. Some observed that the interview represented an idiosyncratic context in which they could reflect on their resistance to normative expectations. That their resistance remained a closed and generally silent process obstructed the key transition in social change processes from a privately experienced contradiction to a publicly expressed challenge of a taken-for-granted meaning (Margolis 1985).

Central to understanding the processes that repressed such transformations of meaning is the pervasiveness of guilt in respondents' accounts of their situations. Guilt can be understood as a feature of women's socialization to relationship rather than autonomy (Eichenbaum and Orbach 1983, 147). Thus, for women, an assertion of independence or pursuit of self-defined goals is equated with rejection of others' needs or with unresponsiveness to others and produces tension and guilt. Looking beyond the individual experience of guilt, Shott (1979, 1324) considers the social patterning to guilt as a "reflexive role-taking emotion." Such emotions are invoked when individuals take on the role of the generalized other and perceive themselves to be deviant or immoral in some way. Individuals are motivated to reduce or avoid such unpleasant feelings as guilt, so that it — and its specter — are "significant motivators or normative and moral conduct and, hence, facilitate social control" (Shott 1979, 1324).

The experience of a respondent can best illustrate the way in which guilt represents both self-control and social control. Ms. Scott, an unmarried woman in her 50s, described how she had resisted bringing her frail mother from Holland to live with her in Toronto. Ms. Scott expressed strong general approval of family commitment and caring and was fond of her mother, whose loneliness and diminishment she felt keenly. It was evident to her that in the conventional division of labor, responsibility for her mother was all hers. Her brother had made this explicit, and her mother's social worker in Holland regarded her as the "significant" relative, as did an uncle who wrote "a stern letter" reminding her of her duty. Ms. Scott also felt the weight of her mother's contradictory injunction that children ought to feel responsible for elderly parents but that Ms. Scott must "live her own life." Ms. Scott imagined that having her mother living with her would curtail her career ambitions and friendships. She felt "tremendously guilty" about these reservations, noting that her sense of duty was "very hard to escape."

Some time before the interview, Ms. Scott had decided to resolve this sense of entrapment by arranging her mother's admission to a nursing home in Holland. Glad that she had finally set a limit on her obligation, she talked about it tearfully and guiltily. She articulated her ambivalence in describing a woman friend in similar circumstances who set limits on her engagement with her mother more easily. On one hand, she was horrified at her friend's harshness, thinking to herself: "Well, I'm appalled at your coldness, you know, you really ought to be more dutiful; you should understand your mother more." On the other, she admired her resolution and self-protection and her ability to act on "her duty to herself." Thus, at one and the same time, this respondent resisted the normative expectations she had internalized yet imposed them on herself and other women.

Hochschild's (1979) analysis of feelings as a neglected aspect of ideology clarifies this inner struggle. Recognizing that feelings are not random experiences but highly structured and tied to normative frameworks, she articulates the notion of "feeling rules" — social guidelines for managing and expressing feelings. She notes that at times of social change, the rules are in flux and unclear. Ms. Scott is faced with competing feeling rules that produce her ambivalence and inner division. The first set of rules is still very compelling and reinforced by the actions of her uncle and her mother's social worker, her brother's choice to absent himself from responsibility, her mother's expectations and Ms. Scott's sadness for her, and her attachment to the imagery of the family as a warm and supportive institution. The competing set of rules, propelling her to want to "live her own life," receives some reinforcement from women friends, from the validation and reward she receives at work, and from the abstract imagery of women's entitlement to self-determination.

This kind of inner division is implicit in the limit-setting processes and awareness of "feeling rules" described by other respondents. For example, they voiced guilt at not doing enough in relation to their mothers, at minding the responsibilities they felt, and at talking about their concerns with others. Accordingly, they judged themselves as inadequate, selfish, and disloyal. They invoked feeling rules in such statements as "I should feel guilty at not being nearer"; "I shouldn't complain about her"; "I've no right to be irritated with him [subject's brother] — he's really very good." Through these processes of self-censorship, women contained their complaint. For most of them, guilt or the specter of guilt stifled articulation of the tension embedded in their situations.

To summarize, women's efforts to set limits on their obligation to their mothers served to resolve some of the tensions between the expectations that they faced as daughters and their own wishes for themselves. However, such resolutions came at the price of inner conflicts that prevented translation of their dilemmas into complaint or demands for more shared responses to their mothers' needs in old age.

Conclusion

This study offers insights into the way social policies and practices, the division of paid and unpaid work, and values concerning gender and family ties structure women's experiences of obligation and frame the contradictions embedded in their accounts of caregiving. The research alerts us to the limits of narrow social-psychological interpretations of the meaning of women's sense of obligation. Formulated as psychological or interpersonal problems, women's dilemmas are subject to individually oriented interventions. Certainly, care relationships between mothers and daughters have individual characteristics and tensions for which micro-level interventions may provide much-needed relief. However, it is crucial to recognize that they are also socially structured relationships, charged with expectations by virtue of the absence of alternative responses to old people's needs.

Recognizing the links between individual experiences and wider social structures also highlights the error of posing caregivers' and care receivers' interests in oppositional terms. Unqualified assertions of caregivers' rights and increasingly common allusions to "intergenerational conflict" cast caregivers' and care receivers' interests as opposites (Binney and Estes 1988). While elderly mothers may appear to be the immediate cause of caregivers' dilemmas, their dependence on female kin is not really a choice and is often not welcomed (Aronson 1990).

The research points to the external constraints, beyond the immediate and interpersonal dimensions of women's situations, that left them to negotiate their responsibilities alone, with little room to maneuver. Recognizing the minimal presence of public services and the relative absence of men from responsibility for care, women themselves saw their sense of obligation as a necessity rather than a choice when they posed the question "Who else is going to do it?"

Ideologically, this material division of labor was powerfully reinforced, both by external pressures, for example, by family members and service providers, and by internal pressures. Women were torn between adherence to prevailing cultural values about femininity, care and family ties and the wish to enhance their own autonomy and interests. In general, they bore these dilemmas privately, since speaking about them at all would violate images of caring and loyalty to loved ones. Borne privately, they understood them as personal problems or failings, rather than as legitimate subjects for complaint. Facilitating this transition in meaning — from a personal problem to a public issue — is an important task for the future.

Turning to the future and thinking of strategies for changing these repressive processes and enhancing women's interests, analysis must address both the material and ideological aspects of women's obligations. In formulating the problem of the costs of unpaid caregiving as a conflict between women and the state, attention has been focused largely on material aspects of the division of public and private responsibility. Solutions are seen in terms of expanded government provision for old people. Generously funded and flexible community care and more humane and self-determined forms of congregate care are heralded as ways of freeing women from the obligation to care by according them real choices in acting on their affections for others and their aspirations for themselves (Dalley 1988; Qureshi and Walker 1989). Thus, it is suggested, neither they nor their elderly relatives would, as at present, be pressed into ties of obligation and dependence.

Whether the provision of such material alternatives would so simply liberate women from the powerful cultural injunction to care is debatable. The experiences of the Scandinavian countries with generous entitlements to public supports (by North American standards) suggest that women continue to dominate in paid caring occupations and to feel more obliged than men to assume informal responsibilities for dependent relatives (Borchorst and Siim 1987). Others note that it is not easy for women to relinquish responsibility for care, even when alternatives are available. Accepting formal help is seen as synonymous with failing to "cope" and being uncaring and, therefore, flies in the face of deeply held images of womanhood (Briggs and Oliver 1985). In short, what is at play is not just a contest for resources and practical alternatives but, even more fundamentally, an ideological struggle about the meaning of gender and the definition of women's needs (Fraser 1989, 144).

Challenging the gender division of care opens a well-developed debate about the sharing of the right and the responsibility to care between men and women (Finch 1984; Saraceno 1987; Ungerson 1987). The obstacles to such sharing — the separation of the paid work world from the domestic sphere, the rhythms and organization of the labor market, the construction of gender identities and associated power differentials — are daunting and, perhaps, account for why this avenue of change has been less addressed. However, drawing attention to the division of responsibility for old people and assumptions about gender roles can, in itself, be an important contribution to the debate at this stage. Making visible what generally passes as unremarkable challenges received ideas and meaning and, cumulatively, can prompt re-examination of service practices, social policies, and research conceptualizations of women as caregivers.

The experiences of the women who participated in this research provide a basis for conceptual exploration of the social processes that sustain the present pattern of care of old people. Their accounts illustrate the tensions embedded in feeling responsibility for their elderly mothers and open the way for understanding the constraining context that obliged them to care. Broadening this preliminary exploration of the intersection of personal and structural forces, as well as working toward more equitable definitions of responsibility and care in research, social policy, and practice, is the challenge for the future.

References

Abel, E.K. 1989. The ambiguities of social support: Adult daughters caring for frail elderly parents. *Journal of Aging Studies* 3:211-30.

Aronson, J. 1988. Women's experience in giving and receiving care: Pathways to social change. Ph.D. diss., University of Toronto, Toronto.

—. 1990. Old women's experiences of needing care: Choice or compulsion? *Canadian Journal on Aging* 9:234-47.

Baines, C., P. Evans, and S.M. Neysmith, eds. 1991. *Women's caring: A feminist perspective on social welfare,* Toronto: McLelland & Stewart.

Binney, E.A., and C.L. Estes. 1988. The retreat of the state and its transfer of responsibility: The intergenerational war. *International Journal of Health Services* 18:83-96.

Borchorst, A., and Ciim, B. 1987. Women and the advanced welfare state. In *Women and the state,* edited by A.S. Sassoon. London: Unwin Hyman.

Bowers, B.J. 1987. Intergenerational caregiving: Adult caregivers and their aging parents. *Advanced Nursing Science* 9:20-31.

Briggs, A., and J. Oliver. 1985. *Caring: Experiences of looking after disabled relatives. London: Routledge & Kegan Paul.*

Brody, E.M. 1981. "Women in the middle" and family help to older people. *Gerontologist* 21:471-80.

—. 1985. Parent care as a normative family stress. *Gerontologist* 25:19-29.

Bulmer, M. 1987. *The social basis of community care.* London: Allen & Unwin.

Chafetz, J.S. 1988. The gender division of labor and the reproduction of female disadvantage. *Journal of Family Issues* 9: 108-31.

Chappell, N.L., L.A. Strain, and A.A. Blandford. 1986. *Aging and health care: A social perspective.* Toronto: Holt, Rinehart & Winston.

Cicirelli, V.G. 1981. *Helping elderly parents: The role of adult children.* Boston: Auburn House.

Dalley, G. 1988. *Ideologies of caring: Rethinking community and collectivism.* London: Allen & Unwin.

Eichenbaum, L., and S. Orbach. 1983. *Understanding women: A feminist psychoanalytic approach.* New York: Basic Books.

Eichler, M. 1988. *Families in Canada today: Recent changes and their policy consequences.* 2nd ed. Toronto: Gage.

Finch, J. 1984. Community care: Developing non-sexist alternatives. *Critical Social Policy* 9:6-18.

—. 1987. Family obligations and the life course. In *Rethinking the life cycle,* edited by A. Bryman, B. Bytheway, P. Allat, and T. Kiel. London: Macmillan.

Finch, J., and D. Groves. 1980. Community care and the family: A case for equal opportunities? *Journal of Social Policy* 9:487-514.

—, eds. 1983. *A labour of love: Women, work and caring.* London: Routledge & Kegan Paul.

Finch, J., and J. Mason. 1990. Filial obligations and kin support for elderly people. *Ageing and Society* 10:151-76.

Fraser, N. 1989. *Unruly practices: Power, discourse and gender in contemporary social theory.* Minneapolis: University of Minnesota Press.

Health and Welfare Canada. 1986. *Aging: Shifting the emphasis.* Ottawa. Health Services and Promotion Branch.

Hochschild, A.R. 1979. Emotion work, feeling rules and social structure. *American Journal of Sociology* 85:551-75.

Hooyman, N.R., and Ryan, R. 1987. Women as caregivers of the elderly: Catch 22 dilemmas. In *The trapped woman,* edited by J. Figueira-McDonough and R. Sarri. Newbury Park, CA: Sage.

Judge, K. 1978. *Rationing social services.* London: Heinemann.

Lee, G.R. 19895. Kinship and social suppor of the elderly: The case of the United States. *Ageing and Society* 5:19-38.

Margolis, D.R. 1985. Redefining the situation: Negotiations of the meaning of "woman." *Social Problems* 32:332-47.

Mills, C.W. 1940. Situated actions and vocabularies of motive. *American Sociological Review* 5:904-13.

Moroney, R. 1980. *Families, social services and social policy: The issue of shared responsibility.* Rockville, MD: National Institute of Mental Health.

Osterbusch, S.E., S.M. Keigher, B. Miller, and N.L. Linsk. 1987. Community care policies and gender justice. *International Journal of Health Services* 17:217-32.

Parker, G. 1985. *With due care and attention: A review of research on informal care.* London: Family Policy Studies Centre.

Parker, R.A. 1967. Social administration and scarcity: The problem of rationing. *Social Work* 24:9-14.

Qureshi, H., and A. Walker. 1989. *The caring relationship: Elderly people and their families.* London: Macmillan.

Rimmer, L. 1983. The economics of work and caring. In *A Labour of Love: Women, work and caring.* edited by J. Finch and D. Groves. London: Routledge & Kegan Paul.

Saraceno, C. 1987. Division of family labour and gender identity. In *Women and the state,* edited by A.S. Sassoon. London: Unwin Hyman.

Shott, S. 1979. Emotion and social life: A symbolic interaction analysis. *American Journal of Sociology* 84:1317-34.

Smith, D.E. 1979. A sociology for women. In *The prism of sex: Essays in the sociology of knowledge,* edited by J.A. Sherman and E. Torton Beck. Madison: University of Wisconsin Press.

—. 1986. Institutional ethnography: A feminist method. *Resources for Feminist Research* 15:6-13.

—. 1987. *The everyday world as problematic: A feminist sociology.* Toronto: University of Toronto Press.

Therborn, G. 1980. *The ideology of power and the power of ideology.* London: Verso.

Twigg, J. 1989. Models of carers: How do social care agencies conceptualize their relationship with informal carers? *Journal of Social Policy* 18:53-66.

Ungerson, C. 1987. *Policy is personal: Sex, gender and informal care.* London: Tavistock.

Walker, A. 1985. From welfare state to caring society? The promise of informal networks. In *Support networks in a caring community,* edited by J.A. Yoder, J.M.L. Jonder, and R.A.B. Leaper. Dordrecht: Martinus Nijhoff.

Jane Aronson's interests center on the influence of health and social policies in shaping women's experiences of caring over the life course, both materially and emotionally. Currently, her research focuses on competing interpretations of older women's needs embedded in their perspective on receiving care and in social policies and practices.

AUTHOR'S NOTE: The work reported in this article was supported in part by the National Health Research and Development Programme of Health and Welfare Canada through a National Health Fellowship, the Programme in Gerontology at the University of Toronto through a seed grant, and the Social Sciences and Humanities Research Council of Canada through a postdoctoral fellowship. For their responses to an earlier draft of this article, I am grateful to Roy Cain, Lynn Kearney, Dorothy Pawluch, Vera Tarman, and Vivienne Walters. Thanks are also due to the reviewers of *Gender & Society* for their helpful comments and Margaret Andersen for editorial advice.

Growing Up And Old Together: Some Observations on Families in Later Life

INGRID ARNET CONNIDIS

Our usual picture of a family includes a mother, father, and their young children living together. But not many families of later life fit this picture. Indeed, this is an increasingly inaccurate portrayal of families for many adults of *all* ages. Nonetheless, much of the research about older families is about marriage and about parent-child relationships. In some ways, this focus is understandable; 56 percent of older persons are married, and the vast majority, about 80 percent, have at least one living child (Connidis, 1989a). However, this narrow focus is a problem for two reasons. First, it overlooks the family lives and the contributions to family life of those who are not married or do not have children. It is as if these individuals are not part of families. Second, the focus on marriage and children ignores the potential significance of other family relationships, for example, those between siblings; between aunts, uncles and their nieces and nephews; and between cousins. The objective of this chapter is to take a more inclusive view in making some observations about family life in older age.

On her first visit to a nursing home, 90 year-old Hagar Currie, lead character in Margaret Laurence's book, *The Stone Angel*, strikes up a conversation with a resident. Hagar speaks in the first person:

"Do you —" I hesitate. "Do you ever get used to such a place?"

She laughs then, a short bitter laugh I recognize and comprehend at once.

"Do you get used to life?" she says. "Can you answer me that? It all comes as a surprise. You get your first period, and you're amazed — I can have babies now — such a thing! When the children come, you think — Is it mine? Did it come out of me? Who could believe it? When you can't have them any more, what a shock — It's finished — so soon?"

I peer at her, thinking how peculiar that she knows so much.

"You're right. I never got used to a blessed thing." (p.104)

Similarly, family life continues to hold surprises. But, relationships do not tend to take dramatic turns in their character - just as individuals do not - simply by virtue of reaching age 65. Poor relationships do not sweeten, nor good ones sour due solely to the passage of time (e.g., re: siblings see Scott, 1983; Wilson and Pahl, 1988).

Aging is characterized by both *continuity and change*. Perhaps no other part of our lives gives a stronger sense of continuity than relationships with our family. And yet, here too, considerable change takes place. Some family members are lost, often through death, but also through divorce and relocation. We gain other family members through marriage - our own or others' - and birth. As well, the relationships which remain continue to evolve. They require ongoing negotiation as conflicting needs and wants are resolved. We do not enter old age with our relationships "set."

Marriage

For those who remain married into older age, marriage provides a basis for continuity. Spouses have typically known each other since at least early adulthood, have shared (or at least been aware of) the challenges, successes, and disappointments of family, work, and leisure, and are still together as they enter a new phase of life, typically without the demands of children and paid work. In many ways, such couples have grown up together.

Research shows that old couples and newlyweds have the highest levels of marital satisfaction (Lupri and Frideres, 1981; See Rosenthal and Gladstone, Chapter 10). Two caveats regarding such research must be noted (Connidis 1989a). First, studies of marital satisfaction in old age are dealing disproportionately with what could be termed the successes, namely, those couples who have stayed together. The more unhappy couples are likely to have divorced or separated at younger ages. Second, most people would experience discomforting inconsistency in saying first, yes, I have been married to this person for 40 or more years and, then, no, I am not very happy with this relationship. The implicit rejoinder - then why have you stayed together for so long? - would be hard for most people to answer to their own satisfaction. Hence, the happiness of long-term marriages may be exaggerated.

Nonetheless, a lifetime together coupled with typical age-related declines in physical ability usually increases a couple's interdependence; that is, husband and wife depend upon one another more than before (Depner and Ingersoll-Dayton, 1985; Kelley, 1981). This interdependence often provides a basis for a renewed sense of companionship and for providing more intensive support should one of the spouses become ill.

This somewhat rosy picture of marriage in later life often follows a challenging period of transition immediately after retirement. During this transition, both members of the couple must sort out their changed life patterns and their respective roles within their marriage. Although the common portrayal of retirement — a husband underfoot in the kitchen of his wife — has some validity, it is only one response. As the roles of women change, retirement is increasingly a "his and hers" experience. Even among more traditional couples, there appears to be a move away from traditional gender roles and behaviour (Brubaker, 1985; Zube, 1982). For men, this may mean greater sensitivity and reflection and, for women, increased independence and assertiveness.

Should one spouse become ill or incapacitated, the other usually becomes the most active provider of care and support, barring his or her own illness. This is true whether the ill spouse is wife or husband (Ingersoll-Dayton and Antonucci, 1988). This point merits emphasis because there has been much media coverage about the burden of care being assumed by women. With respect to marriage, women are much more likely than men to provide care to a spouse but, this is largely because husbands are more likely to become ill and die before their wives. For a surviving spouse who provided long-term care, a key challenge is rebuilding contact with others. This is why the long-term illness of a spouse prior to death does not necessarily ease the transition to widowhood in later life (Martin Matthews, 1991).

Widowhood

Widowhood is experienced quite differently by men and women (Connidis, 1989a; Martin Matthews, 1991). Among men, widowhood signals a major break with the norm, for older men are more often married. Men do not have a ready network of widowers to join when they lose their wife. As well, many of today's older men (and a substantial portion of their younger counterparts) rely heavily on their spouse to maintain contact with their circle of family and friends. Consequently, widowhood often sets men somewhat adrift, as they are less adept at maintaining relationships once on their own. Thus, for men, widowhood is more often associated with isolation and loneliness.

Although the loss of a husband also creates a sense of loneliness among women, this feeling tends to be less pervasive for two main reasons. First, if widowed in older age, women do have a ready network of widows to join. Second, women benefit from the interpersonal skills they have developed over a lifetime and are better able to maintain their ties with other family members and friends. However, unlike men, a significant portion of today's older widows suffer financially when they lose their husband. As well, the number of years they must survive on reduced income and resources is considerably higher, given their greater life expectancy.

Counter to a common assumption about differences between men and women following widowhood, some Australian research finds that men more readily acquire the skills traditionally associated with the opposite sex than do women (Kendig, 1986). Most notably, women tend not to acquire the "handyman" skills of their husbands. Moreover, those who have never driven a car are unlikely to learn how once widowed, thereby contributing to the major transportation problem experienced by the older population, particularly in rural areas.

Older Parents and Their Children

Much of the research on this tie concerns the support that adult children provide their older parents. Terms such as "the caught generation", the "sandwich generation", and "women-in-the-middle" have been created to refer to middle-aged daughters who are "sandwiched" or "caught" between meeting the demands of their children and those of their parents (usually a widowed mother). As well, many of these women must meet the demands of work as well. One reason that this topic has received so much attention is the age of those who do much of the research and produce much of the media coverage: namely, middle-aged adults.

There are two major concerns with the amount of attention paid to the problems of the sandwich generation. First, the likelihood of women being "caught" in this situation tends to be exaggerated. The real possibility of being sandwiched is limited. Estimates are that, at most, roughly half of middle-aged women actually have both living parents and dependent children at the same time (Rosenthal, Matthews, and Marshall, 1989). The parents of many of these women are relatively young and healthy, reducing the likelihood of having to provide care. If one includes labour force participation as a third competing demand, the numbers drop again. In fact, the percentage of women who are actually combining child care, parent care, and labour force participation is quite low among middle-aged women. One estimate ranges from 5 percent among those aged 50 to 54 to 13 percent among those aged 45 to 49 (Spitze and Logan, 1990). Another two percent in each of these age groups is combining parent and child care but not work outside the home (Spitze and Logan, 1990; see also, Rosenthal, Matthews and Marshall, 1989).

A second shortcoming of the focus on the sandwiched middle generation is the tendency to ignore the support that older parents offer their children. Here, middle-aged children tend to demonstrate a common human trait, namely, a failure to notice when one is a burden or responsibility for others. Yet, there is ample evidence of the ongoing support given by older parents to their adult children. Financial support is most commonly provided by the older for the younger generation. Also, although the median age of widowhood in Canada is rising, a significant proportion of married women are widowed before the age of 65 (Martin Matthews, 1991). A substantial source of support for many of these women comes from their older parents and, when this occurs, the well-being of these younger widowed women improves markedly (Bankoff, 1983). Finally, in the wake of an increasing number of divorces, grandparents, especially maternal grandmothers, are often central to the stability of their grandchildren's lives, either as parent substitutes or as regular contacts (Gladstone, 1987; 1988).

While the latter case represents an unusually high level of grandparental involvement, middle-aged bias is apparent in our understanding of grandparenthood. The widely accepted wisdom regarding grandparenting is that it is a predominantly pleasurable, almost benign, relationship devoid of the responsibilities and obligations of parenthood. While this is supported by some research, it is in part a matter of conjecture on behalf of the parent generation (i.e., those most directly engaged in the responsibility and obligations of raising children). However, as a grandmother, Margaret Mead observed:

> I felt none of the much trumpeted freedom from responsibility that grandparents are supposed to feel. Actually, it seems to me that the obligation to be a resource but not an interference is just as preoccupying as the attention one gives to one's own children. I think we do not allow sufficiently for the obligation we lay on grandparents to keep themselves out of the picture — not to interfere, not to spoil, not to insist, not to intrude.... (Blackberry Winter, 1972: 303).

All this said, we must not lose sight of two very important and repeated findings. First, children, especially daughters, typically do provide support to their older parents when it is required (Atkinson et al., 1986; Chappell, 1992). Sons also provide support, but this is most likely to occur when daughters are not available (Horowtiz, 1985). When daughters are in the labour force, gender differences occur, with daughters working outside the home tending to employ the managerial style more typical of male caregivers (Brody et al., 1987; Brody and Schoonover, 1986). Given that a majority of men and women are now in the labour force, there is a growing need for services which can be managed or coordinated by adult children.

Second, when women (and men) are caught between the demands of children, parent/s, and work, they often experience stress, burden, social isolation, and burn-out. There is a clear need to promote policies and programs that support those providing care as well as those receiving it. More generally, we must institute broader social change which is supportive of families, old and young. Currently, the interests of work and family are typically in competition. The need to mesh these interests remains, for they are indeed enmeshed among the individuals trying to meet the dual demands of family and work, more often for women than for men. To date, we have tended to assign priority to work over family. As more men and women are engaged in both enterprises simultaneously, there may be a growing willingness to recognize the importance of family, and to increase the flexibility of the work world accordingly.

Siblings

The older parent's need for care often marks a key transition in the sibling relationship, bringing brothers and sisters together as they seek to provide support to their parent/s. Siblings, now middle-aged adults, move away from their role as children and, ideally, toward sharing responsibility for their parents. Sometimes this transition leads instead to rancour over the uneven contributions made by various siblings, as is regularly demonstrated in letters to Ann Landers and her sister Abbie.

Very few of us have not been touched personally by the sibling relationship, either as a brother or sister, as a parent watching the sibling ties of our children flourish and flounder, or as a child observing the ties between our parents and their siblings. Yet, relatively little research has been directed to questions about sibling ties in adulthood. Periodically, media attention has dealt with this subject but with a marked preference for such topics as major sibling rifts, falling in love with a spouse's brother, and similar titillating topics.

In another passage from Margaret Laurence's *The Stone Angel*, Hagar, who has just declined her daughter-in-law Doris' offer to meet with her minister, thinks to herself:

Doris believes that age increases natural piety, like a kind of insurance policy falling due. I couldn't explain. Who would understand, even if I strained to speak? I am past ninety, and this figure seems somehow arbitrary and impossible, for when I look in my mirror and beyond the changing shell that houses me, I see the eyes of Hagar Currie, the same dark eyes as when I first began to remember and notice myself. (p.38)

There are few who look into our eyes and see us in our youth; certainly not children and, more and more often, not a spouse either. One exceptional relationship in this regard is that between siblings. Indeed, the shared history of siblings is one cornerstone of this relationship in old age, as it provides such a ready basis for reminiscence and a sense of continuity (Cicirelli, 1982; Goetting, 1986; Moss and Moss, 1989).

There are other reasons to expect the sibling tie to be especially significant in older age. At least 80 percent of those aged 65 and over have at least one living sibling, making this tie more prevalent than having a spouse, especially among older women (Connidis, 1989a). Also, when compared to ties to spouse, parents, and children, the tie to siblings is more sociable and less obligatory (Cumming and Schneider, 1961; Connidis, 1989b). Higher rates of divorce and childlessness, and smaller, closely-spaced families may combine to increase the significance of sibling ties to future cohorts of older persons.

Closeness to siblings tends to grow over the years and rivalry tends to decline, unless the tie was originally acrimonious. Contact with brothers and sisters tends to ebb and flow, a common pattern being less contact during middle age and increased contact in older age. In a study of older Londoners (i.e., aged 65 and over), nearly 80 percent considered at least one of their siblings to be a close friend (Connidis, 1989b). In another study of Londoners aged 55 and over (Connidis and McMullin, 1992), 70 percent described their relationship with their siblings as somewhat, very, or extremely close. These findings suggest the viability of brothers and sisters as a substantial source of emotional support in later life.

Contact, confiding, and companionship among siblings are all more likely when the siblings are sisters and when one of the siblings is single, meaning never married (Connidis, 1989c; Connidis and Davies, 1990; 1992). Similarly, when at least one sibling is childless, contact and confiding between siblings is more likely, particularly among sisters. Finally, when at least one sibling is widowed, contact between siblings is higher. Women, those who are not married, and those without children are of considerable concern from a policy perspective because they do not have a spouse and/or child to provide support in later life. These findings indicate the potential significance of siblings as providers of support in older age.

However, the greater involvement of single and childless siblings does not represent a simple case of their dependence. Rather, these family members make significant and unique contributions to the whole family. They provide a disproportionate share of help to older parents and they are more readily available in crisis as they have no competing demands from either a spouse and/or children (see Rosenthal and Gladstone, Chapter 10).

Research on life transitions and their effects on the sibling tie (Connidis, 1992) provides further evidence of the family roles played by single and childless individuals, underlining the continuing significance of the family of origin — our parents and siblings — over the entire life course. This is too often lost in our focus on the nuclear family of procreation, as though one family displaces the other rather than simply adding to it.

What happens to sibling relationships when brothers and sisters marry, have children, divorce, are widowed, or experience the illness or death of family members? Based on interviews (Connidis, 1992) with 60 pairs of siblings from 25 to 89 years old, a few patterns emerge. First, about sixty percent report no change in their relationships with brothers and sisters following marriage, the arrival of children, or widowhood. Just the opposite is true regarding divorce and the divorce or widowhood of one's siblings: about 60 percent report change in their sibling ties following these events. Thus, what we might term crisis events are more likely to have an impact on sibling relationships.

Of all the events, the arrival of children, either one's own or one's siblings, and the poor health or death of family members are most likely to lead to emotionally closer ties between siblings (with 60 to 100 percent reporting this outcome). Comments from a brother in his 40s exemplify the impact of family illness or death:

I was drawn closer to my sister at our father's death. Before that I didn't know her well....Just the shared emotion of it I guess. We never showed each other our emotions because we hardly ever saw each other but on that occasion we did, so [the death of a parent] draws people closer together.

Divorce and widowhood typically lead to greater emotional closeness, very supportive behaviour from siblings, and more frequent contact. Speaking of the aftermath of her brother's divorce, a sister in her 40s observes:

He and I were very close. We'd be together every weekend with our kids. Now he's more on his feet and we don't see each other as much as we did before....We've always been close. The divorce just made it more so.

Marriage, on the other hand, is equally likely to bring greater and less emotional closeness, as well as improved relations and less frequent contact. Says an 81 year-old widow:

After I got married and was away all those years we always kept in contact and I would be at home at times but, of course, then you're not as close to them as when you are living in the same city. As far as feelings or love for them, it has always been the same [but] there's a feeling of closeness now that you don't have when you are living miles away.

Of all these life events, it is marriage which is most likely to place a damper on sibling ties, until the arrival of children, when the sibling tie appears to resurge. The shared concern for children appears to be driven by a mutual interest among siblings in the welfare of the entire family's children. A 41 year-old single woman's comments reflect this:

I think the baby coming has warmed things up a lot and brought things closer....I sort of hold myself responsible for that child's happiness....It would be different if I had my own family I'm sure,...but without that I have the resources, emotionally and financially, to be able to make him a part of my world.

Life crises such as divorce, widowhood, illness, and death tend also to awaken dormant sibling ties across the life course and into old age. Perhaps the ability of siblings to look into one another's eyes and see the children they once were allows them an extra degree of empathy for one another.

Conclusion

In closing, the significance of our family ties extends beyond our personal experience of them. In her autobiography, Margaret Mead brings home the power of our personal lives to shape our world view; to transform our individual concerns to concerns about the world and its future. She writes:

In the presence of grandparent and grandchild, past and future merge in the present. Looking at a loved child, one cannot say, "We must die now so that later others may live." This is the argument that generations of old men, cut off from children, have used in sending young men out to die in war. Nor can one say, "I want this child to live well no matter how we despoil the earth for later generations." For seeing a child as one's grandchild, one can visualize that same child as a grandparent, and with the eyes of another generation one can see other children, just as light-footed and vivid, as eager to learn and know and embrace the world, who must be taken into account — now. (Mead 1972:311).

In turn, the child or grandchild, looking at a loved parent or grandparent, has a personalized concern for the welfare of older people. The changes we can make in families — the greater involvement of both parents; the greater involvement of communities; the greater inclusion of all members — are not small steps. They point to a better future, not just for the private lives of individual families, but for all of society.

References

Bankoff, Elizabeth A. (1983). "Aged Parents and Their Widowed Daughters: A Support Relationship" *Journal of Gerontology* 38(2):226-230.

Brody, Elaine M., Morton H. Kleban, Pauline T. Johnsen, Christine Hoffman, and Claire B. Schoonover. (1987). "Work Status and Parent Care: A Comparison of Four Groups of Women." *The Gerontologist* 27(2):201-208.

Brody, Elaine M., and Claire B. Schoonover. (1986). "Patterns of Parent-Care When Adult Daughters Work and When They do Not." *The Gerontologist* 26(4):372-381.

Brubaker, Timothy H. (1985). "Responsibility for Household Tasks: A Look at Golden Anniversary Couples Aged 75 Years and Older." In Warren A. Peterson and Jill Quadagno (eds.), *Social Bonds in Later Life*. Beverly Hills: Sage Publications. Pp. 27-36.

Chappell, Neena L. 1992. *Social Support and Aging*. Toronto: Harcourt, Brace.

Cicirelli, Victor G. (1982). "Sibling Influence Throughout the Lifespan." In Michael E. Lamb and Brian Sutton-Smith (eds.), *Sibling Relationships: Their Nature and Significance Across the Lifespan*. Hillsdale, New Jersey: Lawrence Erlbaum Associates Publishers. Pp. 267-284.

Connidis, Ingrid Arnet. (1989a). *Family Ties and Aging*. Toronto: Harcourt, Brace.

Connidis, Ingrid Arnet. (1989b). "Siblings as Friends in Later Life." *American Behavioral Scientist* 33(1):81-93.

Connidis, Ingrid Arnet. (1989c). "Contact Between Siblings in Later Life." *The Canadian Journal of Sociology* 14(4):429-441.

Connidis, Ingrid Arnet. (1992). "Life Transitions and the Adult Sibling Tie: A Qualitative Study." *Journal of Marriage and the Family* May.

Connidis, Ingrid Arnet, and Lorraine Davies. (1990). "Confidants and Companions in Later Life: The Place of Family and Friends." *Journal of Gerontology: Social Sciences* 45(4):S141-S149.

Connidis, Ingrid Arnet, and Lorraine Davies. (1992). "Confidants and Companions: Choices in Later Life." *Journal of Gerontology: Social Sciences* 47(3):S115-S122.

Connidis, Ingrid Arnet and Julie A. McMullin. (1992). *Final Report: Social Support and Service Needs of Older Adults: Targeting Groups at Risk*. London: Interdisciplinary Group on Aging, University of Western Ontario.

Cumming, Elaine, and David M. Schneider. (1961). "Sibling Solidarity: A Property of American Kinship." *American Anthropologist* 63(12):498-508.

Depner, Charlene E. and Berit Ingersoll-Dayton. (1985). "Physical Distance and Social Contact Between Elders and Their Adult Children." *Research on Aging* 10(1):56-80.

Gladstone, James W. (1987). "Factors Associated with Changes in Visiting Between Grandmothers and Grandchildren Following an Adult Child's Marriage Breakdown." *Canadian Journal on Aging* 6(2):117-127.

Gladstone, James W. (1988). "Perceived Changes in Grandmother-Grandchild Relations Following a Child's Separation or Divorce." *The Gerontologist* 28(1):66-72.

Goetting, Ann. (1986). "The Development Tasks of Siblingship over the Life Cycle." *Journal of Marriage and the Family* November:703-714.

Horowitz, Amy. 1985. "Sons and Daughters as Caregivers to Older Parents: Differences in Role Performance and Consequences." *The Gerontologist* 25(6):612-617.

Ingersoll-Dayton, B. and T. Antonucci. (1988). "Reciprocal and Nonreciprocal Social Support: Contrasting Sides of Intimate Relationships." *Journal of Gerontology* 43:565-573.

Kelley, Harold H. (1981). "Marriage Relationships and Aging." Chapter 13 in James G. March (ed.-in-chief), Robert W. Fogel, Elaine Hatfield, Sara B. Kiesler, and Ethel Shanas (volume eds.), *Aging: Stability and Change in the Family*. Toronto: Academic Press. Pp. 275-300.

Kendig, Hal. (1986). "Intergenerational Exchange." In Hal L. Kendig (ed.), *Ageing and Families: A Social Networks Perspective*. Boston: Allen & Unwin. Pp. 85-109.

Laurence, Margaret. (1968). *The Stone Angel*. Toronto: McClelland and Stewart.

Lupri, Eugen and James Frideres. (1981). "The Quality of Marriage and the Passage of Time: Marital Satisfaction Over the Family Life Cycle" *Canadian Journal of Sociology* 6(3):283-305.

Martin Matthews, Anne. (1991). *Widowhood in Later Life*. Toronto: Harcourt, Brace.

Mead, Margaret. (1972). *Blackberry Winter: My Earlier Years*. New York: Pocket Books (Washington Square Press).

Moss, Sidney Z. and Miriam S. Moss. (1989). "The Impact of the Death of an Elderly Sibling: Some Considerations of a Normative Loss." *American Behavioral Scientist* 33(1):94-106.

Rosenthal, Carolyn J., Sarah H. Matthews, Victor W. Marshall. (1989). "Is Parent Care Normative? The Experiences of a Sample of Middle-aged Women." *Research on Aging* 11(2):244-260.

Scott, Jean Pearson. (1983). "Siblings and Other Kin." In Timothy Brubaker (ed.) *Family Relationships in Later Life*. Beverly Hills: Sage. Pp. 47-62.

Spitze, Glenna and John Logan. (1990). "More Evidence on Women (and Men) in the Middle" *Research on Aging* 12(2):182-198.
Wilson, Patricia and Ray Pahl. (1988). "The Changing Sociological Construct of the Family" *Sociological Review* 56:233-272.
Zube, Margaret. (1982). "Changing Behavior and Outlook of Aging Men and Women: Implications for Marriage in the Middle and Later Years." *Family Relations* 31:January:147-156.

Ingrid Arnet Connidis is a Professor of Sociology and Director of the Interdisciplinary Group on Aging at the University of Western Ontario. She received her B.A. and M.A. at Western and her Ph.D. at the University of Toronto. Her primary research interests are the family relationships of older persons, especially those who are childless or single (never married); sibling relationships in adulthood; and the composition of various support networks for different groups of older persons. She is author of *Family Ties and Aging* (Harcourt Brace). Her professional interests take on personal meaning through her relationships with her parents, six siblings, four children, and spouse.

AUTHOR'S NOTE: This chapter is a revised version of a presentation at the Queen's University Lectures on Aging: Myth and Fact, Sponsored by the Queen's Gerontology Project and the Department of Sociology, Queen's University, Kingston, Ontario, March 3, 1993. I thank the Social Sciences and Humanities Research Council of Canada (grant numbers 410-92-0393) and The Western Foundation for their support of this research.

The Portrayal of Older People in Canadian Advertisements: Regular vs. Specialized Magazines[1]

MERVIN Y. T. CHEN AND NAN ZHOU[2]

Introduction

Most advertisements in consumer magazines are, in Goffman's term, "public pictures" designed to sell products for advertisers. They are pictures in which the advertiser uses models and/or props to evoke life-like scenes. Within these scenes, Erving Goffman[3] posits that human behaviours can be seen as "displays", such as gender, ethnic, and age displays. In this paper we consider how age is displayed in Canadian popular magazines.

Content Analysis of the Portrayal of Older People in Advertising

How are the aged depicted in advertisements? Today, unlike in the past, the aged are no longer ignored entirely. However, they are to a great extent depicted unfavourably.[4] A major finding in studies of the portrayal of old people in various media is their low visibility in advertising. Content analyses of Canadian and American print ads have found that older people are under-represented in comparison with their proportion in the population.[5] This pattern is especially pronounced for the portrayal of older women.[6] In general, advertising is oriented toward the young,[7] although a more recent study found that when product brands were aimed at older age groups (i.e., 45 and older), older models tended to be used more frequently.[8] Characters past the age of 50 are often portrayed as being physically inactive, with health being a problem,[9] and tend to be seen in non-work or family settings.[10] Also, older models are frequently seen in ads selling a corporate image rather than a particular consumable product.[11] In terms of gender, older men appear more frequently and more often in work scenes[12] and are used as major role advisors much more frequently than older women.[13] Generally, older women are more often negatively stereotyped.[14]

However, these findings are not conclusive. For example, contrary to most studies, Swayne and Greco found that females appeared more frequently than males in commercials. They also found that only a very small percentage of ads containing older people were for products relating to physical ailments. Furthermore, some studies[15] indicated that the elderly were frequently cast in authoritative roles, such as advisors. Ursic et al. (1986) found a significant use of the elderly not only for promoting a corporate image but also for advertising products such as fine wine.

Reactions to the Portrayal of Older People in Advertising

How do older people react to their images in advertising? Research findings are not conclusive. In their own survey and in the studies they reviewed, Festervand and Lumpkin[16] found that older people usually reported that advertising presented an inaccurate image. Their study suggested that such stereotyped depictions of the elderly might evoke not only negative attitudes toward the sponsoring company and/or products, but even limited boycotting of the company or product.[17] Similarly, Smith, Moschis and Moore[18] found that negative portrayal of older people in ads affected their self-perception negatively. Other studies, however, have indicated that the elderly are unconcerned with the way they are being represented in ads,[19] or that they see themselves portrayed positively in advertising.[20]

From a socialization perspective, advertising may have an important effect on the internalization of dominant imagery and ideology, perhaps because it is one of the places where symbolism interacts with the economy.[21] Cues in advertising may provide symbolic models for older consumers' behaviour, may affect their self-image, and may even influence societal attitudes toward the elderly.[22] Thus, how older people are featured in ads has potential implications for the social and psychological well-being of the elderly.

From a broader perspective, advertising is more than a source of purchase-related information to consumers. It is also a means of social communication.[23] It "communicates, directly and indirectly, evaluations, norms and propositions about matters other than the products that are to be sold."[24] Belk and Pollay suggest that advertising serves as a "family album of society." In creating certain impres-

Table 1

Categories of Analysis

Category	Main Description
Age	Direct mention; no mention but known (such as a life celebrity); "look" age: face, hair, hand, wrinkles; clothes; posture.
Gender	Male and female.
Race	White and non-white (Aboriginal, black, and Asia): direct mention; features of face; colour of skin.
Occupation	Non-domestic occupations include high level (top level manager, professional, entertainer, etc.), middle level (middle level white collar occupation, etc.), and low level (service, clerical, construction worker, etc.) and domestic occupations: direct mention; task being performed; tool being used; surrounding; background; relation with others in the illustration.
Role Importance to Ad's Theme/Layout	Important, equally important, and less important or unimportant: direct mention; strategic physical position in illustration (front vs. back, centre vs. side); shot size relative to others in illustration; focal point of attention; product back, centre vs. side); expert vs. non-expert; giving advice/help vs. receiving advice/help.
Place	Residential; business; neither (such as outdoor);no background: surroundings and background of the character.
Activity	Sedentary (sit, read, watch TV, knit, etc.) vs Nonsedentary and "high" physical activity (stand, sports participating, etc.).
Association with People	Alone; either in interaction with or within a group, which was directly mentioned or judged to be: with family; with non-family others; with age peers; with non-age peers.

Table 2

Number & Percentage of Older Characters in Ads

Magazine	n	%
Canadian Living	3	5.7
Chatelaine	10	18.9
Homemaker	1	1.9
Maclean's	9	17.0
Primetime	3	5.7
Reader's Digest	2	3.8
Subtotal	28	52.8
Grand	7	13.2
Today's Times	6	11.3
Vie Nouvelle (F)	7	13.2
Independent Senior	5	9.4
Subtotal	25	47.2
Total	53	100.0

sions, it is selective and biased, just like individual family albums.[25] By studying these images, we may better understand the values and biases of ourselves and of others.

Purpose of the Study

The depiction of older persons in advertising, as compared to the amount of effort devoted to other issues about older people such as health care and retirement, is still a relatively new area of study in both social gerontology and marketing in Canada.[26] There are very few publications on the portrayal of older Canadians in advertising. In surveys commissioned by the Canadian Radio-Television and Telecommunications Commission in 1984 and in 1988, the portrayal of gender in Canadian broadcasting was examined. The results of these surveys indicated that relatively few male and even fewer female characters in the 36-65 age range were depicted in English or French television ads. Similarly, very small numbers of male and female characters beyond age 65 appeared in the ads.[27] Lexchin's study[28] of print ads unveiled that characters over 65 years of age were included in just over 7% of the ads in the two most widely read refereed Canadian

Table 3

Age, Gender, Role Importance, Activity, and Social Relations of Characters by Types of Magazines

Magazine	Regular		Specialised		Total	
	n	%	n	%	n	%
I. Age of Characters						
15 - 49	154	84.6	32	54.2	186	77.8
50 & over	28	15.4	27	45.8	53	22.2
II. Gender of Older Characters						
Male	16	57.1	12	48.0	28	52.8
Female	12	42.9	13	52.0	25	47.2
III. Role Importance						
Important Role	20	71.4	7	28.0	27	
Equally Imp't Roles	8	28.6	18	72.0	26	
Unimportant Roles	0		0		0	
Total	28	100.0	25	100.0	53	

Chi Square = 9.967 $P < .001$

	Regular		Specialised		Total	
IV. Activity						
Nonsedentary	8	61.5	7	70.0	22	
Sedentary	5	38.5	6	30.0	11	
Total	13	100.0	20	100.0	33	
V. Social Relations of Characters						
Alone	18	64.3	8	32.0	26	
Not Alone	10	35.7	17	68.0	27	
Total	28	100.0	25	100.0	53	

Chi Square = 5.508 $P < .01$

Table 4
Ad Characters and Canadian Population by Age Groups

Age Group Ads	Number in Ads	Percentage of Ads	Percentage in 1991 Population*
15-24	93	38.9	14.0
25-49	93	38.9	39.9
50-64	30	12.6	13.6
65+	23	9.6	11.6
Total	239	100.0	

*Calculated from Statistics Canada, *1991 Canadian Census: Age, Sex, and Marital Status*, Cat. 93-310 (Ottawa: Statistics Canada, 1993), Table 3.

Table 5
Ad Characters and Canadian Population by Gender

Age Group	Number in Ads		Percentage in Ads		Percentage in 1991 Population*	
	M	F	M	F	M	F
15-49	55	131	29.6	70.4	50.1	49.9
50+	28	25	52.8	47.2	46.0	54.0

*Calculated from Statistics Canada, *1991 Canadian Census: Age, Sex, and Marital Status*, Cat. 93-310 (Ottawa: Statistics Canada, 1993), Table 3.

medical journals in 1988. In an analysis of advertisements in Canadian consumer magazines, Zhou and Chen (1992) found that the visibility of older characters was marginal: only 5.1% of the characters in their sample were judged to be 50 years of age and older and not one ad included a character that was judged to be 65 years of age or older.

In recent years, specialized magazines targeting the older segment (50 and above) of the population have appeared both in the United States (e.g., *Modern Maturity*) and in Canada (e.g., *Independent Senior*). How are older people portrayed in ads in these magazines? Are they depicted similarly to the way they are depicted in ads in regular consumer magazines? Or, are they different? An extensive literature search did not reveal any study on how the aged are portrayed

Table 6
Products

Older Characteristics

Products	Regular Magazines		Specialized Magazines	
	%	n	%	n
Medicine	21.4	(6)		-
Hygiene	0		8.0	(2)
Food	7.1	(2)	-	
Beer	10.7	(3)	-	
Jewelry	3.6	(1)	-	
Appliances	3.6	(1)	-	
Store	3.6	(1)	-	
Entertainment	3.6	(1)	-	
Car	3.6	(1)	-	
Institution	0		16.0	
Media	25	(7)	8.0	(2)
Travel	-		4.0	(1)
Banks	-		4.0	(1)
Clothing	7.1	(2)	-	
Aging preventive products	10.7	(3)	-	
Old age specific products	-	-	60.0	(15)
Total	100%	(28)	100%	(25)

in ads in those publications. As an attempt to bridge the gap, this paper presents the results of the analysis of the portryal of older persons, judged to be 50 years of age and older, in advertisements in Canadian consumer magazines ("regular magazines" hereafter) and those in magazines targeted at older readers ("specialized magazines" hereafter). The specific research questions asked were: 1) How frequently did ads present older characters? 2) How were older characters portrayed? 3) What are the differences, if any, between the ads in two types of magazines in their portrayal of older characters?

Methodology

Employing a three stage procedure, one sample was drawn from Canadian consumer magazines listed in the *Canadian Media Directors' Council Media Digest 1991/92* and another was drawn from specialized magazines listed in the *Canadian Advertising Rater and Data*. First, all geographic editions of all December 1991 issues of the ten largest circulating regular and specialized magazines in Canada were ordered. Some magazines did not respond after repeated contacts. As a result, six regular and four specialized mgazines were obtained (Table 2). Second, all national ads (i.e., identical ads in all editions of each issue) were identified. Third, all national ads containing a picture of at least one human character were retained for analysis. All regional ads were excluded because ads with regional orientation could distort the results of a national study.[29]

The working definition of an "older character" was any character in an ad who was judged to be 50 years of age or older. In selecting characters to be included, complete human figures and close-up shots were counted but blurry shots, shadow figures, and very small characters in crowded scenes were excluded.

Categories of Analysis

The categories of analysis, similar to those used in N. Zhou and M. Chen (1992), are presented in Table 1. For each category, a character was classified into the proper sub-category through an examination of the content of the ad, both written and pictorial. The more descriptors which could be applied to the ad, the greater the possibility that the character could be classified into a sub-category. A character which could not be classified was placed in an "indeterminate" sub-category.

Coding

Two trained coders (a male/older and a female/younger) completed a content analysis of the data by coding all the characters in the study. The inter-coder agreements were 98%, which was highly acceptable in this type of study.[30] One month after the completion of the analysis, 5% of the characters were re-analyzed by Coder One and the test-retest agreements again were 98%.

Results

Presence of Older Persons, Gender and Racial Compositions

Of the 239 analyzable characters, 53 or 22.2% were older characters (Table 2). As shown in Table 3-I, slightly over one half of the older characters (28) were in regular consumer magazines, the rest were in specialized magazines. Nearly one in ten (9.6%) of the characters were identified to be 65 years of age or older

(Table 4). Not surprisingly, specialized magazines used more older characters in proportion to regular magazines (Table 3-I).

For older characters, the distribution by gender was almost equal. For the younger characters, however, the distribution was heavily skewed toward females (Table 5).

When the two types of magazines were compared, a greater proportion of older male characters were depicted in regular magazines, while the distribution of male and female characters in specialized magazines was almost equal (Table 3-II). In 1991, Canadians of aboriginal, Asian, and African origins accounted for 7.8% of the population.[31] But, there were no non-white older characters found in the sample.

Occupation

Of the characters in regular magazines whose occuptions could be identified, 20% of the occupations were judged to be of low status, 80% were of middle or high status. Of those in specialized magazines, one half represented low status occupations, the other half represented middle or high status occupations.

Importance to Ad's Theme

In specialized magazines, a much smaller proportion of older characters was judged to be playing an important role in the ad's theme or layout. In contrast, a greater proportion of older characters played an important role in the ads in the regular magazines (Table 3-III).

Place

Where a setting could be identified, equal proportions of older characters were depicted in business and home settings. This is in sharp contrast with the finding in our previous study where about two-thirds of the older characters were shown in a residential house setting.[32]

Activity

For those whose activity could be identified, older characters were depicted as physically active in both regular and specialized magazines; but, even more so in the latter (Table 3-IV).

Association with People

While 64.3% of the older characters were seen alone in the regular magazines, 68% were portrayed with family members or with other people of the same or younger age groups in specialized magazines (Table 3-V).

Product Association

Older characters were used to promote a wide array of products in regular magazines. However, in specialized magazines, of the twenty-five older characters, 60% of them were used for commodities targeted at the elderly (Table 6). Examples are denture products, incontinence products, and page magnifiers.

Summary and Discussion

The findings indicate that while Canadian advertisers continue to convey primarily a young image of the population, the use of 22.2% of older characters in the current sample is higher than the 5.1% found in the sample used in our previous study conducted one year earlier.[33] Furthermore, when the type of magazine was controlled, the proportions of older characters used in regular and specialised magazines were 15.4% and 45.8% respectively. Given the intended audience, this difference is no surprise, of course. But, the 15.4% (See Table 3-I) found in regular consumer magazines is much higher than those found earlier in Canada and elsewhere.[34] As for the gender composition of older characters, males and females were relatively evenly distributed. In our sample, visible minorities are still invisible in Canadian advertising.

Advertising that demeans the elderly (or any other group for that matter) is no longer socially responsible or acceptable.[35] We did not find such ads as the 'little old lady' crying "Where is the beef?", or the rocking chair type of ads in this sample. Rather, some fairly positive portrayals of older people appeared in our data. This was especially so in specialized magazines. In these magazines, two-thirds of the older characters were seen in social and "transgenerational" scenes; equal proportions were in high and low status occupations; and, they were cast in equally important roles to the ad's theme or layout. Both types of magazines portrayed old people as being physically active, but this occurred even more so in specialised magazines.

In sum, the findings of this study are in sharp contrast with previous content analyses of magazine ads. This suggests a more positive image of older people in current advertising. There are two possible and interrelated explanations of the findings. The first is an economic interpretation. It is increasingly known that the 50 and over market is a growing and potentially profitable market. In the past, it may have been the marketers' unwillingness and/or fear of turning away the more 'desirable' younger age groups that impeded them from directing advertising efforts toward the aged.[36] The profit potential is now so overwhelming[37] that advertisers may be gradually overcoming their own obstacles and reorienting their advertising themes. Also, Hooyman and Kiyak[38] pointed out that, from their observations, advertisers in print publications have been slower than other mass media to integrate positive images of aging into their advertisements. Maybe the print advertising industry has begun to close the gap.

The second explanation of the increased portrayal of the elderly is political, namely, the onset of political correctness. As mentioned above, advertising that demeans any group is no longer socially tolerated. Offensive ads almost invariably endanger the advertisers and/or the company and open them to the possibility of criticisms or protests and even a boycott of the product. Increasingly, to reduce the risk of negative publicity, advertisers use more positive contents in advertising. To illustrate, the vice-president of a specialised magazine for "mature readers" emphatically stated in an interview that his magazine does not want to offend the readers. They used to have a policy not to publish any ads related to funerals, but, now they do because the ads are, in his words, "nicely done." To what extent these findings reflect a firmly established trend of attitudinal and policy changes by the advertising industry is too early to judge. More longitudinal studies are needed. Also, in Canada, specialised magazines tend to be localized and the volume of their publication is relatively small. To be nationally representative, more of these magazines should be included in the samples of large scale studies.

Notes

1. An earlier version of this paper was presented at the Second Conference on Images of Aging, University of Geneva, Sierre, Switzerland, July 1-3, 1993.

2. The order of the authorship is random. Both authors contributed equally to the project. The authors would like to express thanks to the Social Sciences and Humanities Research Council of Canada for an Aid to Small University Grant which partly supported the project, to the publishers for providing the magazine copies used in the study, and to Janesse Leung and Robert Dann for their assistance in analyzing the data.

3. Erving Goffman, *Gender Advertisements* (Cambridge, MA.: Harvard University Press, 1979).

4. J. Lexchin, "The Portrayal of the Elderly in Drug Advertisements: A Factor in Inappropriate Prescribing?" *Canadian Journal on Aging*, 9 (3, 1990), 296-303; G. P. Moschis, "Marketing to Older Adults: An Overview and Assessment of Present Knowledge and Practice," *Working Paper*, No. 21-89 (Atlanta, Georgia: Georgia State University, 1989); Robin T. Peterson, "The Depiction of Senior Citizens in Magazine Advertisements: A Content Analysis," *Journal of Business Ethics*, 11 (1992), 701-706; D. B. Wolfe, *Serving the Ageless Market* (New York: McGraw Hill, 1990); N. Zhou & M. Y. T. Chen, "Marginal Life after 49: A Preliminary Study of the Portrayal of Older People in Canadian Consumer Magazine Advertising," *International Journal of Advertising*, 11 (1992), 343-354.

5. S. Bramlett-Solomon & V. Wilson, "Images of the Elderly in *Life* and *Ebony*, 1978-87," *Journalism Quarterly*, 66 (Spring, 1989), 185-88; B. Kvasnicka, B. Beymer & R. Perloff, "Portrayals of the Elderly in Magazine Advertisements," *Journalism Quarterly*, 59 (Winter, 1982), 656-58; L. E. Swayne & A. J. Greco, "The Portrayal of Older Americans in Television Commercials," *Journal of Advertising*, 16, (1, 1987), 47-54; A. C. Ursic, M. L. Ursic & V. L. Ursic, "A Longitudinal Study of the Use of the Elderly in Magazine Advertising," *Journal of Consumer Research*, 13 (June, 1986), 131-133; Zhou & Chen, 343- 354.

6. P. England, A. Kuhn & T. Gardner, "The Ages of Men and Women in Magazine Advertisements," *Journalism Quarterly*, 58 (Autumn, 1981), 468-71; W. Gantz, H. Gartenberg & C. Rainbow, "Approaching invisibility: The Portrayal of the Elderly in Magazine Advertisements," *Journal of Communication*, 30 (Winter, 1980), 56-60.

7. England, et al., 468-71; J. S. Francher, "'It's the Pepsi Generation....' Accelerated Aging and the Television Commercial," *International Journal of Aging and Human Development*, 4 (3, 1973), 245-55; A. J. Harris & J. F. Feinberg, "Television and Aging: Is What You See What You Get?" *The Gerontologist*, 17 (5, 1977), 464-68.

8. Peterson, 701-706.

9. Harris & Feinberg, 464-68.

10. Swayne & Greco, 47-54.

11. Gantz, et al., 56-60.

12. Ursic et al., 131-133.

13. Harris & Feinberg, 464-68; Swayne & Greco, 47-54.

14. Ibid.

15. Harris & Feinberg, 464-68; Swayne & Greco, 47-54.

16 T. A. Festervand & J. R. Lumpkin, "Response of Elderly Consumers to Their Portrayal by Advertisers," *Current Issues and Research in Advertising* (1, 1985), 203-26.

17. Ibid.

18. R. B. Smith, G. P. Moschis & R. L. Moore, "Effects of Advertising on the Elderly Consumer: An Investigation of Social Breakdown Theory, " in R. W. Belk, et al. eds. *1984 AMA Educators' Proceedings* (Chicago: American Marketing Association, 1984), 1-5.

19. L. Langmeyer, "Senior Citizens and Television Advertisements: A Research Note," *Current Issues and Research in Advertising* (Ann Arbor: Graduate School of Business Administration, University of Michigan), (1, 1984), 167-78.

20. E. S. Schreiber & D. A. Boyd, "How the Elderly Perceive Television Commercials," *Journal of Communications*, 30 (Winter, 1980), 61-70.

21. J. Dickey, "Women for Sale: The Construction of Advertising Images," in K. Davies, et al. eds. *Out of Focus: Writings on Women and the Media* (London: Women's Press, 1987); J. Williamson, *Decoding Advertisements* (London: Marion Boyars, 1978); J. Williamson, *Consuming Passions: The Dynamics of Popular Culture* (London: Boyars, 1986).

22. Swayne & Greco, 47-54.

23. W. Leiss, S. Kline & S. Jhally, *Social Communication in Advertising*, 2nd ed. (Scarborough, Ont.: Nelson, 1990).

24. G. Andren, L. Ericsson, R. Ohlsson & T. Tannsjo, *Rhetoric and Ideology in Advertising* (Stockholm: A.B. Grafiska, 1978).

25. R. W. Belk & R. W. Pollay, "Images of Ourselves: The Good Life in Twentieth Century Advertising," *Journal of Consumer Research*, 11 (March, 1985), 887-97.

26. Zhou & Chen, 343-354.

27. ERIN Research, *The Portrayal of Gender in Canadian Broadcasting - Summary Report 1984-1988*, Cat. BC92-46 (Ottawa: Minister of Supply and Services, 1990).

28. Lexchin, 296-303.

29. N. Zhou, R. Sparkman & S. Follows, "Geographic Culture, Regional Advertising, and the Myth of the Nine Nations of North America: A Content Analysis of Canadian and U.S. Magazine Advertisements," in N. E. Synodinos, C. F. Keown, T. H. Becker, T. G. Grunert, T. E. Muller & J. H. Yu, *The Proceedings of the Third Symposium on Cross-cultural Consumer and Business Studies* (Honolulu: University of Hawaii, 1990), 1-6.

30. H. H. Kassarjian, "Content Analysis in Consumer Research," *Journal of Consumer Research*, 4 (June, 1977), 8-18.

31. Calculated from Statistics Canada, *Census of 1991, Ethnic Origins: The Nation*, Cat. 93-315, (Ottawa: Statistics Canada, 1993), Table 1A.

32. Zhou & Chen, 343-354.

33. Ibid.

34. Ibid.; Peterson, 701-706.

35. An illustration is a television commercial for a lemonade mix that features an old man. The old man was deaf and his repeated inability to understand the lines about the product was not perceived as entertaining. The commercial was dropped as complaints were filed and decreased sales suggested social rejection of this approach. Cited in R. H. Davies & J. A. Davies, *TV's Image of the Elderly: A Practical Guide for Change*, (Lexington, MA: Lexington Books, 1985), 69.

36. V. Knauer, "The Aging Alienated Consumer," *The Aging Consumer*, Occasional Papers in Gerontology, 8 (Ann Arbor, Michigan: Institute of Gerontology). Cited in D. Loudon & A. J. Della Bitta, *Consumer Behavior*, 3rd ed. (New York: McGraw-Hill, 1988), 228.

37. J. Ostroff, *Successful Marketing to the 50+ Consumers: How to Capture one of the Biggest and Fast-Growing Markets in America* (Englewood, Cliffs, New Jersey: Prentice-Hall, 1989).

38. N. R. Hooyman & H. A. Kiyak, *Social Gerontology: A Multidisciplinary Perspective*, 2nd ed. (Needham Heights, MA: Allyn and Bacon, 1991).

Mervin Y. T. Chen, Ph.D., is a Professor of Sociology, Department of Sociology, Acadia University, Wolfville, Nova Scotia, Canada. He received his Ph.D. from McMaster University in Ontario, Canada. His areas of interest include Sociology of Work, Sociology of the Family, and Social Gerontology. He has published both in English and Chinese. He is the senior author of *Work in the Changing Canadian Society*, Butterworth, 1985. Dr. Chen's articles appeared in *Aging in Canada: Social Perspectives*, edited by V. Marshall, *Journal of Religious Gerontology*, *Journal of Ethnology and Sociology*, *Journal of Canadian Studies*, *International Journal of Advertising*, and *Society/Societé*.

(Joe) Nan Zhou, Ph.D., is an Associate Professor of Marketing, The Fred C. Manning School of Business Administration, Acadia University, Wolfville, Nova Scotia, Canada. He received his M.B.A. from Idaho State University and Ph.D. from the University of Utah. His works have appeared in *Advances in Consumer Research*, *Journal of Advertising*, *Journal of Consumer Research*, *Journal of International Consumer Marketing*, *International Journal of Advertising*, and *Journal of Marketing Education*. He has served as a guest editor for the *Journal of International Consumer Marketing* and is a member of the editorial board of the *Journal of Marketing Education*.

Social Policy for an Aging Society

ELLEN M. GEE AND SUSAN A. McDANIEL

Introduction

As the Canadian population ages, social policy will be challenged. This is not because demographic change creates a policy "crisis," but rather because population aging is part of other societal forces and changes — such as socio-economic development, family changes, value changes, increased control over birth, death, and disease, etc. — all of which have policy dimensions.

The term "social policy" refers to social arrangements aimed at the distribution of social resources and the promotion of the welfare of the individual or the individual and society, and concerned with choices among competing values.[1] The term "social arrangements" means both that social policies reflect power relations (i.e. are political)[2] and that they encompass more than government (or public) interventions; the clause "aimed at the distribution of social resources and the promotion of welfare" suggests that such aims are not always successful; and the phrase "competing values" highlights the contradictions in meshing welfare state social policies with a market-based economy. This latter point relates to conflicts between economic and social policy, given differing underlying assumptions, that may be handled differently in various countries.[3]

This analysis is based on three premises: that historical and present-day tensions regarding principles underlying social policies, and between social and economic policies, will shape the policy agenda of the future; that gender issues will figure more prominently in policy debates as the Canadian population continues to age; and that social policy challenges related to an aging society are not, and will not be, restricted to elderly persons only. Indeed, such challenges encompass all age groups and society as a whole. Given the importance of this third point, this paper is divided into two major sections — social policy issues for *the aged* and social policy issues for *an aging society*. The distinction emphasizes that the social policies typically associated with older persons (such as pensions and health care) comprise only one part of the policy arena as a population ages.

Social Policy Issues Regarding the Aged
Criteria for Resource Allocation to Older Canadians

The criteria for Canadian social policies for the elderly have evolved into a complex mixture combining various principles of allocation — age, need, and merit. This is well exemplified in old-age income policies. Until recently, Old Age Security (OAS) was solely age-dependent — the program was universal, covering all persons aged 65 or over, regardless of income. Some newer programs are based on a combination of age and need (income testing); the Guaranteed Income Supplement (GIS), the Spouse's Allowance (SPA), and provincial income supplements. The Canada/Quebec Pension Plan (C/QPP), private pensions, and private savings arrangements such as Registered Retirements Savings Plans (RRSPs) are based on a combination of age and "merit," with merit generally defined as contributing to one's own income in old age through traditionally defined (paid) employment (or by independent wealth).[4] Thus, merit is related to gender and socio-economic status.

Policies have made some progress in reducing poverty among the elderly in Canada. However, categories of aged persons with high levels of poverty remain, most notably "unattached" women. Within this group, in 1989, 41 percent lived below the poverty line defined by Statistics Canada.[5] There is debate as to whether the overall reduction in seniors' poverty is due to improvements in programs that help those most in need (the GIS and SPA) or the maturation of the C/QPP, i.e. as more people have become eligible for full benefits.[6] Nevertheless, about one-half of elderly Canadians have incomes so low that they qualify for the GIS; and it is clear that OAS and maximum GIS benefits do not pull people out of poverty.[7]

This mixture of criteria — age, need, and merit — contains contradictory principles. In times of economic downturn, these tensions become more manifest and are illustrated in various steps taken in recent years. Age *per se* as a criterion has been eliminated with the OAS "claw-back" (Bill C-28), a recent policy change that attacks the principle of universality,[8] changing the OAS from a universal benefit to a GIS-type benefit that will reduce the later-life income that many people had expected.[9] The need-based programs, which operate as a "safety net," have had a secure footing until recently. Indeed, GIS benefits have improved substantially over the past decade. However, there are signs that some need-based programs are under threat: court challenges to the SPA on grounds that its (non-age-related) eligibility criteria violate the Canadian Charter of Rights and Freedoms could, if successful, result in curtailment of the program, and in 1991 the Manitoba income supplement to low-income seniors was de-indexed.[10] In recent years, reforms have been made in the private pension arena, which covers less than one-half of all workers and even fewer working women, and in private retirement savings plans, which are more accessible to well-off Canadians.

Thus, recent policy directions indicate a move from age-based universality, some threat to need-based policies, and a favouring of the merit criterion. Together, these suggest trends toward decreasing income in later life and/or increasing inequality in income levels among the aged. They reflect a long-standing ideological tension in Canadian society between what Dennis Guest refers to as "residual" and "institutional" approaches to social policy, and a re-surfacing of the residual approach which favours the free market and the meting out of its own justice — rewarding work, thrift and foresight.[11]

Yet, it is doubtful that need-based programs for the elderly will be severely curtailed, given their support by the Canadian public in general and by women's lobby groups.[12] The research and policy challenges for the future involve: the conceptualization of need-based programs as social provisions rather than as "safety nets"; as Sheila Neysmith states, "(n)eed does not have to be equated with means testing. Programs can be universal in *application* and selective in *impact*" (italics in original);[13] the assessment of need in a more flexible way that recognizes the diversity of the elderly population; and the implementation of need-based programs that minimize stigmatization.

While need-based policies and programs, in one form or another, are "here to stay," recent policy directions in Canada stress merit as a criterion of resource allocation. However, as Neysmith notes, the criteria of need and merit are contradictory — they are based on fundamentally different beliefs about the relationship between the individual and society, the role of government in social welfare, and the play of market forces.[14] While we cannot attempt to reconcile these differences, it is possible that the increasingly powerful voice of women will alter, to some degree, the traditional definition of "merit" (which is derived from a male perspective), thereby down-playing conflicts between merit and need.

Issues in Service Delivery to Older Persons

Most older people do not require social services, that is, services that reflect organized societal approaches and the use of knowledge, skills, and resources for the amelioration of deprivations or conditions.[15] Equating an older population with a "service-needy" population is incorrect and reinforces ageist stereotypes of incompetence and dependency. Ingrid Connidis estimates that only about nine percent of the community-dwelling elderly require a community service.[16] Nevertheless, as the aged increase (particularly within the fast-growing category of persons aged 85 and over, who are the most frail) and as the traditional source of family support — female kin — dwindles due to smaller family size and increased female labour force participation, there will be a growing need for services to be provided to the aged.[17]

One important issue is the privatization of services. Since around 1980, social services in Canada have been subject to a trend of privatization — the systematic turning over of social provision from the public to the private sector. This trend has been initiated at the federal level, under the catchwords of "expenditure restraint" (Liberals) and "deficit reduction" (Conservatives).[18] Thus, cutbacks in federal welfare expenditure have shifted responsibility for social services to the provinces. For their part, the provinces, either financially unable or unwilling to provide support for social services, pass on costs to the private sector, to communities, to the voluntary sector, or to individuals. Another determinant of privatization is neo-conservative ideology, which attacks state delivery of social services and favours market mechanisms.[19] This view reflects one side of the ideological tension between residual and institutional approaches to social policy.

A number of potential dangers are inherent in privatization. One is a shift in focus from social services as provision for those in need to social services as cost burdens. Also, a two-tiered system of services could result — the "rich" and the "poor" having access to social services differing in composition and quality.[20] Third, social services may be more at risk of discontinuation if their responsibility lies with the private sector. Other concerns relate to maintaining standards, and an increasing tendency to rely on non-professionals at the front line of service delivery.[21] Detailed research is needed both on the implications of privatization for service delivery to elderly persons and on the unresolved issue of whether privatization actually results in savings, and, if so, at what "cost" in human terms.[22] Also, the unintended and unanticipated consequences of privatization for the health and quality of life of older Canadians need to be explored.

Coordination of services is another issue of policy concern. The federal government plays a relatively small role in social policy regarding the aged; most policy areas affecting the elderly (e.g. health, housing, social services, transportation) are under provincial jurisdiction, although the costs of some of the programs in these policy areas are partially borne by the federal government.[23] Also, municipal governments are involved in service delivery. As there is no single agency or policy responsible for the needs and interests of the elderly, conflicts exist across agencies about how best to serve the elderly and, within a policy area, about how to allocate funds to assist the aged. Thus, neglect of a policy area can occur if it is assumed that responsibility lies elsewhere.[24] Also, lack of coordination results in costly service overlaps and creates a complex system that hampers accessibility. Problems of accessibility are particularly acute for immigrant seniors who may lack working knowledge of an official language.[25]

While centralization may not be the panacea for coordination, one federal agency with an almost exclusively client base of elders — the Department of Veterans Affairs — provides services in a way that eliminates the common coordination pitfalls.[26] Given the thrust of constitutional reform, it is unlikely that decentralization will be curtailed. However, it is possible that agencies at the provincial and federal level will assume an aging mandate, and thus improve the coordination of services to seniors. A catalyst for improvement, at least at the federal level, lies in a demographically induced shift in expenditures; it has been shown that an increase in the aged population will have a greater impact on federal expenditures than on provincial or municipal expenditures.[27] However, this must be viewed in the light of federal legislation such as Bill C-69, which initiated cuts in Established Programs Financing.

Models of Care

Policy conceptualization of the appropriate model of care is especially important with regard to the frail elderly. Until recently, the medical model dominated in the provision of health care and housing for the aged; it was based on physician-centred services, hospital utilization and/or institutional placement, and the equating of health care with medical care. This model has resulted in high use of medical services by older people and, many argue, the unnecessary institutionalization of the aged. Accordingly, it has been criticized for increasing dependency, restricting individual autonomy and choice, and being expensive.[28]

An alternative model of community/home care is advocated by many gerontologists and policy-makers. The goal is to assist people to live independently in their own homes and communities for as long as possible, with integrated health and social services providing a "continuum of care." Policy-makers have readily endorsed this model, given its cost-containment features. For example, the 1991 British Columbia Royal Commission on Health Care and Costs recommended moving health care out of hospitals and into communities and homes. At the same time, it recommended that the number of doctors and other medical workers be controlled and that a cap be placed on payments to doctors and hospitals.

It is difficult to be critical of the *goal* of community-based care — it is humane, it reflects the desires of seniors themselves, it promises individual choice, autononomy and independence, and it appears to be cost-efficient. However, as Robert Evans has observed, "Changes in *what* is provided take place rapidly; in *how* it is provided, much more slowly."[29] The resulting research and policy challenges include the following goals: 1) to ascertain *how* a community-based continuum of care will be implemented in ways that do not, even in the short-run, threaten the health care needs of the elderly; 2) to deal effectively with a medical monopoly that is bound to feel threatened (for doctors are a necessary part of the health care system and institutionalization may be the best alternative for some frail elderly and their families); 3) to ensure that informal care-giving, provided by elderly and middle-aged women for the most part, does not become a substitute for social services; 4) to facilitate the integration of formal and informal care; and 5) to ascertain the "real" costs of community care, as cost containment may be overstated. These challenges become even more difficult due to privatization and lack of co-ordination, as the community care model incorporates a notion of integrated health and social services.[30]

Workplace Policies

In Canada, mandatory retirement has been a social practice buttressed by a combination of social custom and pension incentives/disincentives. Until the 1991 Supreme Court ruling upheld mandatory retirement, research on the topic focussed on its "pros" and "cons."[31] Research must now examine the consequences of mandatory retirement, including the social implications of a decision holding that certain types of age discrimination are justified; that is, benefit the greater good.

At the present time, the effects of the ruling seem to be quite minimal, given a trend towards earlier retirement. However, the long-term consequences may be less benign. Persons facing grim prospects in terms of retirement income — due to, for example, the expansion of the claw-back to the less well off, the low coverage rates and low levels of full indexation in private pensions, and the lack of disposable income to purchase RRSPs in the working years — may find it necessary to work past the age of 65.[32] Many of these will be women (particularly widows and the growing number of divorcées), who will be forced to remain in or re-enter the labour force at low-paying jobs.

Most older workers find themselves in work-places with policies designed for young employees. Canadian corporate policy adjustments for older workers have evolved slowly. More progress has been made in the United States, in response to the end of mandatory retirement.[33] Even more progress has been made in Europe, in particular in the Scandinavian countries, where age structures are considerably "older" than in Canada.[34]

Work-place policies need to be designed and implemented to alter the way work is organized to retain older workers, especially given impending labour shortages in particular industries, occupations and regions. As the work and retirement needs of individuals are extremely varied, no single policy will suffice.[35] Examples include modifications in the work-place, both physical and organizational, to accommodate the needs of older workers; flexible retirement, including part-time work, perhaps in conjunction with partial pensions, reduced work hours, and job-sharing; flex-time policies, especially for employed care-givers; and job retraining. Few such initiatives have appeared in the Canadian corporate sector; indeed, Canadian employers seem eager to rid themselves of older workers — through enhanced retirement packages and other policies that encourage early retirement, as well as practices such as forced downward job mobility, sometimes through job reclassification.

Some limited attempts have been made by the federal government to assist older workers. Examples include the Innovations Program for Older Workers, which offers wage subsidies and training opportunities for older workers to rejoin the labour force, and the 1990 federal budget which provided additional funds to Employment and Immigration Canada for the retraining of older workers. As well, there are various provincial initiatives of minor scope.[36]

The challenge ahead lies in bringing together the key actors — business, organized labour, and government — to adopt policies and practices that will benefit, and take cognizance of the needs of, older workers and older unemployed persons. There is also a need for more research on the aging workforce and the use of such research in policy development. While a shrinking labour force in the traditionally defined working ages will act as a stimulus to multi-sectoral planning, negative attitudes about older workers will simultaneously have to be addressed.

Social Policy Issues in an Aging Society

Social policy is grounded in the distribution and redistribution of social resources. Given the bases of social resources in income, housing, health, etc., it is not possible to examine social policy in a vacuum; the economic and political context in which social policy issues and debates occur matters greatly in a discussion of the broader societal dimensions of aging and social policy. Issues of aging are not limited to the aged, but affect virtually all groups in society.

Intergenerational Equity/Economics of Aging

The contemporary model of distribution/redistribution of societal resources is one of competition amongst stakeholders, with political forces determining the allocation of resources (allowing that some consideration be given to the aim of distributive justice). Broadly, intergenerational equity encompasses the idea that the young and the old should have similar access to opportunities, including social policy benefits. A core aspect is that the young have been deprived of their fair share of opportunities/benefits due to excessive allocation to the old.[37]

While intergenerational/equity conflict has received considerable public attention in the United States, it has not yet emerged as an issue in Canada. However, its underlying basis — pessimism about the economic implications of population aging — is present.[38] As a result, attention in Canada focuses upon *how* (significantly, not *whether*) social policy is influenced by population aging. The aging population has become, in many ways, the paradigm by which social policy is driven.[39] If welfare, health and/or public pension costs are increasing, population aging is seen as the culprit. These arguments continue to be made, despite strong evidence to the contrary;[40] moreover, "solutions" such as increasing immigration and fertility rates are proposed. That these solutions to a problem (that may not be a problem after all) may entail their own set of problems is seldom considered.

federal government has turned to immigration policy — increasing the number of immigrants allowed into Canada in recent years to 220,000 per annum. Such a level, if maintained and assuming no significant levels of out-migration, may be high enough to prevent the Canadian population from declining; it is estimated that the number of immigrants needed annually to prevent declining size ranges, depending upon fertility assumptions, from 200,000 to 310,000.[44] But what about population aging? In order for the age structure to be significantly affected, the number of immigrants needed per year would exceed 600,000! It is doubtful that Canadian society could absorb this number of immigrants per year, especially given that immigrants now come from much more diverse backgrounds in terms of country of origin, religion, language and race.

Even if changes were made in the ages of immigrants allowed into Canada (from the current situation in which 23 percent are under 15 years of age to 30 or even to 50 percent), no long-term effects on the overall population age structure would result.[45] This point seems to be lost on policy-makers. In late 1991, the Minister of Employment and Immigration announced that the age of dependent children of immigrants allowed into Canada would be lowered from 21 to 19, presumably to make for a younger age distribution of immigrants.

Immigration is not a viable mechanism to "solve" population aging. Given that immigration is desirable for other reasons, immigration policy should focus less on demographic manipulation attempts and more on providing services and support to new Canadians. Immigrant programs are being cut back, in cost-saving measures, while immigration remains relatively high.

If we want to reverse the trend of population aging, the key lies in increasing fertility levels. However, a major increase would be required — from current (total) fertility rates of approximately 1.6 to rates about 3.1; that is, to a level approaching that of the baby boom years in Canada.[46] The virtual impossibility of such a task may be a factor in why Canadian policy has generally not focused upon trying to increase fertility levels, but rather on increasing immigration levels.

However, in Quebec, the Bourassa government has launched a pro-natalist policy which is driven by many forces. The policy pays parents bonuses based on the number of children they have, with the third and fourth child worth more than the first or second. One aspect of this policy is to increase the pool of future labour force participants to counter population aging. Fertility levels have increased somewhat in the province, but it remains for researchers to ascertain whether this is due to the policy, other factors such as the baby-boom cohort reaching the end of its child-bearing years, or a growing sense of nationhood.

Child Care Policy

At first glance, it might seem that child care is unrelated to population aging. However, population aging is the direct result of decreased fertility, which is in turn related, among other factors, to the increased labour force participation of women. Thus, an aging population is one with a high proportion of young mothers (and fathers) who are working and have child-care needs. In 1988, 67 percent of Canadian mothers with at least one child under the age of 16 were in the paid labour force; for mothers with at least one child under the age of three, the figure approaches 59 percent.[47] Access to high-quality day-care at reasonable costs is a critical issue for many families with children. Most children with parents in the labour force (or full-time students) are not cared for in licensed child-care settings, despite parental preference for this type of care.[48]

Although a national child-care policy was promised by the federal government in 1987, it was officially abandoned in early 1992. The lack of a child-care policy may be viewed as one factor that increases the opportunity cost of children, and keeps fertility lower than it might otherwise be.[49] The social, personal, and economic costs of continuing to ignore child-care policy must be considered as well.

Informal Care-giving to the Elderly

Many middle-aged women (daughters and daughters-in-law, in particular) are engaged in care-giving to elderly family members.[50] A "care-giving crisis" is upon us, not because of the increased numbers of older persons who are living longer, but rather because of a shortage in the traditional "supply" of care-givers as more and more women enter the paid labour force. This will be exacerbated in the future as the number of younger-generation women declines.[51]

Canadian policies for elder care have taken this family support for granted. However, as the pool of children dwindles, policies that are supportive of children, rather than dependent upon them, will be needed. These policies need not be based on the assumption that the family bears the primary responsibility for aged members; indeed, Alan Walker states that "perhaps the main principle that policy-makers and society in general must recognize is that not all families should be expected to care" and Susan McDaniel argues that one of the policy challenges facing us regarding elder care is dismantling the ideology of familism.[52]

The above notwithstanding, there is a need for policies that assist middle-aged women with elder care. What kind of policies are required? One approach is to provide assistance, in the forms of respite care and adult day-care, to children giving hands-on care to aged parents.[53] Another approach is pension policy reform, most probably in the C/QPP, which would allow for a drop-out provision to allow children to leave the labour force for a period of time to attend to elder care-giving without forfeiting pension credits. Tax deductions or family allowances for elder care are other possibilities. Finally, the gender-based division of labour of care-giving needs to be challenged. Policies that encourage men to be more involved in care-giving seem appropriate.[54] Piece-meal policies will help only minimally, as entrenched values, behaviours, and attitudes as well as wider social and economic factors structure the gender inequalities of care-giving. Perhaps the most we can hope for now are policies that do not reinforce gender inequalities in elder care-giving.[55]

Conclusion

Population aging does not create a crisis in social policy; rather, population aging is, in fact, the *result* of successful social policies that have made it possible for people to live long lives and to control their fertility. Nevertheless, an aging Canada faces a number of policy challenges; changing demographics call for creative ways to deal with individual and social welfare.

Policy aspects of population aging involve complex issues for society as a whole. Policies concerning the aged and other age groups in society are not unrelated. In this paper, the division of the issues into two parts is put forward for analytical purposes only. In reality, the policy issues of the aged and of aging are closely intertwined. For example, work-place policies and service delivery issues are related to care-giving by the middle-aged; demographic policies, designed to counter population aging, have an indirect effect on other social policies aimed at the aged; pension policy influences the economics of aging and informal care-giving.

Ideological tensions in Canada, past and current, play a key role in defining problems and policy solutions. The economic underpinnings of social policy are particularly salient in the 1990s, given the emphasis on economic policy to the neglect of social policy. Ironically, the down-playing of social policy, based on financial consideration, may stall initiatives and innovations important in promoting economic development.

The last point emphasized here is that gender will figure more prominently in social policy as the population ages. Any failings of policies for the elderly are felt more acutely by women, partly given women's greater life expectancy and partly because gender-based injustices accumulate with age. Many social policies (e.g. on child care, informal care-giving, and certain work-place policies such as pay equity and pensions) are of more concern to the daily lives of women. Women (of all ages) are, of course, a heterogeneous group and "there is no guarantee that women will become the agent of change that will reverse emergent trends."[56] Nevertheless, as the social power of women increases, policy issues central to the lives of women, including aged women and the middle-aged women who care for them, will gain more visibility and legitimacy.

NOTES
1. Alan Walker, "Social Policy, Social Administration and the Social Construction of Welfare," *Sociology* 15, 2 (1981), 225-50.
2. For example, John Myles and Jill Quadagno argue that social policies in Canada have been a tool of "national elites used in the struggle to create a pan-Canadian identity in a nation whose construction has always been problematic." In Myles and Quadagno, "Explaining the Difference: The Politics of Old Age Security in Canada and the United States," paper

presented at Donner Foundation Conference, Yale University, May 1991, 5. In a similar vein, Keith Banting argues that interpretations of policy that focus on its function of maintaining social/political stability are valid, in Banting, "The Welfare State and Inequalities in the 1980's," *Canadian Review of Sociology and Anthropology* 24, 3 (1987), 309-38. From a different perspective, Julia S. O'Connor focuses upon class tensions in policy developments, in O'Connor, "Welfare Expenditure and Policy Orientation in Canada in Comparative Perspective," *Canadian Review of Sociology and Anthropology* 26, 1 (1989), 127-50.

3. In comparison with other countries in the Organization for Economic Cooperation and Development, Canada's social spending is relatively low, our degree of social inequality is comparatively high, and our old-age income benefits are modest. See John Myles, *Old Age in the Welfare State: The Political Economy of Public Pensions*, rev. edition (Lawrence, Kansas: University of Kansas Press, 1989); Banting, "The Welfare State and Inequalities in the 1980's"; and O'Connor, "Welfare Expenditure and Policy Orientation in Canada in Comparative Perspective."

4. In the case of the Canada Pension Plan, the age criterion is now more flexible. Since 1987, benefits have been available to persons at age 60 (in contrast to age 65). However, persons who claim benefits before the age of 65 have their benefits reduced by 0.5 percent for each month prior to age 65. Persons may also defer receipt until after 65, but only receive proportionately higher benefits up to the age of 70. The C/QPP functions on a "pay as you go" basis, i.e. one does not really contribute to one's own retirement income. The contributions of today's workers pay for today's retirees; retirees in the future will be paid by tomorrow's workers.

5. Statistics Canada "low-income cut-offs" (poverty lines) are based on a subsistence definition of poverty, and provide lower estimates of the extent of poverty than other measures.

6. Frank C. Fedyk, "Federal/Provincial/Municipal Jurisdictional Issues: Their Impact on Seniors in Canada," paper presented at the annual meeting of the Canadian Association on Gerontology, Victoria, 1990.

7. National Council of Welfare, *A Pension Primer* (Ottawa: National Council of Welfare, 1989).

8. A troubling aspect of the claw-back is that its ceilings are not fully indexed to inflation. Each year persons with less and less income will be subject to it; it has been estimated that persons who are retired in 2019 with as little as $20,000 (1989 dollars) annual income will have OAS benefits reduced by the claw-back. See National Council of Welfare, *Pension Reform* (Ottawa: National Council of Welfare, 1990); Monica Townson, "Pensions: Who's Responsible Anyway?" keynote address presented at the annual meeting of the Canadian Association on Gerontology, Ottawa, 1989. For a discussion of the historical tensions between the principles of universality and selectivity in Canadian social policy, see Keith Banting, "Visions of the Welfare State," in Shirley Seward, ed., *The Future of Social Welfare Systems in Canada and the United Kingdom* (Halifax: The Institute for Research on Public Policy, 1987), 147-63.

9. Robert L. Brown, *Economic Security in an Aging Population* (Toronto: Butterworths, 1991).

10. See Ellen M. Gee and Susan A. McDaniel, "Pension Politics and Pension Challenges: Retirement Policy Implications," *Canadian Public Policy* 17, 4 (1991), 456-72, for a discussion of consequences of recent and possible pension policy changes.

11. Dennis Guest, *The Emergence of Social Security in Canada*, 2nd edition (Vancouver: University of British Columbia Press, 1985).

12. For discussions of a preference for need, as opposed to age, as a basis for social policies for the elderly, see Bernice L. Neugarten, ed., *Age or Need? Public Policies for Older People* (Beverly Hills: Sage, 1982). See Fay Lomax Cook, Victor W. Marshall, Joanne Gard Marshall, and Julie E. Kaufman, "Intergenerational Equity and the Politics of Income Security for the Old," paper presented at Donner Foundation Conference, Yale University, May 1991; Herbert C. Northcott, *Public Opinion Regarding the Economic Support of Seniors* (Edmonton: Edmonton Area Series Report No. 67, Population Research Laboratory, Department of Sociology, 1990).

13. Sheila M. Neysmith, "Social Policy Implications of an Aging Society," in Victor W. Marshall, ed., *Aging in Canada: Social Perspectives*, 2nd edition (Markham: Fitzhenry & Whiteside, 1987), 592.

14. *Ibid.*, 594.

15. Definition taken from Judah Matras, *Dependency, Obligations and Entitlements: A New Sociology of Aging, the Life Course, and the Elderly* (Englewood Cliffs: Prentice-Hall, 1990), 81.

16. Ingrid Connidis, "The Service Needs of Older People: Implications for Public Policy," *Canadian Journal on Aging* 4, 1 (1985), 3-10.

17. Ellen M. Gee, "Demographic Change and Intergenerational Relations in Canadian Families: Findings and Social Policy Implications," *Canadian Public Policy* 16, 2 (1990), 191-99.

18. Andrew F. Johnson, "Federal Policies and Privatization of Provincial Social Services," in Jacqueline S. Ismael and Yves Vaillancourt, eds., *Privatization and Provincial Social Services in Canada: Policy, Administration and Service Delivery* (Edmonton: University of Alberta Press, 1988), 197.

19. A.N. Azim, "Privatization of Social Services: Potential Implications and Consequences," in Jacqueline S. Ismael and Ray J. Thomlison, eds., *Perspectives on Social Services and Social Issues* (Ottawa: Canadian Council on Social Development, 1987), 41.

20. Ibid., 45.

21. Jacqueline S. Ismael, "Privatization of Social Services: An Heuristic Approach," in Ismael and Vaillancourt, eds., *Privatization of Provincial Social Services in Canada*, 1-11.

22. The United States health care system, based on a privatized model, is more expensive, both as a percentage of GNP and on a cost per capita basis, than the Canadian nationalized system, as pointed out in David W. Conklin, "U.S. Health Care: Why Canada's System is Better and Cheaper," *Policy Options* 11, 4 (May, 1990), 15-18.

23. Kenneth Kernaghan and Olivia Kuper, *Coordination in Canadian Governments: A Case Study of Aging Policy* (Toronto: The Institute of Public Administration of Canada, 1983).

24. Barry D. McPherson, *Aging as a Social Process: An Introduction to Individual and Population Aging,* 2nd edition (Toronto: Butterworths, 1990), 367.

25. Carol Martyn, *Hidden Faces: A Survey of Suburban Immigrant Seniors* (Burnaby: Burnaby Multicultural Society, 1991).

26. Arguments for decentralization are that it would eliminate duplication of services between the federal and provincial governments, and it would allow provinces to tailor social services and programs to the needs of their residents. Canadian Council on Social Development, "Constitutional Reform and Social Policy," *Social Development Overview* 1 (Fall, 1991), 3. See A. Margery Boyce and Ellen M. Gee, "Aging Veterans in Canada," in Eloise Rathbone-McCuan and Betty Havens, eds., *North American Elders: United States and Canadian Perspectives* (Westport, Conn.: Greenwood Press, 1988), 181-200.

27. David K. Foot, "The Demographic Future of Fiscal Federalism in Canada," *Canadian Public Policy* 10, 4 (1984), 406-14.

28. William F. Forbes, J.A. Jackson and A.S. Kraus, *Institutionalization of the Elderly in Canada* (Toronto: Butterworths, 1987). It has been estimated that the cost of home care for a person is 11-14 percent of the cost of institutional care; see Mark Novak, *Successful Aging: The Myths, Realities and Future of Aging in Canada* (Markham: Penguin, 1985). However, without factoring in the "hidden costs" of informal care-giving and with no comprehensive, systematic mechanism for assessing costs, it is difficult to assess with any precision the relative costs of institutional versus home care. See Neena L. Chappell, "Long-Term Care in Canada," in Rathbone-McCuan and Havens, eds., *North American Elders,* 73-88.

29. Robert G. Evans, *Strained Mercy: The Economics of Canadian Health Care* (Toronto: Butterworths, 1984), 347.

30. Regarding home-based services, it has been noted that the decentralized Canadian system results in a lack of uniformity in program objectives, criteria, funding sources, services available, personnel and terminology; see Chappell, "Long-Term Care in Canada," in Rathbone-McCuan and Havens, eds., *North American Elders,* 80.

31. See Neil Guppy, "The Magic of 65: Issues and Evidence in the Mandatory Retirement Debate," *Canadian Journal on Aging* 8, 2 (1989), 173-86.

32. See National Council of Welfare, *A Pension Primer.*

33. Joseph A. Tindale, *Older Workers in an aging Work Force* (Ottawa: National Advisory Council on Aging, 1991), 30.

34. For discussions of issues related to later-life employment in a number of different countries, see Jack Habib and Charlotte Nusberg, eds., *Rethinking Worklife Options for Older Persons* (Washington, D.C.: International Federation of Aging, 1990).

35. Tindale, *Older Workers in An aging Work Force.*

36. Ibid., 41-49.

37. Samuel H. Preston, "Children and the Elderly: Divergent Paths for America's Dependents," *Demography* 21, 4 (1984), 435-57.

38. Alan Walker, "The Economic 'Burden' of Ageing and the Prospect of Intergenerational Conflict," *Ageing and Society* 10 (1990), 377-96.

39. Susan A. McDaniel, "Demographic Aging as a Paradigm in Canada's Welfare State," *Canadian Public Policy* 13, 1 (1987), 330-36.

40. See, for example, Ivan P. Fellegi, "Can We Afford an Aging Population?" *Canadian Economic Observer* (October 1988), 4.1-4.34; Brian B. Murphy and Michael C. Wolfson, "When the Baby Boom Grows Old: Impact on Canada's Public Sector," *Statistical Journal of the United Nations* 8 (1991), 25-43; Michael C. Wolfson, "International Perspectives on the Economics of Aging," *Canadian Economic Observer* (August 1991), 1-16.

41. Neysmith, "Social Policy Implications of an Aging Society," 594.

42. Gee and McDaniel, "Pension Politics and Pension Challenges"; Walker, "The Economic 'Burden' of Ageing and the Prospect of Intergenerational Conflict."

43. Fellegi, "Can We Afford an Aging Society?" 4.17.

44. *Ibid.,* 4.4-4.5.

45. Health and Welfare Canada, *Charting Canada's Future: A Report of the Demographic Review* (Ottawa: Minister of Supply and Services, 1989), 24.

46. *Ibid.*

47. Statistics Canada, *Labour Force Annual Averages, 1981-1988* (Ottawa: Minister of Supply and Services, 1989).

48. Status of Women Canada, *Report of the Task Force on Child Care* (Ottawa: Minister of Supply and Services, 1986).

49. Douglas E. Hyatt and William J. Milne, "Countercyclical Fertility in Canada: Some Empirical Results," *Canadian Studies in Population* 18, 1 (1991), 1-16.

50. Elderly persons provide much care-giving, particularly aged wives. However, we wish here to emphasize the care-giving that is provided by a different age group – the middle-aged.

51. John Myles, "Editorial: Women, the Welfare State and Care-giving," *Canadian Journal on Aging* 10, 2 (1991), 82-85. Gee, "Demographic Change and Intergenerational Relations in Canadian Families."

52. Alan Walker, "The Relationship between the Family and the State in the Care of Older People," *Canadian Journal on Aging* 10, 2 (1991), 94-112. Susan A. McDaniel, "Challenges to Family Policy in an Aging Canada," paper presented at the annual meeting of the Canadian Association on Gerontology, Ottawa, 1989.

53. Such support is needed more by spouse care-givers, given that most adult children do not reside with frail elderly parents; however, among those who do, the need is critical.

54. Gee, "Demographic Change and Intergenerational Relations in Canadian Families"; Walker, "The Relationship Between the Family and the State in the Care of Older People."

55. Walker, *ibid.*

56. Myles and Quadagno, "Explaining the Difference," 37.

Ellen M. Gee is Professor of Sociology at Simon Fraser University and has served on the executive of the Canadian Association on Aging, the Canadian Population Society, and the Canadian Sociology and Anthropology Association. Susan A. McDaniel is Professor of Sociology at the University of Alberta, Past President of the Canadian Population Society, and Chair of the Statistics Canada Advisory Committee on Demographic Statistics and Studies.

A Critique of Canadian Aging and Health Policy

VICTOR W. MARSHALL

The state of health policy in relation to aging in Canada needs addressing. We do not have a single policy position in this area; neither do we have a single policy process. This paper briefly reviews aspects of the policy process in Canada, offers views on what such a policy position must include, and identifies some barriers to the development of a sound policy process in this area. Among the barriers which are highlighted are the limitations which often follow from taking the stance of a particular discipline toward health policy and aging. While not denying the many insights which appear in the policy literature, this paper seeks to evidence the weaknesses or oversights inherent in this literature.

The Context of National Health Policy

In Canada, the federal government is constitutionally limited in the health field. Hospital and medical services for the civilian population are under provincial jurisdiction, as is education in the medical and health fields, and the regulation of the health care professions. Nonetheless, a series of initiatives by the federal government has had a major, cumulative impact on health policy at the provincial level. These initiatives include a series of grants begun in 1948 to assist with hospital construction, education, public health programs and the control of specific diseases; the introduction in 1957 of medical insurance for hospital care and in 1966 for physician services; subsequent reforms to the principle of block financing; and legislation which provided incentives to provinces to ensure compliance of physicians with the intent of the medicare legislation. The history of these changes has been documented in several places.[1]

The federal government, through Health and Welfare Canada, has demonstrated its interest in health policy. In the past few years, it has also become intensely interested in aging and health policy. This is evident in several departments, not only Health and Welfare Canada but also Statistics Canada and Veterans' Affairs. Some intergovernmental coordination has been achieved but the degree of federal-provincial coordination has not been great.

Cooperative efforts between federal and provincial sectors in aging and health policy are indicated in the existence of a Federal-Provincial-Territorial Committee on Long Term Care. This mechanism, however, is not judged to be highly influential or successful.[2] Provincial-level policy structures and processes in the aging and health area are highly variable.[3] Indeed, it seems that the more one studies the system in a given province, the greater the limitations which are revealed.

Aging and health policy is also influenced by several interest groups. A major example is the Canadian Medical Association (CMA), whose Committee on the Health Care of the Elderly established an implementation structure to act on its 1987 report.[4] The Canadian Association on Gerontology, the Canadian Public Health Association (and its provincial affiliates), the Victorian Order of Nurses, and any number of health occupations and professions have from time to time attempted to influence the aging and health policy sphere.

Nor should we neglect the local level. Service delivery policies are made throughout Canada at community and district levels, often without guidance, mandate, or financial support from higher levels. From the point of view of the aging individual, or of any other "lay person," aging and health policy may well appear to be highly fragmented.

Finally, it must be noted that those who think about aging and health policy are few in number. There is not much that is systematic about aging and health policy in Canada. It is ill-developed and often ill-advised; its policies are fragmented and sometimes contradictory.

The Desired Scope of a Policy Process for Health and Aging

The appropriate scope for an aging and health policy process should be found within the framework of "healthy public policy." This approach to health policy has been stimulated and promoted by the World Health Organization and the Health Promotion Directorate of Health and Welfare Canada, and it also has a strong influence on health policy in the province of Ontario. This approach incorporates the following four principles:[5]

— healthy public policy should be multisectoral — the health of a people will be enhanced through developments in all sectors, such as the economy, nutrition, housing, the environment and education.
— a guiding principle of healthy public policy is a commitment to equity — principles of fairness should guide efforts to promote health.
— healthy public policy initiatives should, ideally, be broadly participatory.

— healthy public policy takes an ecological perspective which places humans in a broad context of the physical and social world.

Healthy public policy represents a very broad development of health promotion ideas or ideology, in which concerns for healthy life-styles and disease prevention are retained, as are concerns to employ effective health care technology. However, the major thrust of healthy public policy moves well beyond health education and social marketing strategies, and well beyond the health care system, to develop health policies in all sectors of life. The fact that health status is for the most part environmentally determined (in the classic epidemiological triangle of host, agent and environment, the latter is given imminence) leads the policy-maker to examine the health effects of all policies that have an impact on the social or physical environment.

In the specific context of aging, this approach has a number of policy implications:

i) Policy initiatives should include, and perhaps focus on, the well elderly. The importance of medical and health professionals for health policy is circumscribed.

ii) Environmental and ecological theories of aging, grounded in the work of Kurt Lewin and related theorists assume great importance.[6] Adaptation, in the ecological approach, rests on attaining a "fit" between person and environment. Policy initiatives should focus on changing the environment rather than the person.

iii) Policy initiatives to enhance the health of the elderly should focus on income security, housing, and other social determinants, rather than specifically on health or medical matters.

iv) Health promotion/disease prevention goals should be set for people of all ages in a life-span context, and specifically for the aged.

v) In keeping with the emphasis in healthy public policy of encouraging active participation, older people should be included in health-promoting policy initiatives.

vi) The ecological tenets of healthy public policy, applied in the social realm, imply that the "problems" of the aged should not be viewed in isolation from the problems of the society as a whole.

vii) Notwithstanding the previous point, equity considerations should lead to the allocation of resources to the aged in excess of those which might be allocated on "equality" grounds, in order to redress systemic or institutionally based deprivations. For example, compensation should be directed to the aged because they are systemically excluded from full labour force participation.

viii) Socially relevant policies in a wide variety of fields should be examined in light of their health effects (broadly defined) on the elderly. For example, urban design and transportation should take into account the special needs of a less mobile or frail older population, thereby providing an environmental fit which facilitates greater opportunities for independence.

Barriers to the Implementation of a Sound Policy Process

As Geoffrey Weller has pointed out, health policy results from "a tremendous variety of shifting forces, ranging from the character of political and social institutions, the interests of influential groups and the character of technological change, to the rate of population growth, its age and geographic distribution."[7] All these factors which influence health policy can potentially create barriers which detract from the development and implementation of sound viable health policies.

Narrowness of Focus

The first general barrier is a narrowness of focus, which includes four dimensions: demographic determinism, economic reductionism, a focus on the health care system and disease, and ageism.

1. Demographic Determinism

Demographic determinism reflects the view that the major engine of social change is demography. Applied to the aging and health area, this dogma asserts that the major cause of problems is the aging of the population, with associated changes in the age structure such as increased dependency ratios. What often follows are problems with the misapplication of demographic arguments to the aging and health policy field. At the cohort level, this can lead to the equivalent of "blaming the victim." Is the Canada Pension Plan underfunded? If so, blame the surprisingly large increases in the number of old people. Blaming demographic change draws attention away from the fact that sustained high unemployment levels cause major reductions in the amount of money flowing into the CPP fund; it also helps to mask the fact that the contributions of employers and employees could earn more if the fund were not a major source of low-cost loans to the provinces, or if interest rates were higher.

In the health field, demographic change is often unfairly blamed for driving health care delivery financing into a perilous state. In the more general sense, this is an example of what Alan Walker has called the "alarmist demography of despair," and what Ann Robertson has labelled "apocalyptic demography."[8] An important Canadian example of "alarmist" or "apocalyptic" demography is the use by the CMA Task Force on the Allocation of Health Care Resources of the demographic projections by Woods Gordon; their findings suggest that we face a need either to redesign our geriatric care system or face a crisis in which virtually all acute-care beds might come to be occupied by the elderly. Specifically, the Woods Gordon report predicted that we would need to provide 118,000 hospital beds and 276,000 long-term beds by the year 2021.[9] Such arguments represent a misuse, or at best an inadequate use, of demography.

The truth is that demographic changes are not to blame, as some demographers have themselves made clear. In a 1985 paper, Robert G. Evans pointed out that the majority of demographic forecasts of health care costs in Canada indicate that there will be a rise in per capita health care costs, but that the rise will occur at a slower rate than the general expansion in the economy.[10] Frank Denton and Byron Spencer's work in economic demography exemplifies careful research in this area.[11] Examining several scenarios of demographic change, they conclude that "population changes can be expected to have a substantial impact on the cost of health care in the longer term. However, it seems clear that large increases in the cost of health care that occur within a decade or so are not likely to be primarily the result of population changes but rather to reflect changes in the quality of services provided."[12] Using more recent age-specific health costs in a revised model following from the studies on which Evans made his 1985 remarks, Denton, Neno Li and Spencer now argue that in the long run population aging will have a greater impact in increasing health costs than in increasing the growth of the economy.[13] Nonetheless, they remain convinced that we do not face a crisis, given our ability to modify health care delivery, and given the slowness of demographic change.

As Evans shows, the increased health care costs will be concentrated in hospital services rather than in physician's services or in other health services.[14] In this light, an analysis for the Economic Council of Canada by Ludwig Auer is instructive.[15] He has shown that, while hospital operating expenditures in Canada increased at an annual rate averaging 14.9 percent over the period 1961-80, only 1.6 of the increased percentage points could be attributed to population growth. The net effect of changes in the age composition of the population was essentially zero. The largest proportion of the increase was in per capita expenditures (12.7 percent); higher hospital wage rates accounted for about two-thirds of the increase, while increased service intensity accounted for one-quarter.

As a final point, it must be noted that there are different kinds of demographers — social, economic and generalist demographers who claim no other disciplinary allegiance. Whatever their stripe, it seems that demographers contribute to the aging and health policy process largely in relation to the economic impact of the changing age structure of the population. There is an unfortunate tendency among a small set of demographers to assume that the major forces driving social change (including changes in health and social services for the aged) are demographic. There is an even greater tendency for the media to accept and perpetuate this assumption. This keeps many demographers busy just correcting the fallacy of demographic determinism. We should avoid attributing too much causation or determinism to demographic changes.[16]

2. Economic Reductionism

Economic reductionism is the tendency to reduce all policy issues to those of costs: cost escalation, cost savings, cost effectiveness. It seems that economics are always the bottom line. However, we have to recognize that there are other values than cost savings, values which define for us the kind of society in which we wish to live.

We are fortunate in Canada that most of our academic health economists do not focus in their analysis of health policy issues solely on costs. However, there is enough of a problem to warrant comment. To take a prominent example, economist Robert Evans argues that the aging of Canadian society is "too easily projected as a 'crisis' in the collective funding of health care, to the virtual exclusion of other dimensions."[17] Yet, having warned us not to focus so heavily on cost constraints, he urges us to focus instead on choices. The choices, however, are still defined in terms of costs. As Evans puts it, "...the central question remains. Not, Can we (all) afford to grow old? but, How much do we want to spend in the process? What share of our resources do we want to give up, in our youth and middle age, to support ourselves in an increasingly extended old age, and how would we like these resources to be spent?"[18]

Any and all policy issues can be framed in terms of their costs and the allocation of these costs. Attention to these issues is a critically important aspect of public policy. It is not, however, the sole issue of public policy, nor is it necessarily the best way in which to focus public policy (as Ellen Gee and Susan McDaniel argue elsewhere in this issue).

Evans makes it clear that our policy answers cannot be determined solely by economics. In another paper in which he states that health policy questions can be reduced to questions of "value for money," he divides that criterion into two classes: effective use of resources and "the social priorities to be placed on health care relative to 'other things.'"[19] In respect to social priorities, Evans adds, "... the outcomes are outcomes of collective choices, political and social. Policy choices taken (or not taken) collectively lead to the development of particular institutional structures, which in turn govern outcomes in terms of values received (or not) for resources given up."

Without forgetting the economic side of health and aging policy, we need to give more attention to the political and social choices and the development of social institutions to which Evans alludes. Still, on the most basic level, our policy development continues to focus too narrowly on the economic components and outcomes.

3. A focus on the health care system, disease and pathology

As Evans points out, "... the health policy questions connected with aging must be defined more broadly than the health care system itself and *a fortiori* much more broadly than simply questions of health care finance."[20] Most health care is not provided by the formal health-care system but through self-care and informal care. That is, when people become ill, they are likely to attempt first to care for themselves. Second, they are likely to seek care informally, such that, in the case of the aged, upwards of 75 percent of care received by the community-dwelling elderly is provided by family, friends and neighbours rather than by formal care providers.[21]

Hospitals are most likely to provide care for older people with severe health problems, but as the work of Evelyn Shapiro and her colleagues has demonstrated, the majority of older people do not experience hospitalization in a given year. For example, over a five-year period, 42 percent of a cohort of Manitobans aged 65 and over were never admitted to a hospital, and of those aged 85 and over, 35 percent were never admitted over five years. A small percentage of the elderly account for the great bulk of hospital days used by the elderly. Thus, two percent of those aged 65 and over accounted for 20 percent of the days, and four percent of those aged 85 and over accounted for 32 percent of the total days accumulated by all persons in that age bracket.[22] As to nursing-home utilization, while it is high in Canada by international standards, it is nonetheless the case that even in the age 85 and over group, only 32.5 percent are institutionalized.[23] Most older people live at home, with assistance, if and when it is needed.

A serious mistake is made if we limit health policy to the care of the sick. Health policy should not be sickness policy. The vast majority of people spend the vast majority of their later years in reasonably good health, without the need for extensive or intensive care by formal health-care providers. Our aging and health policy should emphasize the promotion of health, with the care of the sick being a very small, but important, component of overall strategy.

4. Ageism

There is a tendency to see aging policy issues as problems of the aged and not of the society as a whole. An overemphasis on the "needs of the elderly" as considerations for health policy neglects the social configurations in which the elderly are embedded. Raymond Illsley has suggested that social policy for the elderly unduly neglects the needs of the elderly.[24] While this is possible, there is, as well, a danger in taking the opposite position of mainly or only consider-ing the needs of the relatively few elderly who need the assistance or protection that policies can provide.

Over the past decade the emphasis on viewing the elderly in a life-course perspective should convince us that, in order to understand the situation of older people, they must be viewed in the context of their entire life course. Health status, social supports, and the broader social and economic contexts in which people will live their final years are profoundly shaped by their contacts with history over the course of their lives. At the familial level, we need only consider that most family care of the elderly is provided by the family to recognize that aging is not solely a concern of the aged. At the societal level, the different age groups are "all in it together." We share life in society, with its economic and social pressures, of which the pressures to provide health and health services to the oldest members of our society are increasingly important.

Public policy is too important to be left to the economists — or to the demographers, epidemiologists, health-care bureaucrats and planners — or to the gerontologists. We cannot afford a too narrowly focused approach to aging and health policy. Public policy in Canada, including health and aging policy, is currently dominated by demographic and economic concerns and by its focus on the health-care system. There are too few inputs from other sources — including sociology, social welfare, philosophy and ethics from the academic discipline side. As well there are too few community inputs from the various groups who will be most affected by the policies.

B. Structural and Processual Aspects of Policy

Turning from the narrowness of the focus to the policy process itself, there are structural aspects of policy-making in Canada that form a second set of barriers having an impact on the outcomes. These include the presence of federal-provincial-territorial boundaries, a lack of policy-making expertise, a lack of basic data upon which to plan and make decisions, and a need for measures to coordinate the various sectors and agencies involved in decision-making.

1. Federal-Provincial-Territorial Boundaries

Canada has been favoured and disfavoured by inter-jurisdictional boundaries concerning health care. It may well be that Medicare would not exist if the government of Saskatchewan had not taken some initiatives, and if our constitutional policy had not allowed a single province to take the step of introducing a medicare system. Yet, provincial boundaries may well impede the flow of information which could foster better public policies; they certainly imply the need for complex inter-jurisdictional coordination mechanisms to sort out provincial from federal responsibilities and to maintain, where appropriate, national standards of health and health care.

The manner in which the provinces are said to have constitutional authority over most health matters is an evolving question. Arguing that the federal government should have a greater place, Donald Wigle states:

> The view that health is primarily a provincial responsibility is widespread. The only health-related interventions that are mainly provincial responsibilities, however, are occupational health and safety, institutional education and health care delivery. The federal government has a general responsibility for the health of Canadians and specific responsibilities to control health hazards involving more than one province or another country. The federal government has taken the responsibility of reducing regional economic disparities and it is only an extension of this principle to suggest that the federal government should address regional disparities in health status.[25]

Certainly, if the broad definition of health which flows from the World Health Organization and the federal government's adoption of the "healthy public policy" framework is to be taken seriously,[26] then the definition of health, along with the legitimate domain of policy intervention, is much broader than the domain reserved for the provinces.

2. Lack of Policy Analysis Expertise

It seems obvious that we have not only too little policy expertise in the area of aging and health, but that this expertise is too narrowly defined in terms of disciplines. In Canada, research training in the health field is not adequately orientated toward the development of a broadly based cadre of health policy researchers. Many provinces provide no training fellowships in this area, and the number available federally, through the National Health Research Development Program (NHRDP) of Health and Welfare Canada, is very small (about 22 fellowships a year) and weighted towards supporting those with interests in epidemiology.

As Wigle has recently observed, Canada lacks many of the organizational apparati for health policy formation.[27] We have no counterpart to any of the 11 National Institutes of Health in the United States, including the National Institute on Aging. We do not have anything like an Administration on Aging, although we have a small Seniors Secretariat lodged within Health and Welfare Canada. We do not have any free-standing counterpart to the Surgeon-General in the U.S. — an office which has done a great deal to further health promotion and disease prevention in relation to aging.[28] Instead, we have an uncoordinated panoply of aging and health policy initiatives at federal, provincial, and local levels.

3. Lack of Basic Data

While data files on social and health issues of aging are becoming increasingly available, systematic comparisons of health service and long-term care data are difficult to make because there are no accepted and uniform definitions of the levels of care across the country.[29] Moreover, provincial resources for the accumulation and exploitation of health data are very limited in most provinces. The Ontario Health Survey (conducted in 1990) provides valuable epidemiological data, but little data useful from a health promotion perspective that would support a broad, multisectoral healthy public policy. The federal health promotion survey (conducted in 1985) focused almost exclusively on life-style issues, while ignoring structural issues, such as the social determinants of health, which are pertinent to healthy public policy concerns.

Other federal and provincial data-bases are useful, but one must ask why other provinces, and the federal government itself, have not followed the lead of Manitoba and Quebec, the only provinces to make data easily available in support of a broad dialogue (i.e. one that extends outside the walls of government) in the health and aging policy domain.

Another weakness about the data available for policy formation is the demand for rigorous evaluation of innovative programs, through experimental designs (randomized controlled trials) in situations where it is difficult and economically prohibitive to do so.[30] The difficulties of generating such evaluation data leave us in a position of continuing to provide services the efficacy of which is unknown, even as we are fearful of innovation in long-term care. Many studies in the acute and long-term care areas, and in community-based programs such as respite care, have small sample sizes which make it difficult to arrive at valid and reliable conclusions. Meta-analysis is difficult because of different operationalizations of concepts (such as coordination and case management, in the long-term care area). Finally, we must abandon any notion that a single research study must carry the burden of supporting policy developments. Rather, systematic pooling and thoughtful comparison of information from many studies, each and all with their respective problems and limitations, can better support sound policy initiatives. Thus, in the long-term care area, the gerontological community has been well served by the systematic reviews of a number of scholars of the limited studies available.[31]

4. Need for Intersectoral Coordination Mechanisms

The assumption that creating a healthy society requires multisectoral initiatives implies a need to foster better mechanisms for intersectoral co-ordination. Perhaps this is most evident in the aging area where a set of issues emerges concerning the links between shelter and health services for the elderly. In almost all provinces, responsibility in this area is still fragmented; the Ministries of Housing, Community and Social Services, and Health all carry significant responsibilities, but interministerial coordination mechanisms are generally weak.

The problems are, however, much more general than may be suggested by identifying the three principal governmental ministries involved. Achieving multisectoral coordination in the policy field is no mean feat.[32] It requires:

— the identification of all stakeholders with an interest in the policy outcome.
— a process to foster the mutual acknowledgment of the stakeholders concerning the interests of the others.
— some process to referee competing claims to the legitimacy of the various stakeholders.
— stakeholders who survive the legitimacy test must then be convinced that the benefits of collaboration outweigh the costs — that collaboration is not a zero-sum game in which the gains of one require the losses of another; but rather that collaboration leads to win-win outcomes.

The policy process in any field includes two phases: policy formation and implementation. Both phases require that a large number of parties work together. The healthy public policy framework increases the number of stakeholders by virtue of its multisectoral nature, and thereby increases the complexity of the entire policy process.

Conclusion

As we move towards the 21st century, so too will the baby-boom cohort be nearing entry to the retirement years. Beginning in 2010, the steady increase in the number and proportion of people aged 65 or older will become a rapid increase, as the first of the baby boomers reaches age 65. It has now been about two decades since policy interests gave much recognition to the fact that Canada is an aging society. This recognition will increase dramatically as the full impact of the aging of the baby boom on later-life issues comes to be anticipated with greater urgency. It is too easy, however, to reduce policy concerns to some demographic formula. The well-being of Canada's future elderly population depends on the current social and economic circumstances. Living out their adult lives through these conditions will shape their social and economic circumstances in the first quarter of the next century. Policy analysts and policy-makers are already alert to the facts of population aging and are adopting a broadly based policy approach. Increasingly too, we find mechanisms initiated to encourage multisectoral health policy in the aging area. Nevertheless, we lack balance in the domain of aging and health policy, relying too heavily on unidisciplinary concerns. We focus too strongly on demographic crises, health-care financing crises, and the sick elderly. We fail to recognize that most older people are healthy most of the time and that health policy should be directed to enhancing their levels of health — their autonomy and well being. We pay no more than lip service to the social determinants of health, whereas we should direct our major policy thrusts towards creating the social and environmental conditions which foster health.

The healthy public policy framework offers some useful general principles to guide aging and health policy. However, we must find effective and efficient ways to overcome the specific institutional and organizational barriers identified in this paper if viable aging and health policies are to become a reality in the future.

NOTES

Work on this paper was supported by CARNET: The Canadian Aging Research Network, funded under the federal Network of Centres of Excellence Program; and by the Centre for Studies of Aging, University of Toronto. I would like to thank Susan McDaniel and Barry McPherson for comments on earlier versions.

1. See, for example, Neena L. Chappell, "Canadian income and health-care policy: Implications for the elderly," in V.W. Marshall (Ed.), *Aging in Canada: Social Perspectives*, 2nd Edition (Markham: Fitzhenry and Whiteside, 1987), 489-504; Anne Chrichton and David Hsu, *Canada's Health Care System: Its Funding and Organization* (Ottawa: Canadian Hospital Association, 1990); Malcolm G. Taylor, *Health Insurance and Public Policy* (Montreal: McGill-Queen's University Press, 1978).

2. As noted in Victor W. Marshall, *Models for Community-Based Long Term Care: An Analytic Review* (with the assistance of Susan Rappolt and Seanne Wilkins). Prepared for the Social Policy Directorate of the Policy, Communications and Information Branch, Health and Welfare Canada, 1989, 140. See also *Future Directions in Continuing Care*, Report of the Federal/Provincial/Territorial Subcommittee on Continuing Care (Ottawa: Minister of Supply and Services Canada, 1992).

3. See the paper by Béland and Shapiro, this issue.

4. CMA, Committee on the Health Care of the Elderly, *Health Care for the Elderly: Today's Challenges, Tomorrow's Options* (Ottawa: Canadian Medical Association); and CMA, *Challenges and Changes in the Care of the Elderly*. Proceedings of two conferences organized by the Committee on the Health Care of the Elderly of CMA (Ottawa: Canadian Medical Association, 1991).

5. Marshall, Victor W., "Lessons for gerontology from healthy public policy initiatives," in Steven J. Lewis and Patricia Baran (Eds.), *Aging and Health: Linking Research and Public Policy* (Chelsea, Michigan: Lewis Publishers, 1989), 319-29; and Pederson, Ann P., Edwards, Richard K., Marshall, Victor W., Allison, Kenneth R., and Kelner, Merrijoy, *Coordinating Healthy Public Policy: An Analytic Literature Review and Bibliography,* Health Services and Promotion Branch Working Paper HSPB 88-1 (Ottawa: Minister of Supply and Services Canada 1989).

6. Lewin, Kurt, *Field Theory in Social Science* (New York: Harper and Row, 1951). These approaches are described in the paper by Haldemann and Wister in this issue.

7. Weller, Geoffrey R.,"The determinants of Canadian health policy," *Journal of Health Politics, Policy and Law* 5, 3 (1980): 405-518.

8. Walker, Alan, "Demand and supply of health care services," in *Aging with Limited Health Resources.* Proceedings of a Colloquium on Health Care (Ottawa: Economic Council of Canada [Minister of Supply and Services], 1987), 27-39; Robertson, Ann, "The politics of Alzheimer's disease: A case study in apocalyptic demography," *International Journal of Health Services* 20, 3 (1990): 429-42.

9. CMA, Task Force on the Allocation of Health Care Resources, *Health: A Need for Redirection* (Ottawa: Canadian Medical Association, 1984); Woods Gordon Management Consultants, *Investigation of the Impact of Demographic Changes on the Health Care System in Canada.* Final Report to the Task Force on the Allocation of Health Care Resources (Toronto: Woods Gordon, 1984).

10. Evans, Robert G., "Illusions of necessity: Evading responsibility for choice in health care," *Journal of Health Politics, Policy and Law* 10, 3 (1985): 439-67.

11. Denton, Frank T., and Spencer, Byron G., "Health care costs when the population changes," *Canadian Journal of Economics* 8, 1 (1975): 34-48; and Denton, Frank T., Li, S. Neno, and Spencer, Byron G.,"How will population aging affect the future costs of maintaining health-care standards?" In V.W. Marshall (Ed.), *Aging in Canada: Social Perspectives,* 2nd Edition, 553-68.

12. Denton and Spencer, 1975.

13. Op cit., 561.

14. Op cit.

15. Auer, Ludwig, Canadian Hospital Costs and Productivity. Appendix A, *Aging with Limited Health Resources.* Proceedings of a Colloquium on Health Care (Ottawa: Economic Council of Canada, (1987a), 179-85; and Auer, Ludwig, *Canadian Hospital Costs and Productivity.* A study prepared for the Economic Council of Canada (Ottawa: Minister of Supply and Services Canada, 1987b).

16. It will be obvious to readers of the paper by Gee and McDaniel in this issue that their work is on the "corrective" side, and not subject to the criticisms I have leveled against a few demographers, and against misleading media coverage of aging issues in particular.

17. Evans, Robert G., "Reading the menu with better glasses: Aging and health policy research," in Steven Lewis (Ed.), *Aging and Health: Linking Research and Public Policy,* 146.

18. Loc. cit.

19. Op cit., 1985, 440.

20. Op cit., 1989, 146.

21. Marshall, 1989, op cit., 49-51; Walker, op cit.

22. Shapiro, Evelyn, "The relevance of epidemiological research on aging to policy making and planning: Evidence from the Manitoba Longitudinal Study on Aging," in *Epidemiology and Aging: An International Perspective,* edited by Jacob A. Brody and George L. Maddox (New York: Springer, 1988), 167-76; and Roos, N., Shapiro, E., and Havens, B., "Aging with limited resources: What should we really be worried about?" in *Aging with Limited Health Resources.* Proceedings of a Colloquium on Health Care (Ottawa: Economic Council of Canada [Minister of Supply and Services Canada], 1987), 50-56.

23. Chappell, N.L., "Long-term care in Canada," in *North American Elders. United States and Canadian Perspectives,* edited by E. Rathbone-McCuan and B. Havens (New York: Greenwood Press, 1988), 76-77; Forbes, W.F., Jackson, J.A., and Kraus, A.S., *Institutionalization of the Elderly in Canada* (Toronto: Butterworths, 1987), 39-40.

24. Illsley, Raymond, "Social policy for the elderly: Adaptation to change," in Johannes J.F.

Schroots, James E. Birren, and Alvar Svanborga (Eds.), *Health and Aging: Perspectives and Prospects* (New York and Lisse: Springer Publishing Company and Swets Publishing Service, 1988), 65-79.

25. Wigle, Donald T., "Health objectives for Canada," in *Aging with Limited Health Resources,* Proceedings of a Colloquium on Health Care (Ottawa: Economic Council of Canada, 1988), 92-101.

26. Epp, The Honourable Jake, *Achieving Health for All: A Framework for Health Promotion* (Ottawa: Minister of Supply and Services Canada, 1986).

27. Op cit., 95-96.

28. Dep, S.G., Abdellah, F.G., Phram, S.R., and Moore, S.R., *Proceedings: Surgeon General's Workshop, Health Promotion and Aging* (Washington: U.S. Dept. of Health and Human Services, Public Health Service, 1988).

29. An overview of surveys in the health field is given in Owen Adams, Tracey Ramsay and Wayne Millar, "Overview of Selected Health Surveys in Canada, 1985-1991," *Health Reports* 4, 1 (1992), 25-52. *The Survey of Ageing and Independence*, completed for Health and Welfare Canada in 1992, represents the largest survey on aging issues conducted in Canada to date, and has the advantage of defining aging issues broadly and over the adult life course. About 10,000 persons aged 45-64, and an equal number aged 65 or older, were interviewed on a range of topics including labour force and family history, retirement planning, health, social integration and well being.

30. The point has been made by others. See Eleanor D. Glor, "An effective evaluation of a small scale seniors health promotion centre: A case study," *Canadian Journal on Aging* 10, 1 (1991), 64-73; Dorothy Pringle, "Diffusion across a semipermeable membrane, or the process through which research influences policy development," in Steven J. Lewis and Patricia Baran (Eds.), *Aging and Health: Linking Research and Public Policy,* 359-77.

31. Notably, Kane, Rosalie A., and Kane, Robert L. (with the assistance of James Reinardy and Sharon Arnold), *Long-term Care: Principles, Programs, and Policies* (New York: Springer; and Weissert, 1987). Cready, C.M., and Pawelak, J.E., "The past and future of home- and community-based long-term care," *The Milbank Quarterly* 46, 2 (1988), 309-88.

32. This draws on Pederson et al., op cit., 38-39.

Victor W. Marshall is Professor of Behavioral Science, Director of the Centre for Studies of Aging at the University of Toronto, and Network Director of CARNET: The Canadian Aging Research Network. He served for five years as Editor-in-Chief of *The Canadian Journal on Aging,* and his book, *Aging in Canada: Social Perspectives* (1980, revised 1987) is a leading source in the field.

Ten Provinces in Search of a Long Term Care Policy

FRANÇOIS BÉLAND AND EVELYN SHAPIRO

There are numerous descriptions of long term care (LTC) in Canada (1-7). But, like any sector of human activity subject to the political decision-making process, LTC undergoes a cycle which goes from policy statements to their evaluation while passing through an implementation phase and returns to a policy statement. In recent years, some Canadian provinces have undertaken a profound revision of the mission, organization and financing of LTC. All of this activity, which examined specific aspects of LTC or the whole sector, has produced a large and varied number of documents. These policy documents are the subject of this text inasmuch as the LTC sector is defined as all the social and medical services dedicated to the aged who have functional limitations; these services are medical and support services which seek to compensate for functional incapacities and to correct them or which permit individuals the maximum possible autonomy and the maintenance of dignity(8).

The documents, prepared by a Ministry or by a group of experts appointed by provincial governments or by commissions of inquiry, royal or not, indicate the policies which they urge the political authorities to adopt. Without assuming that the documents' proposals will be translated into reality, these proposals are important elements in the debate unfolding now in several Canadian provinces on LTC policies. We will seek to identify the areas of agreement and disagreement in order to establish whether the provinces are now reaching similar conclusions about the goals, the means and the ultimate values of LTC or whether the provinces are likely to adopt different perspectives in changing LTC.

It is possible to question the importance of the values, beliefs and ideas in the formulation of LTC policies on the grounds that these policies are largely influenced by the competing interests of the institutional management structures and the political forces which struggle for control. Without denying the importance of these elements, the role of provincial governments in the financing and organization of social and medical services has led them to set up planning bodies and, occasionally, study groups that have produced studies and planning documents which have played a fundamental role in determining the direction of our health and social service system. Planning also depends on values, norms and scientific knowledge (9-12). This is the area which we will explore to identify the public definition of LTC issues in Canada.

The first part of this text presents the types of analysis used by the researchers who have focused on LTC in Canada or, at least, in some Canadian provinces. This research, often descriptive, suggested how the universe of issues in this field could be categorized and provided the framework for analyzing the study and governmental planning documents. The second part of the text describes the process of identifying and collecting the documents. The third part reports the results of our reading of the documents. They are grouped into four broad categories, namely, the fundamental values to which they refer, the organization principles, the service management structure and the financing. Finally we conclude by identifying the similarities in perspective among the documents or their agreement on the elements of LTC which they address.

Some Challenges Facing LTC

Kane and Kane (13) conclude their study of LTC in Ontario, Manitoba and British Columbia by emphasizing that a universal medicare system is an essential foundation for a LTC system. In Canada, the provincial governments had to construct governmental mechanisms not only to reimburse medical fees and insure hospital services, but especially to set up, develop and control a complex and varied network of health institutions. Their role in the field of social services developed in parallel to that of health care services. Canadian LTC is, therefore, embedded not only in the context of a universal health care system but also within governmental mechanisms for planning, implementation and evaluation of medical and social services. This did not happen smoothly and without problems. Chappell et al. (14) emphasize that the system of universal medical insurance is also an obstacle to the construction of a LTC system in the sense that it confirms the importance of medicine and medical care in the whole health care field while LTC is basically not a medical program. According to Kane and Kane (15), LTC comprises personal care, social support and health services for people with limited functional capacities. These services are medical and support services which seek to compensate for functional incapacities and correct them, permitting the maximum possible independence and the preservation of individual dignity. Nevertheless, in Canada, the provincial LTC systems retain the mark of their original affiliation with medicine (16). Consequently, LTC benefits, but at the same time is limited, by historic forces which have directed the organization and financing of medical care.

The question of the medical or social direction of LTC remains unanswered in the majority of the provinces because they have grouped them either under the authority of ministries of health or under the authority of ministries of social services. Some provinces have a sole ministry responsible for both health and social services but Kane and Kane (17), like Schwenger (18), stress that, in these cases, the coordination of LTC does not appear to be less difficult. LTC is then confronted by a question of priority, which is the first issue that we identify here, namely, whether the administrative responsibility falls under medical or social jurisdiction. Manitoba is unique in that it has adopted a medico-social model.

Kane and Kane's (19) definition of LTC emphasizes its social character which make functional incapacities the criterion for determining the need for services. Moreover, the historic link which LTC has with medical personnel and institutions raises the question about the type of services provided to LTC beneficiaries. Kane and Kane raise this question in regards to home care services but it can also be raised in regards to other LTC services in respect to their ability to call on social resources without medical justification. For example, in Ontario certain home care services are not available without medical prescription. Elsewhere, there is a discernible shift of home care from an organization with social goals towards an organization with medical goals. Thus, the Quebec program for intensive home care service (SIMAD) appears to be developing into a program of intensive medical services at home to the extent that the emergencies to which it responds are medical rather than social (20). The second issue, therefore, concerns the capacity of LTC resources to provide both medical and social services within its mandate.

In Quebec, although home care services are under the jurisdiction of the "Centres locaux de services communautaires" (CLSC), which are public organizations with a community, social and health mission, housekeeping services are increasingly provided by private firms under contract to the CLSCs. Thus, services financed by public funds are provided by private, for-profit companies. The CLSCs resorted to this in order to serve a larger clientele with the same budgets because private sector salaries as well as working conditions are inferior to those in the public sector. In fact, among social and health services, LTC is where private enterprise is most prevalent. In 1983 in Canada, 37% of LTC beds were in private for-profit institutions whereas for-profit hospitals are practically non-existent.

Provincial regulation of nursing homes, private or public, is fairly common throughout Canada but methods to evaluate quality of care are little developed and financing methods vary among the provinces but tend to be uniform within each province for private and public institutions. The third issue, therefore, concerns the public or private ownership of organizations providing LTC.

The debate about the ownership of institutional and community services for LTC revolves around the financing of these services and their efficiency. Thus, private enterprise might have a greater incentive to be efficacious and efficient than public organizations. But private LTC establishments in Canada often operate in environments strongly constrained by public parameters, except in the sheltered housing sector where state intervention is not as heavy. Hence the Kane and Kane (21) question: what are the incentives for efficacy and efficiency in a system financed by global budgets that are fixed by a central authority? The authors' response cannot be summed up in a few lines, but they comment that community services supported by the state and without charge are not bottomless pits, that LTC clients do not impose excessive demands, that the demand for LTC has been stable for a certain number of years and that decisions for the allocation of resources to the LTC sector have been made in the past without major political crises. Finally, in this interventionist climate, families have not diminished their support to aged family members, thus contradicting American fears in this area which serve as a pretext for limiting home care services under Medicare and Medicaid without medical prescription (22). In Canada, the development of community services has created the conditions necessary for the application of constraints in the LTC institutional sector. The secret of the efficacy and efficiency of the provincial resources for LTC comes from the systemic approach demanded by hospital insurance policies in the 50's, medicare in the 60's and the methods of managing and financing medical and social services since then. Three issues have been defined here: the efficiency of LTC, the role of the family in LTC and the systemic approach to the organization of these services.

Empirical studies tend to show and observers of the LTC scene tend to believe, that the aged prefer to live in the community. LTC systems which offer home care and community services allow them to exercise their preference. By basing its LTC system on a socio-medical model, Manitoba concretely favoured maintenance at home for the aged. The other provinces have all introduced home care; however, the solidity of their roots in a LTC system varies. In Ontario, home care is fractured into several components according to the origin of the client referral; in Quebec, these services are the responsibility of the CLSC, but their ties with other LTC services are minimal. Thus, the way in which the services are organized and the services which are favoured by the way in which they are financed limit or widen, as the case may be, the choices available to LTC recipients. The capacity to respect these choices is the seventh issue identified.

British Columbia and Manitoba have installed a network of case managers who have more or less broad jurisdictions. In Manitoba, the role of the case manager is responsible for the process of case assessment. This process permits a full assessment of the circumstances of potential LTC recipients and directs them to the appropriate community or institutional services. The Manitoba system has only one entry point. In British Columbia case managers evaluate cases and authorize placement in institutions or plan community services. The users remain the responsibility of the case manager after placement. In Ontario, there are multiple entry points into institutional or community resources. There is not, at this time, a single entry point or a uniform assessment procedure. In Quebec, the CTMSP is the unique assessment instrument used to evaluate the need for institutional placement. Regional groups of experts establish the need for care. Moreover, the interpretation of similar cases varies from committee to committee even though the CTMSP is employed only for institutionalization. Finally, the plan for care proposed by the CTMSP is not necessarily applied by the institution that will receive the individual (23).

The process of case assessment is a fundamental element in the management of a LTC system. The degree to which this system is formalized is an excellent indicator of the degree to which each province plans and organizes the whole LTC system. For example, the position of the CTMSP in the Quebec case shows that this province has only partially succeeded in establishing bridges between the institutional and community components of LTC. The eighth LTC issue concerns the whole admission system, that is, the question of a single entry point, the assessment procedure and the provision of appropriate services.

LTC costs preoccupy the ministries of health, social services or community services of the provinces. Nevertheless, Kane and Kane (24) emphasize that the levels of utilization of community and institutional services have stabilized over the course of the past years. The proportion of aged 65 years or older in LTC institutions in Canada is higher than that in the United States. But this is a misleading comparison because LTC institutions play different roles in the two countries. Thus, in the United States, stays in nursing homes are shorter partly because methods of payment and conditions of insurance coverage play a fundamental role in the selection of clientele and the length of their stays (25). The ninth LTC issue, therefore, revolves around the problem of costs, their control and the substitution of services within LTC.

In summary, this description of LTC issues arising from LTC research in Canada has helped identify nine issues. We now propose to check if these issues are raised in the documents on LTC policy which we have identified. Some of the issues mentioned by Canadian LTC analysts can be grouped under the heading of resource allocation. The first of these issues is most certainly that of LTC costs. But there is more to resource allocation than costs. In effect, there must

Table 1:
Long Term Care Issues in Canada

I. Values

    1. Human Dignaty
    2. Legitimacy of government intervention
    3. Role of family

II. Organizational principles

    1. Patient preference
    2. Equilibrium between the medical and social sectors
    3. Integration of institutional and community services

III. Management of the long term care system

    1. Referral process
    2. Public or private ownership of institutions
    3. Incentives for efficacity and efficiency

IV. Resource allocation

    1. Long term care costs
    2. Mobilization of the capacity to deliver resources
    3. Needs of the population

be a social legitimation for the investment of resources. LTC analysts identify the needs of the aged as this legitimizing element. Finally, the medical or social resources must be mobilized to deliver services which address the needs of the aged. The type of resources mobilized is then one aspect of resource allocation.

Some LTC issues can be grouped under a second heading: management of the care system. One of the dimensions of the management of the system, the one that is a key element of the organizational structure of the LTC system, is the assessment process and case referral. Another of the dimensions of the organizational system is the systems approach, that is to say whether or not LTC systems are operated as an ensemble of services to plan, implement, manage and evaluate. And last, the issue of public or private ownership of community or institutional establishments also falls under this heading.

LTC issues can also be grouped under the heading of organizational principles of the system. We have touched on the question of the degree of integration of the community and institutional services and the equilibrium between the medical and social sectors in LTC. These two dimensions are distinct. Medical services can be provided either in the community or in institutions. For example, to the extent that a medical perspective is dominant, one can envisage the coordination of community services and medical institutions. Finally, users' preferences have been the object of numerous commentaries. This theme brings us to a group of issues which have thus far been ignored, that is, the values in which LTC services are embedded. These values are fundamental in the formulation of policies. We propose that the areas which raise issues about LTC values are the legitimacy of government intervention, the importance of the family in its response to the needs of the aged and the human dignity of LTC users.

The twelve issues that we have identified are strongly interrelated. Thus, the debate about the ownership of LTC organizations has a direct relationship to the legitimacy of state action in the field of health and social services, a legitimacy much greater here than in the United States (26). The balance negotiated between the medical and social sectors is not independent of the historic role of the state in setting up and managing universal health insurance and has a close connection with the type of resources mobilized in response to the LTC needs of the aged. Moreover, these needs are assessed in the LTC system in the light of available family resources and, in a more general way, in the light of the social support network available to the aged. Respect for the dignity of the aged is articulated by respecting their desire to remain at home in their community. As a result, there is a relationship between dignity and respect for the service preferences of the users, preferences that are respected or not according to the range of available community and institutional services. The degree of integration of these services is the ingredient which constitutes, in some way, an LTC sector which can be managed efficaciously as a system. Finally, access to the LTC system has been intensively studied by the LTC analysts to which we have referred. The case assessment process is itself an instrument to determine, and possibly, to control costs.

Our review of the analyses has allowed us to identify twelve LTC issues which are intimately interrelated. Dealing with each one makes it possible to cover them all without sacrificing their individual importance. It is beyond the scope of this paper to analyze the relationships between these issues and to try to constitute them in a system of categories for the analysis of LTC. It is sufficient to note here that they form an interesting descriptive set of challenges to LTC planning and that they offer a framework which we will apply to the LTC policy documents that are identified and examined in this work.

Materials and Methods

The documents that we have identified are of two types: 1) those which signal a policy change by a provincial government such as Ontario's *"Strategies for Change: the Reform of Long-Term Care in Ontario"* and 2) reports submitted to provincial governments by government-appointed groups such as Quebec's Rochon Report, which evaluates the current situation and proposes global or sectoral changes in the social service sector or in the health sector. The first type of document indicates the will on the part of the government to engage in reform, the second type have not received government backing. The latter are included in this analysis because they reflect the current thinking on LTC which influences provincial planning efforts. The potential sources of thought are, doubtless, numerous. We are concentrating on the written documents because by leaving an imprint, they can be consulted and because they have an advantage over verbal communications in that they are the most thorough expression of thinking on LTC. The documents that we sought to identify had to have a direct relationship to LTC planning. Books, scientific articles or popular journals, or even newspapers, can influence a policy decision, force a Minister to act or leave a lasting impression on bureaucrats, technocrats and politicians. But these documents are part of a general public debate on LTC or part of the scientific curriculum rather than indicators of the current thinking within the ministries themselves. The documents of interest in this study are the internal reports to ministers or to councils that are attached to them, documents from Commissions of Inquiry on health, social services or, specifically, documents on LTC and texts from working groups or groups of experts set up by the Ministers who have jurisdiction over LTC. We have set ourselves the task, not to identify and analyze everything that has been written on LTC in the provinces, but to concentrate, in one way or another, on the intellectual products that originate, in one way or another, from the Ministers.

All the provincial ministries that have jurisdiction over LTC and all the provincial councils on the aged were contacted. Those responsible for LTC were identified and all agreed to send us their public documents or those which are available to the public which might be of interest to us. In each province, several persons were contacted in order to identify those responsible for planning medical and social services, those responsible for community services provided at home or in institutions, and those responsible for provincial councils on the aged or the organizations that take their place. Since governmental structures of each province are different, we had to identify the various persons who had to be contacted in each province. The federal authorities were also invited to contribute. The Federal/Provincial/Territorial Committee on Long Term Care and the National Advisory Council on Aging were consulted. During the summer of 1991 we asked each organization, directorate or minister to send us all the study or policy documents published in the last five years on health and social services, in general, and on LTC, in particular. The five year limit is arbitrary but it seemed realistic in that documents of this kind are not produced each year, their period of usefulness can be fairly long and the evolution in thinking can be observed over a short period if several documents are produced by the same province. Finally, from Quebec we obtained documents covering a fairly long time period, the first dating from 1980. Although we did everything we could to identify those responsible provincially for LTC, we cannot be certain that we obtained all the documents relevant to our study.

The direction of the federal documents is similar to that of the provincial documents. The latter, despite their limitations, provided useful information on the present state of LTC in the provinces. The provincial authorities and the councils on aging sent us a rather heterogenous set of documents: brochures, booklets, and pamphlets intended to inform the aged about services to which they are entitled, annual reports from Ministers of health and social services, statistical descriptions on the services provided, a range of presentations to administrators of LTC organizations on policies, recent decisions or ministerial regulations and finally policy documents. We centred our attention on these last documents, but the others were also consulted to ensure that no policy announcement of interest had been missed. From the set of documents received, we kept twenty-three provincial documents for our analysis (see appendix).

Seven provinces sent policy documents; three provinces furnished statistical brochures or annual reports from ministries not related to LTC planning or to its components. The first group of provinces includes British Columbia, Alberta, Ontario, Quebec, New Brunswick, Nova Scotia and Prince Edward Island. The second group is composed of Saskatchewan, Manitoba and Newfoundland. The British Columbia documents date from 1989, 1990, 1991. They are from a group of experts, appointed by the Minister of Health to examine services to the aged, from the Directorate of Continuing Care within the Ministry of Health and from the Royal Commission on Health Care and Costs. The documents from the Ministry of Health treat specific topics such as financing, while the report from the Royal Commission covered the whole field of health services. Ontario set up a task force with expertise in LTC. This group produced a consultation paper and a report which gave rise, in 1991, to a ministerial declaration to the Ontario legislative assembly confirming, in its essentials, the recommendations made by the group of experts. The Ontario authorities also sent us a discussion paper on unregulated housing. For the past ten years, the Quebec Ministry for Health and Social Services (MSSS), the successor to the Ministry for Social Affairs, has produced a number of consultation papers and policy announcements concerning the aged. These documents are mainly concerned with LTC but also with other types of services. The MSSS also produced a series of study and policy documents on health and social services in general, each of which contains a section on the aged and LTC. Finally, the Rochon Commission report is pertinent to our study. In August 1991, the Senior Citizens Office of New Brunswick sent the Ministry of Health and Social Services a report on services to the aged. This report was submitted to the legislative assembly by the Minister the same month. From Nova Scotia, two study documents came to us from the Senior Secretariat and the Department of Community Services. Prince Edward Island, for its part, set up an ad hoc committee on aging which tabled a report in February 1990 on the impact of aging on social services and health.

The study and planning documents that have been identified are recent. Most of the provinces focused on LTC. Two of the three provinces that did not send us policy documents have adopted, within the past couple of years, a medico-social model for LTC. It is fair to say that past in-depth study of their LTC programs has resulted in changes that other provinces are seeking to make. Moreover, in 1992, after the time limit set for our study, Manitoba published a planning document for health services (27).

The twenty-three documents that we have identified, plus the bits and pieces of information obtained from other written sources, have been analyzed with the aid of the framework consisting of the twelve issues confronting LTC. In other words, the documents were divided into twelve categories for analysis and the differences and similarities among them were noted. Few of the policy pronouncements could not be classified in one or another of the issue categories, confirming the adequacy of the framework. Moreover, all the pronouncements could be categorized in one of the four sets of issues: values, management, organizational principles and allocation of resources.

Results

The provincial perspectives on LTC are similar in many ways. The values that guide policy, organizational principles, the management models and the methods for allocating resources chosen by groups of experts, the commissions of inquiry, and internal ministerial work groups are essentially the same. We are tempted to say that the differences among the provincial documents have more to do with the editors' energy, in that some documents appear more elaborate, more detailed, more complete than others, than with fundamental differences in orientation. One has the impression that, except for some differences in emphasis, what one group has written could be endorsed by the others.

Values

Ontario LTC policy is based on the dignity, security and self-determination of the aged (1990). To do this, the family and community are the two social entities that should be supported. The diversity of these entities, based on their own cultural traditions, must be preserved. The LTC system should, at the same time, be accessible, integrated, and involve community participation. A number of Quebec working groups have focused on the health and social services ministry's policy for the aged. The most recent document (1991) repeats the subject dealt with in an older document (1980) by proposing respect for the continuity of life across all ages but particularly during the transition from middle age adult to old age. *"La politique de la santé du Québec"* (1992) includes a chapter entitled, "Social integration of the aged." Health problems, social isolation, and loneliness are perceived as consequences of the separation of the aged from society in general. Also, in order to better understand the role of values in the Quebec documents reference should be made to the document entitled, *"Vers un nouvel équilibre des âges"* (1991), which affirms that whatever is of value for the population in general is of equal value for the aged. The recent proposals for reform of the health and welfare system in Quebec, such as the Rochon Commission report or the document, *"Une réforme axée sur le citoyen"*, apply to all citizens regardless of age. Proposals intended to include citizen participation in the regional planning and management of services and institutions also apply to the aged. Moreover, the logo of *"Une réforme axée sur le citoyen"* and of *"La politique de la santé et du bien-être"* shows an aged woman accompanied by a little boy.

Documents from other provinces also address the values underlying LTC and other policies applying to the aged. Thus, the document from Prince Edward Island proposes respect for the right of the elderly to choose the services that they need: they are partners in decisions that concern them. The document from the Nova Scotia Senior Citizens' Secretariat promises independence and autonomy; British Columbia's Royal Commission stresses their well-being, their dignity and their independence. The documents from Alberta are the sole ones to mention compassion and understanding.

Organizational Principles

The documents we have read speak to two issues concerning LTC organizational principles: 1) the importance of both institutional and community services; and 2) the balance between the medical and social sectors. In the 1990 document, *"Strategies for Change"*, Ontario seeks to enable the aged to live in their own homes and community while it sets up a coordinated, coherent, and integrated LTC system from an operational, financing and planning point of view.

These two organizational principles are common to all the documents that we have consulted. Thus, in Prince Edward Island, the highest priority is given to the informal sector; New Brunswick intends to favour community services and to increase their role in the LTC system. The British Columbia Royal Commission affirms that it is preferable to maintain the aged in an imperfect milieu but in their own community, rather than to institutionalize them. In Quebec, a number of documents repeat the same messages year after year. It is particularly important to develop or to restore autonomy to the aged, to maintain them in their "natural living milieu", to increase their participation in social life and to establish "conditions which permit real quality of life". The Rochon Commission emphasized the change in the philosophy of intervention in LTC which has persisted since the 1920s, namely, to move from an institutional model to a community model, while *"Vers un nouvel équilibre des âges"* praises local projects which bring the aged together. *"La nouvelle politique de la santé et du bien-être du Québec"* repeats essentially the same message.

Housing is conceived as an integral part of LTC policies in the experts' documents and in the policy pronouncements of Prince Edward Island, New Brunswick, Ontario and Quebec.

The subject of health promotion is introduced in several documents through the intermediary of the community role of LTC. The 1992 Quebec document proposes that community services have a role in supporting the integration and participation by the aged in community life. Community services in Ontario would have a complementary role to home care but would also undertake health promotion. Two other documents from Quebec mention this subject. Health promotion is usually associated with health policies in regards to children, adolescents, and middle-aged persons rather than to the aged. In these documents, health promotion is conceived as aiding the maintenance of autonomy, re-education and the maintenance of function among the aged with functional incapacities. Other documents from other provinces also emphasize this dimension of LTC.

Management of the LTC System

The documents consulted refer, without always making the distinction, to the management of the system and to the allocation of resources. Consequently, it was difficult to establish the clear borders between these two sectors. In fact, the three major proposals concerning the management system for LTC are interested in controlling both the provision and costs of services, namely, 1) the necessity for central planning accompanied by the regionalization of administration; 2) setting up a single entry point; and 3) the use of a single case assessment instrument.

An important element in the organization of LTC is the concentration of decision-making in one ministry. In British Columbia, the Royal Commission proposed that the ministerial responsibility for institutional LTC be concentrated into one single administrative unit. Home care and community services are not involved in this recommendation. In Quebec, a single ministry is responsible for health and social services but the community and institutional sectors of LTC are not united into a single directorate.

The need for LTC planning was clearly enunciated in the documents from Ontario, Quebec, and British Columbia. But if, at the ministerial level, the provincial documents promote single directorates, it does not follow that they agree on the centralization of all decision-making. Instead, the documents call for clarification of responsibilities for LTC. Thus, Alberta, British Columbia, Ontario and Quebec agree in giving local or regional units more responsibility in planning, implementing and managing LTC.

Local participation has been the subject of numerous discussions in Quebec. Ontario and British Columbia documents also mention it. Even before the report from the Rochon Commission, the document, *"Un nouvel âge à partager"*, placed emphasis on the implications for the local community in implementing ministry policy toward the aged. *"Vers un nouvel équilibre des âges"* picks up this theme, calling for the prudent broadening of the regional role in LTC planning. In Ontario, the region or subregion is a unit responsible for LTC planning, decision-making and service provision; it is responsible for implementing provincial reform, the management of community programs and home care. Furthermore, it will oversee the coordination of LTC, the management of financial resources and the control of services. The assessment of client needs and admissions to institutions will also be regionalized. The geographical levels of responsibility for the different functions are not the same in all provinces. However, documents from British Columbia, Quebec and Ontario all propose setting up regional or subregional bodies that would be responsible for coordination, not only among themselves but also for coordinating services to patients, either directly through the intermediary of a single entry point into the system, or indirectly by the application of uniform case assessment instruments to direct clients to institutions or community services.

One of the points frequently raised in the provincial documents is a single entry point system into the LTC network. This is raised in different ways in documents from Newfoundland, Nova Scotia and from New Brunswick where a pilot project is under way. Alberta recently instituted an instrument to assess the needs of residents in institutions; Ontario has indicated its intention to adapt it, but this instrument is designed more to determine payments to facilities, not to direct the aged towards the appropriate services. In Quebec the CTMSP instrument is used to decide the level of institutional care required for the aged. It is not the only instrument used to direct the elderly to the most appropriate resource. None of the Quebec documents that we have consulted propose a single entry point to the LTC system, nor the use of the CTMSP or another instrument for case assessment and referral to community or institutional services.

The most complete documents on LTC organization come from Quebec, Ontario, and to a lesser extent, from British Columbia and Alberta. The 1990 and 1991 Ontario documents indicate the development strategies for LTC. The strategies are enumerated in *"Strategies for Change"*. The subjects with which it deals are also in the Quebec documents. These themes are: accessibility to services, coordination of long term care services, support to family and friends, local or regional participation, and the quality of care. The British Columbia Royal Commission also dealt with essentially the same material in the chapters on home care, long term care, and palliative care.

The importance of quality of care is raised in several documents in various ways. The British Columbia Royal Commission emphasized training of personnel and the difficulties that professionals encounter in their relations with the aged. The idea of quality in LTC is somewhat broader than that applied, strictly speaking, to medical services. *"Vers un nouvel équilibre des âges"* extends the definition to quality of life to the extent that the institutions are homes where people live. The components of the definition of quality of life are: the identity of the individual, control of his/her life, privacy, security, and comfort. Ontario documents make explicit references to these components when they discuss respect for cultural diversity, dignity, security and self-determination. The documents bring us back to values by the way they treat the subject of quality of care. The documents do not focus very long on the way in which quality of LTC care will be evaluated.

Allocation of Resources

The aging of the population underlies the reason why the provinces found it necessary to review LTC. Some documents develop the components of a sociology of help to the aged. They focus on the increasing participation of women in the work force and on other factors that reduce social support to the aged. Despite this, the importance of the role of the family in LTC is emphasized as well as the need for formal support services. *"Vers un nouvel équilibre des âges"* also emphasizes the support role which the aged play in regards to other family members. Finally, the role of technology is mentioned in the Ontario and British Columbia documents with the hope that it will reduce costs and maintain the independence of the elderly.

Specific long term care services to which resources ought to be allocated are included in most of the documents. This list is organized around the concept of a continuum of care with a strong community pole. In *"Strategies for Change"*, the six essential elements of a LTC continuum are: 1) mechanisms for access to services which inform, assess and direct people to the appropriate agencies; 2) home care services which are pivotal for the reorganization of LTC in Ontario; 3) community support services which complement home care services; 4) specialized services for education, consultation, evaluation and geriatric treatment; 5) support services to the caregivers of the elderly; 6) LTC institutions. Access organisms are the linchpin for institutional and community LTC. Institution placement can only be authorized by placement committees. Home care services help those with diminished functional capacity to participate in the community; they support family members in their caregiving role. Community services offer a range of services from meal services to housekeeping services. Specialized services bridge the gap between hospital services and the community. LTC organizations must establish operational guidelines and make efficacious use of beds. An increase in the number of institutional beds is not planned. The ownership structure of LTC institutions will not be modified. For-profit institutions will continue to function in parallel with non-profit institutions. Nevertheless, the province reserves the right to plan the distribution of beds and to decide on the financing. Nova Scotia also proposes to maintain coexisting private and public sectors.

LTC financing will require contributions from users. This policy of co-payment is meant to reinforce the objectives of an integrated and coherent LTC system, but service consumption will be tied to cost as much as possible. This principle was outlined in the Quebec document, *"Un financement équitable dans la mesure de nos moyens"*, in which expenditures on the health services were linked to the general state of the economy. In Ontario, those who can pay for LTC services must contribute in order to allow everyone to utilize services according to their needs. Generally, in institutions there will be user co-payments for the costs of administration and shelter, and at home, co-payments for the cost of community services. A recent Ontario document proposes that home support services be free of charge.

In the documents that we have consulted, few provinces committed themselves financially to the objectives of maintaining the aged at home and to their social integration. Certainly, most of them have increased their budgets for home care, but only Ontario, through its minister, has committed itself to invest specific amounts to develop home care and community services. The minister has even asserted his willingness to invest in these resources despite Ontario's economic difficulties.

The documents from other provinces have outlined the components of LTC in more or less the same fashion as Ontario, which stressed specific aspects of a continuum of services. Alberta included health promotion in the continuum, Prince Edward Island and New Brunswick stressed home care and the adaptation of housing for the aged. Prince Edward Island proposes to serve tenants in Senior Citizens Housing. In Quebec, a 1985 document presents a continuum of services. Other Quebec documents stress some aspects of this continuum. Reflecting perhaps the backwardness of Quebec in the area of supportive housing, *"Vers un nouvel équilibre des âges"* devotes a complete chapter to this. Programs to adapt and promote shared housing between generations are proposed. However, the document is silent on the subject of housing specifically for the aged. These units are perceived as ghettos which prevent their integration into society. In a more general way, the document recommends the examination of intermediate types of housing, ie, those between private housing and institutions. It recommends examining the use of communication technology to maintain the aged at home. Finally, although it emphasizes housing, it nonetheless suggests a range of services which constitute a LTC continuum: information services, services to help in the activities of daily living, support services to families, psychosocial services, gerontological, geriatric and psychogeriatric services, and palliative care services.

Discussion

The provinces have based their LTC policies on lofty, generous ideas such as the independence, dignity, continuity of life, compassion, and access to services. However, the increase in the proportion of those aged 65 and over and, especially, that of persons aged 80 and over seems to be the source of the unanimous fear that makes these virtues seem so attractive and makes them lose altitude. Still the work of Densen (28) and Evans (29, 30) and their respective colleagues show that, even in a weak economic climate, the Canadian aged do not weight heavily on federal and provincial budgets, at least not to the point of disequilibrium. These works list three ingredients which are essential in order to adapt social and health services to the need for services that they must face without burdening state budgets: 1) change the practices of health professionals; 2) reorient resources to community services; 3) show the political will necessary to achieve these first two changes. The documents that we have read are a good beginning. At least, if some provinces miss the boat in reforming LTC, it will not be because of a lack of ideas on defining the parameters for action. But, intentions for reform by the provinces and their success rest on an historic foundation which both facilitates and complicates their task.

Several observers of the Canadian social and health service scene have noted the historic weight of the heritage of reforms over the last forty years. The introduction of the universal hospital insurance by the federal government in 1959, followed by universal medical insurance in 1967, and adherence by all provinces to federal-provincial agreements on a universal medicare system in 1971 are often given as developments which make it difficult to adopt LTC policies which recognize the differences between medical care and LTC (31). What is more, the agreements on financing complementary services and the program of financing by sharing costs from the 1970s gave special status to LTC in relation to medical and hospital care by excluding them from the application of the national norms of universal medicare insurance (32). Because LTC services are not subject to the five national rules of universal medicare, the implementation of community services, among others, is left to the decision of the provinces and they can therefore, under certain conditions, charge user fees. In effect, before 1966, most of the provinces had LTC programs for indigent aged. The federal government assumed a part of these costs in 1966. Since then, some provinces have not provided LTC programs except for the population covered by the federal-provincial cost-sharing agreements; others have considerably extended LTC services.

Clearly, there is a difference in status between LTC and medical and hospital services. The provincial documents that we have read demonstrate a large diversity in the treatment of the two programs. In effect, LTC services develop symbiotically with the ministries which direct the health services resources. These ministries have implemented mechanisms for planning, consultation, implementation and surveillance, which already manage most of the components of LTC, either directly or in collaboration with the ministries which have jurisdiction over social services. Historically, the weight of this type of management appeared to have been more important for determining the future of LTC services than the limits imposed on them by a too-powerful medical establishment. In fact, our hypothesis is that the systemic perspective adopted by the provinces in their reform of LTC was made possible only by the availability of the tools for planning and managing medical and hospital services by the provinces, tools which they had to set up following the agreements on universal health insurance. Kane and Kane (33) understood it well because they proposed that an integrated and coherent system for LTC can only develop in the framework of universal medicare.

Did the framework for universal health care prevent LTC from developing according to its own, unique perspective? In certain provinces such as Manitoba, the answer is no. The documents with which we are acquainted show that at the level of ideas, the provinces know how to identify the specific characteristics of LTC. To know if, in each case, this translates into concrete actions is another story, one beyond the scope of this paper. That there are difficulties such as opposition from powerful interest groups, is not surprising. It is, therefore, necessary to assess if Canadian universal health insurance and its management system facilitate the implementation of necessary reforms in the LTC sector or if these reforms would have been easier without them. To our way of thinking, to ask the question is to answer it.

We have emphasized that provincial policy documents were oriented towards the same values, organizational principles, management methods and allocation of resources. This similarity is not unique to the ten provinces. Kammerman (34) had already noted that LTC policies in eight countries (Yugoslavia, Canada, Poland, Great Britain, France, the Federal Republic of Germany, and the United States) have defined the problems they faced in the same terms. These problems are the same as those which we have found in the provincial documents: demographic changes, the entry of women into the workforce, the geographical distance of children from their parents, the isolation of the elderly and their increasing politicization. All the countries stress the development of community services. Their LTC services are basically the same. Differences appear in the emphasis placed on one type of program as compared to another: on the administrative unit responsible for LTC, admission criteria, service costs, quality assessment and the planning and integration of LTC services. All of these leave considerable room for international variation. The Canadian provinces, however, agree on many of these points to such an extent that inter-Canadian differences are fewer than the differences among the eight countries studied by Kammerman (35). They generally agree that LTC management is conjointly medical and social, with the advantage often given to the social; that planning is centralized with the decentralization of administration to regional units; and that the emphasis is on the community services with a single entry point and a unique assessment system. The question of user fees and an acknowledgment of the importance of the quality of services remain either controversial or barely touched, as the case may be.

We will limit our final comments to user fees because the discussion of this subject opens the door to considerations about universal access to LTC, the exclusion of LTC from federal-provincial agreements on the financing of universal health insurance and the criteria for determining the need for LTC.

Canadian universal medicare system covers services considered medically necessary. Historically, the exact meaning of what is medically necessary has remained fluid. It is a mixture of legal exclusions for certain procedures or medical acts, of inclusions determined by negotiations between doctors and provincial governments on professional remuneration and of limits imposed on hospital budgets. LTC is a set of services provided to persons with functional incapacities in order to permit them to maintain their independence. An important part of the services which these people require are the hospital and medical services covered by universal insurance. The paramedical and non-medical parts are more or less available, depending on the province, while the users pay a greater or lesser part of the cost according to schedules which also vary by province. Are these services as necessary as medical services? Where should the line be drawn between necessary services, medical services and insured services? Should all LTC services be part of universal insurance? Or, should the current distance between medically necessary services and the other services be maintained, even though the latter are necessary to LTC users? These questions cannot be answered if the discussion is to be limited to the organization and financing of medical, social and community services.

One must, at the same time, consider the living conditions of the aged as a whole. User fees cannot be discussed without reference to policies in regards to retirement and income protection for pensioners; the institutionalization of the aged is never independent of the availability of sheltered housing; medical, social and community services must be re-examined in light of health promotion efforts; the value placed on the support role of the family and of the milieu cannot ignore the confirmed relationship between the state of the social support resources and both morbidity and mortality (36). Now, each of these sectors, whether it be income, shelter, health promotion, social support, is the object of significant governmental intervention. Some of the these interventions have even preceded universal health insurance and LTC policies. To isolate LTC from other governmental policies towards the aged would lead to incongruities. Ontario's *"Strategies for Change"* proposes that users who have the means ought to contribute to the costs in order to permit others who need them to have access to LTC services. This is the argument which a World Bank document uses to justify user fees for medical services.

The aged are one of the groups of people to whom a multitude of governmental policies are addressed. Taken together, these policies cover the spectrum of social security policies. Already, provincial governments have coordinated some of these policies in an ad hoc fashion. Thus, the institutionalized aged, users of one of the components of LTC, are guaranteed the availability of a fixed part of their income whatever the costs of their shelter. We suggest going beyond these circumstantial arrangements. The objectives that a society wants to attain with LTC for an aged population belong in a policy context that considers income, shelter, health and psychological well-being. Thus, the question of user fees for LTC recipients can only be discussed within an income policy which concerns itself not only with the level of income for the aged which is acceptable to society but with the direct and indirect effects of user fees on access to LTC and to other medical, social and community services.

What is missing in the provincial documents which we have studied is precisely this anchorage of LTC policies in a social security policy. The document which comes the closest is that from Quebec *"Vers un nouvel équilibre des âges"*. But what it gains in the breadth of its vision, it loses in the coordination of the sectors of this general social security policy. The documents show that the provinces understand the social and community role of LTC and that they ought to maintain the important ties with medical services. But, if the values that the provinces associate with LTC are virtuous, they sink, with astonishing unanimity, into the "catastrophism" associated with aging societies. That is unnecessary.

Provincial administrations of health and social services are not without problems, but the provinces have set up viable service resources and have provided themselves with mechanisms for planning and implementing policies. These tools, born out of the adoption of the Canadian universal health insurance system, are the elements needed to adapt the medical and social service resources to current circumstance and structural changes. Moreover, Canada has set up the elements of a social security policy for the aged which will permit the reappraisal of the whole LTC sector in a new way while integrating it with this policy by way of a general policy for health and well-being, rather than by a service policy which would derive its inspiration from current thinking about the ways to produce health.

References

1. N.L. Chappell, "Long-Term Care in Canada," in E. Rathbone-McCuan et B. Havens, *North American Elders: United States and Canadian Perspectives* (New York: Greenwood, 1988).

2. N.L. Chappell et L.A. Strain, *Aging and Health Care: A Social Perspective* (Toronto : Holt, Rinehart & Winston, 1986).

3. W.F. Forbes, J.A. Jackson, A.S. Kraus, *Institutionalization of the Elderly in Canada* (Toronto: Butterworths, 1987).

4. R.L. Kane et R.A. Kane, *A Will and a Way: What the United States Can Learn from Canada About Caring for the Elderly* (New York: Columbia University Press, 1985).

5. V.W. Marshall, *Modèles de soins communautaires de longue durée: Examen analytique* (Division de la santé de la Direction générale de la politique et de l'information, Santé et Bien-être social Canada, 1989).

6. C.W. Schwenger, "Formal Health Care for the Elderly in Canada," in V.W. Marshall, *Aging in Canada: Social Pespectives* (Toronto: Fitzhenry & Whiteside), 505-37.

7. R.W. Sutherland, J. Fulton, "Long Term Care," in *Health Care in Canada: A Description and Analysis of Canadian Health Services* (Ottawa: The Health Group, 1988).

8. R.L. Kane et R.A. Kane, "Long Term Care Versus Tender Loving Care," in S.J. Williams et P.R. Torrens, *Introduction to Health Services* (New York: Wiley, 1964), 216-48.

9. Kane et Kane, 1964.

10. C.E. Lindbloom, "The Science of Meddling Through," *Public Administration Policy* 19 (1959), 79-99.

11. P.A. Sabatier, "Toward Better Theories of the Policy Process," *Policy Studies* (juin 1991), 147-56.

12. P.A. Sabatier, "Knowledge, Policy-Oriented Learning, and Policy Change," *Knowledge* 8 (1987), 649-92.

13. Kane et Kane, 1985.

14. Chappell et Strain, 1986.

15. Kane et Kane, 1985.

16. Schwenger.

17. R.L. Kane et R.A. Kane, "Vacating the Premises: A Reevaluation of First Principles," in C. Eisdofer, D.A. Kessler, A.W. Spector, *Caring for the Elderly: Reshaping Health Policy* (Baltimore: John S. Hopkins University Press, 1989), 490-506.

18. Schwenger.

19. Kane et Kane, 1985.

20. P. Joubert, A. Laberge, J.P. Fortin, M. Paradis, F. Desbiens, *Évaluation du programme québécois de services intensifs de maintien à domicile (SIMAD)*, rapport final de recherche (Réseau de recherche sociopolitique et organisationnelle en santé, Unité de recherche en santé communautaire, Centre hospitalier de l'Université Laval, 1991).

21. Kane et Kane, 1985.

22. E. Ginzberg, "How to Think About Health Care for the Elderly," in C. Eisdorfer, D.A. Kessler, A.W. Spector, *Caring for the Elderly: Reshaping Health Policy* (Baltimore : John Hopkins University Press, 1989), 451-66.

23. J.P. Lavoie, A. Grandmaison, M. Ostoj, "Évaluation du système d'accès à l'hébergement et aux soins de longue durée dans la région socio-sanitaire du Montréal-Métropolitain," *Sociologie et Sociétés* XX (1988), 3-46.

24. Kane et Kane, 1985.

25. L.G. Branch et A.R. Meyors, "Long Term Care in the United States," in E. Rathbone-McCuan et B. Havens, *North American Elders*, 89-107.

26. P.G. Clark, "Ethical Dimensions of Quality of Life in Aging: Antonomy vs Collectivism in the United States and Canada," *The Gerontologist* 31 (1991), 631-39.

27. Manitoba Health, *Quality Health for Manitobans, the Action Plan* (Winnipeg, mai 1992).

28. F.T. Denton, P.C. Pineo and B.G. Spencer, "The Utilization of Adult Education Facilities by the Elderly: A Multivariate Analysis and Some Implications for the Future," *Canadian Journal on Aging/Revue canadienne du vieillissement* 7, 1 (1988), 4-16.

29. R.G. Evans, "Hang Together, or Hang Separately: The Validity of a Universal Health Care System in an Aging Society," *Canadian Public Policy* XIII (1987), 165-80.

30. C. Hertzman, I.R. Pulcins, M.L. Barer, R.G. Evans, G.M. Anderson, J. Lomas, "Flat on Your Back or Back on Your Flat? Sources of Increased Hospital Services Utilization Among the Elderly in British Columbia," *Social Science and Medicine* 30 (1990), 819-28.

31. Chappell et Strain, 1986.

32. E. Shapiro, *The Provincial Role in Community Care,* Neuvième conférence Wilson Abernethy, Center for Studies of Aging, Université de Toronto, 28 février 1991.

33. Kane et Kane, 1985.

34. S.B. Kammerman, "Community Services for the Aged. The View from Eight Countries," *The Gerontologist* 16 (1976), 529-37.

35. S.B. Kammerman, 1976.

36. N. Eustis, J. Greenberg, S. Patten, *Long Term Care for Older Persons: A Policy Perspective* (Monterey: Brooks & Cole, 1984).

Appendix: The Documents

1. British Columbia

- British Columbia Task Force or Issues of Concern to Services, Toward a Better Age. Ministry of Health, April 1990.

- British Columbia Task Force or Issues of Concern to Services, Toward a Better Age: Strategies for Improving the Lives of Senior British Columbians. Ministry of Health, 1989.

- Ministry of Health, *Care Services: Strategic Plan, 1991/1992*, Victoria, 1991.

- The British Columbia Royal Commission on Health Care and Costs, *Closer to Home*, Volume 2, Province of British Columbia, 1991.

2. Alberta

- Alberta Health, *Long Term Care Initiatives, Neo Initiatives in Long Term Care and Geriatric Care,* January 1991.

- Alberta Health, *Operational Plan for Long Term Care and Geriatric Programs,* fall 1990

- Alberta Health, *Long Term Care Institutions Branch, Long Term Care Funding System: A Conceptual Framework,* March 1990.

- The Committee on Long Term Care for Senior Citizens, *A New Vision for Long Term Care — Meeting the Need,* février 1988.

3. Ontario

- Z. Akande: *Nouvelle orientation en matière de soins de longue durée,* déclaration à l'Assemblée législative, ministère des Services sociaux et communautaires, Ontario, 11 June, 1991.

- Ministère des Services sociaux et communautaires: *Nouvelle orientation en matière de soins de longue durée et de services de soutien en Ontario,* document de consultation publique, Ontario, October 1991.

- Ministère des Services sociaux et communautaires: *Stratégies de réaménagement. Réforme globale des soins de longue durée en Ontario,* Imprimeur de la Reine pour l'Ontario, 1990.

- E.S. Lightman: *Document de discussion,* Commission d'enquête sur les logements non réglementés, Imprimeur de la Reine pour l'Ontario, 30 March 1991.

4. Québec

- Ministère des Affaires sociales: *Pour mieux vieillir au Québec,* Gouvernement du Québec, juin 1980.

- Ministère des Affaires sociales: *Un nouvel âge à protéger, politique du ministère des Affaires sociales à l'égard des personnes âgées,* Gouvernement du Québec, 1985.

- Ministère de la Santé et des Services sociaux: *Un financement équitable à la mesure de nos moyens,* Québec, 1991.

- Ministère de la Santé et des Services sociaux: *Pour améliorer la santé et le bien-être au Québec,* Québec, April 1989.

- Ministère de la Santé et des Services sociaux: *Une réforme axée sur le citoyen,* Québec, 1990.

5. New Brunswick

- Santé et Services communautaires, Bureau pour citoyens aînés: *Promotion de l'autonomie des citoyens aînés. Bâtir pour l'avenir.* New Brunswick, April 1991.

- Déclaration de l'Honorable J. Raymond Frenette, ministre de la Santé et des Services communautaires, à l'Assemblée législative, au moment du dépôt d'une politique gouvernementale d'encadrement relative aux personnes âgées, 18 April 1991.

6. Nova Scotia

- Senior Citizens' Secretariat: *Planning with Seniors for the 21st Century. Aging: Independent Living — A Discussion Paper,* Nouvelle-Écosse, 1989.

- Department of Community Services: *Home Care Division, Policy Overview of the Coordinated Home Care Program,* Nova Scotia, 25 September 1990.

7. Prince Edward Island

- Ad hoc Committee on Aging: *The Aging Impact Study,* Department of Health and Social Services, Prince Edward Island, February 1990